Access in London

Access in London

A GUIDE FOR PEOPLE WHO HAVE PROBLEMS GETTING AROUND

*Research and survey work carried out
by Pauline Hephaistos Survey Projects
with assistance from Artsline*

Written by Gordon Couch,
William Forrester and Justin Irwin

**Quiller Press
London**

The guide is based on survey work carried out in 1995 and early 1996 by members of the Pauline Hephaistos Survey Projects group. Over the years, the group has produced some sixteen access guides, and this is the third edition of the London one. The previous London editions were published by Nicholson's.

The group of surveyors included a variety of people, some able-bodied, some wheelchair users and some disabled walkers. We come from several universities and colleges, from St Paul's School in London and from Lord Mayor Treloar College near Alton in Hampshire. A few of the group are 'post-student' age, and are working in a variety of jobs.

The name sounds a bit of a mouthful, but Pauline arises from St Paul, and some of us come from a Christian group attached to St Paul's School. The Hephaistos part of the name arises from the Greek god who was the smithy, and the equivalent of Vulcan in Roman mythology. He was a son of Zeus, who was foolish enough to defend his mother, Hera, during some major row. Zeus kicked Hephaistos off mount Olympus and, after a long fall, he landed at the bottom and broke his leg. In frescoes he is shown with one leg facing one way, and the other turned through 90°. He has been adopted by some as the Greek god for disabled people, and gave his name to a school near Reading which a number of the group attended before its closure.

Assistance with the surveying of the entertainments venues was provided by Artsline, who are described on page 12.

Note that a **LARGE PRINT** version of the book can be obtained from
Access Project, 39 Bradley Gardens, West Ealing, London W13 8HE.

First published 1996 by Quiller Press Ltd
46 Lillie Road, London SW6 1TN

Copyright © 1996 Pauline Hephaistos Survey Projects

Maps and Diagrams: Helen Humphreys
Cover illustration: Pat Drennan
Printed by Biddles Ltd
Design Criteria diagram reproduced from *Designing for the Disabled* by
Selwyn Goldsmith with the kind permission of the publishers
RIBA Publications Ltd.

Contents

List of useful addresses

Artsline
54 Chalton Street NW1 1HS
Tel/Minicom: 0171 388-2227, see page 12

Centre for Accessible Environments
Nutmeg House, 60 Gainsford Street, SE1 2NY
Tel: 0171 357-8182, see page 13

DIAL (UK) National Association of Disablement Information and Advice Lines, for local centres, see page 13

Forrester (William)
1 Belvedere Close, Guildford, Surrey GU2 6NP
Tel: 01483-575401, see page 14

Greater London Association of Disabled People (GLAD)
336 Brixton Road SW9 7AA
Tel/Minicom: 0171 274-7840, see page 15

Holiday Care Service
2nd floor, Imperial Buildings, Victoria Road, Horley, Surrey RH6 7PZ
Tel: 01293-774535, see page 15

London Transport Unit for Disabled Passengers (LTUDP)
172 Buckingham Palace Road SW1W 9TN
Tel/Minicom: 0171-918 3312.

Pauline Hephaistos Survey Projects (PHSP)
39 Bradley Gardens, West Ealing W13 8HE
(the authors of this guide, also referred to as Access Project).

Royal Association for Disability and Rehabilitation (RADAR)
12 City Forum, 250 City Road EC1V 8AF
Tel: 0171 250-3222, see page 17.

Tripscope
The Courtyard, Evelyn Road, Chiswick W4 5JL
Tel/Minicom: 0181 994-9294, see page 18.

Wheelchair Travel
1 Johnston Green, Guildford, Surrey GU2 6XS
Tel: 01483-233640, see page 18.

Acknowledgements

This project has involved a large number of people, without whom the guide would never have been researched or written. The various activities have included:

- ensuring that the necessary financial basis was secure, for which we are particularly grateful to the trustees of the charitable trust, to past members and friends of the group who have contributed by covenant, and to various charitable trusts and companies who have sponsored or supported us;
- careful preparation and planning of what was to be visited and ensuring that the surveyors were well briefed about what to look for;
- undertaking the practical research, by visit;
- writing, proof reading, editing, preparing diagrams and symbols and the host of meticulous and time-consuming activities that are necessary in putting together the text of such a guide;
- publishing, distribution and publicity.

We would like to express our thanks to all of the following, in their different roles, some large, some small:

The surveyors who did the foot and wheel work in London and who contributed to various phases of the project:
Jo Anjari, Max Baird-Smith, John Bhoyroo, Dan Cartland, Josh Carver, Nick Cattell, Gordon Couch, Mark Crouch, Giles Disney, Richard Donaldson, Robert Droy, Nicola Duncan, George Dymond, Polly Ferguson, Alex Frith, Robert Gibbs, Tom Glennie, Ed Hayward, Ben Hayward, Mike Huxley, Justin Irwin, Alice Jacobs, Janet Lascelles, Kate Leach, Adam Making, Dave McGaughey, Garry Mistry, Craig Newport, Polly Peers, Jeremy Rampling, James Rhys, Clare Roberts, Mark Reynolds, James Ross, Trevor Sather, Andy Taylor, Jo Taylor, Ben Thomas, Nick Tjaardstra, David Wallace, Nick Windsor, Julia Williamson, Matthew Woodeson, Mark Worledge, and in particular Rory Mee and Martin Skinner for two months slog during October and November.

Artsline staff who visited entertainment venues, checked write-ups and undertook part of the fund raising:
Pauline Guthrie, Leo Rawlings, Roger Robinson, Brian Vickers and Fred Williams

Those who commented on our draft text, such as Jim Bennett at Tripscope, David Phillips at HCS, John Wagstaff at LTUDP, John Yunnie at BR, and Nick Goss and Alison Hibberd at RADAR.

Past members and friends of the group who have contributed with donations and covenants, and who gave us the confidence to commit ourselves to

the project:
Roger Ayers, Dave Allport, Tim Atkinson, Dave Aubrey, Peter Aubrey, Clive Barter, Matthew Boulton, Neil Brown, Andrew Burton, James Clay, Ian and Rachel Copeland, Gordon Couch, Raymond Couch, Daryl Dob, Paul Fairclough, Peter Filmer, Robert Gibbs, Tom Honey, Bill Hollins, Paul Haines, Duncan and Debbie MacConnol, Mayo and Thalia Marriott, Richard Marshall, Geoff Matthews, Olly Paish, Adrian Rates, Mark Runacres, Marcus Sen, Ted Stewart and Roger Stone.

The trustees of the charitable trust which finances the activities:
Dave Aubrey, Isabel Baggott, Gordon Couch and Mukesh Patel and their honorary auditor Peter Stevenson.

Our sponsors, who provided essential supplementary finance to the charitable trust:

Arthur Andersen & Co Foundation
Britten Pears Foundation*
Chapman CT*
Charles Hayward Foundation
City Parochial Foundation
Coral Samuel CT
Courage CT
Godinton CT
Goldsmiths' Company
Harrison & Crossfield*
Mercers' Company
Newby Trust
Pyke CT
Rayne Foundation
Saint Sarkis CT
St George's Hospital Medical School Rag
Sir Andrew Carnwath CT
Sue Hammerson CT
Taylor Walker*

*contributions made via Artsline

We would also like to thank:
Ealing Community Transport for supplying two accessible minibuses to help with the survey work; and Quiller Press for agreeing to publish the guide which will ensure that it is widely available through conventional bookshops as well as through disability organisations and the disability network.

Abbreviations

BO	box office
BR	British Rail (the pre-privatisation operator of the railways)
CP	car park
D	door width in cm
D, ST	the door width and side transfer distance in **adapted loos**, in cm.
D,W,L	the door width, cabin width, and length of a lift, in cm
DAR	Dial-a-Ride
DaRT	Dial-a-Ride and Taxicard Users Association.
DisEnq	number for enquiries by disabled people
DLR	Docklands Light Railway
ETB	English Tourist Board
Ext	extension
FC	Football Club
GF	ground floor
GFB	ground floor bedroom
GLAD	The Greater London Association of Disabled People
HCS	Holiday Care Service
L	length in cm
LATU	London Accessible Transport Unit
LT	London Transport
LTB	London Tourist Board
LTUDP	London Transport Unit for Disabled Passengers
M	management or administration telephone number
M25	the orbital motorway going right round Greater London
Middx	Middlesex
MSCP	multi-storey car park
NCP	National Car Park
NKS	RADAR National Key Scheme
OB	orange badge, widened here to include any reserved parking for disabled people
PHSP	Pauline Hephaistos Survey Projects
RADAR	Royal Association for Disability and Rehabilitation
RecM	recorded message
RNIB	Royal National Institute for Blind People
RNID	Royal National Institute for Deaf People
ST	side transfer space in cm
UGCP	underground car park
W	width in cm
YHA	Youth Hostels Association
YMCA	Young Men's Christian Association
YWCA	Young Women's Christian Association

16thC, 19thC etc are used for 16th century, 19th century etc.

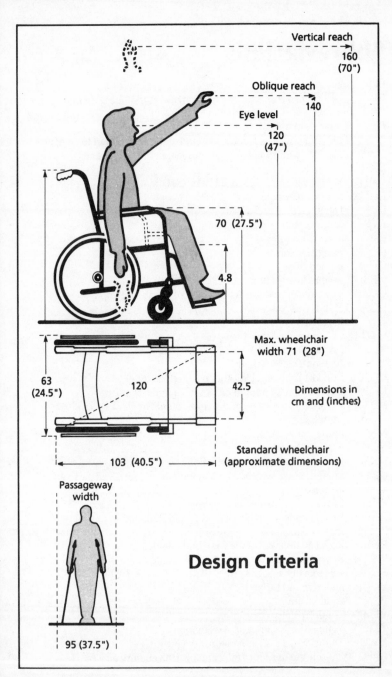

Vertical reach
160 (70")

Oblique reach
140

Eye level
120 (47")

70 (27.5")

4.8

Max. wheelchair width 71 (28")

63 (24.5")

120

42.5

Dimensions in cm and (inches)

103 (40.5")

Standard wheelchair (approximate dimensions)

Passageway width

Design Criteria

95 (37.5")

Introduction

This book sets out to give detailed information about travel, accommodation, leisure activities and tourist attractions for people with mobility problems. This edition contains a unique guide to London's accessible pubs that have a **wheelchair loo** and, as always, we have included our 'good loo guide'. Those using the guide include people who use a wheelchair, elderly persons, those who use a stick or crutches, and possibly those with young children. They include London residents, day-trippers, people visiting relatives in London, and, of course, visitors and tourists. We have included information where possible for people who have hearing or visual impairment. Some will be in need of the guide for only a short time if they are recovering from an accident.

The preparation, research, fundraising and organisation necessary to publish this book was carried out by the members of PHSP (Pauline Hephaistos Survey Projects), working in partnership with Artsline and in cooperation with Tripscope. Artsline were responsible for surveying the entertainment venues, while Tripscope were our consultants on all matters to do with transport. The information is firmly based on the experiences of disabled people, and virtually every entry has been wheeled into or walked into, and measured, by our survey teams. Most of the information gathering was carried out during 1995.

GLAD (the Greater London Association of Disabled People) have estimated that there are tens of thousands of chair users in London, and over 400,000 people with disabilities. In addition, many disabled people come to London as visitors, and this is a guide for everyone.

We assume that this book will be used in conjunction with other guides and information. In particular we recommend the *Eyewitness Travel Guide to London* published by Dorling Kindersley. This contains an area by area account and uses illustrations and cut-aways which often clarify access. In addition a good street plan is essential, and if you're driving into central London, we recommend the *Evening Standard London Parking Map*. A good (and cheap) little book which very adequately covers the history and provides tour ideas for the Capital is *Everybody's Historic London*, published by Quiller Press. We appreciate the expense involved in buying several books and maps, but there's really no way round it, except possibly by borrowing.

In the guide, we have tried to be objective by describing what the barriers are, where they are, and how (if possible) to get around them. **This approach allows you to make up your own mind as to whether or not a visit is practicable, or on how much help you might need.** We have included many places where a real effort has been made to overcome barriers. Do bear in mind, however, that inclusion in the guide doesn't imply accessibility, and what we're doing is to describe the places listed.

PHSP is a small voluntary Christian-based group which aims to educate its own members about what is possible, as well as to collect information. Some of our members get round on legs, some get round on wheels and others have crutches. We try to ensure that the people we meet when surveying understand the need for uncomplicated access to places for everyone. In particular, special arrangements, like having to ask for separate entrances to be opened, asking for the key to the loo, or having to ring first before coming, are much more of a pain than most people realise.

The use of access guides can enable people with disabilities to affect the process of increasing awareness and bringing about change, simply by being there as part of the public. We have found that attitudes (and facilities) in London have changed quite dramatically since the last edition in 1989 and generally for the better. While there is a long way to go, particularly in connection with the vexed question of accessible transport, people seemed much more aware of disability issues and of people's rights to access than they were only a few years ago.

Why travel?

If you already have travelitis (the travel bug), then you will know why so many people do it. However, if you're unsure about it, then perhaps we can encourage you by sharing our experiences. Since the 1970s, when some of our group first wanted to travel, we have been to various parts of France, to Jersey, Norway, Germany and Israel, normally writing guides as we went. Because the group consists of both disabled and able bodied people, we ran into barriers and problems that would normally have been divisive. In practice, we tackled problems together, and found that, given the right information, and with a bit of determination, most things were possible. We gathered this information together on a systematic basis, and have made it available via these Access guides.

Our experiences have been fun, we've learned a lot, and done things that in the normal course of events we'd never have even thought of doing. We do think that 'travel broadens the mind', and in particular it has brought us into contact with many many people. The majority have been interesting, interested and helpful, though occasionally we have met people with attitudes that were more obstructive than a spiral staircase!

Overall it has brought a series of memorable experiences. Each member of the group will have a different tale to tell. We have encountered new cultures, and seen some amazing sights. Even though there may have been a few problems and difficulties, they've been worth it.

If you are still not convinced, we recommend *Nothing Ventured* by Alison Walsh, published by Harup Columbus, London. This includes the stories of several people with disabilities going to all kinds of exotic places, as well as destinations in Britain and in Europe.

Why London?

There is an enormous amount to do, see and discover in London. The West End is up with Broadway in offering a variety of high class entertainment, and there are museums and restaurants which match those you'll find anywhere else. There are pageants, street markets, galleries and night clubs. Although accessibility varies, there are enough historical buildings, art galleries and museums with good access to fill any itinerary. You will find that there is a healthy mix of cultures and races, partly arising from emigration from countries of the old Empire, and partly from the importance of the city as a business centre. You will also find that things become somewhat frantic during the morning and evening 'rush hour' when people are getting to and from work on weekdays.

A brief history

There is no evidence that the ancient Britons settled on the site of what is now London. The Iron Age inhabitants arrived in the south-east of England around 500 BC, and one of their settlement areas was in what is now Heathrow Airport. *Londinium* grew after the Roman invasion in 43 AD. After Roman rule, the Dark Ages saw London controlled by Saxon invaders, who were often in dispute with the Vikings for control of the country. This was until 1066 when William the Conqueror took over, changing Saxon England into Norman England.

London grew in both population and prestige, becoming England's most important city. There was a large palace and abbey at Westminster, where Chaucer and many other famous people are buried. Also the beginnings of the Tower of London. Tudor London saw the reign of Henry VIII, which is best discovered at Hampton Court where he lived. The population increased rapidly. During the Stuart period the bubonic plague hit the city, reaching its peak in 1665 with the Great Plague. London then took another purging, with the Great Fire in 1666. This is said to have been started accidentally by a baker in Pudding Lane, and the site is commemorated by a huge Doric column, known as the Monument. As part of the reconstruction, St Paul's Cathedral and many other famous churches were built.

The effects of the industrial revolution can be seen clearly. There are old power stations in central London, and there was extensive development, including the Docklands, towards the east. Throughout the Georgian, Regency and Victorian eras, London developed enormously. There was a mixture of elegant housing for the wealthy, much of which remains, and of rat-infested tenements for the poor (well described by Dickens in his many novels). This reflected the success of both traders and industrialists and the human cost of that success. The less attractive parts have been, or are being, extensively rebuilt and redeveloped. The architecture of the times can be seen in many of the remaining buildings, with extensive Victorian development in outer suburban areas.

London became the capital of the British Empire, the world's largest city, and the world centre for banking and trade. Since then, its relative importance has declined, but it remains one of the great capitals of the world. *We hope that you have an enjoyable visit, and that the information in this guide will be helpful.*

How the guide is arranged

The guide starts with general information, and a chapter on getting around which provides the basis for visiting. There are chapters on accommodation, on the sights and on entertainment. Where appropriate, we have grouped the write-ups into geographical areas. In particular, we have differentiated between places inside the north and south circular roads, and those outside but within the M25. The M25 is the orbital motorway going right round Greater London with a radius of about 25 to 30 km. The north and south circular roads form an inner ring with a radius of very roughly 10km. There's a bigger area north of the river than there is to the south. The split is shown on the diagram which includes an indication of where central London is, marked as the West End and the City. It also shows which out-of-town shopping centres we have described.

The write-ups on places of interest are grouped into geographical areas. Within sub-sections, write-ups are normally presented in alphabetical order.

We include information about watching sport, about shopping, and on places for a day out, a few of which are outside the M25 ring.

Units and definitions

We have given measurements in centimetres (cm), and metres (m). Although these are the units increasingly being used internationally, many British people still think in Imperial measures. To convert metric measurements to more familiar units, use the following guidelines:

    10 centimetres is about 4 inches (2.5 centimetres =1 inch)
    1 metre is about a yard
    1 litre is about 2 pints
    1 kilo is about 2 pounds

The diagram opposite page 1 gives the approximate dimensions of a standard wheelchair. Chairs vary considerably in size and some electric chairs are considerably larger, so it's worth checking the exact dimensions of yours to

Ring Roads

also showing the Thames, Lee Valley
and out of town *Shopmobility* sites

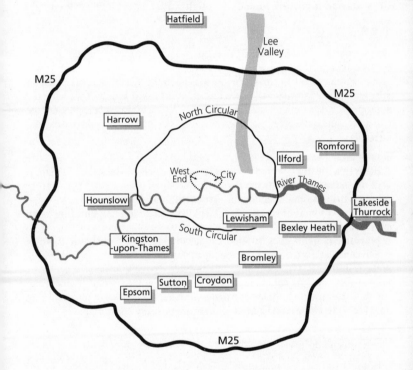

relate to the measurements given in the guide.

Steps are listed by number, with + indicating steps up and – indicating down. Occasionally we list them as ±, in that it depends on which direction you are coming from.

In cafés, restaurants and pubs we have not said each time that the chairs and tables are movable. It is assumed that they are movable, and therefore more convenient for chair users and for others. **Where they are not movable, or if the seats and tables are high up or might cause a problem, we have said so.**

Our definition of a **wheelchair loo** is one where the toilet is unisex; the door opens outward; the door width is greater than 70 cm and the side transfer space is greater than 70 cm. If the loo does not quite meet these criteria, but is adapted for a chair user, then we call it an **adapted loo**, and we give the appropriate measurements and information. Where the cubicle is INSIDE the ladies or gents toilet area, we describe them as being **wheelchair** or **adapted cubicles**.

A **lift** is in a lift shaft, with doors, and a cabin which can be large or small. It goes up and down between the floors of a building.
An **open lift** is a small rectangular vertical lift, usually to take one chair user at a time and bypassing just a few steps – often added in a building as an afterthought.
A **platform stairlift** goes up stairs (attached to the wall) and has a platform which can take a wheelchair, and occupant.
A **stairclimber** is a free-standing and portable device to which a wheelchair may be attached. It needs (usually) two or three people to operate it, but it can enable a chair user to be helped up or down stairs. We would comment that the only versions we've come across of these are not very comfortable to use.

Measurements are given in centimetres (cm) for lift measurements: door width (D), cabin width (W) and cabin length (L). On this basis, you can decide whether the lift is large enough for you to use. Similarly, with loos, we have given the door width (D) and the space for side transfer (ST) from the toilet seat to the wall.

Note that if you are travelling from the USA, and possibly from some other parts of the world, your electrical equipment (battery chargers, for example) may not work here. This is because the supply is at 240 volts and 50 cycles, whereas the American supply is at 60 cycles, and not all equipment will operate on both systems.

Symbols

Some years ago the use of a symbol to denote facilities for disabled people was agreed internationally and everyone is now familiar with the 'wheelchair' sign. In principle, the sign is used in accordance with criteria such as flat or ramped access; doors wider than 80cm, the provision of a large lift and so on. Unfortunately in practice, it has been misused so widely so as to become virtually meaningless, particularly when used in guide books and listings. The assessment of accessibility is made by so many different people with varying perceptions of disability that some places listed as accessible have steps at the entrance or other obvious barriers. **Our approach is essentially descriptive, and we leave readers to make up their own mind about what is accessible for them**.

Symbols are used here to highlight certain data about access and to help overseas visitors there is a key in French and German. We hope that a system like this will soon be used to summarise important access data in conventional guide books.

Disability terms

Throughout the book we have used positive language about disability, and tried to take a positive attitude to obstacles. The barriers are there to be overcome, not simply accepted, and for a long time we have been part of the movement involved in breaking down barriers. Members of our group have a variety of disabilities and, as a result, are handicapped by the world around them.

We talk about disabled people and not 'the disabled'. When people refer to a 'disabled toilet' they imply that the cistern doesn't work, and not that it is big enough for a chair user. We have used the terms **wheelchair loo**, or **adapted cubicle**, to describe a valuable facility. Amazingly (we think) we found places where parking, entrances and other facilities are still described as being for 'invalids'. Emphatically, we do not regard ourselves as being invalid or ill.

The use of language changes, and there is, of course, a danger in worrying too much about precise political correctness. Nonetheless a sensible use of language can help to change attitudes, and to increase understanding, especially if it causes people to ask, 'Why did you say it that way?'. RADAR issue a briefing on the use of disability terms and will send a copy if asked.

General information

Climate

Visitors must take into account the generally mild but unpredictable weather. There are hot spells in the summer and cold periods in the winter but the forecast of 'sunshine and showers' is all too common. When packing, you should allow for chilly winds in the winter (and even the possibility of snow and ice). It may rain at any time, but there are often good spells of several weeks when it will be dry and sunny. If you come in the summer, remember that relatively few buildings have air-conditioning. The temperature can vary from 32°C/90°F right down to –11°C/10°F. Places to go if it's really wet or cold include the big museums, the Barbican and South Bank areas, or some of the very big shops or covered shopping areas. Covent Garden is a possibility, with both shelter and street entertainment. If it's fine, the parks and riverside are particularly attractive.

Emergencies

In the event of accident or emergency, the standard procedure is to telephone the Police, Fire Service or Ambulance by dialling **999**. That way you'll get the right help or advice. The first person you'll speak to is the operator who will ask, 'Which service do you require?' When you then get through, you can explain what is needed.

Normally both doctors and dentists are available only during working hours. If you need to collect a prescription, your nearest police station keeps a list of local pharmacies and their opening times. Two chemists open late are:
   Bliss 54 Willesden Lane NW6 *Tel:* 0171 624-8000
   Open 09.00-00.00 Mon-Sun.
   Boots Piccadilly Circus W1 *Tel:* 0171 734-6126
   Open 08.30-20.00 Mon-Sat.12.00-18.00 Sun.

The Medic Alert Foundation, 12 Bridge Wharf, 156 Caledonian Road N1 9UU *Tel:* 0171 833-3034 *Fax:* 0171 278-0647, provides a useful service for those with medical problems that could be compounded by treatment after an accident. It is of special importance to those who have epilepsy, haemophilia, diabetes or allergies, and to those who need regular dosage of a particular drug. Life membership is available for a nominal fee. Members wear a metal emblem engraved with the telephone number of the Emergency Service and a note of the immediate medical problems of the wearer. Additional medical information is filed at the Emergency Headquarters, where the telephone is staffed 24 hours a day.

SOS Talisman Co, 21 Gray's Corner, Ley Street, Ilford, Essex IG2 7RQ *Tel:* 0181 554-5579 *Fax:* 0181 554-1090 operate a similar service, which works on the basis of including information in a small locket which is worn permanently.

Maps and guides

Amongst the best maps are the Geographers' A-Z series, and *Nicholson's London Streetfinder*. The Geographia *Greater London Street Atlas* covers an enormous area and is particularly useful if you're driving. The A-Z series generally have the better maps while the Nicholson ones use a smaller grid, and are better for what they say in the title, street finding. There are big books covering Greater London, pocket size booklets with enlarged and coloured maps of the central area, and single sheet maps. Some guidebooks include street plans of the central areas.

There are numerous listings about what is happening in London, including pamphlets from the LTB and other tourist offices. The *Evening Standard* which is London's evening paper, has listings, as do some of the national dailies. The most extensive listing of events is in *Time Out* which comes out weekly, and there's also *What's On in London*. These tell you about theatres, restaurants, sporting, musical and special events, and exhibitions. You'd best have a look on the bookstalls to decide which one covers what you are looking for.

There are literally dozens of guide books to London, all with slightly different angles and presentation. We have highlighted only a few. A listing here does not imply that their advice for disabled visitors or residents is particularly good – that's why you need this book! When choosing a guide, check the date of publication, as things change, particularly prices and opening times. There are many specialist guides to particular aspects of London and its history and life. Where relevant, we have detailed these in each chapter.

For general guides to interesting and historic places, we recommend the *Eyewitness Guide to London* published by Dorling Kindersley. It includes good area maps and building cut-aways which are relevant to access. In the chapter on *Places of interest* we have largely used the same geographical areas as they have, and we hope that the two books can be used in parallel. Other guides that we have found useful include the *Rough Guide to London* and *Time Out London*. The *Fodor London Companion* gives a comprehensive and readable background to many of the interesting places and events, as does the less expensive *Everybody's Historic London* published by Quiller Press. The *Guinness Guide to Superlative London* has well integrated access information. Also note *Walking London* by Andrew Duncan, published by New Holland Publishers. It's particularly good for people who want to see things from the 'outside', and yet get a feel for the history and life of the places.

You may have got used to a particular guidebook format, or like a particular style, and others we would mention are:

- the *Michelin Green Guide to London*, which also has some good cut-away drawings;
- Nicholson's *The London Guide*, which includes comprehensive listings of places;
- the London Transport *Capital Guide*;
- the *Blue Guide to London*;
- the *Companion Guide to London*;
- the *Insight Guide to London*;
- Thomas Cooks *Travellers London*;
- *The Best of London* from Gault Millau;
- the *Everyman Guide to London*;
- The *AA Essential Explorer Guide to London*;
- the *New Penguin Guide to London*;
- the *American Express pocket guide to London*; and,

If you are on a tight budget, *London for Free*, published by Harden's Guides, gives hundreds of ideas for activities and visits for which there is no charge. If you are looking for something to do with the children, try *Days Out With Kids*, from Two Heads Publishing.

The London Heritage Guide has colour plates of many of London's historical sites. Published by Pevensey Press, it gives a much more detailed insight into London's history than is possible in a general guide. Finally, two books which are not guide books, but are an excellent read, and can bring the city to life in a different way. The *Faber Book of London* and the *Oxford Book of London*, are both anthologies of prose and poetry about the city and its life.

Telephones

The code for London is either 0171 or 0181. The 0171 code applies to central London and Docklands numbers and 0181 to most subscribers more than 4 miles from Charing Cross. You need to include the code when dialling between these zones. If in doubt consult a phone book. Outside London, different codes apply. If in doubt, ask the operator for advice (dial 100). For emergency services dial 999. For directory enquiries use 192 for UK numbers or 153 for international numbers.

Many new public telephone boxes have no door, making access easier, but it is sometimes harder to hear. Public phones are frequently sited at railway stations, in major stores and shopping centres. Quite often a box will be installed at a lower height so that it is easier for a chair user. Some accept cash payment, but an increasing number use Phonecards, which are prepaid and widely available in small shops. Some now accept credit cards, and it is possible to get a

'Chargecard' from BT. Cards are particularly useful for those who find it difficult to push coins into the conventional coinbox. A few telephones include an induction coupler, which is of value to those using a hearing aid, but the provision is somewhat uneven.

Sadly we report the resurgence of the popular, but inaccessible, red telephone boxes. They have reappeared in Westminster, presumably because they are thought to look nice. What is regrettable is that they have replaced accessible boxes, and parallel provision of telephones that everyone can use has not been made.

Telephone calls from hotel rooms are frequently charged at a considerably higher rate than those from a public callbox.

The management of hotels, restaurants, theatres and so forth often request or even demand that disabled visitors telephone in advance. The same is true for people wanting to travel by train. If special arrangements have to be made, this seems reasonable. **What is unreasonable is that people are expected to telephone numbers that are almost permanently engaged.** Enquiries also meet the frequent request to phone back later. *This can be very frustrating if you're trying to dial into a busy line*, a point frequently not appreciated by the person at the other end. It sounds helpful when someone says, 'Do ring back in an hour's time when the person you want will be here.' Given the difficulty of finding an accessible phone and the probability of encountering busy lines, it is much harder than it sounds. *We hope that people will become more aware of this problem and try to reduce its impact by providing accessible advice and information.*

Specialised information

Contact points

There are many sources of information and who you go to depends on what you want to know. If you need advice or help, you often have to be persistent and try different contacts if your first or second enquiry does not produce a satisfactory answer. We list here some general sources and the major organisations of and for disabled people. Remember that much depends on whom you speak to. They may be new in the organisation; they may be in a hurry to do something else, or the person who really knows is in the loo. On the other hand, you'll often come across people who will go to a great deal of trouble to help.

If a telephone number or address has changed you will almost certainly be able to get the new one from one of the other agencies listed, if not from British Telecom directory enquiries on 192.

Access Committee for England, 12 City Forum, 250 City Road EC1V 8AF *Tel:* 0171 250-0008 *Fax:* 0171 250-0212 *Minicom:* 0171 250-4119. Promotes the changes which will eventually achieve an accessible environment for people with all kinds of disabilities. They support the work of local access groups and officers and publish a quarterly newsletter *Access Action.*

Action for Blind People, 14 Verney Road SE16 3DZ *Tel:* 0171 732-8771. Offers information and advice. Publications include *Ability not Disability* which is a detailed brochure describing their services, and a regular newsletter.

Age Concern, Astral House, 1268 London Road, Norbury SW16 4ER *Tel:* 0181 679-8000 *Fax:* 0181 679-6069. The focal point for all voluntary groups concerned with and for older people. **Extensive information and advice service.**

Artsline, 54 Chalton Street NW1 1HS *Tel/Minicom:* 0171 388-2227 *Fax:* 0171 383-2653, provide an up-to-date telephone information and advice service about all aspects of access to arts and entertainment activities. **They have a great deal of experience and knowledge of what is possible and practicable**. Apart from suggestions about where to go, they may be able to tell you something about the attitudes of management. They can advise about which events are free. **Artsline are concerned to promote participation in the arts by disabled people as well as informing about the possibilities of spectating**. The telephone service currently operates Mon to Fri from 09.30 to 17.30. They are involved in the publication of a monthly magazine DAIL (*Disability Arts in London*) which has up-to-the-minute listings and reviews.

British Council of Organisations of Disabled People (BCODP), Litchurch

Plaza, Litchurch Lane, Derby DE24 8AA *Tel:* 01332-295551 *Fax:* 01332-295580 *Minicom:* 01332-295581. The BCODP is an umbrella organisation working to ensure that disabled people have the major say in policy issues and decisions which affect them.

British Tourist Authority (BTA), Thames Tower, Blacks Road, Hammersmith W6 9EL (administrative offices only), operates the **British Travel Centre**, 12 Regent Street SW1Y 4PQ *Tel:* 0181 846-9000 with mainly step free access. It provides a wide range of information and services of a general nature about travelling in and through Britain. Only limited information for disabled visitors is available. The Centre is due to relocate during 1996, to somewhere else near Piccadilly Circus. The phone number given is the main BTA number, so it will transfer to the new location.

Can Be Done, 7 Kensington High Street W8 5NP *Tel:* 0181 907-2400 *Fax:* 0181 909-1854, is a small tour operator that organises tailor-made holidays and tours in London and elsewhere in the UK, for both groups and individuals. All are 'accessible'. Its director, Jackie Scott, is herself a chair user, and aware of the travel requirements of disabled people.

Centre for Accessible Environments (CAE), Nutmeg House, 60 Gainsford Street SE1 2NY *Tel:* 0171 357-8182 *Fax:* 0171 357-8183. The CAE aims to improve access to buildings and the environment generally, working with and through architects and others. It offers information and training on the accessibility of the built environment for disabled people. It has a useful range of publications including design sheets and reading lists. Expert information can be provided on all technical and design issues relating to access provision. CAE promotes an excellent series of seminars on a wide range of topics, training workshops and an access audit service.

DIAL (UK) (National Association of Disablement Information and Advice Lines), Park Lodge, St Catherine's Hospital, Tickhill Road, Balby, Doncaster DN4 8QN *Tel:* 01302-310123 *Fax:* 01302-310404. DIAL coordinates local groups offering free advice and information on all aspects of disability. Each centre is run by a group of local people with direct experience. The groups operating in the London area at the time of writing are:

Barking and Dagenham, St George's Day Centre, St George's Road, Dagenham, Essex RM9 5JB *Tel:* 0181 595-8181;
Hackney DIAL, 16 Dalston Lane, Hackney E8 3AZ *Tel:* 0171 275-8485;
Islington ARCH, 90 Upper Street, Islington N1 0NP *Tel:* 0171 226-0137;
Lewisham Association of People with Disabilities, 67 Engleheart Road, Catford SE6 2HN *Tel:* 0181 698-3775;
Richmond RAID, The Annex Day Centre, Fortescue House, Stanley Road, Twickenham TW2 5PZ *Tel:* 0181 898-4225;

Romford and Havering DIAL, 1 Angel Way, Romford RM1 1JH *Tel:* 01708-730226;

Waltham Forest DIAL, 1a Warner Road, Walthamstow E17 7DY *Tel:* 0181 520-4111;

Wandsworth DIAL, Atheldene Centre, 305 Garratt Lane, Wandsworth SW18 4DU *Tel:* 0181 870-7437.

Disability Alliance (DA), Universal House, 88 Wentworth Street E1 7SA *Tel:* 0171 247-8776 (11.00-15.00) *Fax:* 0171 247-8765. The DA consists of many of the major voluntary groups and produces *The Disability Rights Handbook*. This is updated every year, and outlines the various benefits to which disabled people are entitled in straightforward language.

This handbook also contains a comprehensive list of the organisations of and for disabled people. Telephone advice is given but the office is not open for personal callers.

Disabled Drivers Association (DDA), National HQ Ashwellthorpe, Norwich NR16 1EX *Tel:* 01508-489449 *Fax:* 01508-488173. The DDA aims to encourage and help disabled people to achieve greater mobility. It has branches all over the country. They publish a quarterly journal *The Magic Carpet*.

Disabled Drivers Motor Club (DDMC), Cottingham Way, Thrapston, Northants NN14 4PL *Tel:* 01832-734724 *Fax:* 01832-733816. The DDMC also aims to encourage and help disabled people to achieve greater mobility. Information is available from the office, and via a bi-monthly journal *The Disabled Driver*.

Disabled Living Foundation (DLF), 380 Harrow Road W9 2HU *Tel:* 0171 289-6111 *Fax:* 0171 266-2922, works to help disabled people in aspects of ordinary life which present difficulty. It has a large showroom and has a comprehensive information service on specialised equipment of all kinds. Advice is given on visual impairment, incontinence, music, sport, clothing and skin care. A publication list is available on application. *An appointment is necessary as you usually get shown round by an expert.* Their showroom is completely accessible and has a **wheelchair loo**. Parking possible if you book. The display includes a special kitchen for visually impaired people.

Disablement Income Group (DIG), Unit 5, Archway Business Centre, 19 Wedmore Street N19 4RZ *Tel:* 0171 263-3981. DIG promotes the financial welfare of disabled people through a programme of advice, advocacy, research, information and training. It publishes *The Journal* quarterly.

Forrester (William), 1 Belvedere Close, Guildford, Surrey GU2 6NP *Tel:* 01483-575401, is a London Registered Guide, and a round-Britain tour escort. He is a chair user himself, and has extensive experience of organising and leading trips and visits, both for disabled individuals and groups. For London visitors, he offers a tailor-made day tour, travelling together by accessible taxi. Specialist tours are available of Westminster Abbey, the British Museum and Houses of Parliament, and an itinerary planning service is offered. Early booking necessary.

Greater London Association of Disabled People (GLAD), 336 Brixton Road SW9 7AA *Tel/Minicom:* 0171 274-0107 *Fax:* 0171 274-7840, is a voluntary organisation working with and through a network of borough associations and London-wide organisations to assist disabled people in London. It provides information to both residents and visitors. It has an Access Consultancy Service with considerable experience of carrying our access audits. Publications include *The London Disability Guide, London Disability News* and *Boadicea,* a newsletter for disabled women. GLAD also undertakes research on issues that affect disabled people throughout London. If you are staying in a particular borough GLAD can put you in touch with the local association.

HAPA, Fulham Palace, Bishops Avenue, Fulham SW6 6EA *Tel:* 0171 736-4443 *Information and Minicom:* 0171 731-1435 *Fax:* 0171 731-4426, organises five adventure playgrounds in London providing facilities for children with disabilities and special needs.

Holiday Care Service, 2nd Floor, Imperial Buildings, Victoria Road, Horley, Surrey RH6 7PZ *Tel:* 01293-774535 (information); 01293-771500 (administration); *Minicom:* 01293-776943 *Fax:* 01293-784647. The UKs central source of travel and holiday information for disabled or disadvantaged people. Produces the *Holiday Care Guide to Accessible Accommodation* which gives details of accessible facilities and attractions across the UK. Also produces an information sheet on *Accessible Accommodation in London* inspected against the National Accessible Standard. They have been instrumental in improving some of the attitudes concerning disability and disabled travellers within the tourist industry.

London Advice Finder (LAF), Resource Information Service, The Basement, 38 Great Pulteney Street W1R 3DE *Tel:* 0171 494-2408. LAF is a database containing details of over 2000 sources of help and advice in and around London. Entries include advice centres, counselling services, specialist legal support, self-help groups, health charities, housing advice agencies, community groups, Citizens Advice Bureaux and disability groups. This was a new service in 1995, and is potentially useful as their database is expanding, provided it is supported by practical experience as well as just being a listing of what the agencies say about themselves.

London Tourist Board (LTB), 26 Grosvenor Gardens SW1W 0DU (address for administrative purposes only). LTB and borough tourist office desks are the main source of tourist information in London. They can tell you whether places will be open and give information about costs and concessions. The amount of specialised information they have for disabled visitors is extremely limited, and the most likely thing to happen is that you will be offered a copy of this guide!

There are desks at the Heathrow terminals, and Waterloo International arrivals hall. The biggest facility is the **Tourist Information Centre**, Victoria station forecourt SW1, by the head of the taxi rank. Step free access. Good bookshop.

In inner London there are *Tourist Information Centres* as follows:

British Travel Centre, 12 Regent Street SW1 (moving shortly);

Greenwich, 46 Greenwich Church Street SE10 *Tel:* 0181 858-6376 *Fax:* 0181 853-4607. They produce a small information book with some access information;

Hackney, Central Hall, Mare Street E8 *Tel:* 0181 985-9055;

Islington, 44 Duncan Street N1 *Tel:* 0171 278-8787 *Fax:* 0171 833-2193;

Lewisham Library, 199 Lewisham High Street SE13 *Tel:* 0181 297-8317 *Fax:* 0181 297-9241;

Selfridges (LTB desk), Oxford Street W1, Basement Services Arcade;

Southwark, Hays Galleria, Tooley Street SE1;

Tower Hamlets, 107a Commercial Street E1 *Tel:* 0171 512-4200 *Fax:* 0171 375-2539.

Outer London *Tourist Information Centres* are at:

Bexley, Central Library, Townley Road, Bexleyheath, Kent *Tel:* 0181 303-9052 *Fax:* 0181 303-7872;

Croydon, Katherine Street, Croydon *Tel:* 0181 253-1009 *Fax:* 0181 253-1008;

Harrow, Civic Centre, Station Road, Harrow, Middx *Tel:* 0181 424-1103 *Fax:* 0181 424-1134;

Hillingdon, Central Library, 14 High Street, Uxbridge, Middx *Tel:* 01895-250706 *Fax:* 01895-239794;

Hounslow, 24 The Treaty Centre, Hounslow High Street, Hounslow, Middx *Tel:* 0181 572-8279 *Fax:* 0181 569-4330;

Kingston, The Market House, Market Place, Kingston-on-Thames, Surrey *Tel:* 0181 547-5592 *Fax:* 0181 547-5594;

Redbridge (Ilford), Town Hall, High Road, Ilford, Essex *Tel:* 0181 478-3020 *Fax:* 0181 478-9149;

Richmond Old Town Hall, Whittaker Avenue, Richmond, Surrey *Tel:* 0181 940-9125 *Fax:* 0181 940-6899. They had some useful access information;

Twickenham, The Atrium, Civic Centre, York Street, Twickenham, Middx *Tel:* 0181 891-1141.

The LTB operates a comprehensive range of recorded information services called *Visitorcall*. They cover events, shows, where to take the children, river trips and the weather. There are as many as thirty-five different numbers. The principal ones are listed in the London Business and Services Telephone Directory. The information is regularly updated, but will include nothing about access.

Royal Association for Disability and Rehabilitation (RADAR), 12 City Forum, 250 City Road EC1V 8AF *Tel:* 0171 250-3222 *Minicom:* 0171 250-4119 *Fax:* 0171 250-0212. RADAR is the central coordinating body for all the voluntary groups concerned with disabled people. It provides advice and information on a wide variety of subjects including access, housing, specialised equipment, benefits available and local authority responsibilities. It is the coordinating group for preparing access guides throughout the country and keeps a list of those currently available. It produces an extensive publications list including, *Holidays in the British Isles*; *Holidays and Travel Abroad*; and a monthly *RADAR Bulletin*. All contain useful information.

Royal National Institute for Blind People (RNIB), 224 Great Portland Street W1N 6AA *Tel:* 0171 388-1266 *Fax:* 0171 388-2034. Promotes facilities for the rehabilitation, training and employment of blind people and provides a range of braille publications. It advises on a wide range of problems and needs. RNIB publishes a monthly magazine, *New Beacon*. Their publication *European cities within reach – London* is promoted as an access guide to London, and usefully mentions a few places which provide audio guides. RNIB publications come from Customer Services, PO Box 173, Peterborough PE2 6WS *Tel:* 01345-023153.

Royal National Institute for Deaf People (RNID), South East Office, 39 Store Street WC1E 7DB *Tel/Minicom:* 0171 813-2480 *Fax:* 0171 916-4546, aims to promote and encourage both the alleviation and prevention of deafness. It is mainly a service organisation, and offers six core services to deaf people, the family, friends and related professional services. These are, information; residential care where needed; a network of Communication Support Units; training; Typetalk, the national telephone relay service; and the testing of devices which assist deaf people. The RNID have a library, a medical research unit and the Tinnitus Helpline.

SHAPE (London), 356 Holloway Road N7 *Tel/Minicom:* 0171 700-8138 *Fax:* 0171 700-8143, is a major provider of training in the arts. In addition it runs the **Shape Ticket Scheme** to enable disabled and elderly people to enjoy a wide range of arts events. Membership of the scheme costs less than £10 a year. Under certain circumstances, they may be able to provide a volunteer to go with you, and provide transport. The number of West End performances at which these facilities can be provided is quite limited, and you need to be well organised at least two to three weeks before the event. If you require an escort, you need to get in touch with them shortly after receiving your bi-monthly programme/newsletter. Seats are normally available at reduced prices, to a wide range of shows, but only to specific performances. Individual members can book up to four seats, and there is the opportunity for groups to join the scheme at twice the individual membership cost.

Shopmobility provides invaluable services and resources in a number of outer London shopping centres. It tries to ensure that disabled people have equal opportunity of access to both shops and services. Most commonly schemes are sited in the centre of shopping areas with adjacent OB spaces. *Shopmobility* offers scooters and both manual and powered chairs for use, and will have valuable local knowledge. There are schemes in Bexley Heath, Bromley, Croydon, Epsom, Harrow, Kingston, Lewisham, Redbridge, and Sutton. Also at Hatfield and Lakeside Thurrock, just outside the M25. New ones are opening (or due to open) at Enfield, Hillingdon, Hounslow, Richmond and Wandsworth, see the map on page 5. Their operating hours and availability vary from place to place. For information contact the *Shopmobility* National Officer, Joss McLeod, 85 High Street, Worcester WR1 2ET *Tel:* 01905-617761. Alternatively get in touch with Lyn Devivo at Kingston *Shopmobility Tel:* 0181 547-1255, or any local *Shopmobility* number. For details of the shopping centres, see the chapter on *Shops*.

Sympathetic Hearing Scheme (SHS), 7 Armstrong Road W3 7JL *Tel:* 0181 740-4447 *Fax:* 0181 742-9043 *Minicom:* 0181 742-9151. The SHS offers a unique service. Everyone with a degree of hearing loss is at a disadvantage. It's a disability which attracts little attention but can be difficult and embarrassing. The Sympathetic Hearing Scheme aims to train people at information desks, ticket offices and behind counters to be thoughtful and helpful. A plastic card they issue may help you get around. It's just like a credit card and is an easy way of saying, 'I can't hear very well, please speak clearly.' The card has the international hard of hearing symbol and some simple instructions and hints on the back for the person you're talking to.

Tripscope, The Courtyard, Evelyn Road, Chiswick W4 5JL *Tel/Minicom:* 0181 994-9294 *Fax:* 0181 994-3618, offers information on journeys of any distance – local, long distance or international. They provide an excellent service and are both experienced and practical. Advice is free, and they are available during 'normal working hours'. Wherever you are starting they can advise you on the easiest and cheapest ways of travelling and on the problems you may meet.

Wheelchair Travel, 1 Johnston Green, Guildford, Surrey GU2 6XS *Tel:* 01483-233640 *Fax:* 01483-237772. Probably the best (and almost the only) source of converted vehicles for hire. Trevor Pollitt who has established and built-up this service over a number of years is well known to us. Wheelchair Travel has a number of adapted minibuses with either tail lifts or ramped access available for hire with or without a driver. In addition they have cars with hand controls, and 'Chairman' cars.

There are an enormous number of groups and societies which are listed in some of the publications mentioned above and at the end of this chapter. We haven't included all the specialist groups because there just isn't space, but we hope that enquirers will be persistent in seeking the right source of information and advice.

Equipment repair and hire

There are a number of places where it is possible to hire special equipment, including wheelchairs, and others where you can buy equipment. We list here some of the principal sources. For local advice, the nearest *Shopmobility* might be a good source, or possibly the local borough disability association.

All Handling (Movability), 492 Kingston Road, Raynes Park SW20 8DX *Tel:* 0181 542-2217 *Fax:* 0181 395-4410. A long established family-run firm who address mobility needs including wheelchairs, scooters, stairlifts and various specialised equipment. Powered and manual chairs are available on hire.

Care & Mobility Ltd, 440 Cranbrook Road, Gants Hill, Ilford, Essex IG2 6LL *Tel:* 0181 518-3458 *Fax:* 0181 518-3394, supply a range of specialist equipment connected with mobility, furniture and bathroom and toilet fittings. They offer a home adaptations service, and have a larger site and assessment centre at Rayleigh in Essex.

GBL Wheelchair Warehouse, Units 1-3 Shield Drive, Brentford, Middx TW8 9EX *Tel:* 0181 569-8955 *Fax:* 0181 560-5380. Ramped access and a **wheelchair loo** on-site. Small CP. GBL is a firm run by chair users. They offer a wide range of chairs, new, ex-demo or secondhand, and have an excellent hire or repair service. If you have a problem, give them a ring. The units are on an industrial estate near the Gillette tower on the A4, and are built where the old Firestone factory used to be.

Homecare Equipment Hire, 93 Northcote Road, Clapham SW11 6PL *Tel:* 0171 924-4058. Located near the junction with Salcott Road, on a busy shopping street, there is +1 step at the entrance, but portable ramps are available. It has a wide range of equipment available for hire. The list is geared to the kinds of things people might need when coming out of hospital after an operation. It is equally applicable to someone visiting London who may need a high-seat armchair, a raised toilet seat, a perching stool/shower stool, or an over-bed table where they are staying. They will send you a list of items available, and offer a delivery service.

Keep Able, 2 Capital Interchange Way, Brentford, Middx *Tel:* 0181 742-2181.

Near the north end of Kew Bridge, on the link road leading behind the swimming pool to the A4. CP. They have a large range of specialist equipment, for bathrooms, toilets, high seat arm-chairs, powered and manual chairs, walking aids and numerous 'gadgets' of one kind and another. They offer an assessment service before you buy, to ensure that you get appropriate equipment.

UK Care, The Old Mission Hall, Chipping, Herts *Tel:* 01763-273933 *Fax:* 01763-273934, are solely a hire company for scooters, manual and powered wheelchairs. They operate a collection and delivery service in the London area.

Repairs to NHS equipment

We made some enquiries about what to do if you are visiting London and you have trouble with any equipment that may have been supplied by your local NHS Trust. An obvious question is, 'What do I do if my wheelchair breaks down ?'

Unfortunately we didn't get any straight answers. The problem is that each NHS Trust has its own contracts for things like repairs, and each Trust may have different conditions. If it is something fairly straightforward like a puncture, and you can get it repaired at modest cost, then the thing to do is to get it fixed. Take the bill back to your own NHS Trust Supplies office/depot, and they'll probably pay up. One thing you need to bear in mind is that if you have to 'call out' one of the private suppliers listed here, there may be a significant charge over and above the cost of the repair. Possibly the best thing we can suggest is that you take with you the phone number of your own NHS Supplies office and then, if you have a problem, at least you can ring up and say, 'Help! What should I do?' Alternatively, go through the NHS Trust Supplies office nearest to where you are staying. Organisations who have been most helpful to us on various occasions are the AA and RAC. If you are a member or are staying with a member, there may be some simple repairs that they can help with.

Escalators

Elderly people and some disabled walkers find escalators difficult and they're obviously a problem for most solo chair users. Our own experience, however, is that they are a safe and easy way of changing levels for a chair user with one or two sensible able-bodied friends and most of our survey teams have learned how to cope. The pusher must be strong enough to control the chair safely and smoothly over a kerb. On an escalator the trick is simply to balance the wheelchair on the back wheels at the point of balance. The person behind pulls or pushes the chair on to the escalator, placing the wheels in the middle of a step as it opens up. The person in front pushes gently and horizontally against the chair and is only there to steady the chair if necessary. It's much easier than it sounds, though don't try it unless your able-bodied friends are strong enough. If you're intending to use the tube, see the write-up on LRT.

Facilities for those with hearing impairment

An increasing number of venues and auditoria are now making provisions for people with reduced hearing. Two systems are commonly used. Induction loops consist of a loop of wire right round the area, carrying an electronic signal which can be picked up on a conventional hearing aid. In practice, there are sometimes technical problems. There may be a good signal in one part of an auditorium and not in another. There are cinemas with two or three loops where you can see a film in one, and tune in to the soundtrack of another! If you need to use the loop signal, it is usually worth ringing in advance to ensure that it's switched on and working. They can probably advise about the best place to sit, and it is possible to 'tune' the system while you are there, if it is unsatisfactory. If you're lucky, this can be done while the adverts are showing before the main film.

The other system is called Sennheiser, based on an infrared signal with special earphones to pick up the sound. You will sometimes be asked for a nominal deposit to ensure the return of the earphones. Sennheiser systems can be highly directional, and you may have to sit in designated seats.

A number of telephones now have an induction coupler, and a few ticket offices use a mike behind the glass with a coupler outside, but their use is not yet widespread. A number of arts centres listed have special activities, for people with hearing impairment, and there are occasional 'signed' performances at theatres. For the latest information ask **Artsline** or **RNID.**

Minicom/Typetalk

Minicom and Typetalk are communication systems for those who find conventional phones difficult because of hearing or speech loss. For easy communication with someone who is hard of hearing, or for communication between deaf people, Minicom provides a simple and convenient method. The equipment consists of an add-on to a conventional phone which has a keyboard, and a display panel. Textphone terminals are called Minicoms, and hence the widely used name. Alternatively, it is possible to hook-up a computer and screen to provide the 'text' part of the signal, although you need the right software to make it all work. It's a way of avoiding the need to buy another piece of equipment, if you can utilise what you already have. The RNID offer a Uniphone, where all the necessary equipment is incorporated into one terminal. With developing technology, an increasing number of 'one piece' terminals will no doubt become available. Consult either BT or the RNID.

For a conversation, a Minicom terminal is needed at both ends. If you speak, the phone will work conventionally. If you use the keyboard, then the display at the other end will show your message. Thus a hearing person can talk to a deaf person, or two deaf people can type messages to each other.

For communications by or with someone who has hearing or speech loss, the Typetalk service can be invaluable. One end of the conversation can then be on a conventional phone. The other needs to be a Textphone. A deaf person can use it to communicate with someone on an ordinary phone and vice versa. The conversation goes via a Typetalk operator who provides a friendly and entirely confidential service. If you speak, the phone works conventionally. If you are hard of hearing, the Typetalk operator types in the message from the hearing person which is then displayed on your small panel. If you type in your conversation, rather than speak it, the operator will read the message out to the person you're ringing. Any reply will then be typed back to you. The service is funded by BT and run by the RNID. It is available throughout the country, and can be used for international calls. You pay the same charge as you would for a conventional call, and if your calls take longer as a result of using Typetalk, there is a rebate available.

For information on Minicom/Typetalk, contact: **Typetalk,** John Wood House, Glacier Building, Harrington Road, Brunswick Business Park, Liverpool L3 4DF *Tel:* 0151-7099494 *Minicom:* 0800-500888 *Fax:* 0151-7098119.

Braille terminals are available for deaf-blind people. They are more complex than the simple Typetalk phone, and if this facility might be of use, contact: The **National Deaf/Blind League**, 18 Rainbow Court, Paston Ridings, Peterborough PE4 7UP.

If you're deaf or hard of hearing, or have loss of speech, it's a brilliant service, although naturally it takes a bit of getting used to. Minicom terminals are becoming more widely used, and this allows those who are hard of hearing both to get and to provide information by phone.

Facilities for those with visual impairment

It is difficult for us to describe the special facilities for the visually impaired, as none of our surveyors quite understands what is involved. In particular, we recognise that the print size of this book is too small for some. **A LARGE PRINT version is available**, from PHSP Access Project, 39 Bradley Gardens, West Ealing W13 8HE. The print size used here is the result of a compromise with the publishers over the amount of information included and the eventual size and cost. The first edition of the guide was made into a Talking Book, and we hope that this will be done again.

The RNIB have published a special guide to London in a series on European cities. It has about fifty pages of general advice, and a list of places with audio tours. The amount of information is limited. It is available in large print, in braille and on tape, and will hopefully be updated and enlarged.

A good number of major museums and a few theatres, now provide a range of items/exhibits which can be felt and handled, and some lay on special exhibitions from time to time for visually impaired people. If you have a particular area of interest, it's best to contact the museum direct. **Artsline** may also be able to help.

Loos

Finding suitable loos is a serious problem for many people, and particularly for disabled people whose needs are more exacting. In the guide, toilets are referred to as loos since its sounds slightly more informal. American readers will be used to calling them the John or the bathroom. In Britain the bathroom is the room with a bath, and not necessarily with a toilet.

There are far more **adapted loos** around now than there were when the guide was first published. Quite a few McDonalds, Burger King and Pizza Hut restaurants have one, as do new shopping precincts, and a small, but increasing, number of pubs. We include a chapter entitled the *Good Loo Guide*, which covers much of central London.

You would be well advised to get hold of one of the special NKS keys available from RADAR which will open approximately half the adapted loos including most of those provided by local authorities and those on rail stations. **You can get an NKS key from RADAR**. They ask for pre-payment for keys, which cost less than £5 including postage. If you're wanting to send money from abroad, note that small cheques, even ones made out in sterling, are of little value as the bank may charge well over £5 for processing a cheque drawn on a foreign bank. RADAR will send a key to your UK address, and will help if they can.

For the distinction we have made between a **wheelchair loo**, an **adapted loo**, and unisex toilets and those in the ladies or gents areas, see the section on *Units and definitions*.

Price concessions

A number of places offer price reductions for chair users, or blind people, and/or, sometimes, for a friend or escort. Reductions are sometimes available for others such as pensioners or those on benefit. Sometimes the concession is for those who are registered disabled. The problem is that concessions are highly capricious and can depend as much on who's on the door as it does on official policy. The offer of price concessions for entrance is a well intended gesture, particularly in view of regulations which say that chair users may not enter some places without a friend or escort. We have always taken the view that the right of access is even more important, even if you have to pay for it. This essentially comes from our experiences over past years when people's rights to access have not been so widely recognised, and people have told us that 'you cannot come in'.

Because of their variability, and because they may apply to some disabled people and not to others, we have tended not to detail price concessions. The whole subject is confused, and the rules sometimes change. **Artsline** (0171 388-2227) will be able to advise about the up-to-date situation at particular venues. Places where there are well established concessions for chair users include most major museums; the two theme parks; many historical buildings; the South Bank (National Theatre and Festival Hall complex); the Barbican; the Colliseum; Fairfield arts complex in Croydon; the Royal Opera House; the Tower Bridge Walkway and the Tower of London. There are many others.

The Royal Shakespeare Company who use the Barbican Theatre have a particularly positive and practical approach to the question of concessions, which is worth a mention. They say that all tickets are half price for disabled people whose choice of seats is limited by their disability. For members of the audience who *need* to come with a companion, both tickets are half price.

Specialist books and publications

There are a large number of these, and listings can be obtained from the Centre for Accessible Environments, Disabled Living Foundation, GLAD, RADAR, SCOPE and other major disability organisations. Several have already been mentioned in the descriptions of the various specialist organisations. A few of the more important ones not highlighted elsewhere are:

Arts and Disability Directory Published by the Arts Council, 14 Great Peter Street SW1P 3NQ.

Chariot is a well produced and attractive magazine with all kinds of articles and discussion which tackles disability issues in a challenging but readable form. It is available at some large supermarket bookstalls or from Output UK Publishing, 61 Ditchfield Road, Widnes, Cheshire WA8 8RS *Tel:* 0151-423 4711.

Directory for Disabled People by Ann Darnbrough and Derek Kinrade has established itself as the main handbook for disabled people in Britain, and for those involved in disability issues. It includes sections on specialist equipment, employment, holidays, benefits and sports activities, and is regularly updated. The 1995 edition was published by Prentice Hall/Harvester Wheatsheaf, Marylands Avenue, Hemel Hempstead, Herts HP2 7EZ.

Disability Now is a monthly newspaper published by **SCOPE**, 12 Park Crescent W1N 4EQ *Tel:* 0171 636-5020, which covers a wide range of topics of interest to disabled people.

Door to Door is a publication from the Department of Transport prepared by Tripscope and regularly updated. It provides basic information about transport for disabled people. Although general in nature, it includes useful sections on personal transport schemes, buses, trains, air and sea travel and so forth. Available from Social Services Security offices and disability organisations or direct from Department of Transport, Door to Door Guide, Freepost, Victoria Street, Ruislip, Middx HA4 0NZ.

Disability Rights Handbook is a comprehensive guide to the social services for disabled people and is updated regularly to cover changes in welfare provision. It is available from **Disability Alliance (DA)**, Universal House, 88 Wentworth Street E1 7SA *Tel:* 0171 247-8776.

The London Disability Guide is a valuable resource book for disabled residents published by **GLAD**. It covers a variety of subjects including such things as benefits, education, employment, health services, housing and mobility. It also has an excellent list of relevant organisations who may be able to offer information, advice or help. Available free on receipt of a large stamped addressed envelope and about £1 in stamps. Braille, large print and tape versions are available.

Wheelchair stairlifts

While the provision of a ramp is always preferable, several venues and museums have installed stairlifts to help overcome the access barriers inside buildings. There are several types, the most common being the platform stairlift which goes up an inclined stairway. Others include open (vertical) lifts and portable stairlifts of the Gimpson or Scalamobile variety.

While this is clearly a facility that is much needed, our experience in going round surveying is that a significant number of the platform stairlifts are not working. Vertical open lifts to bypass a few stairs are simpler, and are probably less likely to go wrong. There are several problems and, too often, finding the operator who has the key and who knows how to work it can take an age. Minimising the cost means that they can be of somewhat lightweight construction. Maintenance and testing isn't always as thorough as it should be and some are not built to carry electric chairs. When used for this they break down as a result of the load. We have even come across one venue (the Purcell Room) with a perfectly good stairlift to bypass four steps which was not used for nearly two years. It almost fell on someone once, when being improperly handled – and as a panic reaction, the management discontinued its use! Fortunately that has been sorted out.

The final type is the portable Gimpson or Scalamobile. These are really a last resort to overcome step barriers. They are relatively cheap (hence they are attractive to those who control the budget). They are relatively horrendous to ride in, and there is a fundamental feeling of insecurity, however competent the operators. Properly operated, they are perfectly safe, but it doesn't necessarily feel that way. They can only accommodate certain types of chair, as the clamps are not universal, and they certainly cannot take an electric chair. We have commented on our experience with their use at Buckingham Palace.

The bottom line is, of course, that if you are a chair user or a disabled walker, using one of these devices may be the only way to get into some places. All of them are intended to be helpful, and to open more possibilities, and unquestionably their use is making places more readily accessible than they were.

If it's really important to you, telephone first to check that the necessary equipment is working. The best practice for such stairlifts is to install robust well-engineered equipment which is strong enough to carry electric chairs, and to test the lifts every day so that repairs and maintenance can be carried out as soon as there is a problem.

See the section on *Definitions and units* for the descriptions of different kinds of lifts.

Travelling and getting around

This chapter is written initially from the point of view of someone arriving in London, possibly for the first time. It can readily be used, however, by residents, and there is a section on facilities that are only available to people who live in London boroughs. There is a brief section for those arriving by air, and one detailing rail (formerly British Rail) services.

We describe the main rail termini together with stations that have step free access within a roughly 50km radius. There is advice and information for car and mini-bus users, and then sections on using London Transport underground trains and buses. These are equally applicable to residents and visitors.

London is big, and much of its public transport system was designed a century ago. There has been limited investment in improving the facilities and, until quite recently, the needs of disabled passengers have not really been considered. While attitudes are now more positive, the necessary changes to help disabled passengers are still inadequately funded. In particular the provision of accessible buses in central London, which is feasible without massive expenditure, has been limited to the circular *Stationlink* route. Diagonal links across the West End and City, to the sights, entertainment venues and shops in central London are urgently needed, and could be provided by a small network of low floor buses.

Travelling around in London is one of the biggest problems for the disabled person who wants to be both independent and mobile. Since the last edition of the guide in 1989 progress has been slow and patchy. Small sections of the system like the Docklands Light Railway (DLR) have step free access. In 1998 the Jubilee line extension will be opened, providing an invaluable section of the tube with step free access. More black taxis are now wheelchair accessible. For car users, there are more OB spaces in London. For London residents, Dial-a-Ride and Taxicard services, provide limited door-to-door services.

In so far as disabled people remain deeply concerned and angry about the lack of progress towards a fairer society where everyone can take part on an equal basis, the slow progress with developing an accessible transport system is probably the issue where they have most justification in calling for rapid change.

However, with the right information and with a little determination and planning, you should be able to get to most of the places you want, although you may have to use taxis or bring your own transport. If you need advice and/or up-to-date information about particular journeys, **Tripscope,** The Courtyard, Evelyn Road, Chiswick W4 5JL *Tel:* 0181 994-9294, are both experienced and practical. Advice is free, and available during normal working hours.

Note that we are looking at things largely from the point of view of someone making their own plans and bookings. If you are arranging your trip through a tour company, it is essential to make your needs clear, and to make sure that the person you are dealing with has really understood. Too often they think that 'goodwill' is a substitute for knowledgable action. It is important for you to understand the probable limitations of the 'system' and also to check that things can be (and are) organised to your satisfaction. There can be a difference between what the friendly sounding booking clerk says, and what actually happens when you turn up. You'll sometimes meet someone at your destination who'll say, "I don't know anything about that…"

Arriving

You may arrive in London by plane, train, coach or in your own transport, and each is discussed.

By air

If you fly into London, you will have needed to find out from the airline about access problems en route. Excellent general advice about flying is given in a free booklet called *Flying high*, published by the **Disabled Living Foundation**. It was produced in conjunction with British Airways, and includes sections on planning your journey, things to be aware of at the airport, and personal toilet on-board the aircraft (particularly if you are unable to get to the loo).

A new book researched by **Tripscope** and published by **RADAR** is called *Access to air travel*. This details where to contact the airlines, and the different procedures followed. Some require that a disabled passenger must be accompanied, others do not. Some use common procedures for frequent flyers, others do not. The book lists which airlines will carry an electric chair, and which can provide assistance for passengers who are blind, partially sighted or hard of hearing. If you're flying either to or from London, both books are invaluable.

Airports were one of the first places to provide facilities for disabled passengers, and they have been quite good for the past twenty years or so. At certain times they can become extremely congested. If you use the biggest airports, there should be step free access through the terminal to the aircraft door, but occasionally this may not be so either because of a breakdown, or possibly for security reasons. Both Heathrow and Gatwick have little buggies to take elderly and/or disabled walkers through the terminal to the departure lounge. Chair users normally have to transfer to an alternative 'loading' chair in order to get to a seat on the plane. At smaller airports, access to the aircraft will almost certainly be via a flight of steps. If you make prior arrangements it is normally possible to carry you up in an ambulance-type carrying chair.

Virtually all airports have **adapted loos** on both sides of the security desks. However, there are only a few of them, and if you want to use a loo you would almost certainly be wise to do so before the departure gate. There are, usually, **adapted loos** in the arrival areas where you are waiting for luggage, but they're not always well signed, and you may have to ask. Not all are unisex.

Transport links to and from the airports

There are accessible transport links to and from the three major airports. At Heathrow it's by bus to and from central London, and on the underground. The Piccadilly line platforms on both Heathrow tube stations have step free access, but you can only go to three stations, see the detailed write-ups on the tube. There are plans for a step free route to and from Heathrow and Paddington by train, but this is unlikely to be operational before 1998, and may even take longer to implement. If Terminal 5 is built at Heathrow it will almost certainly be accompanied by greatly improved public transport links.

To and from Gatwick and Stansted the accessible transport link is by train.

Heathrow

Heathrow airport, 234 Bath Road, Harlington, Hayes UB3 5AP *Tel:* 0181 759-4321 *Minicom:* 0181 745-7010, for general enquiries. There are four terminals, three (1, 2 & 3) of which are linked by underground passages with step free access, although there are several hundred metres between them. Terminal 4 is on a separate site. It can be reached by the underground with only single steps involved (getting on and off the trains). In one direction you have to go via Hatton Cross and change trains. There is also a bus link between the terminals, and an accessible bus is available, see below.

Heathrow has a service called **Travel-care** *Tel:* 0181 745-7495 *Minicom:* 0181 745-7565 *Fax:* 0181 745-4161. They provide a useful booklet called *Travellers' Information – Special Needs Edition* which has practical advice and includes a plan of every terminal showing the location of the main facilities, including **wheelchair loos**. Not all of these are unisex, so if you need this facility, make sure you locate an appropriate one. If you have difficulty in going between terminals, there is a *Help bus* available (*Tel:* 0181 745-5185) which has a lift and wheelchair spaces. Minicom phones should be available at all the information desks.

Gatwick

Gatwick airport, Gatwick, West Sussex RH6 0NP *Tel:* 01293-535535 *Minicom:*

01293-513179. The booklet *Welcome to London Gatwick* includes some information for passengers with disabilities. It does not include terminal plans. There are two terminals with a short train link between them with step free access. **Travel-care** (*Tel:* 01293-504283) offer help to anyone who has a problem.

Stansted

Stansted airport, Stansted, Essex CM24 1QW *Tel:* 01279-680500. A modern and relatively small terminal. A *Passenger information guide* is published, including some information for disabled passengers and a clear plan of the terminal. This shows the location of **wheelchair loos**.

By coach

Coach travel offers good value, if you can manage the steps involved getting on and off. Things have certainly got easier during the last few years as more disabled people have made use of the network. The most important thing is to inform the coach company of your needs when booking. So long as they, and you, are happy, the only general advice is to arrive in good time and make your needs known to staff. Note that there is a useful coach station at Heathrow Airport, although car parking is some 300m away. The main coach station is at Victoria, although some coaches arrive and depart at a 'drop off' point in Pancras Road, opposite Kings Cross station. A Senior Coachcard is available for discounted travel on National Express for those aged 55 or over.

Victoria Coach Station, 164 Buckingham Palace Road SW1W 9TP *Tel:* 0171 730-3466 *Fax:* 0171 730-6597. London's central coach station and the arrival and departure point for most coach services to places all over Britain and the continent. It is some 500m from Victoria rail station, and has been extensively modernised. Short-term parking can be arranged in the coach station itself if advanced warning is given, or there is an NCP in Semley Place.

The main entrance is on the corner of Elizabeth Street. There is step free access throughout with good signposting. If you need assistance, contact the Help Point on extension 235. Given notice, it is possible to help passengers to get on and off, but the operator needs to be aware of your needs at both ends of your journey. On-board loos, where provided, are tiny, and for all practical purposes should be regarded as 'inaccessible'.

On arrival at Victoria, there are signs leading to the office which provides information and assistance to disabled travellers. It is next to Gate 21 Lane B, and if you are coming by taxi you can ask to be set down by the office. There are two **wheelchair loos (D90 ST80 NKS)** nearby.

By rail

There is a huge network of rail lines through the London suburbs. It is more dense south of the river, where there are fewer tube lines. You can pick up maps of the system called *The London and South East map* from a number of information points.

A booklet called *Rail Travel for Disabled Passengers* is available. This includes practical advice, and contact phone numbers. It also contains details of concessionary fares, and of the Disabled Persons Railcard. This offers reduced fares for you and an adult companion. It is valid for a year, and at the time of writing cost £14. Cards are available from **The Disabled Persons Railcard Office,** PO Box 28, York, YO1 1FB. The booklet and other leaflets are available at main stations.

If you do not want to drive in London you can park, or stay, near a station with step free access to the platform. Remember that there is a step up into the carriage, but if you can manage this, you can take the train to central London. Then you can use a taxi. As there are so few journeys 'inside' London that it is possible to make by train without major access problems, we will describe the network in detail in this section on *Arriving.*

The map shows the main peripheral stations with step free access. The range of options, although limited, is growing. City Thameslink station has step free access and is potentially of great use as a central destination. It is unfortunately not open after 9 pm or at weekends. Charing Cross can be a really useful central destination.

There was a problem with writing this section, since British Rail is in the middle of being privatised, and split up into a number of different operations. It was difficult enough getting coordinated information about the limited services available to disabled passengers when there was a single authority for BR. In spite of various assurances, it is almost certain that if there are separate companies, information will be fragmented as well.

There is a statutory framework under which the privatisation is taking place, and if you are interested in the intended policies, get hold of a copy of '*Meeting the needs of disabled passengers – a code of practice*' published in 1994 by the **Office of the Rail Regulator**, 1 Waterhouse Square, Holborn Bars, 138 Holborn EC1N 2SU *Tel:* 0171 282-2000 *Fax:* 0171 282-2040. This does require some minimal provisions to be made for disabled passengers, in consultation with the Disabled Persons Transport Advisory Committee (DPTAC) c/o Department of Transport, Great Minster House, 76 Marsham Street SW1P 4DR *Tel:* 0171 271-5256. The code says useful things about architectural standards and design issues, but little about the practicalities of making arrangements. The existence of the code, and the consultation process is a sign of progress, but with privatisation it may well be a question of two steps forward and two steps back, at much the same time. If the Regulator uses his powers, services for disabled passengers may improve.

There was a problem with writing this section, since British Rail is in the middle of being privatised, and split up into a number of different operations. It was difficult enough getting coordinated information about the limited services available to disabled passengers when there was a single authority for BR. In spite of various assurances, it is almost certain that if there are separate companies, information will be fragmented as well.

We have included some of the principal enquiry numbers for different railway lines, current towards the end of 1995, and supplied by British Rail. When trying to make use of them ourselves, we have found that the performance is variable and some lead to an ansaphone. There is a joint BR/Railtrack project entitled *The Informed Traveller* that aims to provide *a* single enquiry point for all who travel by rail, but this may take a long time to achieve.

We have found that knowledge about the accessibility of different parts of the network is patchy. The RADAR publication *A guide to British Rail for disabled passengers* was last published in 1991, and there is no sign of a new edition.

It is regrettable that the new suburban rolling stock coming into use on BR services make little or no provision for disabled passengers and, in particular, chair-users. The design seems basically to maximise the number of seated passengers, and not to leave three or four 'slots' away from the entry doors, which could either be used by standing passengers, by mums with a push-chair or by a chair user. On long distance trains, the provision of only one or two pre-bookable spaces for a chair user is an inflexible arrangement, making it difficult to travel at peak times or to make a journey at short notice.

Virtually all the central main line stations in London, being termini, have flat access everywhere. In addition, most have portable ramps for easing the transfer of chair users into and out of the trains. Most, though not all, have taxi pick-up points just outside or inside the station.

Stations in and around London with step free access, some via service lifts, include:

(a * indicates that there is some reservation, either about the whole of the station having step free access, or about the hours of operation, or that the station is not staffed. **If the station is listed without comment, there should be step free access throughout the day**)

Thames line
Paddington

access to platforms 13 and 14 for suburban services is via a ramp which is half way up platform 12. Most of the trains that go to and from Reading go from the main line platforms. **Wheelchair loo (D82 ST78)** inside the first aid room on platform 1.

Maidenhead
   *step free access to platforms 4 and 5. Goods lift (W300 L300) to bypass the steps to other platforms but with restricted hours of operation.
Reading

Chiltern line
Marylebone
   wheelchair loo (D100 ST85 NKS) just inside the door to the ladies.
Wembley Stadium
   * long (50m+) and steep ramp up to road level. Not generally staffed.
High Wycombe
   flat access to platforms 1 and 2. Platform 3, the platform for trains to Marylebone, reached by ramped underpass from the end of platform 2.

North London lines
Euston
   both side entrances to the station have steps (+4 from Melton Street, +14 from Eversholt Street). Ramped entrances from the Euston Road and the bus station. **Wheelchair loo (D75 ST80 NKS)** off the concourse near the end of platform 1.
Watford Junction
   main CP over 100m away. Two OB spaces just outside. **Wheelchair loo (D95 ST75NKS)** by the ticket office.

Richmond to North Woolwich line through north London
Richmond
   see write-up under South West Trains.
Kew Gardens
   ramped access in both directions, although southbound there is a locked gate.
Homerton
   via ramps in both directions.
North Woolwich

Thameslink
St Pancras
   wheelchair loo (D70 ST70 NKS) near the end of platform 7.
St Albans
   * flat access to platform 1 and platform 4 at peak times. At other times, and for platforms 2 and 3, staff assistance is required to cross the track.
City Thameslink
   * closes early on weekdays, and is closed at weekends. **Wheelchair loo (D80 ST75 NKS)** in a corner of the concourse, past the ticket barrier and the lifts, on the right.
Blackfriars
   * ramped access from about 100m to the east next to Puddle Dock, but not

well marked. It's about 300m long. Platforms 1, 2, 3 and 4 have step free access, but platform 5 for northbound Thameslink trains can only be reached via a stepped subway.

East Croydon
steepish ramp leading to all platforms. **Wheelchair loo (D95 ST90 NKS)** on platform 4.

Gatwick

Great Northern line
Kings Cross
wheelchair loo (D90 ST130 NKS) on platform 8.

Potters Bar
Welwyn North both platforms have flat access via separate entrances.

Stevenage
* need an NKS key for the lift 'out of hours'. Out of service when surveyed.

West Anglia line
Liverpool Street
recently rebuilt, and on two levels, with lift (D90 W145 L210) access to eastbound Circle line. **Wheelchair loo (D85 ST75 NKS)** off the ticket office at platform level.

Enfield Town
Walthamstow Central
has flat access from street level on either side, Priory Avenue or Selbourne Road.

Chingford

Great Eastern line
Liverpool Street (see above)
Ilford
* some platforms with flat access, others via a platform stair lift (W67 L80). **Wheelchair loo (D85 ST110 NKS)** through the foyer on the left.

Romford
* steep bumpy ramp to the left of the main station bypasses +11+12 steps. The ramp is closed in the early evening and you may have to get a staff member to open it. All platforms have ramped access.

London Tilbury and Southend
Fenchurch Street
lift (D125 W150 L190) to platforms. **Wheelchair loo (D90 ST120+ NKS)** at platform level.

Barking
* all eight platforms can be reached using a service lift (D180 W180 L200) to platform 1, and then steepish ramps, and long distances.

Upminster
* service lift (D200 W200 L200) to platforms, 1, 1a, 2, 3, 4 and 5 so that

interchange between Fenchurch Street trains and the District line is possible.

Kent Link line

Victoria
  wheelchair loo (D70+ ST70+ NKS) by the main toilets on the right side of the station, looking towards the platforms.
Charing Cross
  wheelchair loo (D70+ST80+ NKS) off a corridor linking to the street.
Cannon Street
  * lift access to all platforms, but the station is closed at weekends.
London Bridge
  being rebuilt when we surveyed, but there should be step free access everywhere, a **wheelchair loo** and a step free link to the Jubilee line.
Dartford
  platforms accessible via lifts. **Wheelchair loo (D140 ST95 NKS)** unisex cubicle just inside the ladies entrance.
Orpington
  * the Crofton Road entrance gives flat access to platforms 1 and 2. The Station Approach gives flat access to platforms 5, 6, 7 and 8. Platforms 3 and 4 can only be reached via ±26 steps.
Grove Park
  * ramped access to all platforms except platform 1 which is a branch line to Sudbridge Park and Bromley North only (with ±29 steps).
Sevenoaks
  lift access to all platforms. **Wheelchair loo (D75 ST70)**. Need to get a key from the staff.
Woolwich Arsenal
  * ramped access to both sides of the station through gates which can be opened by NKS key. **Adapted loos (D70+ ST60 NKS)** on platform 1 and opposite the station entrance.

South London lines

Victoria (see above)
London Bridge (see above)
Richmond (see below under South West Trains)
Anerley
  * not always staffed. The platforms have step free access on either side, and there is a nearby road bridge providing a step free link between the two sides.
Wimbledon
  (see below under South West Trains)
Epsom
  * large service lifts, although one was out of action when we surveyed.
Epsom Downs

South West trains

Waterloo

  step free access everywhere, including Waterloo East via lift and ramps. **Wheelchair loo (D70+ ST70+ NKS)** in the foyer above the ladies, off the main concourse. Getting to and from the station is difficult, see write-up on the South Bank in the section on *Arts centres*. Note the link to Bank station.

Brentford

  * unstaffed station with step free access on either side, and a road bridge linking the two platforms. The angle of the track means that the step getting on and off trains is particularly big on both sides.

Richmond

  * a key station on the District line tube, South London lines, and at the end of the line to North Woolwich. The platforms are reached via –22 steps, but there are service lifts (D160 W190 L290) to all platforms. **Wheelchair loo (D90 ST200 NKS)** at platform level near the end of platform 6.

Wimbledon

  lift access to all platforms, and link between BR trains and the District line. **Adapted loo (NKS)** on platforms 7/8 was temporarily closed when we surveyed.

Kingston

  * only one platform is accessible, but trains run from this platform on a loop to and from Waterloo.

Guildford

  step free access to all platforms via ramped underpass. **Adapted loo (D80 ST35 NKS),** large cubicle, on platform 2.

Windsor & Eton Riverside

  wheelchair loo (D85 ST75 NKS) off the concourse.

Hampton Court

  * has +2 steps at the entrance which can be bypassed by a ramp at the side towards the back of the station.

Enquiry numbers for disabled people wanting to make rail journeys, given to us by **British Rail**, and by **Tripscope** are:

Blackfriars 0171 620-5760
Cannon Street 01732-770111
Charing Cross 01732-770111
City Thameslink 0171 620-5760
East Croydon 01273-324487
Euston 0171 922-6482
Fenchurch Street 01702-357889
High Wycombe 0171 922-9522
Kings Cross 0171 922-9091
Liverpool Street
  01473-693333 (Anglia Railways Ltd)
  01206-564777 (Great Eastern Railway)

Links to and from Accessible Rail Stations

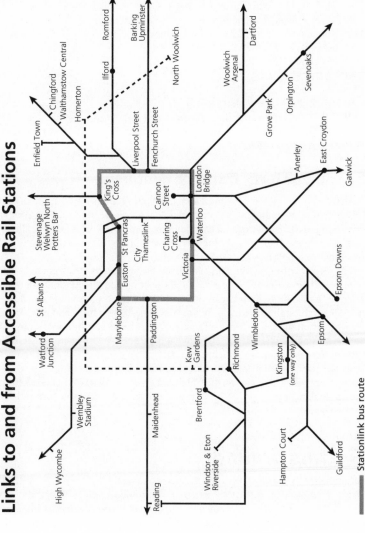

Stationlink bus route

01702-357889 (LTS Rail Ltd)
0345-226688 (WAGN Railway)
London Bridge
01273-324487 (Network SouthCentral Ltd)
01732-770111 (South Eastern Train Co. Ltd)
0171 620-5760 (Thameslink)
Marylebone 0171 922-9522
Paddington 0171 922-6793
St Pancras 0171 922-6466
Reading 01734-579334
Victoria
0171 922-9696 (Gatwick Express Ltd)
01273-324487 (Network SouthCentral Ltd)
01732-770111 (South Eastern Train Co. Ltd)
Waterloo 0171 922-4500

By train or ferry from the continent

With the opening of the Channel Tunnel, the possibilities for easier transport links across the channel have improved considerably. In particular, for car drivers, the *le Shuttle* service for carrying cars from Calais to Folkestone allows people to stay in their cars during the journey, thus greatly simplifying (and speeding) getting across.

The *Eurostar* trains from Paris and Brussels all have two designated chair spaces, with an adapted loo nearby, and these bring you directly into Waterloo International station, in the heart of London. Waterloo International has step free access through to the main station concourse using ramps and lifts. There are **wheelchair loos** on both sides of customs control, and the only major problems are the lack of a link to the underground and the poor pedestrian exits from the station. You almost 'have' to leave by taxi, by using *Stationlink,* or on another train. See the write-ups on pages 42 and 164 for additional details.

The large modern ferries on the Calais to Dover run all have lift access from the car deck to upper parts of the ship, and also have well adapted **wheelchair loos** on board.

Getting around

As undoubtedly the most flexible and convenient method of transport for many is the car (in spite of traffic jams and parking problems), we will consider this first, followed by taxis and minicabs. Then we will describe the facilities on London Transport tubes and buses. The rail network has been described already in terms of getting into the centre from the suburbs. Even Londoners find the variety of possible routes confusing, and may be largely unaware of the range of facilities.

By car or minibus

For many disabled people, getting around by car or adapted minibus is the only practical way, since much of the public transport system is inaccessible. Drivers have to face a fairly aggressive driving style and congestion, especially during rush hours. There can also be parking problems. Having said that, driving is certainly more disciplined than it is in other large European cities like Paris or Rome.

Your reaction to driving in London will depend very much on experience as well as on driving skills and temperament. Londoners tend to be very positive and to go quite fast. Driving speeds have dropped over the years due to congestion. Major junctions are now controlled by traffic lights, and far more lanes have been clearly marked in recent years. This makes it easier for visitors. Problems include the one-way streets and no-right-turns, which seem to crop up everywhere. The secret is not to panic and just press on. Make sure that you've got a good map. If you have a navigator, so much the better, but if you have a map you can at least stop and sort yourself out, working out another route if necessary.

Parking at or near your destination isn't always as difficult as people make out. If you can plan in advance, it may be possible to reserve a space at some major sites (but bear in mind that there are few such spaces) or even at a nearby CP. There's an excellent map for central London called the *Evening Standard London Parking Map*. The write-ups do NOT say how to get out of the CP. For a disabled person using a CP it is clearly useful to know whether there is a step free access route out, for example via a lift.

A leaflet entitled *Information for Orange Badge holders* is issued by the **Parking Committee for London**, New Zealand House, 80 Haymarket SW1Y 4TE *Tel:* 0171 747-4700. You should note that because of the pressure on parking in Central London there are special rules for OB holders, and these vary (confusingly) from borough to borough. Some allocated spaces are for Red Badge holders only, and are intended for those who live or work in the area. It is a special badge issued locally. The general position is that in the boroughs of Kensington & Chelsea, Westminster, and in the City itself, the usual relaxation of parking rules on single yellow lines does not apply, and meter parking is not free either. During the past five years there has been an enormous increase in the provision of on-street OB spaces in central London, although they are quite scattered. Most are marked, clearly, in the *London Parking Map* mentioned above. You need to remember that although it is illegal to clamp a vehicle displaying a valid OB, the car can still be removed if it is deemed to be causing an obstruction.

One way of making constructive use of your car or minibus, and also of the accessible transport facilities, is to drive into the Docklands, park near a station there and use the DLR for some of your sightseeing/visiting. Equally you could park at Richmond and use the train in to Waterloo (for the South Bank) or at East Croydon and go to City Thameslink, Charing Cross or Victoria. With the opening of the Jubilee line extension, the possibilities for parking just outside the centre, and coming in to stations such as Westminster, London Bridge and Caledonian Road, will be greatly increased.

Car/van rental

Probably the best (and almost the only) source of converted vehicles for hire is **Wheelchair Travel**, 1 Johnston Green, Guildford, Surrey GU2 6XS *Tel:* 01483-233640 *Fax:* 01483-237772. Full details are in *General information.*

It is possible to hire vehicles with the 'Chairman' conversion from **Gowerings Mobility**, The Old Barn, 18 Church Gate, Thatcham, Newbury, Berks RG13 4PH *Tel:* 0800-220878 or 01635-871502 *Fax:* 01635-873201. These can take a chair user in the car. You have to collect the vehicle from Newbury.

By taxi and minicab

Taxis and minicabs are widely available. London taxis are of unique design, adapted from the old-fashioned hackney (horse-drawn) carriage of Victorian times. Black cabs are licenced by the police, and every vehicle carries its licence number. They operate a meter on which the fare is recorded. If you order one by phone, the charge will start from where the cab is when you phone, so you pay for the distance it has to come to pick you up.

Taxis can be hailed (stopped) in the street. An increasing proportion of them are wheelchair accessible, and carry portable ramps to help a chair user to get in. **By the year 2000, all will have this facility**. However, there are a few snags. The largest cabs are Metrocabs, but there are relatively few of them. Some drivers don't want to be bothered with the ramps, and we've even heard of a few who carry their golf clubs in the boot instead! The space inside the cab is quite low and restricted, so if you're a chair user you may be sitting side-on with your head bent at a funny angle. If you are side-on, you may have a somewhat lively ride, and someone needs to hang on to your chair quite hard. In addition, the design is particularly difficult for people with arthritis, as the main seat is back some distance away from the door, and you have to bend down to get in. One American who wrote to us said that it was undignified for an elderly gentleman to have to crawl on his knees to get to the seat, as he couldn't easily bend down.

The newer vehicles include a fold-out dickie seat on a hinge, which means that it can be unfolded and will swing right out outside the cab. You can then sit on it outside and swing in while sitting on the seat. This may help some, but cab drivers aren't necessarily quick to spot when you might need this facility. You will also be sitting perched on a small seat which is without the support of arms.

If you want to take a wheelchair accessible cab, the story is that it's a bit of a lottery. You can only book from a home or hotel address, and not (for example) from a theatre or museum. Even if you book a day in advance, if you're only going a short distance, the cab company may come back and say "sorry, we haven't got a cab in your area at the moment...". If it's a big fare, say to go to Heathrow, your chances are greatly increased. This is clearly not right, but we regret to say that is how it is.

The principal companies with radio-controlled cabs are:
Computer Cab Tel: 0171 286-0286
Dial-a-Cab Tel: 0171 253-5000
Radios Taxicabs (London) Tel: 0171 272-0272

For specific journeys that are important, **Tripscope** may be able to help, as they know a number of individual drivers with accessible cabs in various parts of London who are reliable when a booking is made.

Minicabs are conventional cars, and because you can transfer sideways into a seat, they may be easier to use than a London taxi. They can only be ordered by phone, or by prior arrangement, but cannot pick you up in the street. You can go to a minicab office and order one. Unlike black cabs, minicabs are unlicensed, and the standards of driving and of service are considerably more variable. The place where you are staying or visiting or eating at will probably know a reasonably reputable local company.

If you cannot use the public transport system, and do not wish to drive around, taxis and minicabs are almost your only option.

London transport services

London Transport, 55 Broadway SW1 *Tel:* 0171 222-1234, *Minicom:* 0171 918-3015 runs both the buses and tubes. Its principal function is to provide a fast mass transport system which best meets the needs of Londoners. As with other services, it has recently become even more cost conscious than in the past. It is only recently that the needs of disabled passengers have been seriously addressed, and the provisions that have been made are restricted because they are seen as being too costly.

A GLAD survey showed that over 400,000 Londoners could not use the normal public transport system because of their disability. There will be tens of thousands of visitors who will have problems, and probably many more who will be deterred from coming altogether.

Special provisions, particularly for passengers who need step free access, are minimal, and most are shown on the Accessible Transport map. Things will, however, improve considerably in 1998 when the Jubilee line extension opens. The only central service is the *Stationlink* bus which is due to start operating in both directions early in 1996. The DLR reaches Tower Gateway and the Bank. The District line has accessible stations at both ends of the line, and links with the accessible Piccadilly line stations as they use the same stations between Acton Town and Barons Court. Hammersmith has lifts on both platforms linking to street level, and offers the opportunity of changing direction. There are two stations with step free access at the end of the Central line, and there is a step free interchange between the Central and District at Ealing Broadway (but 32 steps to the street). The Northern line has a single accessible station in the north, and two nearby stations in the south, each of which is step free in one direction.

There are buses with lifts for chair users on the main routes going from Victoria and Euston stations to and from Heathrow Airport, although not all buses now have this facility.

In addition to the routes shown there are a number of bus services, known as Mobility Buses, which operate perhaps once or twice a week using wheelchair-accessible vehicles, to enable people to get to shopping centres and other destinations. A number of daily midibus services in the west London boroughs of Ealing and Hounslow are operated by wheelchair accessible vehicles. Details of these can be obtained from the **LT Unit for Disabled Passengers (LTUDP)**, 172 Buckingham Palace Road SW1W 9TN *Tel/Minicom:* 0171 918-3312 *Fax:* 0171 918-3876.

LTUDP produce various free maps, guides and leaflets, including *Access to the Underground,* a *Tactile Tube map* of the central part of the system, and *Harnessing London Transport – a Guide Dog Owner's Guide.* They produce maps of all the Mobility Bus services, which are mainly in the suburbs.

Waterloo to City link

There is an important link between Waterloo International station and the Waterloo-City line. This means that you can get from the main concourse on Waterloo to and from the DLR network. Consequently you can come in from suburban stations to Waterloo or Waterloo East, and go to the Bank, Tower Gateway and to Island Gardens, using a step free route.

The route involves taking the lifts from the Waterloo concourse down to the level under the main station where the International ticket office is and where arrivals come in. Go down the ramp alongside the road, and turn left past the underground ticket office. Go through the bypass gate (operated by NKS key) where the trolley barriers are and out through the double doors, turn right and take the ramp down to the Waterloo-City platform.

At Bank there is a gently inclined Travolator followed by a steepish slope, to take you up to the ticket office ring, and from this level there are staff operated lifts either down to the DLR platform using two lifts, or up to King William Street using a third lift, but you need staff help throughout.

Going the other way involves a little extra time at Waterloo. There is lift/ramped access at the Bank station via the Travolators to the Waterloo-City train, but note that the ramps are steepish. At Waterloo, the arrivals platform only has stepped access to get out (about +30). However, what happens is that the trains go into a siding for a few minutes before returning to the Bank via the ramped departure platform. Consequently, if you cannot manage the stairs, you should tell the driver when leaving Bank (he has to walk the length of the train to change ends) that you need to go via the sidings. The LTUDP tell us that this procedure is currently being 'formally clarified'. The route from the departures platform is up the ramp, through the gate bypass into the International station and then up in the lifts to the main Waterloo concourse.

Buses

Apart from the fragmentary suburban services already mentioned, the main 'accessible' bus service is *Stationlink* which, as its name implies, links the main line railway stations using vehicles that have a tail lift. Currently the service only goes in one direction, operates hourly, and stops in the early evening. There are plans to increase the service in 1996 using low-floor vehicles, so that buses travel both ways round the circuit. This is an essential improvement, as it takes over an hour and a half to get all the way round.

There are accessible buses going from both Victoria and Euston to Heathrow. These operate throughout the day at regular intervals, and at Victoria serve both the rail and coach stations.

One very constructive change that is under way is a trial of over sixty low floor buses. These have no steps at entrance or exit and, using a simple extending ramp, can enable chair users to travel relatively easily. They are much easier for parents with buggies and baby carriages, people with heavy luggage and for elderly people with shopping trolleys. Such buses have been in regular use in other countries for years, and have proved their value to the travelling public, even if they are slightly more expensive to buy and run. There would be enormous benefit if a policy were adopted to replace existing vehicles with low floor units when they become due for 'retirement'.

These low-floor buses have not yet been used on key central London routes in ways which would integrate with other wheelchair accessible facilities.

The underground (tube)

London Underground has recently decided to allow chair users the freedom to travel anywhere they choose on the tube system. Previously, chair users were banned from using the deep sections of the system. London Underground require (and this is not unreasonable) that you can cope adequately by yourself, or with the companions who are travelling with you. While this change is welcomed, it does not include freedom to make choices open to everyone else, for example, about using escalators.

London Transport is in the process of looking in detail at the system, and of preparing proposals for making modifications (such as the provision of ramps, platform stairlifts or of other kinds of lift), provided that a business case can be made out to secure funding from central Government and/or from the European Parliament. In the context of access, we would say that the main point is the fundamental right of people to be able to use as much of the public transport system as is sensibly possible.

Because the system is old, there are steps and escalators at the vast majority of stations. There is a book called *Access to the Underground* published by the LT Unit for Disabled Passengers. It is based on research work originally done by the Richard Cloudsley School. Unfortunately, because of the nature of the system, the guide is a statement of inaccessibility. Because of the different routes possible and the complicated interchange stations it's quite difficult to work out what you can do.

There is also a *Guide to London Underground* for blind travellers, by Angus McKenzie. It is available in braille, large print, or on cassette. It consists of:
- **Tube help**, a broad description of all the lines, routes and problems;
- **Tube list,** an alphabetical list of stations with interchange and guide dog access information;
- **Tube map,** a list of stations, in order on each line, with indications of noises made en route, and details of which side the doors open;
- **Tube ways,** with information about all the central interchange stations.

The guide is available from the LTUDP, or from the Guide Dogs for Blind People Association, Hillfields, Burghfield, Reading, Berks RG7 3YG *Tel:* 01734-835555. The author, Angus McKenzie, can also provide various formats on disk from 57 Fitzalan Road N3 3PG.

In this section we will present some of the information from *Access to the Underground,* and will highlight the small number of step free access routes available. These routes and the stations involved are shown on the Accessible Transport map. In fact, some remarkable journeys are possible, even for a chair user. You could get from Heathrow to Caledonian Road (not far from Kings Cross), with just one step, and note that **there's a step in and out of the trains anyway**. You could also go from Heathrow to Epping, or to Richmond or Liverpool Street or Chesham, all with just the single step access involved in getting on and off trains.

The stations on the Underground that have step free access or just a single step are:
  Barking (using BR lift, and ramps)
  Caledonian Road (lift plus a single step)
  Chalfont & Latimer
  Chesham

Chorleywood
Dagenham Heathway
Earls Court (Piccadilly line only, via a lift and the Warwick Road entrance)
Elm Park
Epping
Hammersmith (both stations and all platforms)
Heathrow terminals 1,2 & 3
Heathrow terminal 4
Hillingdon
Hounslow West (platform stairlift)
Kensington Olympia
Kew Gardens (although you may need to give prior notice to use the westbound exit. You could stay on the train to Richmond, and then come back the other way).
New Cross (although this doesn't link with anywhere accessible)
Richmond
Roding Valley
Sudbury Town
Upminster
Upney
Uxbridge
West Finchley
Wimbledon
Woodford, and
Woodside Park.

On the map showing accessible transport links (pages 48-49), we have included a few stations with step free access in one direction only. For example the southern part of the Northern line could be used to get to and from Woodside Park by using Borough station to go north, and getting off at Elephant and Castle. Similarly it would be possible to go from Ruislip to Caledonian Road, and on the return journey to get back to the accessible platform via either Hillingdon or Uxbridge.

At Stratford there is lift access to the westbound Central line platform, and to the DLR. If the eastbound platform were made accessible it would make a really good junction, especially in view of the Jubilee line extension in 1998. At Liverpool Street the eastbound Metropolitan/Circle line platform can be accessed by lift. Some stations such as Hyde Park Corner have step free access if you can use escalators. Note that escalators and lifts aren't always operational, although London Underground have been undertaking an extensive replacement programme, as many of them were really old.

Docklands Light Railway (DLR)

The DLR is London's only major fully accessible transport system. It links Island Gardens, just across the river from Greenwich, to Stratford, Tower Gateway or the Bank. A new extension goes through the northern docklands to Beckton. **All the stations have step free access with a lift or ramp from street to platform. The coaches have special spaces for a chair user.**

Unfortunately there have been some problems with the serviceability of the lifts. When we did one survey, as many as 15% of the lifts were not working, however during the summer of 1995, when we did a check, they were all operating. Unfortunately as the line runs at a high level over much of its length, the lifts are essential as you might otherwise have to manage anything up to 60 or 80 steps. At the Bank there is lift access in three stages. From street level the lift is tucked away out of sight a short distance along King William Street. There is an intercom to access it. At a lower level there are two further lifts down to the DLR platform. You need staff assistance to use the route as the lifts to the Northern line are only used by passengers during rush hours, and the final lift needs a staff member with a key. If you want to make enquiries about the serviceability of lifts at DLR stations you want to use on a particular day, ring 0171 538-0311.

Links in London with step free access

As explained, these are few and far between. There's *Stationlink*. There are a tiny number of tube links, mainly at suburban stations. One of the few central links involves the Piccadilly line at Hammersmith, Earl's Court and Caledonian Road (where there's a single step).

The DLR is extensive, but only in the east. There is step free access from Waterloo via the International Station, down on to the Waterloo-City line, see page 42. This opens a whole range of possibilities. If you are arriving from, say, Guildford or East Croydon, you can go to the Bank, and then you can use the DLR to go to Island Gardens, and hence Greenwich or to Stratford, or Beckton, all with step free access.

What is not immediately apparent is that a number of the accessible links and facilities are not available in the evenings or, sometimes, at weekends. *Stationlink* stops in the early evening. The Waterloo-City line does not operate on Sundays nor after about 21.30 on weekdays, and City Thameslink station is closed at weekends and evenings.

In addition to the routes shown, which are simplified for clarity of presentation, there are just a few other useful step free routes. The LTUDP will have details, but they are relatively complicated, and require a knowledge of where there is (and isn't) an island platform with trains on different lines using opposite sides. From Hammersmith, for example, if you wanted to get to the accessible platform at Liverpool Street, you could take the Hammersmith & City line (not shown) whose station is 200m from the District line station. Using this line you can also get to the Chesham (Metropolitan) line via Baker Street, where there is a step free change. By judicious use of the Hammersmith interchange where there are lifts, it is possible to get step free to and from Heathrow, Chesham, Epping and Upminster. When the Jubilee line extension is opened, there will be a step free link at Green Park from the Piccadilly line to the Jubilee line, although not up to the surface. At Westminster, there will be a step free link both to the surface, and to the District/Circle lines – and these open up all kinds of possibilities.

The lift at Liverpool Street goes down to underground station ticket office. Through the barriers there is a signed step free route to the eastbound platform of the Circle, Metropolitan and Hammersmith & City lines. Thus you can get to the District and Piccadilly (via the Circle) or link to Upminster. In order to get to Chesham there is a fairly neat trick. All you need to do is to take an eastbound Metropolitan line train one stop to Aldgate. The line finishes at Aldgate, so the trains reverse back, and return via the westbound platform. Thus you can link to the Circle line going the other way, and to the Hammersmith & City line westbound.

In 1998 the Jubilee line extension is due to open, and this will increase the number of stations with step free access considerably. These new stations are shown on the Accessible Transport diagram. This shows the journeys that are possible with step free or single step access. The Piccadilly Line is particularly useful, with a number of accessible stations, including Hammersmith, Earls Court and Caledonian Road. The Piccadilly links to Richmond via the District at Hammersmith. Westminster will also be an important interchange.

Using the Ealing Broadway interchange it is possible for a chair user to travel very cheaply from Heathrow, via Hammersmith, back to Ealing Broadway and then by Central line right out to Woodford or Epping. It is also possible to go from Heathrow to Barking or Upminster.

The *Stationlink* service goes to main line stations that are accessible from the main rail lines, but not by underground.

What is essential is a rolling programme making other links possible, at low cost. An accessible link is needed at Whitechapel, and at Shadwell, to connect with the DLR. Stratford needs step free access to its other platform, and making both Mile End and Ealing Broadway fully accessible, would bring substantial benefit in offering new possibilities for step free journeys.

For getting around **by boat** see chapter on *Open air activities.*

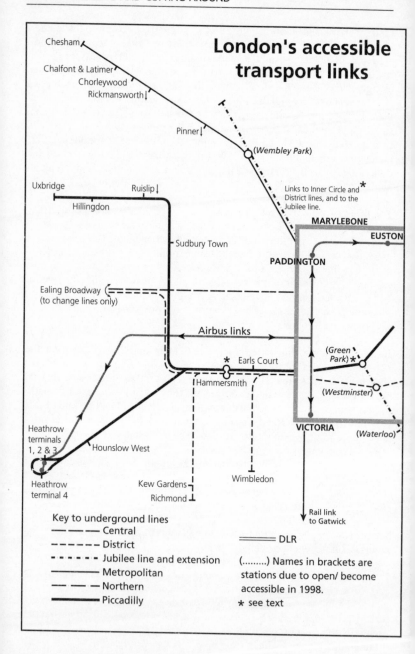

London's accessible transport links

Chesham

Chalfont & Latimer
Chorleywood
Rickmansworth↓

Pinner↓

(Wembley Park)

Links to Inner Circle and *
District lines, and to the
Jubilee line.

MARYLEBONE

Uxbridge   Ruislip↓   EUSTON

Hillingdon

PADDINGTON

Sudbury Town

Ealing Broadway (
(to change lines only)

Airbus links

(Green
Park) *

* Earls Court

Hammersmith   (Westminster)

Heathrow
terminals
1, 2 & 3   Hounslow West   (Waterloo)

Heathrow   VICTORIA
terminal 4   Kew Gardens

Richmond   Wimbledon

Rail link
to Gatwick

Key to underground lines

— — — Central
- - - - - - District
· · · · · · Jubilee line and extension
———— Metropolitan
— — Northern
▬▬▬ Piccadilly

═══ DLR

(.........) Names in brackets are
stations due to open/ become
accessible in 1998.
* see text

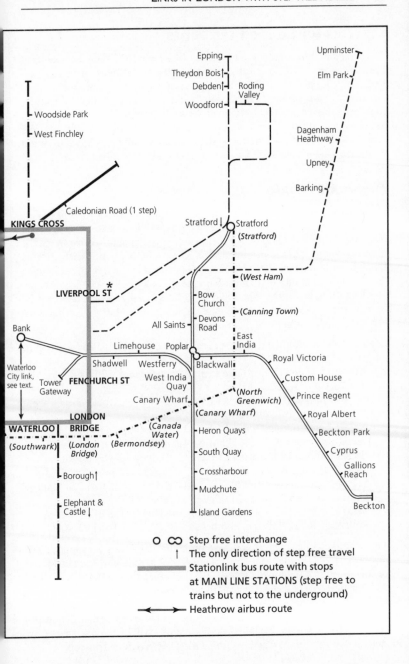

Services for London residents

The principal improvement in the transport system for disabled residents in London has been the provision of Dial-a-Ride services, and the use of the Taxicard. Both have gone through changes, in particular due to cuts in funding (and threatened cuts). Taxicard is funded by borough councils, and Dial-a-Ride by ring-fenced money from central Government. The provisions vary from borough to borough, and from year to year – all of which is most unsatisfactory. **All schemes have tight limitations on the number of journeys any individual can make**. Dial-a-Ride is administered by London Transport, Taxicard by LATU.

Dial-a-Ride (DAR)

DAR use wheelchair accessible minibuses, and provide a door-to-door service for those unable to use ordinary buses or trains. The idea is excellent. You can ring up and they will organise a driver to take you shopping, to visit friends or to go to church, either alone or with companions. DAR can be used by people living in sheltered housing, where several people may want to go to the same destination, either on a regular basis or one-off outings. The concept is good, although it requires a little organisation to make use of the service. The schemes operate from somewhat variable bases. Each will have its own criteria for eligibility and conditions of membership.

Dial-a-Ride is administered in six major areas, each covering a group of boroughs. These are:

- **Central London Dial-a-Ride Ltd,** Hathaway House, 7 Woodfield Road W9 2BA *Tel:* 0171 266-6109;
- **North London Dial-a-Ride Ltd,** Finchley Garage, Woodberry Grove, North Finchley N12 0DP *Tel:* 0181 445-3147;
- **North-East London Dial-a-Ride Ltd**, 400 Roding Lane South, Woodford, Essex IG8 8EY *Tel:* 0181 498-8204;
- **South London Dial-a-Ride Ltd,** Unit 6, Hallamshire Industrial Estate, 45 Weir Road, SW19 8UG *Tel:* 0181 784-6095;
- **South-East London Dial-a-Ride Ltd**, Unit 2 Lagoon Road, St Mary Cray, Orpington, Kent BR5 3QX *Tel:* 01689-896233;
- **West London Dial-a-Ride**, G2 Capricorn House, The Bilton Centre, Walmgate Road, Perivale, Middlesex UB6 7LR *Tel:* 0181 970-0095.

The central enquiry point if you have problems or queries not satisfactorily resolved by your local DAR office is **DaRT Dial-a-Ride and Taxicard Users Association,** 25 Leighton Road NW5 2QD *Tel:* 0171 482-2325 *Minicom:* 0171 284-2081 *Fax:* 0171 284-2079. DaRT membership is open to anyone who uses Dial-a-Ride or Taxicard services and, among other things, they campaign for adequate funding for the services. A specific goal is to ensure that all transport becomes accessible for disabled people. As they will be moving shortly, we suggest you get their new address from GLAD, RADAR or Tripscope.

Taxicard

This provides a complementary service to Dial-a-Ride, and is also for those who cannot use public transport. The card gives a reduced price taxi ride but, like all schemes, it has its limitations. Basically you pay a flat fee of £1.50 if the taxi meter shows anything up to £10.80. The scheme will pay for any extras such as evening, night or weekend journeys, but not for additional passengers. If the cost is over £10.80, you pay the extra.

The snags are that when you make a phone booking, the driver will start the meter wherever he is when he receives the radio message. Additionally he is technically charging waiting time if you are a little bit slow in getting out of the house, although this running time should never cost more than £1.50. When you try to make a booking, if there are no taxis immediately available (particularly if you require a wheelchair accessible cab), the taxi company may not be able to let you know until the last minute that it hasn't got a cab for you.

The limitations on the permissible number of journeys vary from borough to borough and some have withdrawn from the scheme. As an example, if you live in Hillingdon, you are currently allowed only 50 journeys a year, whilst in Lambeth it was 144 when we drafted the text, but early in 1996 they withdrew from the scheme altogether, amidst much protest. Because of the somewhat bureaucratic procedures for the driver who needs to reclaim his money from the Taxicard scheme, there are some taxi drivers who refuse to accept payment by Taxicard.

Cabs which display the Taxicard logo (Computer Cabs or Rainham Radio Taxis) can now be hailed on the street, or picked up at a taxi rank. There are currently about 2,500 of these cabs, but this only represents about 15% of the total. If you use a taxi, you must ask first whether Taxicard will be accepted.

The scheme provides door-to-door transport on a flexible basis. Several people can travel together (thereby reducing the cost per head), and the journey is subsidised. If you need further information, contact the **London Accessible Transport Unit (LATU),** Britannia House, 1 Glenthorne Road, Hammersmith W6 0LF *Tel:* 0181 748-7272, who administer the service.

Travel permits (bus passes)

These can now be used on the buses, tubes and on rail services within the Greater London area, and are available to elderly, disabled and/or blind people, resident in London. Who is entitled to a permit can vary from borough to borough, and the first point of contact in order to find out is your local Social Services Department.

The permits offer free travel after 09.00 Monday to Friday, and at any time over the weekend. These are extremely valuable to a lot of people but as the public transport system presents major access problems, they will not be applicable to most users of this guide. A detailed leaflet is available from LATU.

Accommodation

Accommodation in London tends to be expensive. There is a shortage of good, cheap accommodation in general and an even greater dearth of reasonably priced places to stay that are accessible. We've included hotels in various price ranges, as well as campsites, self-catering accommodation, youth hostels and University of London halls of residence. We have concentrated on lower cost accommodation, and included a good number of places with ground floor bedrooms (GFBs), parking, also those that have step free access and, in some cases, wheel-in showers.

Choosing where you stay is likely to result from a combination of location, cost and accessibility. There is a 'trade-off' between spending more money in the centre of London, or for service and comfort, and maybe being able to walk or wheel to many places you want to visit, or staying further out and travelling in – by whatever means. Almost whatever you decide, it will be a compromise.

Since the last edition of the guide, things have improved considerably. There is now really good, cheap and accessible accommodation at the **Rotherhithe Youth Hostel** and, during university vacations, at **Rosebery Hall**. Also note the **London City YMCA.** With the extension of the DLR, it is possible to have step free access from accommodation in the **Windsor House Travel Inn** (which has adapted rooms) to the Tower of London, to the City and to Greenwich. A new **Formule 1** hotel is opening in Barking, and another is planned. There are some reasonably priced motel rooms a little way out of the centre, and these can provide a good base. Note in particular the **Sleeping Beauty Motel** in Leyton. Also the **Travel Inns** and **Forte Travelodges** around the outskirts of London, since all the new ones have adapted rooms.

The three **Ibis** hotels in Euston, Greenwich and near Heathrow, are recommended for value and accessibility. Of the more expensive hotels, the **Copthorne Tara** and **Mount Royal Hotel** have the best adapted rooms. Ones that are in particularly good locations, from the visitor's point of view, are the **Tower Thistle** and the **Regent Palace,** but neither is cheap, nor has particularly good access.

A major difficulty is finding accommodation where there is a wheel-in shower. A shower is much easier for many people with disabilities to use than a bath, and the ones we've found, in order of increasing cost, are:

- the Formule 1 hotel at Barking
- Sleeping Beauty Motel, Leyton
- Rosebery Hall, EC1
- the Rotherhithe Youth Hostel
- the London City and Ealing YMCAs
- Hotel Ibis, Greenwich
- the Shalimar hotel, Hounslow
- the Oak Lodge hotel, Enfield and

• the Mount Royal hotel.

Staying in a hotel which has ground floor bedrooms (GFBs) eliminates dependence on a lift. Applying Murphy's Law (or whatever version of it you know), if a lift is going to go wrong, it will be when you're on the second floor and in a hurry to go and meet someone. If you're on the GF in the first place, Murphy is defeated and doesn't apply. A few of the places listed are guest houses on the outskirts of London. A chair user travelling with several family members or friends, or a disabled walker can probably cope in the majority of the places we've included, but note that some have cramped bathrooms, so be careful! Some of the accommodation is better suited for disabled walkers.

It may be worth considering staying at one hotel for two or three nights, and moving to another base in order to visit different places, especially if you don't have a car or you find that taxis are difficult. Using a central hotel with less than ideal access could substantially reduce travelling distances. Alternatively, staying outside London near to an accessible rail station (at East Croydon, for example) is a possibility for some.

If you want advice, the main source is **Holiday Care Service (HCS)** – see write-up on page 15. The standards of accessibility which are demanded from hotels which HCS list are admirably high, but as a result they tend to be in the top price bracket. HCS list only four places in London as being suitable for the independent wheelchair user, whatever exactly that means. Unfortunately most of the hotels in their London list fall into a somewhat ambiguous category, where the hotel may have a maximum of three steps between facilities. It may, alternatively, have step free access, but inadequate bathrooms – a very different kettle of fish – and why *three* steps is a criterion and who specifically it affects is a mystery!

The real problem is that the listings are based on value judgements which we would regard as imprecise and therefore of limited use. Rather than describing the facilities and barriers which they have assessed in arriving at their standard, they list them as either being:

• accessible to a chair user travelling independently (category 1);
• accessible to a chair user travelling with assistance (category 2); or
• accessible to someone with limited mobility, but able to walk a few paces and up a maximum of three steps (category 3).

What we have done here, as in the rest of the guide, is to adopt a descriptive approach and 'let the user decide'. We appreciate that this may not gel well with the need within the tourism industry for standards, but it is important that the standards adopted are informative, AND that they don't cut off other almost equally accessible accommodation which might be much cheaper and better located.

Indicated price information is based on the cost of a double room (or two single rooms) and includes the cost of TWO people staying, including breakfast and VAT. The figures should only be used as a rough guide, and it might be noted that a number of hotels have weekend reductions, which are not taken into account here.

£   £0-£40   ££   £40-£60   £££   £60-£100   ££££   £100+

We have listed the information within the various sections by price so that the cheapest places appear first, and the most expensive ones last. If a hotel is on the borderline, we have used a dual indicator. For example, the Travel Inns which cost about £40 to £42 a night, are listed as **£/££**. If a hotel is on the £60 borderline it is listed as **££/£££**.

Camping & caravan sites

Perhaps a tent is not the most obvious accommodation for someone visiting London. However, many disabled people go camping, and the relatively low cost can make it an attractive proposition. At peak times it is sensible to book in advance. In our view the London campsites are reasonably well adapted. Note that the sites have provision for only one wheelchair loo and/or bathroom which could be a problem if your visit coincided with that of several other chair users.

Approximate opening times are given here but they may vary from year to year. **Most of the sites cost less than £5 per person per night.**

Crystal Palace Caravan Site Crystal Palace Parade, SE19 1UF *Tel:* 0181-778-7155. Near the Crystal Palace National Sports Centre. Terraced site with sloped tarmac paths and gravel chip/grass pitches. Ramped office. **Wheelchair loo (D80 ST175) and shower with flat access** in both ladies and gents washroom/toilet areas. Open all year round. **£**

Dobbs Weir Caravan Park Charlton Meadows, Essex Road, Dobbs Weir, Hoddesdon, Herts EN11 0AS *Tel:* 01992-462090. Take the Hoddesdon exit from the A12 and follow signs to Dobbs Weir. A 16 acre site with beautiful surroundings and some on-site fishing spots with step-free access. Reasonably flat with tarmac paths and grass pitches. **Wheelchair loo (D75 ST80) and shower (D80 ST60) with a pull down seat, but with a lip at the entrance.** The shower has a seat but is effectively +1 step. Open April-October. **£**

Picketts Lock Sports and Leisure Centre Picketts Lock Lane, Edmonton, N9 0AS *Tel:* 0181 345-6666. Situated behind the leisure centre, with flat access, tarmac paths and grass pitches. **Ramp to wheelchair loo and shower (D90 ST70+ NKS).** The shower is wheel-in, with a seat. Open all the year round, though in winter the shop and washrooms are closed, and there is no site warden. Campers can use the washing facilities in the centre about 100m away. **£**

Sewardstone Caravan Park Sewardstone Road, Chingford, E4 7RA *Tel:*

0181 529-5689. On A112 between Chingford and Waltham Abbey about 4km south of junction 26 on the M25. Hilly site with tarmac paths and grass pitches. Reception and shop +1 step. Ramp planned. Combined **wheelchair loo/shower (D75 ST160)** with ramped access and grab bars. Open March-October. **£**

Self-catering

If you're thinking of a longish stay in London, and/or you're in a small group, self-catering offers particular attractions. Facilities are extremely limited and tend to be heavily booked. Costs per head vary depending on how many people are staying. As in other sections, we list places in ascending order of cost (the least expensive first). Rates start at around £150/week and are up to some £350/week (in 1995).

Lee Valley Boat Centre, Old Nazeing Road, Broxbourne, Herts EN10 7AX *Tel:* 01992-462085. At the Old Mill and Meadows site there are four riverside chalets for hire. One is adapted for chair users with a shallow ramp at the front. It can sleep 3/5 people and there are two orthopaedic beds. **The bathroom has D75cm and there is ST75 for the loo.** The bath has a cradle. Weekly rates are offered, and also weekend and mid-week rates. Good value.

John Grooms Association 10 Gloucester Drive, Finsbury Park N4 2LP *Tel:* 0181 800-8695 (Holidays); 0181 802-7272 (General Enquiries). *Fax:* 0181 800-8696. Adapted flat at Number 4. Ramped entrance and step free throughout. Three twin GFBs. **Wheelchair loo (D91 ST100)**. Bathroom D83cm with side-opening bath. Movable hoist for helping people out of bed. Kitchen, laundry room, lounge, low payphone.

Gloucester Lodge, 131 Gloucester Terrace W2 6DX *Tel:* 0171 262-5771. Two GF flats +4 steps. Bathroom D62cm.

Tudor Grange, 114 Westcombe Park Road, Blackheath SE3 7RZ *Tel:* 0181 858-6554 *Fax:* 0181 293-1866. Just west of the junction with Glenluce Road. Flats set up for providing accommodation with care if needed, adjacent to a nursing home. Available for short or long-term lets. Catering can be provided if needed. On-site CP. Main entrance +5 steps with ramped bypass. Step free to all the flats, some on the GF, others via lift (D79 W110 L145). Flat 15 seen: D72cm, bathroom D78cm ST104.

Kensbridge Apartments 64 Eccleston Square, SW1V 1PH *Tel:* 0171 834-0985 *Fax:* 0171 373-6183. On the east side of Eccleston Square, 50m south of the junction with Belgrave Road. Main entrance +5 steps, then flat to two GF units. Bathroom D62cm.

Hostels

Youth hostels

There are six Youth Hostels in the London area with varied degrees of accessibility. Only two, at Hampstead and Rotherhithe, are really of interest to people with disabilities. They provide inexpensive accommodation for both individuals and groups. Accommodation is mainly in small dormitories or family rooms. They are only **open to members** but membership is available on arrival. Opening times and charges are detailed in a booklet from the Youth Hostel Association (YHA) Trevelyan House, 8 St Stephen's Hill, St Albans, Herts, AL1 2DY *Tel:* 01727-855215. Hostels are mainly for young people but there is no age limit, and people of all ages use them. **Booking is essential** especially if you have specific requirements. **The new Rotherhithe YH has good adapted rooms.** The provision was made under the auspices of the **London Hotel for Disabled People Project** who also sponsored the adapted rooms in the Copthorne Tara Hotel. Please note that for comparison purposes, the indicated prices relate to the cost of TWO people staying. Prices were around £14 to £22 per person in 1995.

Hampstead Heath YH 4 Wellgarth Road, NW11 7HR *Tel:* 0181 458-9054 *Fax:* 0181 209-0546. Golders Green underground is about 400m away down a steep hill. Flat entrance, and flat to dining room. No lift. Flat to a dormitory of 10 beds with an en suite wheelchair bathroom. D77, loo has ST and there is a flat access shower. The warden was willing to allow mixed sexes to use the dormitory if there was a group booking. **Wheelchair loo (D75 ST70+)** by reception. **£**

Rotherhithe YH Island Yard, Salter Road, SE16 1PP *Tel:* 0171 232-2114 *Fax:* 0171 237-2919. Turn left out of Rotherhithe Underground station and it's 400m on the left. No on-site CP but plenty of parking on the road. Flat to reception, restaurant and lounge and a low-level pay-phone. There are **six adapted bedrooms,** two on each floor. Step free access throughout via two lifts (D80 W105 L150). The adapted rooms have two normal beds and one bunk-bed. Bathroom and loo en suite with a sliding door. **Flat access shower with hand rails and ST80+** to the padded seat with an adjustable back. **Loo with ST70+**. There is an **adapted loo (D85 ST65)** on the left as you enter the hostel. They have a policy of keeping the adapted rooms available for disabled visitors for as long as possible. However, since the facilities are such good value they are liable to get booked up, especially at peak times. **£/££.**

YMCA/YWCAs

London City YMCA 8 Errol Street EC1Y 8SE *Tel:* 0171 628-8832 *Fax:* 0171 628-4080. By the junction with Lambs Buildings. Flat entrance. Lift (D85

W110 L130). Flat to dining room. Five adapted rooms on the first floor, one twin, four single. **Two wheel-in showers** and **two wheelchair loos (D75 ST110)** off the corridor. There are three other slightly larger rooms on other floors with en suite bathrooms which are less spacious than the off-corridor facilities on the first floor. **Wheelchair loo (D74 ST100)** on the GF to the right of reception and turn left. **£**

Helen Graham House YWCA 57 Great Russell Street WC1B 3BD *Tel:* 0171 430-0834 *Minicom:* 0171 405-2177 *Fax:* 0171 242-2749 Opposite the British Museum. Main entrance +4 steps, but ramped side entrance (ring bell). Five rooms with adaptations for deaf visitors, such as strobe lights for door and fire alarm. There are eight GF rooms in all, with a shared bathroom area including a flat access shower with seat. **££**

YMCA Ealing 25 St Mary's Road, Ealing W5 5RE *Tel:* 0181 579-5076. About 500m from Ealing Broadway shops. Adjoining CP with some spaces on gravel. Flat entrance. Heavy door to the lift, locked by combination with keyboard 115cm high. Flat to dining room. Two lifts (D75 W110 L130) giving access to **twelve adapted bedrooms.** Room 317 seen: D74cm, bathroom D78cm (sliding), no ST to loo but flat access shower. **Wheelchair loo (D70+ST70+)** on the GF, past reception on the left. **£/££**

YMCA Kingston 49 Victoria Road, Surbiton, Surrey KT6 4NG *Tel:* 0181-390-0148 *Fax:* 0181 390-0065. On the corner of Brighton Road. Ramped entrance bypasses +2 steps. Flat to dining room and bar. Lift (D80 W120 L130) gives step free access to bedrooms on the second, third and fourth floors. **Three adapted rooms.** Room 201 seen: D70cm, bathroom D70cm but no ST. **Wheelchair loo (D75 ST95)** past the dining room entrance on the left. **££**

London University Halls of Residence

London University has a number of halls of residence. During the vacations some are opened as hostels with rooms let. The facilities tend to be basic, but as a cheap way of staying in central London it is hard to beat, especially if you want a single room (which is proportionately more expensive in a hotel). Halls will generally be available from March-April, July-September and December-January, but exact dates will vary.

Nearly all the halls we visited mentioned that they tend to get large bookings months in advance, since they provide ideal locations for conferences. They will usually have room for some casual visitors but **booking is essential** if you want an adapted room. They will be less busy at Christmas and Easter than they will be in the summer.

Advance bookings should be in writing and addressed to the Bursar at the relevant hall. The central **University of London Accommodation Office**, Union Building, Malet Street, WC1E 7HU *Tel:* 0171 636-2818 can supply further information. We recommend you look at **Rosebery Hall** or **Linstead Hall.**

Canterbury Hall Cartwright Gardens WC1H 9EE *Tel:* 0171 387-5526 *Fax:* 0171 383-7729. Entrance +1 step. Four lifts (D62 W120 L90) but with heavy manual doors. Step free access to dining room and a TV room via the lifts. Eight GFBs, D70cm and spacious. Few have en suite facilities. Bathroom D70cm. **£/££**

Connaught Hall 36 Tavistock Square, WC1H 9EH *Tel:* 0171 387-6181 *Fax:* 0171 636-6591. At the Bedford Way corner of Tavistock Square. Main entrance +5+1 steps, but there's a ramped entrance on the right of the building on Bedford Way. Lift (D100 W175 L90) access throughout. Dining room and bar in the basement. Twenty GFBs, D70cm, bathroom D70cm (not en suite), shower cubicle D69cm, +1. **Adapted loo (D84 ST10)** on the GF. **£/££**

Linstead Hall Prince's Gardens, Kensington SW7 1LU *Tel:* 0171 594-9438. Reservations via Imperial College Conference Centre, Watts Way, Prince's Gardens, Kensington SW7 1LU *Tel:* 0171 594-9494 *Fax:* 0171 594-9505. At the east side of the square. Parking if reserved in advance. Flat entrance. Eating arrangements vary, and meals may be in the Sherfield building, some 400m away. Important to check this when booking. Bedrooms on "Lower Gallery" floor are step free via lift (D86 W95 L163). Flat A29 with two rooms and a kitchen: D73cm, on the same level as an **adapted bathroom D73cm, ST65.** **£/££**

Ramsay Hall 20 Maple Street W1P 5GB *Tel:* 0171 387-4537. Corner of Maple Street and Fitzroy Street. Main entrance +5 steps, but there's a ramped way in from Maple Place. Three lifts (D80 W165 L95) give step free access to all the facilities, including the dining room in the basement. Ten GFBs with ramped access on the same corridor as the **wheelchair loo (D75 ST80)**. Bedroom D77cm. Shower cubicle D63cm and +1. Although step free, long distances are involved between the bedrooms and the various facilities. **£/££**

Rosebery Hall 90 Rosebery Avenue EC1R 4TY *Tel:* 0171 278-3251 *Fax:* 0171 278-2068. Corner of Gloucester Way. Step free to the new Myddelton Wing. There is another lift (D80 W96 L140) in this wing linking six floors with a **wheelchair loo (D85 ST75) and wheel-in shower D69cm on each floor.** Each floor has a kitchen. Both single and twin rooms. In the old building there are adapted cubicles in the ladies (+1) and gents loos. Dining room in basement. Excellent value, but a possible problem is the lack of parking. **£/££**

Weeks Hall 16 Prince's Gardens, Kensington SW7 1NA *Tel:* 0171 589-9608. Reservations as for Linstead Hall. Opposite junction with Ennismore Gardens Mews. On-site CP across the road if you book. Entrance ramped bypassing +1 step. Flat throughout via lift (D72 W110 L89). One adapted room with en suite bathroom (not seen). Meals are usually served in Linstead Hall some 250m away, but arrangements vary. Check when you book. **££**

Hotels

The information below is divided into six sections:
- inner London (W1, W2, WC1, WC2, E1, NW1, W8, SW5 and SW7) *(nearly all the hotels in these areas are numbered, and are shown on the hotels location map)*
- outer London northwest
- outer London northeast
- outer London southwest
- outer London southeast and
- outside the M25.

Some hotels are as much as 30km from the city, and we have included a few just beyond the M25, where there are GFBs in guest houses, at very reasonable prices. The intention is to give the widest possible choice.

Hotels listed by **Holiday Care Service** in their category 3, but not included in our survey (and all relatively expensive), are the:

Heathrow Hilton; Hilton on Park Lane; **Intercontinental** W1; **Langham Hilton** W1; **Le Meridien** Piccadilly W1; **London Mews Hilton** W1; **Sheraton Park Tower** SW1; **The White House** NW1 (category 2), and **Westland** W2.

The Copthorne Tara Hotel in Kensington has ten fully accessible and well adapted rooms. These were sponsored by the **London Hotel for Disabled People Project**. It is still quite expensive, even with the discounts available through HCS, and cost £80/night for two people in 1995. **The Mount Royal Hotel** also has well adapted rooms, but cost over £160/night for two people. They charge more for their adapted rooms!

A number of hotel chains have made it company policy to provide facilities for disabled guests. Notable ones, as far as London is concerned, are the **Ibis** chain, the **Travel Inns**, and **Forte Travelodge**. Note that Travel Inns have plans for a 300-bed hotel in the Old County Hall on the South Bank opposite Westminster. If this development takes place it would provide some budget price adapted rooms in an ideal central location.

It is worth mentioning that what is described as an 'adapted' room by the hotel may not be suitable for everyone, particularly if the adaptations were made a few years ago. Adaptations cover (as they say) a multitude of sins. It is in this area that the ETB/HCS standards can be of value. The listings produced by the chain will only say that they have 'adapted' rooms, and booking personnel probably won't know about details.

Check with the hotel if you are in doubt. But be careful, the person you speak to may not know the necessary details, and may say, helpfully, that "they've had people in chairs staying before, and they didn't have any problems", as though that tells you everything!

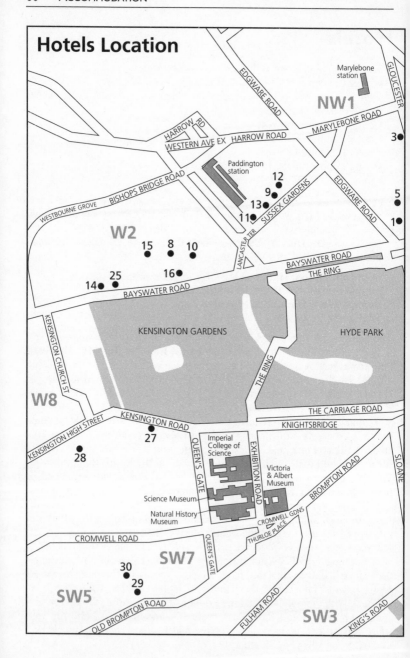

Hotels Location

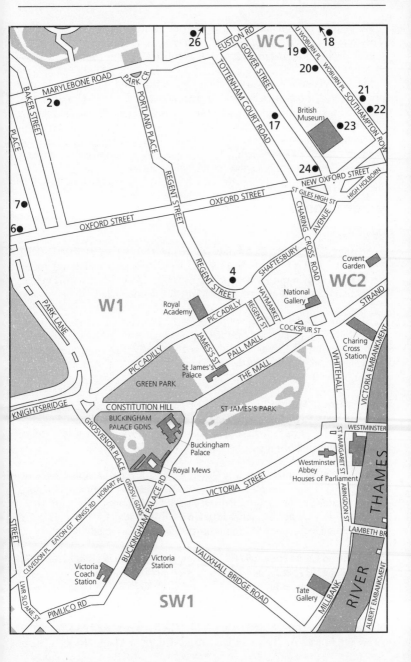

We weren't always allowed to see things (for example if rooms were occupied when our surveyors called), but when that is the case, we say so. As a rule if a specific facility is not mentioned, such as a lift or a GFB, then you should assume that the hotel does not have one.

Many hotels offer reduced weekend rates. It is possible to arrange cheaper prices through reservation agencies, particularly out of season. Unfortunately it is difficult for agencies to advise about access, and about the adapted rooms. If you have particular needs it is always preferable to negotiate directly with the hotel management, as you've then got the best chance of getting what you need. In our real and wonderful world, subject to 'market forces', this means that if you are disabled, you may have to pay more as well.

Inner London

W1

1. Edward Lear Hotel. 28 Seymour Street W1H 5WD *Tel:* 0171 402-5401 *Fax:* 0171 706-3766. Entrance +1 step. Flat to the lounge and dining room. Four GFBs. Only room 1A has en suite facilities: D69cm, bathroom D63cm, cramped. Room 3 spacious, D65cm. Many fire doors. £££

2. Blandford Hotel 80 Chiltern Street W1M 1PS *Tel:* 0171 486-3103 *Fax:* 0171 487-2786. Just off the Marylebone Road, a short distance from Baker Street underground. Entrance +2+2 steps. Lift (D64 W102 L69). Dining room in the basement, step free via the lift. Three GFBs: D69cm, bathroom D60cm (sliding), small. £££

3. Hart House Hotel 51 Gloucester Place W1H 3PE *Tel:* 0171 935-2288 *Fax:* 0171 935-8516. Just north of the junction with Blandford Street. Entrance +3+1 steps. Downstairs to the dining room. Four GFBs, varied in size. Room 2 seen: D68cm, bathroom D49cm, cramped. £££

4. Regent Palace Hotel Piccadilly Circus W1A 4BZ *Tel:* 0171 734-7000 *Fax:* 0171 734-6435. On the corner of Sherwood Street, and listed primarily because of its location. NCP nearby on Brewer Street. Flat entrance. Three lifts (D93 W109 L114). Dining room and bar flat. No GFBs. Room 4003 seen: D76cm, card operated lock, spacious. Bathroom not en suite, and small. £££

5. Bryanston Court Hotel 56-60 Great Cumberland Place W1H 8PD *Tel:* 0171 262-3141 *Fax:* 0171 262-7248. Just south of the junction with George Street. NCP around 300m away. Entrance +1+1 steps. Lift (D58 W77 L87). Flat to dining room. Two GFBs. Room 99 seen: D69cm, bathroom D58cm. £££

6. Cumberland Hotel Marble Arch W1A 4RF *Tel:* 0171 262-1234 *Fax:* 0171 724-4621. Marble Arch underground 50m. NCP 100m. Main entrance +1 step.

Three lifts (D105 W150 L180). Flat access via a side door to part of the dining room. Two adapted rooms (not seen). **Wheelchair loo (D85 ST70+). ££££**

7. Mount Royal Hotel Bryanston Street, Marble Arch W1H 8AE *Tel:* 0171 629-8040 *Fax:* 0171 499-7792. By the junction with Portman Street. NCP 50m. Main entrance +4 steps and then an escalator to first floor reception. A separate entrance to the right has a push button to open which takes you through to a lift (D110 W150 L120) to the first floor reception. Flat access to dining room and bar. **Wheelchair loo (D89 ST350)** past reception, go to the end of the lobby, turn right just before the Glen Miller bar; go to the end of the corridor, turn left and it's on your left. Main lifts (D85 W130 L130) to the left of reception give step free access to **five identical adapted rooms** on the third floor. Three connect with the twin room next door. Room 307 seen: D91cm (with an ultra-clever voice control system to open the door), bathroom D94cm to a wheel-in shower with a retractable seat and ST 96cm. **££££**

W2

8. Caring Hotel 24 Craven Hill Gardens, Paddington W2 3EA *Tel:* 0171 262-8708 *Fax:* 0171 262-8590. By the junction with Leinster Gardens. Main entrance +1+1 steps. Flat to three GFBs. Room A seen: D69cm, bathroom D48cm. Breakfast room is downstairs. **££**

9. Beverley House Hotel 142 Sussex Gardens, Paddington W2 1UB *Tel:* 0171 723-3380 *Fax:* 0171 402-3292. 60m east of the junction with London Street. Small CP with 7 spaces; must be booked in advance. Entrance +1+1 steps. Dining room down a flight of stairs. Four GFBs, D68cm, bathroom D63cm, small. **££/£££**

10. Lancaster Hall Hotel 35 Craven Terrace W2 3EL *Tel:* 0171 723-9276 *Fax:* 0171 706-2870. 30m south of the junction with Craven Road. Flat entrance. Two lifts (D77 W105 L132). Flat to dining room and bar. No GFBs. Step free access via the lift to other floors. Room 309 seen: D73cm, bathroom D57cm, small. **£££**

11. Mitre House Hotel 178 Sussex Gardens, Hyde Park W2 1TU *Tel:* 0171 723-8040 *Fax:* 0171 402-0990. CP in front of hotel. Entrance +3+1−1 steps. Lift (D70 W105 L110) to dining room in the basement. Flat to GF bar and lounge. Five GFBs. Room G1 seen: D69cm, bathroom D70cm, cramped. **£££**

12. Camelot Hotel 45 Norfolk Square, Paddington W2 1RX *Tel:* 0171 723-9118 *Fax:* 0171 402-3412. On the south side of the square near the junction with Norfolk Place. Flat entrance. Five GFBs, two with flat access, three with +1 step. Lift (D79 W104 L101) gives step free access to some other rooms. Breakfast room downstairs in the basement. **£££**

13. Delmere Hotel 128 Sussex Gardens, Paddington W2 1UB *Tel:* 0171 706-3344 *Fax:* 0171 262-1863. 50m west of the junction with Norfolk Place. Two CP spaces. Main entrance +1+1 steps. Five GFBs, with ±1 step to each. Room 18 seen: D72cm, small bathroom. Flat access from reception to lift (D78 W76 L124) and then step free to rooms on the fourth floor with en suite bathroom. Dining room via the lift, then –1. **£££**

14. Royal Bayswater Hotel 122 Bayswater Road W2 3JH *Tel:* 0171 229-8888 *Fax:* 0171 221-2283. Near Kensington Gardens. 30m east of the junction with Queensway. Queensway NCP nearby. Entrance +2 steps. Dining room flat. Lifts (D78 W145 L93) give step free access to most bedrooms. Room 205 seen: D70cm, bathroom D70cm. **£££**

15. Henry VIII Hotel 19 Leinster Gardens W2 3AN *Tel:* 0171 262-0117 *Fax:* 0171 706-0472. Step free throughout via two lifts (D66 W87 L107) including the basement dining room. Fifteen GFBs. Room 1 seen: D68cm, bathroom D64cm, then roomy. **£££/££££**

16. Charles Dickens Hotel Lancaster Gate W2 3NZ *Tel:* 0171 262-5090 *Fax:* 0171 723-1244. 50m east of junction with Leinster Terrace. Entrance +4 steps. Two lifts (D89 W107 L167). Flat access to six GFBs and +7 to seven more. Step free via the lifts to others. Room 1023 seen: D76cm, bathroom D63cm. Bar +5. **££££**

WC1

17. Langland Hotel 29 Gower Street, Bloomsbury WC1E 6HJ *Tel:* 0171 636-5801 *Fax:* 0171 580-2227. 50m north of the junction with Keppel Street. NCP in Bedford Square. Main entrance +2+1 steps to foyer, then –4 to reception. Four GFBs are step free from the foyer. None with en-suite toilet. The GF loo is –4 from the foyer via a passage 68cm wide, D71cm and no ST. Rooms 14 and 15 have a shower and are larger. The dining room is downstairs, but they will serve breakfast in your room. **££**

18. Mabledon Court Hotel 10 Mabledon Place, Bloomsbury WC1H 9AZ *Tel:* 0171 388-3866 *Fax:* 0171 387-5686. Entrance +1 step. Lift (D61 W79 L88). Dining room in the basement, D65cm, –1 from lift. Five GFBs. Room 7 seen: D58cm, bathroom D55cm. **££/£££**

19. Tavistock Hotel Tavistock Square WC1H 9EV *Tel:* 0171 636-8383 *Fax:* 0171 837-4653. CP 150m away in Bedford Way, left out of hotel entrance. Entrance +1 step. Two lifts (D85 W155 L105). Flat to dining room and bar. No GFBs. Bedroom D70cm, cramped, bathroom D55cm. Separate loo D55cm. **££/£££**

20. Royal National Hotel Bedford Way WC1H 0GD *Tel:* 0171 637-2488 *Fax:* 0171 837-4653. Between Bedford Place and Woburn Place. UGCP (NCP) with lift access to the hotel. Flat entrance to foyer and lifts. Eight lifts (D90 W163 L101). Flat to dining rooms and bar. Three adapted rooms: D85cm, bathroom D83cm, no ST space. Large hotel with quite long distances involved. Substantial weekend discounts. **£££**

21. Imperial Hotel Russell Square WC1B 5BB *Tel:* 0171 837-3655 *Fax:* 0171 837-4653. On the corner with Southampton Row. UGCP (NCP) but without lift access. Step free to four lifts (D89 W173 L95) and first floor dining room and bar. Flat to part of GF lounge. Flat from a separate entrance to Day and Night Bar (coffee bar and light meals). Note the 24-hour **wheelchair loo** across the road. No GFBs. Room 514 seen: D69cm, bathroom (sliding) D53cm. Some bedrooms are a considerable distance from the lifts. **£££**

22. Bonnington Hotel 92 Southampton Row WC1B 4BH *Tel:* 0171 242-2828 *Fax:* 0171 831-9170. Flat to three lifts (one D70 W91 L193; two D65 W70+L70+), bar, and dining room which has +2 steps to some parts. No GFBs. **One adapted room.** Room 213 seen: D87cm, bathroom D88cm with ST. **Wheelchair loo (D85 ST110)** on the GF 30m past reception and the bar, by an emergency exit. **££££**

23. Montague Park Hotel 12-20 Montague Street, Bloomsbury WC1B 5BJ *Tel:* 0171 637-1001 *Fax:* 0171 637-2516. 40m south of the junction with Russell Square. 300m from the British Museum. NCP 200m away. Entrance +3+1 steps but a portable ramp is available. Flat to dining room, +4–2 to bar, +4–1 to patio. Two GFBs. Room 40 seen: bedroom D69cm, bathroom D72cm with ST. Rooms vary. **Wheelchair loo (D70+ ST130)**, right past reception towards bar. Turn right just before the bar and it is on the left. **££££**

KENILWORTH HOTEL

24. Marlborough Hotel Great Russell Street WC1B 3QD *Tel:* 0171 636-5601 *Fax:* 0171 636-0532. On the corner with Bloomsbury Street, 200m from British Museum. NCP nearby. Valet parking available. Ramped entrance and step free to two lifts (D76 W105 L137), dining room and bar. **Four adapted rooms.** Room 118 seen: D88cm, bathroom D77cm, ST70. **Wheelchair cubicles (D90 ST100) in the ladies and gents loos,** to the left past reception, through the double doors labelled Brasserie Bar, then turn right. **££££**

WC2

25. Charing Cross Hotel The Strand WC2N 5HX *Tel:* 0171 839-7287 *Fax:* 0171 839-3933. Forms part of the Charing Cross Station facade, on the left. Flat entrance via revolving doors. A side door can be opened. Some unavoidable cobbles outside. Lift (D93 W185 L121). Dining room on the first floor. Flat to GF bar. No GFBs, but step free access via lift. **Three 'adapted' rooms:**

bedroom D74cm, bathroom D65cm, no ST. ££££

E1

Tower Thistle Hotel St Katherine's Way E1 9LD *Tel:* 0171 481-2575 *Fax:* 0171 480-5487. By the northern end of Tower Bridge. Relatively expensive, but well located. On-site CP with three OB spaces at ground level. Ramp bypasses +2 steps at the entrance. Lift (D102 W170 L140) to dining room, bar, bedrooms and **wheelchair cubicle (D70 ST90) in both ladies and gents** on the upper foyer level. Studio room 301 seen: D74cm, bathroom D63cm no ST. ££££

NW1

26. Hotel Ibis Euston 3 Cardington Street, Euston NW1 2LW *Tel:* 0171 388-7777 *Fax:* 0171 388-0001. Opposite Euston Station on the corner of Starcross Street. UGCP next door but with a stepped exit. Can use the hotel courtyard for unloading, +1 step through the bar. Flat main entrance. Two lifts (D107 W147 L150). No GFBs. **Eight adapted rooms.** Room 135 seen: D74cm, bathroom D74cm, ST70+. **Wheelchair loo (D70+ ST70+)** left past the shop, and immediately right down to the end of the corridor. Then on the right. ££/£££

W8

27. De Vere Park Hotel 60 Hyde Park Gate, De Vere Gardens, Kensington W8 5AS *Tel:* 0171 584-0051 *Fax:* 0171823-8583. By the junction with High Street Kensington. Entrance +1 step. Lift (D107 W107 L136). Flat to dining room and bar. Six GFBs. Room 604 seen: D69cm, bathroom D72cm. £££

28. Copthorne Tara Hotel Scarsdale Place, Kensington W8 5SR *Tel:* 0171 937-7211 *Fax:* 0171 937-7100. Off Cheniston Gardens, about 250m from Kensington High Street. UGCP but no lift access. Valet parking available. Flat entrance. Four lifts (D115 W190 L135). Step free access to all facilities. **Ten well adapted rooms**, catering for people with a wide range of disabilities, although **none have a wheel-in shower. Wheelchair loos (D70+ ST70+)** on the first floor. Big hotel with long distances inside. Book through HCS for a significant discount. £££ **(with discount)**

SW5

29. Swiss House Hotel 171 Old Brompton Road, South Kensington SW5 0AN *Tel:* 0171 373-2769 *Fax:* 0171 373-4983. Opposite the junction with Gledhow Gardens. Entrance +2+1 steps. Reception and dining room down a flight of stairs. They can serve breakfast in your room. There are +3 to three GFBs, D85cm, bathroom D69cm. £££

SW7

30. Kensington Edwardian Hotel 40 Harrington Gardens SW7 4LT *Tel:* 0171 370-0811 *Fax:* 0171 373-5138. 40m east of the junction with Collingham Gardens. Entrance +6 steps. Two lifts (D79 W94 L99). Dining room in the basement, flat from lift. Nine GFBs. Room G8 seen: D65cm, bathroom D56cm. **£££**

Outer London northwest

Claremont Hotel. 154 High Street, Wealdstone, Harrow, Middx HA3 7AT *Tel:* 0181 427-2738 *Fax:* 0181 427-0181. On the corner with Claremont Street. CP at rear. Entrance –2 steps with portable ramps. Dining room and lounge with flat access. Three GFBs. Room 1 most suitable: D69cm, bathroom D65cm, then spacious. **£/££**

Arena Hotel 6 Forty Lane, Wembley, Middx HA9 9EB *Tel:* 0181 904-0019 *Fax:* 0181 908-2007. By the roundabout at the junction with Tudor Gardens. On site CP and +3 steps at the entrance. Flat to dining room and bedrooms. Seven GFBs all with en suite bathrooms. Room 12 seen: D62cm, bathroom D74cm (inwards), ST70. Also Room 11 seen: D62cm, bathroom D67cm. **£/££**

Wembley Park Guest House Hotel 8 Forty Lane, Wembley, Middx HA9 9EB *Tel:* 0181 904-6329 *Fax:* 0181 385-0472. By the roundabout at the junction with Tudor Gardens. On-site CP. Main entrance has +2 steps. Flat to dining room and GFBs. Two GFBs (unseen), one with bathroom. **£/££**

Adelphi Hotel 4 Forty Lane, Wembley, Middx HA9 9EB *Tel:* 0181 904-5629 *Fax:* 0181 908-5314. By the roundabout at the junction with Tudor Gardens. On-site CP. Entrance +2 steps. Flat to bedrooms and dining room. Four GFBs, two with en suite bathrooms. Room 1 seen: D66cm, no bathroom. GF bathroom has D65cm and is small. **£/££**

Travel Inn 362 Uxbridge Road, Hayes UB4 0HF *Tel:* 0181 573-7479 *Fax:* 0181 569-1204. 30m east of the junction with Yeading Lane. Opened in November '95. CP with ramp up to the main entrance. Flat to reception and twenty-one GFBs. Two adapted rooms (not seen) with bathrooms. Flat access to *The Grapes* Beefeater restaurant and bar, 50m away, where guests eat and drink. This has flat entrance and a **wheelchair loo** (not seen). **££**

Regal Guest House 170 Golders Green Road, Golders Green NW11 9BY *Tel/Fax:* 0181 455-7025. At the junction with Ravenscroft Avenue. Three CP spaces, with –1 step to the entrance. Flat to dining room and two GFBs. Back room seen: D66cm, shower and loo ensuite but cramped. **££**

Welcome Lodge Scratchwood M1 Motorway, Hendon NW7 3HB *Tel:* 0181 906-0611 *Fax:* 0181 906-3654. Large CP. Step free to dining room and fifty-two GFBs, D69cm, bathroom D63cm with ST. ££

Shalimar Hotel 215 Staines Road, Hounslow, Middx TW3 2LR *Tel:* 0181 577-7070 *Fax:* 0181 569-6789. On-site CP. Ramped entrance. No lift. Flat to dining room and bar, and −1 step to patio. Eight GFBs. **One adapted room:** D85cm, bathroom D72cm, ST and a wheel-in shower. ££

Elm Hotel Elm Road, Wembley, Middx HA9 7JA *Tel:* 0181 902-1764 *Fax:* 0181 903-8365. At junction with St Johns Road. On-site CP. Flat to reception, dining room, bar and six GFBs. Room 8 seen: D68cm, bathroom D56cm, and cramped. Four more GFBs +3 steps. ££.

Master Brewer Motel Westbury Avenue, Hillingdon UB10 9NX *Tel:* 01895-251199 *Fax:* 01895-810330. By the junction with Long Lane. 250m from Hillingdon tube station which has step free access, although there are some slopes en route. On-site CP. The Motel has two main blocks. Entrance to the main building is flat with revolving doors. A side door can be opened on request. Flat to reception, bar, and part of the dining room. **Wheelchair loo (D73 ST150)** to the right of reception. **Two adapted rooms** in the new block 150m from reception, step free between. You can park nearby. Room 302 seen: D72cm, bathroom D76cm, ST75. Over fifty GFBs. ££

Granada Lodge M4 Service Area, Heston TW5 9NA *Tel:* 0181 574-7271 *Fax:* 0181 574-1891. On the westbound side of the M4 going out of London. If you're on the eastbound side come off at the services; follow the signs which will lead you to the hotel on the other side, and at the end of the route, go down Phoenix Way. On-site CP with two OB spaces. Shallow ramp at the main entrance, then flat to GFBs. **Three adapted rooms**. Room 101 seen: D71cm, bathroom D80cm (sliding), and ST100. Room service after 18.00, and they can send breakfast over. **Adapted loo (D84 ST62)** in the Lodge near Room 105. 50m to the main services building for meals. Two **wheelchair loos (D75 ST75)** in the services. ££

Ibis Hotel, Heathrow 112 Bath Road, Hayes, Middx UB3 5AL *Tel:* 0181 759-4888 *Fax:* 0181 564-7894. On the A4 near the airport. CP. Kerb at the entrance, otherwise flat. Two lifts (D79 W125 L135). **Three adapted bedrooms**, D77cm, bathroom D76cm, spacious, but fixed rails prevent ST. **Wheelchair cubicle in both ladies and gents loos** on the first floor. ££

Clive Hotel Primrose Hill Road, Hampstead NW3 3NA *Tel:* 0171 586-2233 *Fax:* 0171 586-2233. By the junction with Fellows Road. Disabled guests can leave their cars at the front of the hotel. There are +3 steps at the entrance, bypassed by a steepish ramp. Flat to reception, dining room, bar and lifts (D80

W115 L135). No GFBs, but step free to all rooms. No rooms seen. **£££**

Earls Court International Lillie Road SW6 1UQ *Tel:* 0171 385-1255 *Fax:* 0171 381-0215. Just west of the junction with Ongar Road. UGCP, with lift (D114 W170 L120). Main entrance flat. Lifts give flat access to bedrooms, dining room and bar. 500 identical bedrooms. Room 415 seen: D68cm, bathroom D62cm, ST96 (partly obstructed by the sink). Room service available for disabled guests. **Wheelchair cubicles (D70 ST100) in ladies and gents loos** on the GF. To reach them, turn left after main entrance, and they are 20m on your left. **£££**

Collonade Hotel 2 Warrington Crescent, Maida Vale W9 1ER *Tel:* 0171 286-1052 *Fax:* 0171 286-1057. By the junction with Warrington Gardens. Restricted CP. Main entrance +2+3 steps, but there is a flat back entrance by the parking spaces, leading to reception and GFBs. Dining room and bar are downstairs. Eight GFBs. Room 2 seen: D68cm, bathroom D63cm, no ST. Lift (D70 W200 L118) to upstairs rooms. **£££**

Raglan Hall Hotel 8 Queens Avenue, Muswell Hill N10 3NR *Tel:* 0181 883-9836/5700 *Fax:* 0181 883-5002. 80m from the roundabout at the junction with Muswell Hill. CP. Main entrance has +5+1 steps, but there is an alternative ramp and +1, or a step free route through the back. Flat to the dining room and part of the bar. Ten GFBs. Room 33 seen: D80cm, bathroom D60cm, no ST. **£££**

The Bridge Hotel Western Avenue, Greenford, Middlesex UB6 8ST *Tel:* 0181 566-6246 *Fax:* 0181 566-6140. Corner of Greenford Road. CP with two OB spaces. Ramped entrance, then flat to dining room, bar and lounge. **Two adapted GFBs:** D75cm, bathroom D80cm (sliding) with ST. Connecting rooms available. **Wheelchair loo (D70+ ST70+)** past reception. Substantial weekend discount. **£££**

Novotel 1 Shortlands, Hammersmith W6 8DR *Tel:* 0181 741-1555 *Fax:* 0181 741-2120. Turn into Chalk Hill Road from Shortlands. Four OB spaces at ground level. Flat to lifts (D100 W220 L120) to first floor reception. Step free to 15% of dining room, and to one of the bars. **Four adapted rooms.** Room 8035 seen: D91cm, bathroom D82cm, ST200. **Wheelchair cubicles (D85 ST85) in ladies and gents loos** on the first floor. Go to left of reception, through the telephone area and turn right; they are on your right. **Adapted loo (D85 ST48)** on the GF (in front of you as you go through the main entrance). **££££**

Hilton National Wembley Empire Way, Wembley, Middlesex HA9 8DS *Tel:* 0181 902-8839 *Fax:* 0181 900-2201. Opposite the junction with Linden Avenue. Ground-level CP. Flat to reception, dining room, bar and lifts. No GFBs, but lifts (D64 W169 L96) give flat access to all rooms. Room 204 seen: D79cm, bathroom D60cm (staff can remove bathroom door). **Adapted cubicles (D75 ST51)** in both ladies and gents loos on the GF: go to right of reception, turn left and loos are on your left. **££££**

Sheraton Skyline Hotel, Heathrow Bath Road, Hayes, Middx UB3 5BP *Tel:* 0181 759-2535 *Fax:* 0181 750-9150. Big hotel on the A4 near the airport. CP. Entrance +2 steps with ramped bypass, automatic doors. Two lifts (D100 W163 L170). Flat to dining room. **Two adapted bedrooms** with card operated lock: D80cm, bathroom D80cm with ST. Long distances between facilities. **££££**

Outer London northeast

Formule 1 West Bank, Highbridge Road, Barking, Essex IG11 7BA *Tel:* (provisionally) 0181 507-0789. This hotel chain is not staffed in the normal way and is geared to 'automated' convenience. Apart from the times when reception is open, there are no staff there at all, and no courtesy phone for calling anybody. The hotel is scheduled to open in August 1996, and a second Formule 1 is planned to open in the London area shortly after. We have used them in France, and the description is based on that experience.

On-site CP. If reception is shut on your arrival, place your credit card in the machine outside and answer the questions on the screen. If you have pre-booked (which is necessary if you want one of the adapted rooms), the screen will tell you the code you have to punch in both to get into the hotel, and then into your room. **You should make a record of the numbers, and certainly not leave your room, or the hotel without a written record. There really is no one around to help.**

Of the GFBs, three are adapted for chair users. The standard bedrooms have a double bed, a single bunk and washbasin, and are not big enough for a chair because the gaps are small. The adapted rooms simply have the double bed rotated with one side of the bed against the wall, leaving a gap of over 80cm, adequate for most chairs. There is a **wheelchair shower/loo (D80+ ST100+)** with a sliding door and a curtain inside to separate the WC area. We were told that they have now incorporated a folding seat into the design. An extra piece of plastic sheet may be useful to keep your chair dry!

These hotels are very basic. The ones we have used have been well kept, but they are simply a place to sleep, and you are, of course, vulnerable to the noise etc from others staying there. The price for a room with breakfast for three people will be around £30. For London, that is remarkable. The hotel is about 1km from Barking underground station which is accessible (see chapter on *Travelling*). **£**

Sleeping Beauty Motel 543 Lea Bridge Road, Leyton E10 7EB *Tel/Fax:* 0181 556-8080. By the junction with Russell Road. On-site CP. Ramped entrance. Step free access throughout using lift (D78 L138 W90). GF has reception, dining room, bar and **four adapted rooms,** two with a bath (102/104) and two with a wheel-in shower (105/106). All have D75cm, bathroom D75cm, ST125. **£.**

Sunningdale Hotel 35 Lonsdale Road, Wanstead E11 2PH *Tel:* 0181 989-3435. 35m from the junction with Cambridge Park Road. On-site CP. Entrance +1 step. Flat to family bedroom (D76cm, with up to five beds, shower cubicle). There is –1 to dining room, bathroom (D70, no ST) and two more GFBs (both with D67). **£**

Travel Inn Redbridge Lane East, Ilford, Essex IG4 5BG *Tel:* 0181 550-7909 *Fax:* 0181 550-6214. By the junction with Roding Lane South. CP. Flat entrance and step free to the fifteen GFBs. **Three adapted rooms** near reception. Room 1 seen: D85cm, bathroom D79cm, ST83. Ramp to breakfast room. Flat to adjacent *Beefeater* restaurant and bar. Staff said *Beefeater* building has a lift up to dining room level (not seen). **£/££**

Travel Inn Winsor Terrace, Beckton E6 4NT *Tel:* 0171 511-3853 *Fax:* 0171 511-4214. On the corner of Woolwich Manor Road and next to Beckton DLR station. The DLR gives step free access into Tower Gateway and Bank stations, among other places. On-site CP. Flat entrance. Twenty GFBs, **two adapted**. One seen: D75cm, bathroom D85cm, ST85. **£/££**

Forte Travelodge The Beehive, Beehive Lane, Gants Hill, Ilford, Essex IG4 5DR *Tel:* 0181 550-4248. Opposite the junction with Ethelbert Gardens. CP with four OB spaces. Flat to reception and all fifteen GFBs. One adapted GFB (not seen). Restaurant and bar in Harvester building 40m away with flat access via pub entrance on the left. **£/££**

Grove Hill Hotel 38 Grove Hill, South Woodford E18 2JG *Tel:* 0181 989-3344 *Fax:* 0181 530-5286. 60m west of the junction with Grove Crescent. CP. Entrance +3+1 steps. Then flat to dining room and the two GFBs. Room 22 seen: D83cm, bathroom D68cm, no ST, shower cubicle +1. **££**

Oak Lodge Hotel 80 Village Road, Bush Hill Park, Enfield EN1 2EU *Tel:* 0181 360-7082. A small privately owned hotel in a residential district. CP. Flat entrance. Lounge and dining room on the GF, and **one GFB with a wheel-in shower and loo. £££**

Outer London southwest

Travel Inn Leatherhead Road, Chessington, Surrey KT9 2NE *Tel:* 01372-744060 *Fax:* 01372-720889. Located near Chessington World of Adventures, next to the *Monkey Puzzle* pub, see write-up on page 227. CP. Ramp to reception. Twenty-one GFBs, including **two adapted**. Room 9 seen: D77cm and bathroom D75cm (sliding), no ST. The pub next door has a **wheelchair loo (D80 ST70)** to the right as you enter. **£**

Forte Travelodge Epsom Road, Morden, Surrey SM4 5PH *Tel:* 0181 640-8227. 100m south of junction with Central Road. CP with two OB spaces. Flat to reception and all fifteen GFBs. **One adapted GFB,** room 1: D85cm, bathroom D81cm, ST113 (slightly obstructed by the sink). Restaurant and bar in *Harvester* building 60m away. **££**

Kew Hotel 339 Sandycombe Road, Richmond, Surrey TW9 3NA. *Tel:* 0181 948-2902. On-site CP. Kerb then flat entrance, and flat to dining room. Two GFBs, cramped bathroom D58cm. **££**

Trochee Hotel 21 Malcolm Road, Wimbledon, SW19 4AS *Tel:* 0181 946-1579 *Fax:* 0181 785-4058. At the end of Malcolm Road off Worple Road. Three parking spaces. Entrance +2 steps. No lift. Flat to dining room, bar and lounge. Five GFBs, D68cm. Rooms vary, and none with en suite facilities. Bathroom D72cm, cramped. **££**

Wimbledon Hotel 78 Worple Road, Wimbledon SW19 4HZ *Tel/Fax:* 0181 946-9265. By the junction with Elm Grove. CP. Main entrance has +2 steps, then flat to dining room and room 1: D69cm, ensuite bathroom (not seen). Other bedrooms upstairs. **££**

Hotel Antoinette 26 Beaufort Road, Kingston KT1 2TU *Tel:* 0181 546-1044 *Fax:* 0181 547-2595. 60m north of corner with Lingfield Avenue. Two buildings 50m apart. Step free to dining room, bar, and lift (D81 W83 L123) to all 44 bedrooms in the main building. Room 403 seen: D67cm, bathroom D51cm and cramped. **Adapted cubicles** in loos to the left of reception, **gents (D66 ST100), ladies (D69, no ST)**. The separate Garden building has ten GFBs with flat access. Room 108 seen: D75cm, bathroom D72cm, no ST. **££**

Quinns Hotel 48 Sheen Road, Richmond, Surrey TW9 1AW *Tel:* 0181 940-5444 *Fax:* 0181 940-1828. About 700m from Richmond Station, on the corner with Church Road. Ten spaces in low level CP. Entrance +1+3+1 steps, then –2 to reception. Eight GFBs on the same level, only two with en suite facilities. Room 32 seen: D69cm, bathroom D71cm, ST54. Five bedrooms can be reached from a lower side entrance (reached from the CP via a slope and –3 followed by +1), only one with en suite facilities, room 18: D68cm, bathroom D63cm, no ST and a standard shower cubicle. The dining room is at the lower level, –16 from reception. A lift is planned. **£££**

Windmill on the Common Clapham Common Southside SW4 9DE *Tel:* 0181 673-4578 *Fax:* 0181 675-1486. Opposite the junction with St Gerards Close. On-site CP. The building contains a pub, a hotel and a restaurant. Hotel has two entrances, reached from the CP by a 15m shallow ramp. The main hotel entrance has +2 steps, then flat to reception but –3–1 to the **adapted GFB**, restaurant and pub. An alternative way in (flat with bellpush to summon staff) is 20m to the left and gives step free access to the adapted GFB, restaurant and pub. Equally, you can approach the room step free via the pub. Room 107 seen: D84cm, bathroom D77cm, ST93 and connecting door to room 106. **Wheelchair loo (D74 ST90)** off the pub conservatory. **£££**

Outer London southeast

Travel Inn 104 Coombe Road, Croydon CR0 5RB *Tel:* 0181 686-2030 *Fax:* 0181 686-6435. 100m west of the junction with Conduit Lane. On-site CP. Slope up to flat entrance. Nineteen GFBs, **two adapted**. Room 4 seen: D80cm, bathroom D78cm (sliding), ST100. Restaurant in the *Beefeater* about 100m away, with ramp bypassing +1 step at the entrance, then +1 inside, and flat to part of the restaurant and bar. **Adapted loo (D80 ST62)** off the restaurant. **£/££**

The Lodge Clacket Lane, M25 Motorway Service Area (westwards), Westerham, Kent TN16 2ER *Tel:* 01959 565789. (*booking* 0800-834719) *Fax:* 01959-561311. Located between junctions six and five. CP with OB spaces. Flat access to twenty-eight GFBs with three adapted. D88cm, bathroom D85, ST140. Main services building 50m away, step free throughout. **££**

Wellesley Hotel (and **Croydon YMCA**) 1 Lansdowne Road, Croydon, Surrey CR0 2BX *Tel:* 0181 681-3381 *Fax:* 0181 686-9461. **Near East Croydon Station, which is fully accessible**. By the junction with Walpole Road. UGCP but only available overnight and at weekends as it is shared with an office block. Needs prior booking. Flat entrance to hotel reception. The YMCA which is attached is closing for refurbishment during 1996/97. Small lift (D69 W102 L69) in the hotel. Flat to dining room. Room 215 seen: D69cm, bathroom D67cm with ST140, partly obstructed. **££**

Hotel Ibis Greenwich 30 Stockwell Street, Greenwich SE10 9JN *Tel:* 0181 305-1177 *Fax:* 0181 858-7139. On the corner of Greenwich High Street. Large pay and display CP at back. Entrance +4 steps, ramped alternative. Flat to the dining room. Lift (D80 W106 L139). **Two adapted bedrooms**: D83cm, bathroom D86cm, ST88, with wheel-in shower. Also 10 other GFBs. **Wheelchair loo (D75 ST70)** on the left of reception. **££**

Clarendon Montpelier Row, Blackheath, SE3 0RW *Tel:* 0181 852-4442 *Fax:* 0181 318-4378. Opposite the junction with Prince Charles Road. Parking possible at the front. Entrance +4 steps, but there's an alternative door about 6m away on the right which can be reached via a steepish ramp. Small lift

(D76 W82 L82). Flat to dining room and bar. Seven GFBs. Room 14 seen: D75cm, bathroom D80cm +1. **£££**

Croydon Park Hotel 7 Altyre Road, Croydon, Surrey CR9 5AA. *Tel:* 0181 680-9200 *Fax:* 0181 760-0426. Less than 200m from the **fully accessible East Croydon Station**. UGCP, no lift access but flat via road, or a flight of stairs. Entrance flat. Two lifts (D107 W182 L135). Flat to dining room. **One adapted GFB**: D64cm, bathroom D74cm, ST70. **Wheelchair loo (D70+ ST70+)** by the lifts. **£££**

Scandic Crown Hotel 265 Rotherhithe Street, Rotherhithe SE16 1EJ *Tel:* 0171 231-1001 *Fax:* 0171 231-0591. 70m north of the junction with Silver Walk, by the Thames. On-site CP. Entrance +1 step with a ramp, to a central reception and two separate buildings. **One adapted room** on the GF of Wharf building reached via an open lift (W100 L164) bypassing +8 steps. Room 1111 seen: D73cm, bathroom D73cm, no ST. Twelve GFBs in the Wharf building which contains the dining room and bar with step free access. **Adapted cubicles in both ladies and gents (D85 ST48).** Eighteen more GFBs in Block A. **££££**

Outside the M25

Allbrown House 15 Princess Avenue, Windsor, Berks SL4 3LU *Tel:* 01753-862704. Parking space. Front entrance +1+1 steps. Flat from rear parking spaces to rear entrance, which has a ledge. Two GFBs. Front GFB has D68cm. Rear GFB has D73cm and shower cubicle. Split level of ±1 on the GF. GF loo with no ST. **£**

Old Hall Farm New Bungalow, Old Hall Farm, Tandridge Lane, Oxted, Surrey RH8 9NS *Tel/Fax:* 01342-892508. Turning is 500m south of the junction with Miles Lane and 150m north of the railway bridge. Bungalow is 300m down turning. Parking. Main entrance has +2–1 steps. Or you can go through the garage for +1 to the GF. Flat access throughout GF, including the dining room. GF bathroom with D74cm, ST200 (slightly obstructed by bidet), bath and shower cubicle (+2–1). Two GFBs, D72cm. **£**

Travel Inn North Terminal, Longbridge Way, Gatwick Airport, Horley, Surrey RH6 0NX *Tel:* 01293-568158 *Fax:* 01293-568278. 500m north of the North Terminal; by the Texaco garage. On-site CP with OB spaces. Flat to dining room, bar and **adapted loo (D86 ST50). Six adapted GFBs**. Room 10 seen: D85cm, bathroom D82cm (sliding), ST88. Another twenty GFBs. Other rooms step free from the lift (D79 W105 L125). **£/££**

Forte Travelodge Church Road, Lowfield Heath, Crawley, West Sussex RH11 0PQ *Tel:* 01293-533441 *Fax:* 01293-535369. 150m off the A23 just south of

Gatwick Airport. On-site CP. Separate OB spaces near entrance. Flat to dining room and bar. **Three adapted GFBs.** Room 1 seen: D78cm, bathroom D80cm, ST93. Lift gives step free access to other bedrooms. **£/££**

Forte Travelodge South Mimms Service Area, Bignells Corner, South Mimms, Potters Bar, Hertfordshire EN6 3QQ *Tel:* 01707-665440 *Fax:* 01707-646933. At junction twenty-three of the M25. Separate building to right of main services building. CP with four OB spaces. Flat to all twenty-five GFBs. **Two adapted GFBs.** Room 1 seen: D85cm, bathroom D74cm, ST117. Self-service restaurant in main services building. **££**

Forte Travelodge Reigate Road, Dorking, Surrey RH4 1QB *Tel:* 01306-740361. On the A25 east of Dorking and 60m west of junction with Punchbowl Lane. On-site CP. Ramp to bypass +8 steps. Flat main entrance and throughout GF. Will have three adapted rooms on the GF. 50m from a *Little Chef* with step free access between. *Little Chef* has a ramp to bypass +4 and is then step free. **Adapted loo (D74 ST62)** at the back of the restaurant. **££**

Granada Pavilion M2 Motorway Junction 4/5, Rainham, Gillingham, Kent ME8 8PQ *Tel:* 0800-555300. Large CP with three OB spaces. Ramped entrance with automatic doors. Twenty-four GFBs with **two adapted**: D85cm, bathroom D90cm, but no ST. **££**

New Denham Guest House 14 Poplar Road, Willowbank, New Denham, Uxbridge, Middlesex UB9 4AW *Tel:* 01895-237083 *Fax:* 01895-234651. At the eastern end of Poplar Road. CP. Main entrance has +1 step. Three GFBs. GF bathroom has D64cm and no ST. **££**

Forte Crest Gatwick Porey Cross Road, Horley Surrey RH6 OBA *Tel:* 01293-771621 *Fax:* 01293-771054. By the A23. CP. Flat entrance with automatic doors. Three lifts (D105 W145 L155). Flat to dining room but – 3 steps to bar. Forty-four GFBs, D76cm, bathroom D71cm. **£££**

Places of interest

This chapter covers many of London's main historical buildings and attractions. **Entries are divided into inner and outer London and further split into small geographical areas.** They are then listed alphabetically. Where there are groups of sights quite close to each other, like HMS *Belfast,* Hays Galleria and the London Dungeon, they will be listed and described together, and cross-referenced from the appropriate chapter.

An increasing number of the sights are accessible without much hassle, and a great variety of things can be seen with minimal difficulty. There are, of course, problems in some places, usually because the buildings are old, or because there are long distances involved.

Good places for getting views of and over London are limited. They include the Tower Bridge Walkway, Waterloo Bridge, Primrose Hill, Greenwich Park, Alexandra Palace and Westminster Cathedral Tower.

There are plenty of opportunities for seeing famous buildings and getting a feel for important aspects of London's life and history without actually going inside the buildings. Some major sights do not have an 'inside' which you can visit, such as Admiralty Arch, the Albert Memorial, Big Ben, Cleopatra's Needle, Mansion House, Marble Arch, the Monument and Trafalgar Square. In each case some sense of the history comes from the facade and the location.

There are statues all over the place. The *Eyewitness* guide we recommend describes some of these. There are more extensive descriptions in other books, and you can pick up an enormous amount of interesting information about London and its history from a study of the statues – most of which, by their very nature, can easily be seen. There's a particularly good description by Margaret Baker in *London Statues and Monuments* published by Shire Publications, Princes Risborough, Bucks HP17 9AJ.

As elsewhere, our write-ups are descriptive and a listing does not mean that a site is fully accessible.

Inner London
City area

This comprises the City itself, together with the area just to the north and east. It includes the Tower, which is not strictly in the City, Tower Bridge and St Katherine's Dock. The write-up covers two areas in the Eyewitness guide; the City and Smithfield/Spitalfields.

The so-called 'Square Mile' is an area of highly concentrated commercial buildings where millions of pounds change hands every hour.

Parking is particularly difficult so it's a good idea to use a taxi or minicab if you can, or the DLR (which now goes to Bank). Note the possibility of using the Waterloo-City line discussed in the chapter on *Travelling,* and that City Thameslink station has step free access, although it is not open at weekends. There are CPs at Minories, West Smithfield and the Barbican where you will probably find space. For a leaflet on parking facilities contact the City Parking Office *Tel:* 0171 332-1548, otherwise see the *Evening Standard London Parking Map.*

The pavements are narrow, and can be crowded during the week. However, it's a fascinating area and there are many old and famous buildings. If you need specific information, for example about opening times, the **City Information Centre** just south of St Paul's Cathedral (*Tel:* 0171 332-1457) is helpful, but we found that they knew little or nothing about access. The **City Access Group** publish a leaflet with a map showing the location of **wheelchair loos**, and giving other details (c/o Access Officer, Corporation of London, Social Services Department, Milton Court, Moor Lane EC2Y 9BL *Tel:* 0171 332-1995).

All-Hallows-by-the-Tower, Byward Street EC3 *Tel:* 0171 481-2928. An interesting church with facilities for brass rubbing. Pepys watched the Great Fire from the tower. The −3 steps at the entrance are neatly bypassed by a steepish ramp. Once inside, most things can be seen. **The Brass Rubbing Centre** is a friendly spot, with tables at a suitable height for most chair users; some of the brasses are mounted on mobile plinths which you can put on your knees if you like. On the south side by the font there are +2. Two small crypt chapels are −20 with three 90° turns. The church has a museum about London's history with a length of Roman pavement, but access involves steep and narrow steps (−10−3, W65cm) and an awkward turn. Audio guide available.

 80%

Bank of England Museum see chapter on *Museums & galleries.*

The Barbican is a sizeable area bounded by London Wall, Moorgate and Aldersgate Street, which has been redeveloped on two levels. There are historic sites, tower blocks of flats, offices, pubs and shops, both at ground level and on the high-level walkway which covers much of the development. The most interesting places are the Barbican Centre (see chapter on *Arts centres*), St Giles's church, restored after extensive bomb damage, and the Museum of London (see chapter on *Museums & galleries*). Signposting around the area has been greatly improved.

Broadgate is a developing complex, not yet finished, built around Liverpool Street station. It consists mainly of office blocks, but there are shops, markets, bars and restaurants. Broadgate Arena is a skating rink in winter and an entertainment venue in the summer. Access is pretty good with ramped/lift routes to most places, but a lack of signposting makes it confusing to a stranger. There's a **wheelchair loo** in Liverpool Street station and several others, in and around the development.

A really bad feature is that some of the vital lifts which you need to use to gain step free access, are part of 'private' buildings. They are under the control (and view) of security personnel and cameras. To use a lift you have to communicate through an intercom (provided it is working). This means that a chair user, who is 'obviously' disabled, will probably be able to use the lifts with much less hassle than a disabled walker. Our experience in this respect was distinctly mixed.

Guildhall, Gresham Street EC2 *Tel:* 0171 606-3030. This has been the administrative centre of the City of London for nearly 900 years. The current building dates from the 15thC. Guildhall Yard outside has been pedestrianised, with some bumpy surfaces. You can visit the famous Great Hall and Livery Hall, unless there's a council meeting. Flat entrance, and +3 steps into the Hall can be bypassed by a signposted ramped route. To go to the Old Library (where there are occasional events) a platform stairlift bypasses +10, then the split levels in the chamber are bypassed by temporary ramps. The crypt is about –30 (steepish), although there is a Gimpson Staircrimber, commonly 'unserviceable', we were told. **Two wheelchair loos (both D90 ST100)**, one on the GF near the Great Hall and the other in the office area past reception on the second floor. You will be escorted to both, for security reasons.

 **80%**

Just around the corner in Aldermanbury (with two OB spaces opposite) is the **Guildhall Library, Clock Museum and Bookshop**. All are reached via +5 with a ramped bypass. The museum has been rehoused, and is flat inside. The bookshop is quite small. In the library there is a reading room, and a platform stairlift to the maps area, bypassing +12. The staff can get the books which you have found on the microfiche. *49 Gresham Street* is a nearby pub, see *Pubs* chapter.

Leadenhall Market, Leadenhall Place EC3, is a small but attractive Victorian market near the Lloyds building, with a variety of clothes and food shops, and several pubs and cafés. It's generally flat and compact but the main roadway is cobbled, and there are kerbs. The *Half Moon* pub has flat access to the bar and to the gents loo, which has a large cubicle (D66 ST60). The nearest **wheelchair loo** is at Fenchurch Street Station.

Lloyds of London, 1 Lime Street EC3, is an interesting modern 'inside out'

building with the piping, ducting and the lifts built on the outside. The public gallery has regrettably been closed. Lloyds has been the heart of the insurance market, although recently under threat because of the massive losses sustained by some of its backers.

Monument, Monument Street EC3 *Tel:* 0171 626-2717. A giant Doric column commemorating the Great Fire of London. It is 62m high and lies the same distance from the supposed site of the outbreak of the fire in Pudding Lane. There are +311 spiralled steps, so it can hardly be described as accessible!

Museum of London see chapter on *Museums & galleries.*

Old Bailey (Central Criminal Court), Old Bailey Road EC4 *Tel:* 0171 248-3277. On the corner with Newgate Street, this is *the* central court complex where many famous cases are tried. All the courts have a public gallery. Courts 1 to 4 are entered from Newgate Street, with +60 or so steps. Court 18 is a further +17. From the entrance in Warwick Passage, Courts 13 to 16 are +30; Courts 5 to 8 +30+40, and Courts 9 to 12 are +30+40+40! Although it is not one of London's more accessible places, we have been told that, on the 'other side' of the facility, for the court officials, lawyers, witnesses and those charged, there are changes being made to make some of the courts accessible.

St Katharine's Dock, E1 *Tel:* 0171 488-2400. A busy and attractive area alongside Tower Bridge, forming one of the earlier stages of the Docklands Development. The area includes the docks themselves, offices, a variety of small shops, a restaurant and the *Dickens Inn* which has a **wheelchair loo** with lift access. The small CP entered from Thomas More Street will disappear with further development, eventually substituted by an UGCP. Currently there is an UGCP at Safeways about 250m away off Nesham Street, with OB spaces and lift (D200 W220 L300) access, and a useful CP at the Tower Thistle Hotel with limited space at ground level. It's ideal if you have a high vehicle, and you may be able to pre-negotiate a space with the hotel management. The area is generally flat but is a conservation area and there are some fiendish teeth-rattling cobbled sections and the odd kerb or step to get over.

There are no major access barriers, although the one or two routes with steps are (of course) not signed. If you come along the pedestrian route around the Tower moat and under Tower Bridge Road there's 1 step followed immediately by a small hump bridge. The step free route to the dock then involves going about 100m straight ahead alongside International

House and parallel with Tower Bridge Road, bypassing a shorter route involving –1–2+3. When you are leaving, while there is a route via the riverfront towards the Tower (and in front of the hotel), there are steps at the end (+5–5) by the bridge, and a minimum of +2–1 large steps by the hotel entrance. To get to the pier for boarding river boats follow the riverside walk from the Tower past the Tower Hotel.

Alongside one of the docks is the *Dickens Inn* pub/restaurant, see write-up under *Pubs*. It is an excellent facility, but gets crowded in the summer. There are several restaurants and bar including a Carvery and a Coffee Shop in the **Tower Thistle Hotel**. This has a ramped bypass to the +2 at the entrance. Inside there are large lifts and the restaurants are on the first floor. It also has **adapted loos**, see write-up under *Accommodation*. The Riverside Delicatessen and Sandwich Bar in Ivory House has flat access. In the middle of the dock there's a rather curious monument called the **Coronarium Chapel,** a multi-faith building opened by the Queen in 1977 (her Silver Jubilee year).

St Paul's Cathedral see chapter on *Places of worship.*

St Bartholomew the Great see chapter on *Places of worship.*

Tower Bridge (Walkway & Museum), SE1 *Tel:* 0171 378-1928 *Fax:* 0171 357-7935. One of London's landmarks, completed in 1894. It houses a museum with an imaginative presentation of the history of the bridge, and there are superb views from the walkways joining the towers.

Entrance in the north-west tower. To avoid steps, approach it along the main Tower Bridge Road. Step free access throughout the five floors via a lift (D150 W350 L150), bypassing some 200 steps. The walkways include good viewing points for children (with two steps, and handrails) and a ramped platform for chair users, so that all visitors can get good views and photographs. Visiting the engine room and the shop at the end of the visit involves either a step free route of about 400m, or –21–11 and 50m. We were told that a lift was being installed to link the main tower with the engine room. **Adapted loo (D90 ST65)** on the second floor of the south-east tower by the lift, and a **wheelchair loo (D90 ST75)** by the engine room.

Tower of London, Tower Hill, EC3 *Tel:* 0171 709-0765. One of London's prime tourist attractions. It is both a fortress and a royal palace, and its history goes back some 900 years. There are CPs at the Tower Thistle Hotel and Minories. Tower Gateway DLR station has step free access. OB holders may be able to negotiate parking on the riverfront – but ring first. *There may*

be long queues to get in on popular days such as bank holidays and summer weekends.

They have a really detailed 'Access' leaflet which (unusually) adopts the same kind of descriptive approach as we do. If you want to explore as much as possible, try and get a copy. It's good. There is a **wheelchair loo (D85 ST85)** outside the Tower on the right hand side as you go down Tower Hill, just past the Tower Pageant.

The Tower consists of a group of buildings with two surrounding walls. The area is roughly 200m square and many of the paths and courtyards are

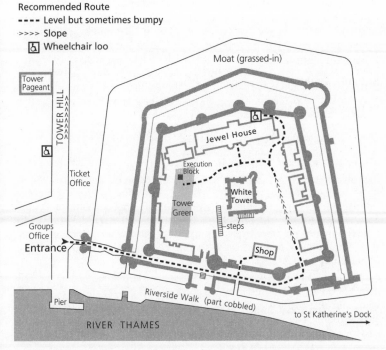

Tower of London

Recommended Route
- - - - Level but sometimes bumpy
>>>> Slope
🔹 Wheelchair loo

Moat (grassed-in)

Tower Pageant

TOWER HILL

Jewel House

Execution Block

Ticket Office

White Tower

Tower Green

steps

Groups Office

Entrance

Shop

Pier

Riverside Walk (part cobbled)

to St Katherine's Dock →

RIVER THAMES

cobbled and sloping. Since the buildings are several hundred years old, access to many of them is difficult, but it's possible to see quite a lot from outside. The **Crown Jewels** have recently been rehoused with flat access. You go past on a moving walkway. There are +3 steps to the viewing platform if you want to take a more leisurely look. The flat/sloped route round takes you through the Middle and Byward Towers and along Water

Lane parallel to the river. On the left is the Gallery shop with step free access. Turning left through the arch you go up the hill past the White Tower, turn left again, and the entrance to the Crown Jewels is in the middle of the courtyard at the top. Ahead is Tower Green where executions used to take place, and you'll probably see some of the famous ravens. You have to go back by the same route, and the whole distance is about 600/700m, partly cobbled.

The **White Tower** has +12+20+10 steps, but only +24 if you use the exit (D76cm) on the far (north) side. The basement is −15 from the north exit side. A complete visit involves over 200 steps, some irregular and steep. The **New Armories** have been moved, and are +48. Two **wheelchair loos (D85 ST85)** behind the Jewel House (by its exit). Go straight ahead past the White Tower, instead of turning left towards Tower Green. The attendant in either the ladies or gents has the key.

The **Ceremony of the Keys** is the ritual of locking up the Tower, which takes place every day between *21.30 and 22.05* and has done every night for some 700 years. Apparently, it was a little late one night in 1941 when a bomb blew the escort off their feet. Admission by ticket only from the Keys Clerk (address as above), and, although there are no steps, disabled visitors should mention their disability when applying. Book well in advance, and give alternative dates if possible.

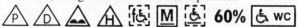 **60%**

Tower Hill Pageant, 1 Tower Hill Terrace, EC3 *Tel:* 0171 709-0081. The pageant is a series of tableaux, models and screens showing London's history. You sit in a 'time car' to make the fifteen minute trip. There is also a fully ramped museum. Flat entrance from Gloucester Court, or through McDonalds, avoids −12 steps from Tower Hill. Lift (D109 W180 L140) access down to the ride, bypassing the steps. One of the carriages on the time car is well adapted, and should cope with any size of chair. **Wheelchair loo (D75 ST74)** on the dark ride level.

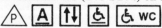

Wesley's House & Chapel, 49 City Road EC1 *Tel:* 0171 253-2262. About 150m from Old Street tube station. Small reservable CP outside the chapel. Via the back entrance to the House, there are −15 steps to the basement, then +1−1, and +15 to the GF, +21 to first floor and +21 to the second. The front door gives flat access to the GF, which has two rooms. Audio guide available describing the rest of the house. The Chapel is flat with lift (D80 W105 L140) access to the basement, containing a small museum with uneven but step free access, and a **wheelchair loo (D85 ST75)**.

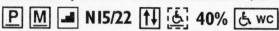 **N15/22** **40%**

Southwark

Described in the *Eyewitness* guide as Southwark and Bankside. The south bank of the river opposite the City, has developed rapidly during the last few years. There is a pleasant riverside walk along much of it, and a park near Tower Bridge. The walk goes under the bridge to a development called Butlers Wharf. London Bridge station is nearby and in 1998 will have accessible Jubilee Line platforms. There are **wheelchair loos** in London Bridge Station and Hays Galleria.

The Anchor, 34 Park Street SE1 *Tel:* 0171 407-1577. One of London's most famous riverside pubs dating from just after the Southwark fire of 1676. The present building is 18thC. The bars are not particularly accessible. There is a step or so at every entrance, and then –4 or –2 inside. The pub is split up and relatively cramped. However, the riverside terrace outside is ramped, and has pub tables but with fixed benches. The view is excellent.

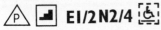 E1/2 N2/4

Bankside Gallery see chapter on *Museums & galleries.*

Bramah Tea and Coffee Museum see chapter on *Museums & galleries.*

Britain at War Experience, 64 Tooley Street SE1 *Tel:* 0171 403-3171. This attempts to recreate the fury of the London blitz. You can sit in an Anderson shelter and hear the raids overhead. Ramped entrance. There is a route without steps, but you need staff help. There's a door to bypass the +1–1 into the simulated lift (to the underground). The Rainbow room has +3, but you can see in, while the Blitz area which otherwise involves –11+11 can be accessed via a 'fire exit'.

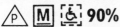 90%

Design Museum see chapter on *Museums & galleries.*

Hays Galleria, Tooley Street EC1, is an attractive development on the riverside on the site of an old tea wharf. It's just opposite the London Dungeon. The centrepiece is an arched courtyard with a remarkable working sculpture of a fantasy ship in the middle. There are good views of HMS *Belfast* and Tower Bridge from the river frontage, and a number of pubs and restaurants. Most of the shops have flat access and there are some stalls. What is disappointing, is that the new *Horniman* pub and *Wall Street* restaurant have split levels. The planning permission regulations don't seem to work somewhere along the line.

On the approach to the Galleria there are some cobbled roads (presumably left to retain some of the original character of the place). There is an overhead walkway from London Bridge station with a lift D75cm at the end to bypass the escalator and steps. You need to use an intercom to use the lift. Around the Galleria there are ramped bypasses to all the steps, though they're not always obvious. There's one eating place *(Café Rouge)* with flat access, and the upper, rather cramped parts of the *Horniman at Hays* pub, are step free. There are −5 to the bar, or −2 through a side entrance.

The situation over loos would be laughable if it wasn't so infuriating. **There are three wheelchair loos on site,** one off the reception area of Counting House (near Tooley Street), one off the reception of Shakleton House (to the right of the four curved steps in the centre) and one ostensibly public one, with a green door, to the left of the four curved steps and close to the *Café Rouge*. The problem is that you'd never know they're there and the public **wheelchair loo (D75+ ST75+)** is kept locked with the key at Shackleton House. It is not signed or indicated, and it's not used (quote from staff on site). **To use the loo, ask one of the security staff or go to Shackleton House.**

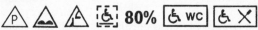

HMS Belfast, Morgans Lane, Tooley Street SE1 *Tel:* 0171 407-6434. This cruiser saw service during the Second World War, and supported the Normandy landings. She was active until 1965 and served in Korea. Now permanently moored on the riverside and run by the Imperial War Museum. CP on the corner of Tooley Street by Tower Bridge. The shop and ticket sales point are somewhat congested, and accessed via a threshold and D75cm. Entrance flat, with an open lift down to the level of the quarterdeck bypassing −4 steps. The lift is on the right side of the gangway, reached along the exit route. There is a steepish ramp to the boatdeck on an upper level.

They have gone to considerable lengths to make parts of the ship accessible, but it's difficult, as there are narrow gaps and doors to gun turrets, and high thresholds/bulkheads (which were designed to keep water out during rough weather). The decks are quite rough with various ridges and protrusions. Chair users will find that help is vital especially to get inside, as ramps put over the bulkheads are very steep. You can get close to some of the smaller guns on the boatdeck. Towards the bow, where the anchors are laid out, there is a barrier 25cm high to get over.

Going up inside to see the bridge and wireless room, and down to the engine room and living quarters, involves steep ladders and well over 100 steps, and is only possible for the relatively agile. In spite of this, there's enough to see in the accessible parts of the ship to make it an interesting visit, but note that a considerable amount of help is needed for a chair user to get around. There's a **wheelchair loo (D90 ST100+)** on the quarterdeck level with portable ramps to help you get over the bulkhead threshold (35cm high) to get to the loo. You need to ask, and the ramps involved are pretty steep.

 **N 100** 40%

George Inn, 77 Borough High Street SE1 *Tel:* 0171 407-2056. A National Trust property which is the only traditional galleried coaching inn left in London. Cobbled approach with tables outside. Entrance to the Southwark bar via −1 step, and there's an awkward turn because of a staircase just L120cm in front. Most chair users could probably manage with just a little help. The bar to the left is flat, but has a small step further in. *It is very atmospheric.* Around the same courtyard is the *Alicante Sandwich Bar,* and the *Guinea Butt* wine bar, both with flat access.

 **EI**

London Dungeon, 28 Tooley Street SE1 *Tel:* 0171 403-0606. A series of dark vaults under the London Bridge railway arches with gruesome waxworks representing some of the grimmer aspects of British history. Flat but slightly rough access throughout. It's also dark inside, with eerie sound effects. If you visit at a busy time, there are unavoidable bottlenecks on the route which make things quite slow. Flat/ramped to *Pizza Hut* restaurant, and the shop. **Wheelchair loo (D80 ST85)** immediately on the left inside the door marked ladies just past the Mystical Forest Area. Not signed outside.

Old St Thomas's Operating Theatre, 9A St Thomas' Street SE1 *Tel:* 0171 955-4791/806-4325. West of Guy's hospital and about 60m from Borough Street. The museum is in the loft of a church, used in the 19thC as an operating theatre. The standard access route is difficult even for the fit and able. It involves +1+2 and then +34 up a spiral staircase with a door 55cm wide en route and only a rope handrail. This leads to the ticket desk. There is then +17, through D73cm, and −2. Access to the operating table is +1+2−2, OR +1+10−6 via the balcony. There is an easier route, using a lift in the adjacent post office, although there are still some steps involved. As it involves post office staff, it is normally only available for pre-arranged groups.

Shakespeare's Globe Museum see chapter on *Museums & galleries*

Southwark Cathedral see chapter on *Places of worship.*

Docklands

An extensive area to the east of London where there has been massive redevelopment, mainly of business and commercial premises. It is served by the **only** step free access transport system in London, the DLR. This runs at a high level from the Bank or Tower Gateway to Island Gardens, just the other side of the river from Greenwich. Docklands is interesting to see from the railway, but there are relatively few places to visit. The main part is north of the river. Some starts at London Bridge and is described under Southwark. St Katherine's Dock is described in the City section. A book called *Travelling Light* published by the DLR, PO Box 154, Poplar E14 9QA, provides a well written and interesting account of what you can see in the area, and its history.

The dominating landmark is the Canary Wharf office development which includes the tallest building in Britain. There's Tobacco Dock and the London Arena, and all three have encountered severe financial problems during their early years. You will also find an interesting little farm, and the City Airport.

Docklands Visitors Centre, 3 Limeharbour, Isle of Dogs E14 *Tel:* 0171 512-1111. Crossharbour DLR station is about 250m away. CP outside. Step free access. A small interesting exhibition explaining the development of Docklands. If you want to understand what is going on, it's a good place to start. **Wheelchair cubicles (D80 ST75) in both gents and ladies loos.**

DLR see chapter on *Transport*.

London Arena see section on *Music venues*.

Mudchute Farm, Pier Street, Isle of Dogs E14 *Tel:* 0171 515-5901. The mudchute was formed from silt out of the Milwall docks together with waste clinker from local industries. The area is now wonderfully quiet, and there's a delightful (and totally unexpected) urban farm with sheep, cattle, pigs, goats, chickens, rabbits and riding stables. There's even a llama. Local groups organise riding for disabled people. On-site CP with flat access to the main building and yard. Rough slightly hilly paths around parts of the farm. To see it all you'd need to go some 300/400m. **Wheelchair loo (D75 ST100)** in the main building. Step free access to the café.

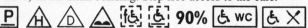

Tobacco Dock see chapter on *Shops*.

Holborn and the Strand areas

This comprises four areas in the Eyewitness guide, with important sites and sights like the British Museum, the Royal Opera House, the Strand and Soho. It includes Bloomsbury, Covent Garden and Trafalgar Square.

British Museum see chapter on *Museums & galleries*.

Central Registry Office see entry on Somerset House later in this section.

Chinatown is centred around Gerrard Street just north of Leicester Square. It has brightly coloured Chinese gates at each end, and is pedestrianised with smooth surfaces throughout. Most restaurants have at least 1 step at the entrance, but a few are step free or have only a tiny lip. A really good place to go for the Chinese New Year celebrations.

Covent Garden is the area behind the Royal Opera House in Bow Street, running parallel to the Strand. It's a pleasant place on a sunny day and is often crowded, especially in the evening. It is a development on the site of the old Covent Garden fruit and vegetable market. There are plenty of small shops and stalls and there is frequently open-air entertainment from buskers, small music groups and Punch & Judy shows. It's generally an animated scene.

There are NCPs at the Southern end of Monument Street, and in Parker Street on the corner of Drury Lane. Access by underground from the Piccadilly line involves less hassle than most stations. Getting off the train there are +19 steps, a lift and then –1.

Little thought has been given to the needs of disabled visitors except in the provision of loos. Surfaces are rough and consist of cobbles or rough paving. The shops are mostly small, and up 1 or 2 steps. However, there are a good number of market stalls and much of the area is under cover, so it's a good place to go if the weather is uncertain. There's an open-air crafts market (that is, open at the ends but roofed over) on the south side.

Wheelchair cubicles (D80 ST80) in both ladies and gents loos in the passage on the south side between the Jubilee Hall Sports Centre and the LT Museum. The loos are said to be open most of the time but, if the cubicles are locked, ask a stallholder to call one of the security staff who have keys. These loos replace a specially adapted toilet which was down 19 steps!

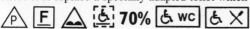 70%

The *Punch & Judy* is the main pub and must rate as the most inaccessible in London, with bars involving either +30 or –30 steps; (mind you, this didn't deter one of our more intrepid survey teams!).

The *Rat and Parrot* pub in Tavistock Street has a slightly bumpy entrance, but a spacious GF. It is close to the loos.

The *Old Orleans* pub/restaurant and *Sheila's* both have **wheelchair loos,** see *Pubs* chapter.

St Paul's Church, Henrietta Street WC2 *Tel:* 0171 835-5221 is London's chief church for the theatrical profession. It backs on to Covent Garden, with the entrance on the other side. Outside there is a quiet garden with several seats, some shaded, which provides a nice spot for a rest or a picnic. Step free access from either Henrietta Street or Bedford Street (via Inigo Place). Access to the church is via +4, and inside it is flat.

London Transport Museum see chapter on *Museums & galleries.*

Theatre Museum see chapter on *Museums & galleries.*

Dickens's House, 48 Doughty Street WC1 *Tel:* 0171 405-2127. Doughty Street is parallel to Grays Inn Road. Entrance 1 step, then two rooms of memorabilia with flat access and −1 to shop. The rest of the house has steps, −14 to the basement and wine cellar, +19 to the first floor and a further +20 to the second floor. From the GF there are two small lips into the garden.

 EI NI4/39 20%

Fitzroy Tavern, 16 Charlotte Street W1 *Tel:* 0171 580-3714. On the junction with Windmill Street. A traditional pub which was a meeting place for artists and writers between the wars, who gave the area the name *Fitzrovia.* Two entrances have flat access.

 80%

Leicester Square is now pedestrianised, with a small park and seats in the middle. Buskers and portrait sketchers can often be found in the northwest corner. It is surrounded by major cinemas, and the new Warner West End a short distance away has flat/lift access throughout. There's a **wheelchair loo** in the *Moon under Water* pub (but entrance +2 steps), and one in *McDonalds* (**step free D80 ST120**) at the junction of Swiss Corner and Panton Street.

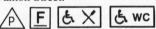

Lincoln's Inn Fields WC2, is a large area of lawyers offices, behind the Royal Courts of Justice. It has been well maintained since the first buildings were erected nearly 500 years ago, and is worth a look. The area is mostly flat, although surfaces can be bumpy. Access to the New Hall and Library is via about 40 steps, and we couldn't see any way round these.

E40

Photographers Gallery see chapter on *Museums & galleries.*

Piccadilly Circus, is small but crowded, with its famous lights and the statue of Eros. It has been partly pedestrianised. Leicester Square is nearby, and en route is the Trocadero entertainment and shopping centre. There are **wheelchair loos** in the *Trocadero,* and in *Burger King* (**D70+ ST70+**) on the north side by the junction with Glasshouse Street.

Pollock Toy Museum see chapter on *Museums & galleries.*

Public Record Office and Museum, Chancery Lane, WC2 *Tel:* 0181 876-3444. By the junction with Carey Street. This is due to move to Ruskin Avenue, Kew at the end of 1996 (see entry under Outer London, later in this section). The two offices share the same phone number. The Office is the principal repository of public archives, state papers and also some aspects of family histories. There are useful leaflets outlining which records are held where, so a phone call might save considerable wasted effort. The Museum includes exhibits such as the *Domesday Book*. Main entrance +4+7+3 steps, with a platform stairlift to bypass them. It is then step free to the museum. **Adapted loo (D80 ST80 but there's a fixed rail in the way)** on the right along the main corridor.

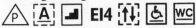

Royal Courts of Justice, Strand WC2 *Tel:* 0171 936-6000. Situated at the junction between the Strand, Aldwych and Arundel Street. The buildings have a magnificent Gothic facade. The large complex of courts is spread between four buildings. These are the Main, West Green, Queens, and Thomas More buildings. Courts 1 to 30 and 64 to 76 are in the Main building, 31 to 38A in West Green, 39 to 50 in Queens and 51 to 63 in Thomas More. A map is available which shows the easiest routes for disabled people to get to various parts of the complex, and they have gone to considerable lengths to make the place more accessible. Signposting is quite good.

> **Main building.** The principal entrance from the Strand has +3+4 steps. 50m away (towards Aldwych), is an entrance for disabled visitors which gives access to the Main building (to the right), West Green (straight on up the ramp) and to Thomas More (turn left just before West Green). Access to the GF of the Main building is via a ramp (bypassing –5) and two platform stair-lifts (bypassing –5 and +16). This brings you to the Hall which is enormous, and of considerable interest. On the other side of

the principal entrance, about 50m away (towards the City) is the Quad-rangle entrance, giving access to courts 64 to 76 via a lift (D85 W125 L110).

Royal Courts of Justice

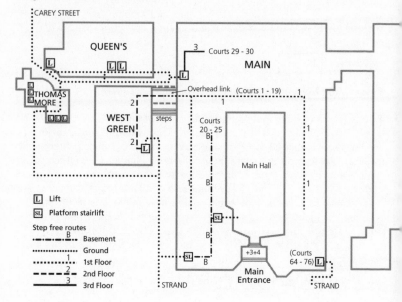

In the Main building, courts 1 to 19 are on the first floor, with step free access only from the second floor of the West Green building described below. Courts 20 to 25 are in the basement, step free using the disabled visitors entrance described above. Courts 26 to 28 are at the Carey Street end, and involve +4 steps. Courts 29 and 30 are on the third floor and have step free access via the Queens building, and a route which leads to a lift (D85 W125 L110) in the corner of the Main building. **Wheelchair loo (D95 ST70)** in the basement. **Wheelchair loos** off the main Hall are accessed by portable ramps, bypassing 2 (for gents) or 2+2 to a unisex cubicle. **Adapted cubicles (D85 ST55)** in both ladies and gents on the first floor. There is a GF restaurant at the Carey Street end of the Main building, but it has +4.

The **West Green** is reached step free from the disabled persons route to the Main building. Go straight ahead and up the ramp, and West Green is on your left. All the courts are then accessible using the lift (D75 W125 L100) to the left of the entrance. The second floor of this building links to the first floor of the main building via a walkway.

The **Thomas More** building is on eleven floors. It has step free access from the entrance described above, and there is a short ramp just before the entrance. Two sets of lifts (D90 W135+ L110+), one by the entrance and the other round the corner. **Wheelchair cubicles (D85 ST70) in both ladies and gents** by the second set of lifts.

The **Queens building** can either be approached from a side exit from Thomas More or from Carey Street, both step free. Three lifts inside, give step free access to all the courts. Two are by the main entrance (D100 W200 L110) and one is by a side entrance (D85 W120 L150).

We were told that a new flat entrance is under construction at the Bell Yard. Also that there are some courts in St Dunstans House, Fetter Lane EC4, with step free access using a lift, and nearby adapted loos.

 90%

St Catherine's House, 10 Kingsway WC2 *Tel:* 0171 242-0262. At the junction with Aldwych. The indexes to the central register of births, marriages and deaths are kept here. Entrance +1+2 steps, but there's a flat alternative via a side door. The office dealing with births has a split level of +2. **Wheelchair loo (D80 ST100)** on the GF through double doors to the left. It is signed, but you need to ask for the key at the customer service desk. The office hopes to relocate within the next couple of years, and we were told that one of the criteria in the selection of new premises will be improved access for disabled people.

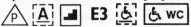 E3

Sir John Soane's Museum see chapter on *Museums & galleries.*

Somerset House, Central Registry Office, The Strand WC2 *Tel:* 0171 936-7000. A huge and imposing classical building. You can go through the archway into the magnificent courtyard. The **Courtauld Institute Galleries** are immediately on your right (see chapter on *Museums & galleries*). At the far side of the courtyard is the Registry Office where among other things, wills and probate records are kept. It may be possible to park in the courtyard if you phone security at least 24 hours in advance. The entrance has +1+3+1 steps, but there is a ramped bypass, some 20m to the left, with a bell to alert security staff to come and open appropriate doors. Inside it is step free to the parts you may need to visit to see a will, or deposit a probate application. Lift (D85 W105 L105) to the first and second floors. Probate enquiries are dealt with on the second floor. **Wheelchair loo (D85 ST80)** at this level.

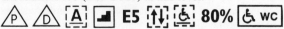

Trafalgar Square is the home of Nelson's column with its famous lions, and of a thousand pigeons. It was conceived by Nash, and mainly built in the 1830s. It is one of London's best known landmarks, and around it are some major sights. The square is flat and quite small. The only step free access is via various road crossings, and there are ramped kerbs at some of them. There are **wheelchair loos** in the nearby galleries, in the *Lord Moon of the Mall* pub and in Charing Cross station (NKS). Around the square are: the National Gallery, Portrait Gallery and St Martin-in-the-Fields Church.

Trocadero, Coventry Street W1 *Tel:* 0171 439-1791. A major development right by Piccadilly Circus, between Shaftesbury Avenue and Coventry Street, bounded by Windmill Street and Rupert Street. It has changed hands several times in recent years, and has recently been taken over by the Burford Group. It contains shops, a MGM multi-screen cinema (see the section on *Cinemas),* and is home to several hi-tech entertainment venues. These currently include Virtual World, Emaginator, Alien War and Funland. In the summer of 1996 Sega World is due to open. The Guinness Book of Records Exhibition, which has been there for some time, will move during 1996. The entertainments vary over time.

Access on the GF is flat from Coventry Street, but from Shaftesbury Avenue there are –5–5–5 steps to Coventry Street. Access was not considered when the building was originally converted. To the right from the Coventry Street entrance there's a service lift. This is fairly busy, and has manual doors, so if someone leaves them open on another floor it can take a while to get it sorted. Split levels inside are dealt with using small open lifts with a 'call button' to summon someone from security to operate. There are **wheelchair loos** in several of the facilities.

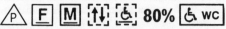

Westminster & St James's

This is covered in two sections of the *Eyewitness* guide. The area includes some of London's most important sights, in particular the Houses of Parliament, Westminster Abbey and Buckingham Palace. Behind the Whitehall government offices there is St James's Park, an attractive area with a lake, fountains and a bandstand.

Buckingham Palace, The Mall SW1. Contact **Royal Collection Enterprises**, St James's Palace SW1A 1JR *Tel:* 0171 839-1377. The palace is the Queen's London home and lived in by members of the royal family, and their staff. When the Queen is in residence, the Royal Standard is flown. Following the fire at Windsor Castle, it was decided to open the State Rooms in the palace for two months each summer to raise money to help pay for the repairs at Windsor. *It is an interesting visit, and there are some impressive works of art on display.*

Chair users are admitted only by prior arrangement. Contact the Special Access Office at St James's Palace. While some 4500 people visit every day, only about twenty-five chair users are allowed, because of perceived problems of evacuation. In 1994 and 95, all the places were booked for the whole period long before the palace opened. One of our surveyors, who uses a chair, applied well in advance in both years and failed to get in, so there is clearly a demand that is not being met and action is needed to meet this.

The main 'line of route' for the tour involves a little under 150 steps. Tickets are purchased from an office in Green Park, and the entrance is about 300m away in Buckingham Palace Road through the Ambassadors Entrance (near the Queens Gallery).

Arrangements can be made for those with disabilities to drive through the palace gates (with appropriate security checks) and to park near an alternative entrance on the other side of the Grand Hall. In 1993 this was ramped, but in 1994 the palace decided to use Scalamobile stairclimbers – which are neither particularly comfortable nor convenient. Our surveyor found that it was an unpleasant way of getting up the initial +13 steps, and we suspect that others found the same. Electric chair users have to transfer to a manual chair, which is a major disadvantage. After the initial steps, access is step free. There is a lift (D80 W105 L175) to the main rooms on the first floor (bypassing about +55). **Wheelchair loo (D115 ST115)** in Lady Barringtons Corridor, off the Marble Hall at the lower level. Because of your starting point, you follow a slightly different line of route to everyone else, as you have to go to and from the lift. They have orgainsed a special shop for buying souvenirs, as the main one is out in the garden –2–10. The main line of route is out through the gardens into Grosvenor Place, but if you want to return by the same route you came in, you can use the stairclimber in reverse.

We are not quite sure how they will handle visitors with disabilities who come with friends who say that "150 odd steps are no problem – in the event of an evacuation we'll simply go down them, just like the ones we've come up". In principle there is strict rationing for chair users.

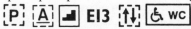

On special occasions and for distinguished foreign visitors, there are processions going to the palace, often starting at Victoria Station. The **Changing of the Guard** both at Buckingham Palace and at Horse Guards Parade, Whitehall, is a regular attraction for visitors. Mounted Life Guards pass the palace regularly at *10.50 and return at about 11.35, except on Sunday when they're an hour earlier.* The Changing of the Guard takes place between 11.10 and 12.30 in the palace forecourt, *every day in summer and alternate days in winter.* **It is possible for disabled people to get permission to watch from inside the railings** since there is often a considerable crowd outside. If you are inside, remember that you're there for well over an hour, with no loo. To get permission you should write to the Master of the Household, Buckingham Palace SW1 (*Tel:* 0171 930-4832). For other information, eg about the times of the events, contact the army's administrative offices (*Tel:* 0171 930-4466), and ask for the public information office.

Cabinet War Rooms see chapter on *Museums & galleries.*

Christie's, King Street SW1 *Tel:* 0171 839-9060. Famous auction house. Well worth a visit to exhibitions and auctions. Be careful not to nod or sneeze as you might be buying something expensive. Entrance +3+1 steps to reception and collections, then −2 to valuations. The mezzanine floor where auctions take place is +14+10, or use the service lift (D110 L90 W200).

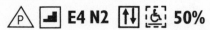

Houses of Parliament & Westminster Hall, Parliament Square SW1 *Tel:* 0171 219-3000. The Palace of Westminster has been the home to the two Houses of Parliament since the 16thC. The present mock Gothic building was built in Victorian times. For security reasons a tour of the Palace of Westminster is no longer possible for the public except at the invitation of a Member of Parliament. However, you can get into the public galleries when the House is sitting via step free routes. Overseas visitors wanting to make a tour should contact **The Public Information Office, House of Commons SW1A 2DG** *Tel:* 0171 219-4272. This is also the number for general information about the Palace and the work of Parliament.

The main 'line of route' for members of the public visiting the building when the Houses are not sitting is shown on the plan, together with the location of the principal lifts. There are some fifteen lifts in different parts of the building, but only the two of greatest relevance to visitors are shown.

Although normal access through St Stephen's Entrance to the Central Lobby involves about 30 steps, there is an alternative route via the Chancellor's Gate (*Tel:* 0171 219-3090) to the principal floor level.

Alternatively, if you make prior arrangements, it may be possible to be dropped off, or even to park, using the New Palace Yard entrance, and then use the other lift shown. The police or staff on duty will escort you everywhere because of security. There are wheelchair spaces below the Bar in the House of Lords, and at the back of the Strangers' Gallery in the Commons (the public gallery) which is steeply stepped; access is by ramp from a lift. It's about 300m to walk or wheel from St Stephen's Entrance via the step free route. The view from the Gallery is somewhat restricted, and our surveyor could only see about a third of the chamber. There were three chair-users there at the time. **Wheelchair loo (D90 ST70)** off the Peers' Lobby and an **adapted loo** with restricted ST off the Lower Waiting Hall.

To get to the Committee Rooms, there is a lift from the corridor beyond the Lower Waiting Hall to the main committee corridors, upstairs. If you go on a 'tour' of the Commons and Lords by invitation, you will find that there is flat access throughout the main floor, and through the Commons lobbies. The flat area is shaded on the plan. Towards the end of the tour, able-bodied visitors walk down the 5 steps to St Stephen's Hall and then the –30 into Westminster Hall. Those unable to do this can ask to get down to New Palace Yard via the lift, and from there, Westminster Hall is reached via a single low kerb.

The Education Unit run a special visits programme for schools and would be pleased to discuss arrangements for disabled students (*Tel:* 0171 219-4750).

In a recent comment from an MP who was temporarily disabled, the Palace of Westminster was described as being extremely 'wheelchair-unfriendly'. He was looking at the building from the point of view of working in it, not just visiting. He described struggling with lifts that were too small, corridor doors which are too heavy to open without help, and a series of steps that would 'challenge a mountain goat!' There have been long deliberations about improving access within the Palace, and the Minutes of Evidence to the Commons Accommodation and Works Committee entitled *Access to the Palace of Westminster* by disabled people published 17 March 1995, makes interesting reading. It is available through HMSO or the Parliamentary bookshop.

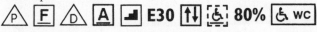

Parliament Square and **Westminster Bridge** The square has statues of famous statesmen such as Disraeli and Churchill. It was Britain's first official roundabout (an oddity, given that it's square!). From the bridge you can get fine views up and down the Thames. Westminster Pier is a starting point for river trips to the Tower or Greenwich. **Wheelchair loo (D80 ST80 NKS)**, just outside the QE II Conference Centre. The toilets are unmarked,

The Palace of Westminster

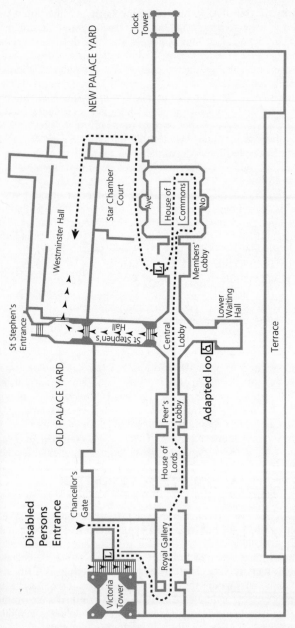

NEW PALACE YARD

Clock Tower

Westminster Hall

Star Chamber Court

Aye

House of Commons

No

Members' Lobby

St Stephen's Entrance

St Stephen's Hall

Central Lobby

Lower Waiting Hall

OLD PALACE YARD

Adapted loo

Terrace

Peer's Lobby

House of Lords

Disabled Persons Entrance

Chancellor's Gate

Royal Gallery

Victoria Tower

······· Line of route for disabled visitors
➤➤ Stepped access
Ⓛ Lift

and the entrance is at the junction of Broad Sanctuary and Storey's Gate, just across the road from the Midland Bank at the corner of Central Hall. There's another **wheelchair loo** by the pier for river trips. To reach the pier from the bridge and bypass the steps, you need to go nearly 100m east along the Embankment, and then come back towards the bridge. The loo was 'double locked' when we visited, with an NKS lock, and another one as well. There was no attendant to answer the intercom button. We hope you'll be luckier. It had just been rebuilt, so it's probably really good, *if* you can get in!

The **Parliamentary Bookshop** is on the corner of Whitehall and Bridge Street. Step free access into the small shop which has some interesting publications and reports produced by Parliament and its committees.

Passport Office, Clive House, 70 Petty France SW1H 9HD *Tel:* 0171 799-2290. Roughly half way along Petty France. Entrance +1–6 steps, but there's a signed alternative where the +1 is ramped, through a staff entrance to a lift (D85 W85 L160) which bypasses the –6. Flat into office area, and there are lots of seats. Ramped access to an **adapted loo (D80 but obstructed ST because of the sink, NKS).**

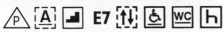

Royal Mews, Buckingham Palace Road SW1 *Tel:* 0171 940-4832. The entrance is between Palace Street and Bressenden Place on the other side of the road. The stables and coach houses were designed by Nash in 1825. You can see all the royal coaches used on different occasions. The mews are basically flat. There's 1 small step en route to the main courtyard, a small lip into one display room and 2 small steps into a second which can be bypassed by using the exit door. You'll find a few stretches of rough cobbled surface. The whole tour is about 500m. **Wheelchair loo (D80 ST70)** in the corner of the courtyard, just past the state coach display, about 150m from the entrance.

St James's Park and **Green Park** SW1. These are both attractive, well shaded, and centrally located by Buckingham Palace. They are flat and have tarmac paths throughout. Both have good maps at key entry points. There are refreshment facilities in St James's Park towards Horseguards Parade at the end of the lake. There's also a bandstand with occasional performances. From the nearby bridge over the lake in St James's there's a unique view of the Whitehall offices, and by taking a judiciously framed photograph, you can persuade your friends that you've been to Istanbul. **Wheelchair cubicles (D85 ST90 NKS)** inside both the ladies and gents, on the north side of the park at the junction with Marlborough Road.

St Margaret's Church see chapter on *Places of worship.*

Sotheby's, 38 New Bond Street W1 *Tel:* 0171 408-8080. Famous auction house with up to three sales a day. Items are put on show three days before. Flat entrance to reception, then +8+8 steps to the first floor and +7 to main gallery. Our survey team was told that all stairs can be bypassed by a service lift. We were told that you should phone (*Tel:* 0171 408-5189) at least a day in advance to use it. Hmmm.

Westminster Abbey see chapter on *Places of worship.*

Westminster Cathedral see chapter on *Places of worship.*

Whitehall runs from Westminster to Trafalgar Square and is a wide street flanked by government offices. There are several important statues of military leaders, including Monty (Field Marshall Lord Montgomery) from WWII and Earl Haig from WW1. Part way along is the Cenotaph, which is the national memorial to those who have died in war. The annual ceremony of remembrance is held there in November. Horseguards Parade, with its daily Changing of the Guard ceremony (see entry on Buckingham Palace) is just beyond the Cenotaph towards Trafalgar Square.

Downing Street, SW1 is half-way up Whitehall, and has a well known resident at No 10 (and another at No 11). It is no longer possible to go down it, and you have to view the houses from behind the railings at the end of the road.

Banqueting House, Whitehall SW1 *Tel:* 0171 930-4179. Opposite Horseguards Parade. It is the only bit of the Palace of Whitehall left which the public can see, as Wolsey's wine cellar is under the Ministry of Defence. Charles I was beheaded just outside in 1649. It contains the Banqueting Hall on the first floor, with magnificent Rubens paintings on the ceiling. There is 1 step at the entrance, then +17+6 inside. Seats around the walls. An area called the undercroft is –3 from the entrance, but there is a ramped bypass behind the door to the left of the steps. They show a video about the building and its history. **Wheelchair loo (D80 ST80+)** at the bottom of the ramp, which could be accessed even if you are not visiting the Hall upstairs.

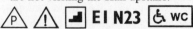

Kensington and Chelsea

This includes three of the areas in the *Eyewitness* guide. Some of the important sights, such as the major museums, Kensington Gardens and Hyde Park, and the famous Harrods department store, are described elsewhere in the guide.

Chelsea Physic Garden, Swan Walk SW3 *Tel:* 0171 352-5646. Located in the triangle formed by Royal Hospital Road, Chelsea Embankment and Swan Walk. It was established in 1673 by the Society of Apothecaries to study plants used for medicinal purposes. Main entrance in Swan Walk has −3 steps, but there's a flat alternative about 50m away. Gravel paths throughout. Size: about 200m by 200m. Shop with step free access, and **wheelchair loo (D85 ST80)** near the flat entrance.

Chelsea Royal Hospital, Royal Hospital Road SW3 *Tel:* 0171 730-0161. A unique retirement home for soldiers; there are always Chelsea Pensioners around in their distinctive uniforms who are happy to chat. It is possible to visit the gardens and some of the Wren buildings, including the Great Hall and the Chapel. Three OB spaces by the Chelsea gate. From either gate the grounds are flat, and it's about 150m to the main courtyard and hall. +10 steps to the chapel, and the same number to the Great Hall. Museum +2 steps.

[P] F /D ◢ N10/10 [&] 50%

Kensington Palace, Kensington Gardens W8 *Tel:* 0171 937-9561. Part of the spacious palace is used as a private home for members of the Royal family. The other part, including 18thC state rooms, is open to the public. It is situated near the middle of the Broad Walk, some distance from the nearest roads. By phoning in advance, disabled visitors may get permission to park outside the palace.

Entrance +1+1+1 steps. On the GF there are −2 to the Court Dress Collection. The state appartments are on the first floor +13+9+9. **Wheelchair cubicle (D75 ST115) in the gents and an adapted cubicle (D75 ST62) in the ladies loos**, both on the GF. Café at the Orangery about 50m away, +6 with a portable ramp available.

[P] /D ◢ E3 N2/3 [&] 80% [& WC]

Regent's Park

Described in one section of the *Eyewitness* guide. The area includes the north end of Baker Street, the Marylebone Road, the Regent's Canal, Little

Venice and Camden. Pay and display parking is possible round the Inner Circle, and on Chester Road. There are a substantial number of OB spaces on the Inner Circle (not marked in the *Evening Standard* parking map). There is also pay and display parking around long stretches of the outer circle. Note the **wheelchair loos** in Regent's Park and the one opposite Madame Tussauds.

Camden is just north-west of Regent's Park, and the canal passes through. There are many shops and stalls on Camden High Street. Camden Market is open Thursday to Sunday and is flat. Much of it is covered. It can be congested, with narrow gaps between stalls. Camden Lock Market, across the canal, has three courts: east, middle and west. There are two levels, but both have ramped access from Chalk Farm Road. A lift from Camden Lock Place goes to the upper level. The surfaces are rough in places, and it's often crowded. **Adapted loo (D86 opens in, ST60)** on the first floor of West Court, accessed via the road or the lift. The key is available from the nearest shop. The *Pizzeria Avanti* in Middle Court, accessed from the street via the towpath, has a ramped side entrance and a **wheelchair loo (D84 ST76)**. The *Fusilier and Firkin* pub has step free access, including the loos.

On Camden High Street roughly opposite the the station, there's a *McDonalds* with a **wheelchair loo (D84 ST83)** and step free access, and also a *Burger King* with a **wheelchair loo labelled 'ladies' (D83 ST72)**.

Little Venice. The Regent's Canal was opened in 1820, joining the Grand Union Canal and the busy port at Paddington Basin to the river Thames at Limehouse. A hundred years ago it was busy with horse-drawn barges. Now it is a quiet waterway taking people on a scenic route through parts of London not otherwise seen.

Little Venice itself provides a quiet retreat from the general 'rush' in London. Near the junction of Blomfield Road and Warwick Avenue are the Rembrandt Gardens. Opposite 60 Blomfield Road is *Jason's Canal Trip* ticket office and restaurant. **Two wheelchair loos (D75+ ST70+)** in the restaurant. Getting on and off the boat involves going through a gap 60cm wide and ±3 steps. Staff there are used to carrying chairs and their users. They use a narrower plastic chair to carry you in if your chair is too wide to get through the gap, and you can transfer back into your own once on board. On the boat the chairs and tables are movable.

{P} {&} 80% ▲ | & WC | & ✗ |

There were two nearby pubs, the *Warwick Castle* with 1+1 steps at the entrance and the *Bridge House* with +1. Neither had **adapted loos**. From Westbourne Terrace Road Bridge there is ramped access down to the towpath where the *Waterside Café* has −1−3 and movable tables and chairs.

The Canal Bus departs from here, and the one we saw, *Water Buffalo,* had +1–3 to get on board and fixed seating so that a chair user would have to transfer.

London Central Mosque see chapter on *Places of worship.*

Madame Tussauds and the Planetarium see chapter on *Museums & galleries.*

Primrose Hill rises gently up from Prince Albert Road, and you can get fine views over London on a good day. **Wheelchair loo (D80 ST100)** in the Children's Playground at the bottom of the hill, about 100m from the park entrance. The attendant has the key.

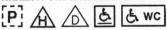

Regent's Park. Manager's Office, The Storeyard, Inner Circle, Regent's Park NW1 *Tel:* 0171 486-7905. A large and attractive area just north of Marylebone. The park was enclosed in 1812, and Nash developed a grand design consisting of a garden suburb including a pleasure palace for the Prince Regent. Only eight villas were ever built. It is fairly flat, and most of the paths are tarmac. There's a largish lake with boating, and in the north-east corner is London Zoo. The ring road round the outside is nearly 8km long. Information office on the Inner Circle close to the junction with Chester Road. They publish a programme of summer entertainments, including recitals in Queen Mary's Rose Garden, performances on the bandstand and children's events in the playgrounds. There are a number of OB spaces on the Inner circle.

To the north is Primrose Hill and, off the Inner Circle, there's a small open-air theatre with step free access – an attractive spot during warm summer evenings. Queen Mary's Garden has an attractive rose garden. We found three places selling refreshments: a cafeteria on the Broadwalk (near Chester Road); a restaurant on the Inner Circle in Queen Mary's Garden, near the theatre; and another cafeteria by the tennis courts towards York Gate. All have flat/ramped access.

There are several **wheelchair loos**:
- just off Chester Road where Broad Walk crosses it, **cubicles (D90 ST90)** in both ladies and gents;
- by the boating lake **unisex (D90 ST120)**, near Hanover Gate; and
- by York Bridge (near the cafeteria), **cubicle (D75 ST100) in ladies.** Gents not seen, but probably similar.

Adapted cubicles (D90 ST45) in both ladies and gents, in Queen Mary's Garden near the end of Chester Road, and another **unisex (D75 ST60)** in the Children's Playground just inside Gloucester Gate. All of them seem to be kept locked with a nearby attendant who has the key.

[P] [F] △/D [⚹] **95%** [⚹ WC] [⚹ ✗]

London Zoo, Regent's Park NW1 *Tel:* 0171 722-3333. The zoo is in the northern part of Regent's Park, and the Regent's Canal passes alongside. The Zoological Gardens, opened in 1828, was the first institution in the world dedicated to the study and display of animals. It has recently been in danger of closure, and has had to rethink its functions and the way it works, particularly in the field of conservation. A considerable amount has been done to improve the facilities for disabled visitors, although some problems remain. Both electric and manual chairs are available for hire near the main entrance, which is useful as the zoo is big. You are advised to book in advance, on extension 576. Volunteers may be available to help people in chairs get around, if you ask.

The main entrance is on the Outer Circle. Parking facilities for disabled visitors are poor, considering the size and importance of the zoo. For OB holders there is a single space on the road outside, plus three possible OB spaces in the staff CP, available on a first-come-first-served basis after 09.30. The main zoo CP is nearly 500m away. There are usually taxis available outside when you leave, so if this is a viable option for you, you could save yourself a long walk/wheel.

The zoo is triangular in shape with sides approximately 500m/500m/800m. The main entrance is, oddly enough, somewhere near the middle of the triangle, because the road (the Outer Circle) passes through the triangle, and the various houses and terraces on the far side are reached via one or other of two ramped tunnels. A full visit could well take you between 2 and 3 km, and there are some steepish slopes, particularly through the tunnels (each has a 30m slope at both ends), and also on the far side of the Outer Circle. A chair-user would need to be very fit to get round on a solo basis.

We have done the write-up splitting the zoo into three areas, and it would be perfectly feasible to reduce the distances involved, by sticking with the displays within about 400m of the main entrance to the south, and still see a lot which is of interest.

Just to the right of the entrance is the **Information Kiosk** which has a leaflet with information for disabled visitors and a large print map. There are plenty of maps around, and some signposting, but the maps are somewhat stylised and diagrammatic rather than precise and 'access-friendly'. In addition there is information about events that day and about animal feeding times, which may help you plan an itinerary.

There are quite a number of animal enclosures where hedges or walls may obstruct your view if you use a chair. One important thing to note is that, with modernisation, it is necessary to go inside far fewer buildings in order to see the animals. Many of the displays can be seen by walking round outside. If the animals or birds happen to be on the ground when you are going past, you'll find some of them difficult to see from a chair-users eyeline. Fortunately, of course, you'll find many of the animals are up in branches or high up in their cages.

Our description starts with the buildings and houses near the entrance, then those further away to the south-east, and finally those accessed by the tunnels under the Outer Circle.

Near the main entrance

There are **wheelchair cubicles (D85 ST70+)** in the gents at the side of the Aquarium, and in the ladies to the left of the main entrance. There is a **wheelchair loo (D95 ST70)** by the *Regent Café*. This is in the coffee shop, on the left of the counters.

The **Reptile House** has ramped access, bypassing +2 steps.

The **Aquarium** has +5 at the entrance and −8 at the exit. It also has a low level of lighting, but you rapidly get accustomed to this, and after a couple of minutes, can see very adequately. As signed at the entrance, if you can't manage the steps, ramped access can be provided through a side exit reached by going up the path at the side. Ask at the Information kiosk about 30m away.

The **apes and monkeys, cranes and birds** are all seen from outside. Further over, past the restaurant, the same is true of the **flamingos, parrots and macaws,** although the flamingos are particularly difficult to see from a chair, because of the hedges. **Elephants and rhinos** may well be seen easily from outside, but if you need to go into the house, there are +5, bypassed by a steepish ramp on the side of the house nearest the penguins. The **café/restaurant** by the fountain has ramped bypasses to the +2 at the entrance. It does, however, have fixed seating inside, as do many of the catering facilities on-site.

Further away, on the main site

Wheelchair loo (D90 ST95) in the children's zoo near the Discovery Centre.

The view of the big cats **(leopards, lions and tigers)** is good, as there are big glass panels coming down to about 40 cm off the ground. A ramped route leads through from the macaws down to the penguins, and there's plenty of cover in this area. There are, however, some steps, and it isn't always easy to spot the way round. In particular, as you approach the penguin enclosure this way there are −5, and you have to go some way round to the right to bypass them.

The **penguin** enclosure presents problems for a chair-user, simply because it has a high wall around it about 130cm high. The **children's zoo** is step free throughout, and well laid out. There are lots of farm animals, with opportunities to touch and even hold. There is –1 to the Discovery Education Centre. The **tropical bird house** has a flat entrance at one end and +2 at the other.

Across (or under) the Outer Circle

As already mentioned, the ramps for the tunnel are quite long. This side of the zoo is slightly more hilly than the main part.

Giraffes and zebras may be seen outside but, if they're not, you can enter the house via a ramp and +1. On a dry day, you can see the antelope and oryx from the canal bridge. On the other side of the canal is the Snowdon aviary with outdoor cages. There is also a route through inside via +1. All the other birds can be seen from outside.

The **small mammals** can be seen with step free access and under cover. There are –21 to the **Moonlight World**. To get into the **invertebrate house**, the normal route is via +14, but there is an alternative, up a steep and somewhat bumpy ramp. This is signed and some 60m to the right. The house is step free inside.

Areas with a reasonable amount of cover and interest in the event of rain include the 'big cats' enclosures and tropical bird house, the aquarium and reptile house, the small mammals house and the Cotton Terraces. Note that the only exit from the zoo which does not involve narrow revolving gates is back via the main entrance.

Outer London
Brentford & Chiswick

Chiswick House, Burlington Lane, Chiswick W4 *Tel:* 0181 995-0508. Situated just off the A4 some 500m past the Hogarth roundabout on the left as you are going towards Heathrow. Well signed. A palladian villa built around a central octagonal room. On-site CP, but there's a 600m walk over a roughish path, and including a step. Disabled visitors should use the main gate 30m BEFORE the CP entrance, and follow the drive to the forecourt of the house. Entrance +1 step (D66cm), then the GF is step free. The link building (D50cm) houses the Restoration Exhibition. Inside there are –12 to a small wine cellar or +16 spiral stairs to the first floor, which is *the* floor to see. Alternative, easier, steps on the grand staircase can be used if you ask. Café some 50m from the house is step free. **Wheelchair loo (D80 ST130 NKS)**, on the left side of the café. Some of the paths around the house and through the gardens are gravelled.

[P] [F] ◢ EI N16 [🚻] 40% [♿ WC] [♿ ✕]

Hogarth's House, Hogarth Lane, Great West Road W4 *Tel:* 0181 994-6757. A Georgian house now a gallery housing many of Hogarth's engravings. Parking is possible by the Reckitt & Coleman office building, although the signs imply that it is elsewhere –3 steps through the gate can be bypassed. The path to the house is over roughish ground. Entrance +1, and the GF is flat. +13 narrow steps to the first floor. The main attraction is the collection of prints, and staff are willing to bring particular examples downstairs if you are interested.

[P] /D\ /▲\ [■] EI NI3 [♿] 50%

Kew Bridge Steam Museum, Green Dragon Lane, Brentford, Middx *Tel:* 0181 568-4757. Housed in a 19thC water pumping station, it has five Cornish beam engines, two of which are 'in steam' at weekends. CP outside. Flat entrance, and then three rooms have flat access. +5 steps to one wing, then +15+5 to the top gallery. +6+5+3 to the big engines. The *Babcock café* is up a steep ramp, D72cm (bypassing another D55cm) and then –2. A few exhibits are outside on the gravel.

[P] [M] [■] N20 [♿] 30%

Public Record Office at Kew, Ruskin Avenue, Kew, Richmond, Surrey *Tel:* 0181 876-3444. The entrance is between Ruskin Avenue and West Park Avenue. Four OB spaces in the CP.

Only half of the new building was open during our survey, but we were told that the building would be step free, with lift access to all floors. The part of the building that was open was step free to the foyer and café. You need a readers ticket to view any records. This can be obtained at the foyer office, but you will have to give a reason as to why you want to see something. **Wheelchair cubicles** inside the gents and ladies loos (gents D75 ST85). A lift (D94 W108 L146) goes to all floors. **Adapted cubicles (D75 ST56 NKS)** in the loos on levels one and two. If necessary, books or documents can be brought to where you are sitting. Fixed tables in the reading rooms, but movable chairs and plenty of legroom.

[P] [M] [↑↓] [♿] 90% [♿ wc] [h]

Fulham

Fulham Palace, Bishop's Avenue, Fulham SW6 *Tel:* 0171 736-5821. Site of the home of Bishops of London from the 8thC until 1973. Includes extensive gardens and a museum. It is only open occasionally, but used for events. You need to ring first. On-site CP. **Adapted loo (D85 ST57)** on your right as you enter the palace. It is labelled 'gents' but there is only one cubicle.

Greenwich

Greenwich is situated a few km to the east of London, and has some spectacular classical buildings, as well as a large park and the (Old) Royal Observatory with its famous meridian. You can get there by river, which is a very pleasant way to come, or by using the DLR to Island Gardens and then the foot tunnel under the Thames which has lift access at both ends. Its history is tied up with the Tudors, with things naval and the study of navigation.

Small covered CP near the *Cutty Sark*, on your left as you approach the riverside by road. The *Gipsy Moth* pub has a **wheelchair loo**; there's one off the foyer in the Ibis hotel, and in the public toilets by the junction of Carlton Road and The Avenue.

The riverside and the area around the Maritime Museum and Royal Naval College is all fairly flat. In the park, and towards the old observatory and Blackheath, there's a steep hill.

Tourist Information Centre, 46 Greenwich Church Street SE10 *Tel:* 0181 858-6376. On the *Cutty Sark* side of the junction with Creek Road. Ramped entrance with a small lip. **Adapted loo (D83 ST57, impeded by a movable bin).** The tourist office produces a useful leaflet which includes some access information.

Cutty Sark, King William Walk SE10 (by Greenwich Pier) *Tel:* 0181 858-3445. A famous tea clipper that sailed both the Atlantic and Pacific in the 19thC. The middle deck has flat access via a cobbled area. The shop is on this level –16 steps to the lower deck. The cabins have D55cm and a threshold 23cm high. +5 to the bows. The upper deck is +12 (steep) with a 46cm threshold at the top.

Gipsy Moth IV, King William Walk SE10. This is the boat in which Sir Francis Chichester sailed around the world in 226 days in the 1960s. It is a tiny vessel, and a visit involves steep steps (+9–4) to the cockpit W66cm. Inside there are more steep steps and some narrow gaps.

A **riverside walk** goes from the two ships past the pier and the Royal Naval College to the Trafalgar Tavern. This is about 400m. The walk is flat or ramped throughout, but there are some cobbles. The *Cutty Sark* (pub), *Yacht Tavern* (in Crane Street) and the *Trafalgar Tavern* all have seating areas on the GF. The *Cutty Sark* and the *Yacht* have **adapted loos**.

 **80%**

Greenwich Park SE10 *Tel:* 0181 858-2608. A large expanse of over 200 acres stretching up the hill from Greenwich and linking with Blackheath. The park was originally the grounds of the royal palace, while Blackheath was common land and was often a meeting point for groups entering London from the east. These included Wat Tyler's group of rebels at the time of the Peasants Revolt. The park was described in outline in the introduction to Greenwich, and it's important to note the steep hill up from the river.

In parts of the park the squirrels are so tame that they will eat out of your hand, but be careful, some may bite! There is a bandstand, with occasional performances, and a superb view of London from the end of Blackheath Avenue near the observatory. There's alternative car access from Blackheath to the viewpoint, where you can park.

National Maritime Museum, Romney Road, Greenwich SE10 *Tel:* 0181 858-4422. An extensive museum whose exhibits illustrate the key role that seafaring has played in British history. It was built in the 19thC as a school for sailors' children. Parking is possible in the museum grounds with prior permission (*Tel:* 0181 312-6608). The museum is large, and the layout complicated. *Unfortunately some of the biggest and most popular special exhibitions have been held recently in parts of the museum with stepped access.* **All the exhibition areas in current use can be reached step free using internal lifts.**

Large parts of the museum are currently closed, and there is an extensive development programme. This involves opening a new entrance and installing a lift to link the previously 'inaccessible' floors. The museum will probably reopen fully during 1998. The new main entrance will be through the middle spur, and should lead to a lift which will link all four levels in the spine (see diagram).

There are three entrances to the grounds, from Romney Road, Park Row, and from Greenwich Park itself. We suggest approaching from the park side, as it is then step free to the (temporary) entrance, and from the exit. Go up King William Walk, left into the park, then into the museum grounds. A bit further on and you reach the temporary entrance near the café, with an open lift 20m away to bypass the steps. The layout of the museum is not easy to describe, as, when it is all open, at least four different levels are involved, in what are effectively different buildings. We have therefore made a diagram, with both a plan and elevation.

We call the **side nearest the park the** *SPINE, with an EXTENSION* where the main public lift is, and the café. **The three legs coming off the spine, rather like a letter E, we call** *SPURS*.

In the extension, by the GF café, the three levels are linked by lift (D125 W135 L150). **Wheelchair loo (D90 ST175)** in the basement. The whole of

National Maritime Museum

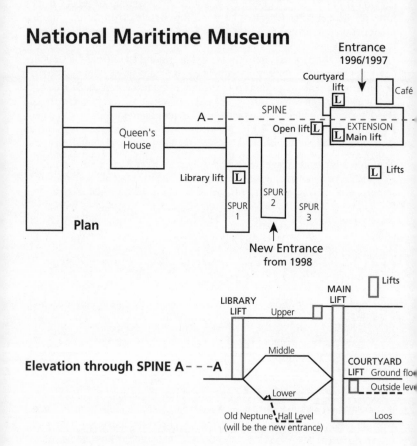

the top floor can be accessed step-free, as there is an open lift bypassing 10 steps. At the far end of the top floor there is a staff operated, private lift (D75 W95 L130), which can take you down to the exit near the Queen's House. There is also a **wheelchair loo (D75 ST90)** near this exit, at ground level.

[P] [D] [A] [↑↓] [♿] 90% [♿ WC] [♿ ✗]

Adjacent to the Maritime Museum and further along the collonade is the **Queen's House.** This was designed by Inigo Jones for Queen Anne of Denmark, and the other buildings towards the river were carefully sited so that the Queen had an uninterrupted view of the river. It has recently been restored and furnished as it would have been in the late 17thC. Along the collonade there are –4, and then +3 into the GF of the house. Unfortunately most of the rooms are on the first floor with +35 spiralled steps. There is an alternative straight staircase, also with +35, normally used as the exit, which would provide an easier route for a determined chair user with some strong friends. If you ask at the Museum, ramps can be put down for the steps along the collonade, and a Gimpson Stairclimber should now be available to carry chair users up to the upper floor of the House. Although slightly alarming to use, it's worth an effort, as the upstairs rooms are exquisite.

Royal Naval College, King William Walk SE10 *Tel:* 0181 858-2154. These impressive buildings were designed by Sir Christopher Wren, and replaced the old Tudor palace. The future of the college is uncertain, at the time of writing, as the government are looking for alternative ways to utilise the buildings. The only parts open to the public were the hall and the chapel. It is about 100m from the road, and parking is difficult both because the roads are busy and for security reasons. The normal route to the hall involves +15 steps, then +3+15 and there's a further +6 to a raised section. If you ask at the entrance lodge, someone will escort you across the face of the building, round the side and down the back. By this route you can have flat (if somewhat bumpy) access and avoid the first +15, but it's about 100m further. The entrance to the chapel is opposite that of the hall, and involves –1+1+3+14.

The Old Royal Observatory and Flamsteed House, Greenwich Park SE10 *Tel:* 0181 858-4422. Famous for the meridian (0° longitude line) which passes through it. Just over 100 years ago, Greenwich Mean Time became the basis of time measurement for most of the world.

The site has been recently refurbished, but is step free only in limited parts. Flat entrance, followed by –1 step into the courtyard (where the meridian is). Part of the courtyard is cobbled. Then step free into the garden where there's a **wheelchair loo (D72 ST80)** on the right down a dead end passage between buildings. There's then +1 and –3 to rooms on the GF containing exhibits. It is possible to bypass the +1–3 into the Meridian building by getting some doors off the courtyard opened. –1 to shop and –1 at its exit.

The normal line of route, operated as a one-way system, is to go from the courtyard through Flamsteed House. This involves +4, D74cm and then +17 to the first floor where there's a D60cm. Stairs –3–7–7. The route continues via the basement –20+16, to the gardens. Access into the Meridian building is described above. Inside there are +20 to the first floor gallery and +17 spiralled and W66cm to the dome, where there's an early telescope. The exit is via the shop as outlined above.

[P] [H] [△] [!] [&] 20% [& WC]

Thames Barrier Visitors Centre, 1 Unity Way, Woolwich SE18 *Tel:* 0181 854-1373. The barrier is a key part of the flood defence system protecting London. It is 500m wide and consists of ten huge movable steel gates. The viewing point and Visitors Centre is situated off the Woolwich Road past Charlton Station, and is well signed. CP within 50m of the exhibition and shop at the far (east) end of the site. From here there's a well-signed lift (D90 W100 L120) to the top of the embankment. This bypasses +9+9. Small café with flat access on the top. You can get down nearer the river edge, via –11–11 or, further back, –27. Notices helpfully warn chair users of the dangers of flooding, but this doesn't happen too often, or too suddenly, so you'd probably get a bit of warning! **Adapted loo (D70 ST77, but inward opening door)** near the bottom of the lift. A round trip to the centre and embankment would involve about 400m from the CP.

You can take a boat to either Greenwich (*Tel:* 0181 305-0300) or Westminster (*Tel:* 0171 930-3373). The pier has ramped access from the upper embankment level, and the boat we saw going off had movable chairs on the deck which was accessible without steps. The boats do vary, however.

Hackney

Sutton House, 2 Homerton High Street, Hackney E9 *Tel:* 0181 986-2264. A Tudor house, surviving in something like its original form, in spite of having been among other things a girls school in the 17thC, and a squat in the 1980s. Limited opening times. Parking in Sutton Place or Isabella Road, off the High Street. It is built around a courtyard. Small lip at the main door. On the GF there is a small concert hall, several rooms, a shop, café and a **wheelchair loo (D93 ST84)**. There are four floors, but no lift. The chapel is in the basement, down about 20 steps. First floor +6+13, second floor +16. The main part of the house is the GF.

Nearby is **Victoria Park,** which was the first public park in London created for ordinary people and not for royalty. It has become known as the People's Park.

[P] [M] [◢] N35 [♿] 40%

Hampstead and Highgate

Hampstead Heath *Tel:* Superintendants office 0181 348-9908, or write to Aztec House, 397 Archway Road N6 4EY. A huge area covering nearly 800 acres, just 7 km from the centre of London. It includes the Kenwood estate. It is quite hilly in parts, and the approach through Hampstead village is up a steep hill. The Corporation of London, Guildhall EC2, who are responsible for the heath, publish an excellent diary/guide which lists various events including performances in the bandstands and at Kenwood, children's activities and fairs. In the middle of the guide is a map showing the principal facilities.

The Heath is best approached from its lower reaches near Parliament Hill. There is a CP in East Heath Road at the South End Green end, from where it is possible to enjoy a pleasant wander across the Heath without encountering severe slopes. Another recommended access point is at the end of Parliament Hill which is a Mecca for kite-flying enthusiasts. If you can climb up, you can get an excellent view over London; or, if you feel less athletic, you can take the path to the left and enjoy a less exacting amble towards Highgate Ponds.

Six wheelchair loos are shown on the Corporation of London listing/map mentioned above, and these are:

- in the heath 'extension' to the north. In the red tile complex next to the sports pitches, some 400m from Wildwood Road and 600m from Hampstead Way **(D80 ST130).** When surveyed, the paths were rough and muddy, due to construction work;
- 100m from the entrance on North End Road (on the west side of the heath) **(D85 ST90);**
- on what is called East Heath, almost due south from Spaniards Inn.

Gravelly paths, and in a hilly area. The loo is in a brick hut complex hidden amongst some trees;

- about 200m from the entrance from Nassington Road, to the south of the heath. It is between the athletics track and the playground. About 800m from Gospel Oak station. **(D100 ST150+)**;
- next to Highgate Road on the east side (locked when we visited);
- Highgate Ponds by Millfield Lane. Steepish ramp **(D85 ST115)**.

Highgate Cemetery, Swain's Lane N6 *Tel:* 0181 340-1834. Full of graves and tombs that reflect high Victorian taste, and mainly known for being the burial place of Karl Marx. It is divided into two sections, west (with 16 acres, and can only be visited by pre-arranged groups), and east (with 37 acres). There is a flat entrance to the east side, and the paths are rough and bumpy. Long distances of over 500m are involved, depending on what you want to see. The west section is on a steepish hill, and there are few paths. Most chair users would need a pusher in the western part, but there's plenty of interest. It's quite often used as a location for horror movies!

Jack Straws Castle, North End Way NW3 *Tel:* 0171 435-8885. By the roundabout at the junction with Spaniards Road. The pub is named after one of Wat Tyler's lieutenants in the Peasants Revolt of 1381. On-site CP, but a slope up to the pub (or 10 steps). Entrances +1 on the left, or +3. The GF is step free, but there are +19 to a first floor function room and a further +18 to another bar and restaurant.

P ⚲ ◢ EI ♿ **40%**

Kenwood House (The Iveagh Bequest), Hampstead Lane NW3 *Tel:* 0181 348-1286. On the northernmost edge of the Heath, it is a handsome period house with a fine picture collection. Open-air concerts are held in the grounds, and concerts and poetry readings are held in the Orangery on the GF. Access for disabled visitors is from the East Lodge on Hampstead Lane via a gate (normally closed) with an intercom. It is then about 200m to a small CP by the house with two OB spaces. The normal route via the West Lodge involves a 400m walk from the road. Ramped access to the GF if you go about 60m round to the front from the OB spaces. This bypasses +15 steps. The GF is flat, and includes various displays of paintings and antiques, as well as a shop. The first floor is +3+18+6. The cafeteria and **adapted loo (D85 ST74 but inward opening door)** are both near the OB spaces.

The audience area for concerts is about 450m from the house reached by gently sloping gravel paths. The orchestra perform under a shelter on the other side of the small lake.

Spaniards Inn, Spaniards Road NW3 *Tel:* 0181 455-3276. Where the road joins Hampstead Lane. Famous pub that Dick Turpin is said to have frequented, and also numbers famous poets amongst its previous patrons. On-site CP, and then flat to right hand entrance. 75% is step free from this entrance. +13 steps to the Turpin bar. Garden –3 from the pub although there's a ramp from the CP.

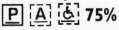 75%

Places of Worship

London has an enormous number of historic and important places of worship, of which we have only surveyed a selection. Most were built with architectural barriers of one kind or another and our experience has been that ecclesiastical authorities have been generally slow in providing ramps or stairlifts to bypass these. However, many famous churches now have step free routes to get in, and these bypass the obstacles which were built many years ago as an integral part of the Gothic architecture.

Westminster Abbey, Westminster Cathedral, St Paul's Cathedral, St James's Piccadilly and St Bartholomew-the-Great provide sharp contrasts in style and beauty. If churches are your special interest, get a copy of *A Guide to London's Churches* by Mervyn Blatch, published by Constable. Note that some of the smaller churches are locked during the day, especially those in the city. If you want to see a particular church, it might be worth phoning in advance.

Reflecting the fact that both Londoners and visitors to the city have a wide variety of belief and practice, we have included descriptions of some of the more prominent mosques, synagogues and temples. Of particular interest, and with good access, are the Brahma Kumaris World Spiritual University, the London Central Mosque, the Peace Pagoda in Battersea Park and the Swaminarayan Hindu Mission. Most synagogues are kept locked except at the times of meetings or services. It is therefore essential to ring first.

Abbeys & Cathedrals

St George's RC Cathedral, Lambeth Road, SE1 (Cathedral House *Tel:* 0171 928-5256). The cathedral, opposite the Imperial War Museum, was rebuilt after its destruction in World War II. A ramp at the entrance bypasses +2 steps. Flat inside with plenty of space for chair users at the sides and front. Induction loop.

[P] [F] [A] [&] 90% [(?)]

St Paul's Cathedral, Ludgate Hill EC4 *Tel:* 0171 236-4128. Admission charge. Christopher Wren's masterpiece still dominates London's skyline. The dome is thought to be the second largest in the world and contains the famous Whispering Gallery. UGCP in Ave Maria Lane, and Orange Badge holders can use the coach space on Ludgate Hill. The floor area is approximately 80m by 200m.

The main entrance has +10+4 steps, with both revolving and swing doors at the top. A flat entrance is 60m away, to the right. Go down the side of the cathedral, and it is tucked away by the corner where the South Transept starts, before you reach the South Porch. The entrance is locked, but ringing the bell will bring assistance. A platform stairlift (W65 L85) or service lift (D80

W105 L135) bypasses +22 (spiral). These give access to the main floor which has flat access throughout, except for the American Memorial Chapel which is +4.

The crypt is also reached by the service lift (bypassing –38 from the main floor). It contains Nelson's tomb, a large chapel, the cathedral Treasure, and a shop. There are **wheelchair cubicles (D80 ST75)** just inside the door of both ladies and gents loos. The –3 steps down to Nelson's tomb have been ramped. To get through to the chapel beyond, ask one of the staff to open the barrier just past the Treasure exhibition.

There are hundreds of steps from the first floor to the other galleries: +259 to the Whispering Gallery, +116 to the Stone Gallery, and +155 to the Golden Gallery. All are narrow. The service lift goes to within about 30 steps of the Whispering Gallery, but we were told that it is strictly for 'private' use.

Just outside the cathedral past the coach park on the south side, and near the junction with New Change there is a 'Tardis' **wheelchair loo (NKS)**, available 24 hours a day. Note that City Thameslink station is nearby, and also the *Old King Lud* pub.

[P] /D\ [A] [■] E24 [↑↓] [♿] 80% [♿ WC]

Southwark Cathedral, Borough High Street SE1 *Tel:* 0171 407-3708 *Fax:* 0171 357-7389. Though much restored, the building retains its traditional Gothic style. Shakespeare's brother Edmond is buried here. It is situated beneath and to the west of London Bridge. OB holders can park on Winchester Walk or Cathedral Street. The entrance is reached either by –20 steps from Borough High Street; a ramped, cobbled, approach from Montague Close; or through Green Dragon Court with a 50m zigzagged route from Bedale Street. Entrance +1 –1 or +3 –7 from the refectory in Montague Close. Inside there are various steps and ramps. Flat or ramped access is possible to the North and South Aisles and Transepts, but the choir and the other 50% of the Cathedral have +3. The shop has +3 in places, and the refectory (a Pizza Express franchise) is +7. Induction loop.

[P] /▲\ [■] E2 [♿] 50% [⁽?⁾]

Westminster Abbey, Broad Sanctuary SW1 *Tel:* 0171 222-5152. Admission charge to parts of the Abbey. The church, used for many national occasions and royal events, contains the tomb of the Unknown Warrior and those of many famous people. Some parking is available by prior arrangement, in the Dean's Yard, 150m away. There are +1+2 steps at the main entrance, which can be bypassed by the signed, ramped entrance via the Cloisters. Use the bell to summon help. This entrance is usually an exit. Once inside, the majority of the ground level is flat. Exceptions are: the chapel of Our Lady of the Pew, leading to St John the Baptist chapel (+1+2); the chapel of St Nicholas (+1+2); and the chapel of St Edmond (+2). The upper chapels have +12+1+2. These include the Lady chapel, and the Confessor's chapel, which contains the

Coronation Chair and Stone, and is reached through a narrow door (W52cm). Induction loop.

The Cloisters give access to the Chapter House (+10), the Abbey Treasures exhibition (−3 bypassed by portable ramp), and to the Abbey Gardens, which have flat access, but restricted opening times. The Abbey bookshop has flat access on the right of the main entrance. **Wheelchair loo (D80 ST80 NKS)** across the road, in front of the Queen Elizabeth conference centre.

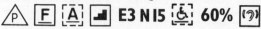

Westminster RC Cathedral, Ashley Place SW1 *Tel:* 0171 798-9055. One of London's rare Byzantine buildings, its red-brick tower stands in sharp contrast to the nearby Abbey. Entrance +3+2 steps, bypassed by a long ramp 30m to the right of the building. Flat inside to all main areas. Numerous side chapels are +1 or +2. The book and souvenir shop are −3. Induction loop.

The tower lift (D80 W120 L140) goes to the top, but there is +1−1 to the balconies. The views are interesting, but not brilliant, and access is limited due to obstacles at the top.

Churches

All-Hallows-by-the-Tower see chapter on *Places of interest.*

All Souls, Langham Place W1 *Tel:* 0171 580-3522. Opposite Broadcasting House at the top end of Regent Street, the church is often used as a recording studio. The +7 steps at the entrance can be bypassed by a ramp on the left. Inside, a lift (D74 W135 L105) bypasses +3 into the church, and also −18 to the lower floor which contains a meeting hall, the reference library and an **adapted loo (D70 ST68)**. Induction loop in the church.

Brompton Oratory, Brompton Road SW7 *Tel:* 0171 589-4811. A quiet and attractive church with a stunning interior, located almost next to the Victoria and Albert Museum. Entrance +6+1 steps, with a ramp on the left to an alternative door. Ask at the house or ring the bell next to the ramp for assistance.

Central Hall, Storey's Gate SW1 *Tel:* 0171 222-8010. The 'Cathedral' of Methodism, used on Sundays for worship and at other times for meetings and exhibitions. Entrance +3+13 steps, bypassed through a side door about 100m away, on the corner of Tothill Street and Matthew Parker Street. This has +1, but there is a portable ramp just inside. Ring the bell for assistance, but due to the size of the building, you may have to wait awhile. Built in 1912 Central Hall has numerous split levels and large staircases. Two new lifts (D80 W96 L102 and D200 W300 L350) have greatly improved access. Roughly 95% of the building is step free, although quite long distances may be involved. The Lecture Hall and Library have +5, bypassed by a platform stairlift. The Great Hall on the third floor has four chair spaces, and an induction loop. Café in the basement. **Wheelchair loo (D80 ST150)** on the third floor. A new **wheelchair loo** is being constructed on the third floor, and there are firm plans to build another in the basement, in mid 1996.

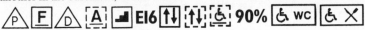

Church of the Holy Sepulchre (St Sepulchre without Newgate), Holborn Viaduct EC1 *Tel:* 0171 248-1660. At the junction of Holburn Viaduct and Snow Hill. Henry Wood, the founder of the 'Proms', is buried here. Entrance +1+2 steps, then swing doors. Flat inside.

City Temple, Holborn Viaduct EC1 *Tel:* 0171 583-5532. The City's main nonconformist church. Entrance +3 steps, bypassed through a (locked) side door. The GF contains the chapel, church and the hall. Six other floors contain conference halls and meeting rooms. **Adapted loos (D63cm)** on first floor, reached by lift (D85 W85 L180). Infrared hearing system in the church.

Farm Street Church, Farm Street W1 *Tel:* 0171 493-7811. Also called the **Church of the Immaculate Conception**. By the junction with Carlos Place. Entrance +5 steps, but there is a step free alternative from Mount Street via the church gardens. Bookshop –7.

![P A E5 80%]

St Bartholomew-the-Great, West Smithfield EC1 *Tel:* 0171 606-5171. Apart from the Tower Chapel, this is London's oldest church. There are twelve OB spaces outside St Bartholomew's Hospital. The main entrance is 50m along a passage just off the West Smithfield roundabout. Flat, then –1 step into the church. Level throughout with uneven surface, except for the Lady Chapel (+1), then +5 to the choir. **Wheelchair loo (NKS)** on the West Smithfield roundabout.

St Bride's, Fleet Street EC4 *Tel:* 0171 353-1301. A Wren church with strong journalistic links, about 500m from St Paul's Cathedral. Fleet Street entrance +2+1 steps, but there is level access from Salisbury Court. Flat inside. The crypt (–21) contains remnants of earlier churches on the site, and a section of Roman pavement.

 E3 80%

St Clement Danes, Strand WC2 *Tel:* 0171 242-8282. Another Wren church, best known for its oranges and lemons. Blitzed in World War 2, it has now become the RAF church. It stands on an island in the middle of the Strand. Entrance +1 step, then level. The balcony is +25, and crypt –22.

 E1 70%

St Giles, Cripplegate, St Giles Terrace EC2 *Tel:* 0171 606-3630. Milton's burial place. In the middle of the Barbican development. Entrance +3 steps.

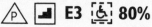 E3 80%

St James's, Piccadilly W1 *Tel:* 0171 734-4511. Poet William Blake was baptized here, and it was supposedly Wren's favourite church. Ramped entrance from Piccadilly through the foyer into the church. The Wren café, on the right of the church, has +1 step from Piccadilly.

 80%

St Lawrence Jewry, Gresham Street EC2 *Tel:* 0171 600-9478. The church of the corporation of London with a fantastic ceiling. Entrance +1 step. Flat throughout except for –2 to small private chapel. Induction loop.

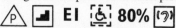 E1 80%

St Magnus the Martyr, Lower Thames Street EC3 *Tel:* 0171 626-4481. There has been a church on this site just next to London Bridge for more than 1,000 years. Wren completed this building in 1676. Flat entrance and level access throughout.

St Margaret's, Parliament Square SW1 *Tel:* 0171 222-6382. The parish Church of the House of Commons, where Sir Winston Churchill was married. Entrance +3+1 steps, with a permanent ramp at the north entrance. Flat inside except for +1 to the enquiry desk.

 E4 90%

St Mary Le-Bow, Cheapside EC2 *Tel:* 0171 248-5139. Houses the Bow

Bells, 'within whose sound a true cockney is born'. Entrance +5 steps. Flat inside. The Court of Arches, which decides ecclesiastical law cases and confirms the election of bishops, is held in the Crypt, which is –17.

 E5 80%

St Mary Le-Strand, Strand WC2 *Tel:* 0171 404-7538. An 18thC building in Baroque style. Entrance +9 steps, then flat inside.

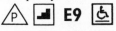 E9

St Martin-in-the-Fields, St Martin's Place WC2 *Tel:* 0171 930-1862. On the corner of Trafalgar Square. Often called the 'Parish Church of London'. The main (west) entrance has +5 steps, bypassed by the ramped North entrance. This gives flat access to the nave. **Wheelchair loo (D95 ST95)** in the north porch is +1. Ask the staff for a key. The crypt is –3–10 from Duncannon Street or –2–27 from the ante-chapel. There are regular concerts (*Tel:* 0171 930-0089).

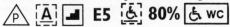 E5 80% wc

St Mary Woolnoth, Lombard Street EC3 *Tel:* 0171 626-9701. Between Lombard Street and King William Street. Sumptuous interior by Hawksmoor. Entrance +8 steps.

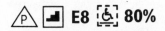 E8 80%

St Marylebone Parish Church, 17 Marylebone Road NW1 *Tel:* 0171 935-7315. Where poets Elizabeth Barrett and Robert Browning were married after they eloped. Entrance +5 steps, bypassed by a ramp on the right, which leads to +1. The inside is level. Lift (D75 W98 L122) to the crypt, where there is a pastoral centre, a small chapel, a café, and a **wheelchair loo (D74 ST80)**. The balcony has +20.

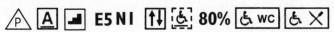 E5 N1 80% wc X

St Olave's, Hart Street EC3 *Tel:* 0171 488-4318. The church where Samuel Pepys is buried. Entrance –1–2 steps. Flat inside, but rather cramped.

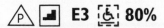 E3 80%

St Paul's Church see write-up on Covent Garden in the chapter on *Places of interest.*

St Peter-Upon-Cornhill, Cornhill EC3 *Tel:* 0171 220-7571. Now used as a Christian study centre, and only open to the public by prior arrangement with the caretaker. Only the back entrance, in St Peter's Alley, is used, which has

+1 step into the courtyard, then +1 into the church.

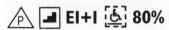 **El+I** 80%

St Stephen Walbrook, 39 Walbrook EC4 *Tel:* 0171 626-8242. Most famous as the place where the Samaritans were formed in 1953. Entrance +1+13 steps.

 **El4** 80%

Temple Church, Inner Temple Lane EC4 *Tel:* 0171 353-1736. One of the few circular churches still in existence. South side entrance +1 step.

 **El** 80%

Wesley's Chapel see chapter on *Places of interest.*

Mosques, Synagogues and Temples

Al Khoei Mosque, Chevening Road NW6 *Tel:* 0181 960-6378. Near the junction with Salisbury Road. CP can be used with advanced warning. Entrance +5 steps, then flat.

Wheelchair users may use the prayer room without removing shoes or transferring from chair. We were told that stick users must use a wheelchair, although presumably disabled walkers can use the prayer room if their shoes are removed.

[P] ◢ **E5** ⟨&⟩

Brahma Kumaris World Spiritual University, Global Co-operation House, 65 Pound Lane, Willesden NW10 *Tel:* 0181 459-1400. The international centre for Brahma Kumaris was opened in 1991. A worldwide organisation with an emphasis on meditation and spiritual development. Courses run daily, weekly, or more long term. UGCP on Pound Lane with twenty-two spaces of which only four are not on a steep incline. The main entrance and GF are flat. A lift (D80 W110 L138) gives step free access to all other floors. The seven floors contain numerous rooms, including a seminar room and auditorium. Roof garden –3+25 –1 steps. **Wheelchair loo (D85 ST90)** on the GF, and **another (D85 ST85)** on the third floor.

[P] **[M]** **[↑↓]** ⟨&⟩ **90%** ⟨& WC⟩

Central Synagogue, 38 Hallam Street W1 *Tel:* 0171 580-1355. Entrance +7 steps. The GF is level. Chair spaces at the rear of the main worship area. Women normally use the upper gallery (about +30), but if this causes a problem, they can remain at ground level. Hall for meetings –24. Induction loop.

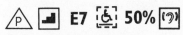

London Buddhist Vihara, The Avenue, Chiswick W4 *Tel:* 0181 995-9493. 50m from the junction with Bedford Road. Entrance +3 steps, then flat to the main hall, shrine, sermon hall and shop. Library +1. Staff said that all visitors, including chair users, must remove their shoes before entering the shrine room.

[P] 🔲 E3 [⚙] 80%

London Central Mosque (Islamic Cultural Centre), 146 Park Road NW8 *Tel:* 0171 724-3363. A beautiful building with a gold dome, on the south-west side of Regent's Park. It was built in 1977, and provides a focus for the Islamic community in London. The entrance is on Park Road by the junction with Hanover Gate. On-site parking controlled by a security barrier. 'Casual' visitors may well not be allowed to use this. The pedestrian entrance is to the right of the security barrier. There are +3 steps to the main square, which leads to the Mosque. If you go straight ahead with the square on the right, you will find a ramp giving step free access.

Once inside, there is a bookshop to the right, and an enquiry desk to the left. Also a prominent display, with clocks showing the five times of prayer – at dawn, noon, mid-afternoon, sunset and night.

10m in front of the main entrance are the Mosque doors. Inside these there is an uncarpeted (non-sacred) area where shoes must be removed before going on the carpet to pray. However, everything is visible from this area, including the fine carpet, chandelier and dome. Although women pray in a separate gallery (+20), women visitors are allowed to look inside from this non-sacred area, provided they are suitably dressed. Women are asked to cover their heads.

For praying, the main GF part of the mosque is for men only. Gents loo and wudhu in the basement are –20 or so. Wudhu is ritual washing before praying, principally of the feet. For disabled men we were told that there is a toilet available on the GF for washing, or that there is a lift (D75 W75 L100). Women pray in an upper gallery (+20). Unadapted ladies loo and wudhu on the GF. The lift bypasses the +10+11 to the first floor library. Provided visitors are sensitive to, and have an interest in, Islamic culture, staff at the mosque are very welcoming. It can make an interesting visit.

[P] [A] [↕] [⚙] 70%

London Peace Pagoda see write-up on Battersea Park in the chapter on *Open air activities.*

London Jamme Masjid, Brick Lane E1 *Tel:* 0171 247-6052. Between the junctions with Princelet Street and Fournier Street. Entrance +5 steps, then flat to the main prayer hall. Worshippers must first visit washing rooms for wudhu (see write-up on the London Central Mosque). These are –3 or –5.

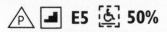 **E5** **50%**

New London Synagogue, 33 Abbey Road NW8 *Tel:* 0171 328-1026. Four parking spaces in the driveway (phone in advance). Entrance +2 steps, then +5–5 to the prayer hall. Alternative entrance +1 at the side of the synagogue. **Wheelchair loo (D85 ST75).**

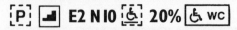 **E2 N10** **20%**

Swaminarayan Hindu Mission, 54 Meadow Garth, off Brentford Road, Neasden NW10 *Tel:* 0181 965-2651. A new and beautiful temple complex. Visitors from all religions are welcomed. At the time of our visit the building was still being completed, but step free access was being provided throughout. We were told that OB spaces were to be provided near the main entrance. There are two main buildings, linked by a 20m ramp. Note that **all** visitors should remove their shoes before entering either building.

The prayer hall contains a reception point, shop, function rooms and areas for worship, all on one level. There are seats and wheelchair spaces on both sides of the worship area. **Wheelchair cubicle (D80 ST85) in both the ladies and gents loos.** The temple is on two floors, with a lift (D85 W105 L160). On the first floor there is an exhibition called 'Understanding Hinduism'. Assistance for disabled visitors should always be available.

West London Synagogue for British Jews, 34 Upper Berkeley Street W1 *Tel:* 0171 723-4404. Flat access through main gate for services. At other times the only entrance is via 33 Seymour Place with +1 step. Step free inside using a lift (D75 W120 L122). All worship is on the GF. The sanctuary has a split level of –4 bypassed by a portable ramp if advance warning is given. **Wheelchair loo (D75 ST85)** on the GF. Induction loop.

Museums & galleries

London has one of the greatest collections of museums and galleries in the world. The variety of subject, size, price and interest, is vast. Much effort and thought has been put into providing improved access for disabled visitors. Staff are usually helpful, although not always aware of all the facilities provided. Several museums provide facilities for partially sighted visitors to touch and feel some exhibits.

Patience is sometimes required to get special step free access routes opened up. Art and historical collections are valuable, and security is important, so it is not always possible to leave particular doors open. It may also take a little time to find the right person to operate stair lifts where they are used to bypass steps.

Some major museums and galleries are large, making it difficult to walk or wheel all the way round in a single visit. You would do well to look at the plan when you arrive, and select some of the things of greatest interest.

Note that a large number of museums now have an entrance charge. They all used to be free. The Natural History Museum and the Science Museum waive their charge late in the afternoon, and it can be quite interesting to visit museums for a short time, and focus on selected display areas. Alternatively, make a day of it, and don't feel you need to rush around. Along with the introduction of a charge, the presentation of many exhibits has been improved, and facilities, such as catering and the provision of loos, have been upgraded. In the text we have indicated where there was a charge in 1995. At most museums and galleries there is a reduced charge for chair users, and/or their companion however the situation for people with other disabilities is less clear. One of the difficulties arising from the introduction of charges is that the museums are one of the few places with **adapted loos** in many areas, and charging for entry makes them MUCH less 'accessible', not physically, but on practical grounds.

If you require more detailed information, there are many guidebooks around. Nicholson's *London Museums and Galleries Guide* and the *Museums and Galleries of London* in the Blue Guide series, are two which stand out. They are both well presented and informative.

Inner London

Apsley House see the Wellington Museum.

Bank of England Museum, Threadneedle Street EC2 *Tel:* 0171 601-5545. Historical and financial displays, including some real gold bars! The nearby Bank station has step free access from the DLR. Entrance +4+3 steps, then ±3 to exhibits. All can be bypassed by portable ramps, available on request. Large print and braille guides are available. **Wheelchair loo (D90 ST85)** at the rear of the museum. The cinema, used by groups, has chair spaces and an induction loop.

⚠️(P) 🔦(A) ▪️ **E7 N3** ♿ **80%** ♿ wc 💬

Bankside Gallery, 48 Hopton Street, Blackfriars SE1 *Tel:* 0171 928-7521. Admission charge. Situated on the South Bank to the east of Blackfriars Bridge this small gallery has one floor. Ramps bypass +2 steps at the entrance, and there is flat or ramped access throughout. The gallery has been awarded a substantial sum of money from the National Lottery, and in the enlarged gallery in the old power station, access will be considered.

⚠️(P) (A) ▪️ **E2** ♿ **90%**

Barbican Art Gallery see section on *Arts centres.*

Bramah Tea and Coffee Museum, The Clove Building, Maguire Street, Butlers Wharf SE1 *Tel:* 0171 378-0222. Admission charge. Just east of Tower Bridge, this small museum displays the social and commercial history of two of the world's most important commodities, and smells gorgeous. CP about 100m away. The museum is on the first floor of an office block, which causes some access problems at weekends. All visitors use the intercom button at the main entrance, then a lift (D80 W128 L137) bypasses +25 steps to the first floor. The lift is not programmed to stop at the first floor: during the week the security guard will re-programme it as necessary. At the weekend, museum staff should assist, but one of our survey teams found this unreliable. Once inside there is flat access everywhere and a central coffee shop. **Wheelchair loo (D85 ST 90)** on the GF, kept locked. The security guard has the key during the week; at the weekend, museum staff will telephone security, whose office is five minutes away in Shad Thames !

(P) (A) ▪️ **E25** ⬍ ♿ ♿ wc

Britain At War Theme Museum see chapter on *Places of interest.*

British Library see write-up on *New British Library.*

British Museum, Great Russell Street WC1 *Tel:* 0171 636-1555. DisEnq (RecM) 0171 637-7384. One of the largest museums in the world, approximately 200m by 200m, and on three main floors. It houses the national collection of archaelogical remains and will soon house all the national collection of ethnography – the study of the races and cultures of mankind. 95% of the museum has step free access via one of the four lifts.

   Limited parking in museum forecourt in Great Russell Street can be arranged in advance (*Tel:* 0171 323-8387). Alternative parking 100m away in well signposted UGCP in Bloomsbury Square.

Main museum entrance has +12 steps, bypassed by a well hidden open lift (W115 L200) to the left. Alternative entrance in Montague Place, with flat access, but *we found it easier to use the main entrance as the bulk of the museum is much more easily reached.* **Plans of the museum, and an excellent booklet for disabled visitors, are available at the information desk.**

The **main GF** has level access to numerous exhibition galleries, and to the gift shop, the book shop and the café. The restaurant, which is rather nicer, is +6+6, bypassed by the poorly signposted staff canteen lift (D90 L130 W136), opposite the entrance to the café. Ask the nearest member of staff if you want to use this. **Wheelchair loos off room 25 (D85 ST75)**, and another off room 28 **(D75 ST70)**, although this one often seems to be closed. Ask a member of staff for assistance. Both are unisex, and poorly signposted but due for a refit in 1996.

The galleries on the **GF** which do not have flat or ramped access are:
   gallery 3A (–8–8–5 from gallery 3, although the –5 can be bypassed by an open lift. There is a lengthy alternative involving going outside the museum to get step free access. Ask for assistance);
   gallery 6 (+1+16 from gallery 7);
   gallery 8 (25% of exhibits +3);
   gallery 11 (+2+9+9 from gallery 10, bypassed by a service lift in gallery 12);
   gallery 14 (+8 from either gallery 12 or 15; there is an open lift here which is not operational, and, staff told us, has never been operational); and gallery 33B (+18 from gallery 32), from where 33 and 33A are then a further –3, although they have flat access from the Montague Place entrance.
The **basement** can be reached with staff assistance by the service lift in gallery 12, bypassing a minimum of –24. Galleries have step free access, except for +3 between galleries 82 and 87, which can be bypassed with staff assistance, via the lecture theatre.

The **first floor** can be reached by the south lift (D90 L112 W140) near the information desk, or by the service lift in gallery 12 or the staff canteen lift (D90 L130 W136) near gallery 2. Lifts bypass a minimum of +25. Step free access everywhere, except to:
   gallery 36 (–3 from level M of south lift);
   gallery 43 (+10+8 to 50% of display);
   gallery 69A (upper section) +14, and
   galleries 90-94 which are +3–3, bypassed through offices at end of gallery 66, although on one of our visits no staff were available to unlock the doors.

This +3–3 is the link from the main section of the museum to the **Montague Place** entrance. From this entrance there is access via north lift (D84 W140

L100) to 5 small levels of galleries, and then –3 to the first floor of the bulk of
the museum. On the ground level an open lift bypasses –4 to gallery 34, and
on level 5 the +6 to gallery 94 can be bypassed by an open lift.

The museum is extremely large with very limited seating throughout.
Wheelchairs are available. When we visited, the willingness of the staff to
help was highly variable, and we were told that the lifts are sometimes out of
order, so it is important to be aware of all four of them, even if some of the staff
are not. The museum hopes to redevelop considerably once the British Library
has moved out and this should make access considerably easier.

[P] (D) [A] [◼] EI2 [↑↓] [♿] 80% [& WC]

BT Museum, 145 Queen Victoria Street EC4 *Tel:* 0171 248-7444. The museum
of British Telecom detailing 150 years of telecommunications. A 70m ramp,
signposted from Queen Victoria Street, bypasses +8+15 steps at the entrance. This
leads to the upper of two display floors. The lower level is –7–13, bypassed with
staff assistance by using the ramp outside, with a portable ramp for a further +1.

(P) (H) [A] [&]

Cabinet War Rooms, Clive Steps, King Charles Street SW1 *Tel:* 0171 930-
6961. Admission charge. This is where Winston Churchill held many vital
Cabinet meetings during World War II. The rooms are laid out as they were
when the war ended. Flat access from the St James's Park side, or –15 steps
from King Charles Street. Step free to the ticket office, then a lift (D84 W110
L150) bypasses the –16 down to the rooms. Step free throughout at the lower
level. The 150m route ends in a small shop. **Wheelchair loo (D90 ST70 NKS)**,
opposite the lift. A free audio guide is available.

(P) [M] [↑↓] [&] [& WC] [👁]

Commonwealth Institute, Kensington High Street W8 *Tel:* 0171 603-4535.
Admission charge. A tent-like building housing displays from different
Commonwealth countries. It was built with serious access barriers. The main
entrance has +14 steps, but the West Entrance has flat access, as well as 2 OB
spaces directly outside. From this entrance ask staff to use the service lift (D100
W100 L200+) to reach each of the three floors of galleries. Once inside, 60%
of the Lower Gallery is flat. There are –5 to the New Zealand section, and a
further –4 to Bangladesh, Papua New Guinea, and Pacific Way. The Middle
Gallery has flat access everywhere, except for +8 to the water display next to
Swaziland. In the Upper Gallery there is +1+1 or +1–1 to Malta, and +1 to a
small section of both Malaysia and the Caribbean Eye. The shop is –16 from
the Middle Gallery. The restaurant has +3 directly next to the West Entrance,
although there is a ramp from the lawn. **Adapted loo (D90 ST60)** just off the
Middle Gallery. There are plans for a major overhaul of the whole building,
with access improvements.

The entrance to the **Conference and Event Centre** just past the West Entrance has +3. There is a ramped entrance 10m to the left, which leads to the foyer and a **wheelchair loo (D90 ST95).**

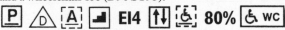 EI4 80%

Courtauld Institute Galleries, Somerset House, Strand WC2 *Tel:* 0171 873-2526. Admission charge. Picture galleries with permanent display of works by van Gogh, Manet and Rubens amongst others. Parking can be reserved in advance (*Tel:* 0171 873-2531). Entrance +2 steps, then +5 to lift (D110 W180 L145). Alternative step free route is via the West door. Ask a member of staff. From this a platform stairlift bypasses +5. Then the lift gives access to both floors of galleries which are step free apart from +1 to room eleven. Coffee shop and **wheelchair loo (D85 ST90)** in the basement.

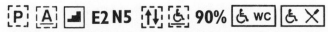 E2 N5 90%

Crafts Council Gallery, 44A Pentonville Road N1 *Tel:* 0171 278-7700. On-site parking if you phone first. Ramped entrance bypasses +6 steps, then lift (D90 W108 L145) access between the two floors. Café on first floor with a ramped entrance. **Wheelchair loo (D70+ ST70+)** on GF. Induction loop in the conference room.

 E6

Design Museum, Shad Thames SE1 *Tel:* 0171 407-6261. Admission charge. Classic design from the past 100 years, and state-of-the-art innovations from around the globe. CP next to museum on corner of Curlew Street and Shad Thames. Entrance +5 steps with a ramped bypass. Displays on the first and second floors, reached via a lift (D80 W125 L165). Ask staff. Coffee shop on the GF, and a **wheelchair cubicle (D85 ST75) in both the ladies and gents loos.** Wheelchairs available.

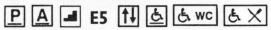 E5

Florence Nightingale Museum, 2 Lambeth Palace Road SE1 *Tel:* 0171 620-0374. Admission charge. Small museum on the site of St Thomas's Hospital, celebrating the life and achievements of the Lady of the Lamp. Six OB spaces opposite. Flat entrance and step free throughout. Small cinema with one chair space. **Wheelchair loo (D82 ST120)** by the gents to the right of reception. It is roughly 100m around the museum.

Freud Museum, 20 Maresfield Gardens, Hampstead NW3 *Tel:* 0171 435-2002. Admission charge. Sigmund Freud moved to this house in 1938, and the museum contains the famous couch on which his patients lay for analysis.

Parking space can be reserved. Entrance +1 step, then level through the GF.
First floor +21.

[P] ▟ EI N2I [👤] 50%

Guards Museum, Wellington Barracks, Birdcage Walk SW1 *Tel:* 0171 930-
4466. Admission charge. Displays of various army costumes and weapons.
Entrance +6 steps, then –41. Both can be bypassed by a lift (D75 W120 L165).
Phone in advance for use. Inside, the museum is level, and is about 100m around.
Wheelchair loo (D90 ST120) in the staff area. The GF shop is +1.

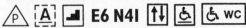 ⚿ [A] ▟ E6 N4I [↑↓] [👤] [👤 wc]

Hayward Gallery see section on *Arts centres* under the South Bank.

ICA (Institute of Contemporary Arts) see chapter on *Arts centres.*

Imperial War Museum, Lambeth Road SE1 *Tel:* 0171 416-5320. Admission
charge. A fascinating collection of historical military equipment, with numerous
changing exhibitions. It is housed in a building that, more than 150 years ago,
was a lunatic asylum. Parking for visitors with disabilities can be arranged (*Tel:*
0171 416-5262). The main entrance is 50m from the road on a tarmac path
through Geraldine Mary Harmsworth Park, and has +9+1+3 steps, bypassed
by a flat disabled persons and schools entrance on the right-hand side. Go to
the right of the big guns, and then down the right side of the building (ignoring
the signs on the wall which seem to point both ways). The door was NOT
labelled when we visited (it says Schools Entrance over the top, and is nearly
150m down the side). Ring bell for assistance. This leads to the lower ground
floor. Diagrams of the building are available, but do not mark the location of
all the lifts.
      There is flat, ramped or lift access to all exhibits on all four floors, with the
exception of two small sections of the lower ground floor. The pair of lifts
(D90 W160 L150) by the main staircase serve the lower ground, ground and
first floors, and a separate lift (D80 W110 L150) must be used to reach the second
floor. This goes from the first floor – turn right from either of the main lifts until
you reach the far wall, and go through the door marked 'disabled lift'.
      The self-service café and the shop are both flat from the GF. Every floor
contains a **wheelchair loo (all D70 ST100+)**, reasonably well marked on the
plan, and signed. There is an **adapted loo (D88 ST48)** in Geraldine Mary
Harmsworth Park where there is also a picnic area.
      The museum has gone to considerable lengths to make the building step
free via the new lifts. When we visited, the 'Blitz experience' exhibition on
the lower ground floor was +6, but there was an unsigned ramped alternative
for chair users. The collection of exhibits there was a bit like a maze, and it
was difficult for anyone to know where they were. The upper floors were
much easier.

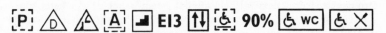

Jewish Museum, Raymond Burton House, 129 Albert Street NW1 *Tel:* 0171 284-1997. Admission charge. Displays of ceremonial art and the history of the British Jewish community. Flat entrance then lift (D80 W102 L140) access between all three floors of exhibits, and a lecture room on the first floor. **Wheelchair loo (D80 ST80)** in the basement.

London Canal Museum, 12 New Wharf Road N1 *Tel:* 0171 713-0836. Admission charge. Illustrated history of London's waterways, with plenty to do for children. Flat throughout the GF. First floor +24 steps. To see the boats in the wharf there are +8–1.

[P] [M] ◢ N24 [↑↓] [♿] 60%

London Dungeon see chapter on *Places of interest.*

London Planetarium, Marylebone Road NW1 *Tel:* 0171 936-6861. Admission charge. Next to Madame Tussaud's, and recently reopened after extensive changes during which a lift was installed. The main feature is a 'cosmic perceptions' show, illustrating how the stars and planets were formed, and how we view them. There are +29 steps to the ticket office, bypassed by a staff controlled lift (D80 W108 L150). Ramped access from ticket office to auditorium, with two chair spaces. Induction loop. 'Planet Zone', one of the exhibition areas, is –21 from ticket office, bypassed by a platform stairlift. To exit the building you need to return to the ticket office. Only three chair users are allowed in the building at any one time.

London Toy and Model Museum, 23 Craven Hill, Paddington W2 *Tel:* 0171 262-7905. Admission charge. Museum full of teddy bears, toys and models, including two model railways, one of which can be used for children's rides. Extensively refurbished in 1995. Ramp bypasses +3 steps at the entrance. Step free inside via lift (D73 W144 L130) to lower floor. Flat access to café and garden which has a split level of –6 bypassed by an open lift. The shop is +6 bypassed by another open lift. **Wheelchair loo (D80 ST75)** near the shop.

London Transport Museum, Covent Garden WC2 *Tel:* 0171 836-8557. Admission charge. Museum detailing the history and effect of the capital's transport system. Recently modernised. Ramped entrance to GF and step free throughout. A lift (D135 W108 L146) links the two other floors. In the shop, staff can open the ramped exit to avoid –3 steps. The **wheelchair loo (D90 ST115)** opposite the entrance has an inward-opening door. Another **wheelchair loo (D86 ST106)** in the café.

 **90%**

Madame Tussaud's, Marylebone Road NW1 *Tel:* 0171 935-6861. Admission charge. Near Baker Street tube. One of London's busiest and most popular tourist sites. The +16 steps at the main entrance lead to a public lift (D114 W185 L113), which travels to the third floor where the exhibition starts. Chair users can take a staff lift (D80 W108 L185) to the third floor, and then follow the usual route, using the same lift to move between the five floors and bypass ±30 or so steps between floors. Most of the exhibits can be reached on the flat, although there are –4 to the 200 Years room, and –4 to the Superstars room, both on the third floor. The excellent Spirit of London ride is +9 from the GF, although this can be bypassed by +4 through an unmarked door on the right just before the +9. The ride has to be boarded while it is moving. Ramped access to the café and **wheelchair loo (D84 ST86)** which is poorly signed. A platform stairlift (W72 L146) bypasses 20+ steps to and from the shop. **The museum is strict about only allowing three chair users to visit at any one time** and it does get extremely busy. It is therefore sensible to telephone in advance to ensure entry.

 **EI6 N 100** **80%**

Madame Tussaud's Rock Circus, London Pavilion, 1 Piccadilly Circus W1 *Tel:* 0171 734-8025/7203. Admission charge. Moving and static wax figures, detailing the development of popular music before and since The Beatles. A ramp 5m to the left of the entrance bypasses +2 steps to the ticket office. Access is by escalator, bypassed by a service lift (D110 W162 L210) linking both exhibition floors. *If you want your photo taken with Freddie Mercury you'll have to ask especially.* Top floor contains a café with limited seating on fixed bar stools, and the Music Revolution theatre which stages a twenty minute show to end your visit. Two chair spaces, while other seating is on benches with no backs. Flat access to the shop through staff areas, and a **wheelchair loo (D80 ST80)** on first floor of exhibits. With staff assistance, there is step free access throughout. Sennheiser sound system throughout.

 **90%**

Museum of Garden History (Tradescant Trust), Lambeth Palace Road SE1 *Tel:* 0171 261-1891. Admission charge. Located just south of Lambeth Bridge, and situated in an old church, this small museum is famous for having Bligh of the Bounty buried in its garden. Entrance +1 step to the shop, then +2/ramped to the museum. Restaurant is a further +2/ramped by pass and seats +2. Flat access to the small garden with a bumpy paved surface.

 **80%**

Museum of London, London Wall EC2 *Tel:* 0171 600-3699 ext240. Admission charge. The museum provides a lively account of London's history from prehistoric times right up to the present day. Interesting and well laid out, with excellent access. The main entrance is on a high level walkway. Access is via the lift (D80 W110 L135) in Aldergate Street, which comes out 50m from the museum entrance. Parking can be arranged if you phone.

Inside there is flat, ramped, or lift access everywhere. Lift (D80 W135 L100), next to the Lord Mayor's Coach, bypasses –10 steps from the upper level to the lower level. The staff lift, next to reception, can be used to reach the intermediate level, housing the education department and the lecture hall (four chair spaces and an induction loop). This floor has one of the **wheelchair loos (D90 ST70)**. Cubicle **(D93 ST71)** inside the ladies near the Coach, and there is a **wheelchair loo (D90 ST70)** in the café just outside the main entrance. The gift shop is flat from the upper level, wheelchairs are available, many exhibits are at low level, and seats are available throughout.

Museum of Mankind, 6 Burlington Gardens W1 *Tel:* 0171 437-2224. *Information desk:* 0171 323-8043. The ethnography department of the British Museum, containing some spectacular exhibits showing how people live and dress. The museum is steadily closing as its stock is transferred to the British Museum. Parking is possible if you ring in advance. Entrance +8 steps, bypassed by a staff route. Ring the bell, and someone will help. The alternative involves a platform stairlift, and two portable ramps.

Inside it is step free to all galleries via a service lift (D110 W138 L85). Flat access on the GF to café, museum shop, and film theatre, which has an induction loop. **Wheelchair cubicle (D74 ST71)** in the ladies, and an **adapted cubicle (D79 ST67)** in the gents. Both on the GF.

Museum of the Moving Image see section on *Arts centres.*

National Army Museum, Royal Hospital Road, Chelsea SW3 *Tel:* 0171 730-0717. Quiet museum with an excellent Story of the Army gallery. Access has improved immensely. Entrance +3 steps with a ramped bypass. The turnstile can be bypassed. Step free access is possible to most of the museum by using two lifts. The first (D122 W200 L135) on the right after the entrance, serves the upper levels of each floor. The other lift (D80 W100 L140), reached by a steep ramp from the GF, serves the rest of the museum. There are +7 at the exit of the Victorian Soldier gallery, which can be avoided by doubling back. The lifts do not serve the small gallery and lecture theatre on the lower level, but a platform stairlift (W70 L85) can be used to bypass the –8. The museum has a shop and café. The **wheelchair loo (D80 ST110)** on the GF is signposted.

[P] [A] [◢] E3 [⇅] [⬇] 90% [♿ WC]

National Gallery, Trafalgar Square WC2 *Tel:* 0171 747-2885. Charge for special exhibitions. Fine collections of various painting schools from the 13th to the early 20thC. Limited parking only available for pre-arranged groups (*Tel:* 0171 747-2424). Main entrance on Trafalgar Square has +35 steps. Flat entrances in Orange Street or through the new Sainsbury Wing, 500m left of the main entrance. The forty-six galleries on the GF of the main building all have flat access. There are three lifts, each serving different sections of the lower floor. The lifts at Orange Street (D80 W133 L114) and near the Central Hall (D79 W107 L140) serve more galleries, and the lift (D80 W107 L140) near the main entrance gives access to the café and an **adapted loo (D100 ST60 NKS).** To gain flat access to this lift it is necessary to avoid the Central Hall, and go via room forty five. There is a **wheelchair cubicle (D80+ ST85+NKS)** in both the ladies and gents loos by the Orange Street entrance.

The **Sainsbury Wing** has five floors, with the middle one at entrance level. The top floor contains the galleries which link to the main building. All floors are accessible via the lift (D118 W170 L183). The restaurant is on the first floor, near a **wheelchair loo (D85 ST85 NKS).** A second **wheelchair loo (D85 ST85 NKS)** is on the lower floor. Signposting is good, as is the detailed floorplan available. Both shops are step free, although the smaller one has a platform stairlift (W82 L125) to bypass +5 to part of it. The Gallery has a theatre with three chair spaces and a cinema with eight spaces. Induction loop in both. It also has a touch sensitive Micro Gallery. CD Rom guides are for hire, giving details of every single artefact. The building is extremely large, with a frontage about 200m long.

[P] [D] [A] [⇅] [♿] [♿ WC] [♿ ✕] [👁] [(?)]

National Portrait Gallery, 2 St Martin's Place WC2 *Tel:* 0171 306-0055. Charge for special exhibitions. Situated to the north of Trafalgar Square the museum has over nine thousand works, including contemporary portaits of famous British people. It has one reservable parking space (contact Head of Security, ext 217). The +2+12 steps at the main entrance can be bypassed by using the ramped entrance in Orange Street. The GF (level one) contains about a sixth of the exhibits and two lifts. The lift (D107 W170 L160) near the main entrance is after the +2+12, but the other lift (D116 W400 L176) is flat from Orange Street. Both serve levels 1,3,5 and the basement. There are stairs to the two other levels, mezzanine two (+11+9) and mezzanine four (+7+8). A somewhat precipitous portable stairclimber can be provided on request. One of our surveyors discovered, however, that this did not fit his wheelchair. **Three wheelchair loos (D75+ ST75+),** in the basement; on level one, and on level five. Facilities for disabled visitors include touch tours, thermoforms, and induction loops in the lecture theatre and education centre. The gallery shop is +1 from the pavement, to the left of the main entrance.

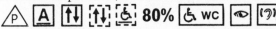

Natural History Museum, Cromwell Road, Kensington SW7 *Tel:* 0171 938-9123. Admission charge. Massive museum full of models and remains, of all types of animals, plants, gems and minerals. Well presented. Most famous for the dinosaur skeletons and the model of a blue whale. The Romanesque frontage is hugely impressive, and the interior is cathedral-like, designed to show off the wonders of creation. The museum is split into the **Life Galleries** covering both existing and extinct animals, and the **Earth Galleries** (the former Geological Museum) which tell the story of the development of the earth.

There are four OB spaces in Exhibition Road with time limits, and parking can sometimes be arranged in the CP at the end of Museum Lane. There is a sloped approach, and then +10 steps at the main entrance in Cromwell Road. Alternatively, use the flat service entrance from Museum Lane off Exhibition Road. It is 200m from the main entrance and the car park attendant will show you through. This leads to the basement where lifts (D110 W180 L140) gives access either to the main entrance, or the *Gallery restaurant.* **Nearly all of the galleries are flat or ramped.** The dinosaur exhibition has its own lift (D79 W89 L130) to a viewing gallery. The balcony above the blue whale has +4+16, although a service lift can be used on request, which we didn't see.

The GF three shops have step free access, as does the *Waterhouse café* in gallery 11, although this has high tables (107cm) and chairs. The self-service Gallery restaurant in gallery 35 has 90% flat access. **Adapted loo (D83 ST65)** at the far right of the entrance hall, and a **wheelchair loo (D85 ST112)** by room 24. Another **(D85 ST190)** is in the basement by the service entrance. The museum is well signposted throughout.

The Earth Galleries are closed until summer 1996. The press office told us that it will have a step free entrance on Exhibition Road, **wheelchair loos** and lift access to all floors. *This should provide a much easier route for all visitors with disabilities.* When the museum is fully refurbished it will be roughly 300m from the main entrance to the most distant exhibits.

New British Library, 96 Euston Road NW1. At the time of writing the planned opening date is late 1997. The press office told us that the building "is fully appropriate for the wheelchair user", and that it will contain a 250 seat auditorium for public events, with step free access and an induction loop. Updated information can be obtained on *Tel:* 0171 412-7111.

Percival David Foundation Of Chinese Art, 53 Gordon Square WC1 *Tel:* 0171 387-3909. Claims to house the finest collection of Chinese ceramics outside of China. Entrance +4 steps, then flat or lift (D69 W122 L86) access to three floors of galleries. **Wheelchair loo (D70 ST200+)** on the third floor.

Photographer's Gallery, 5 and 8 Great Newport Street WC2 *Tel:* 0171 831-1772. Small and interesting gallery with changing displays, housed in two separate buildings. No 5 has a steepish ramp, but is step free to reception, two galleries, the café and **two wheelchair loos, ladies (D80 ST100), gents (D80 ST80).** The print sales room and the library are +19 steps. No 8 is step free throughout, and contains another gallery and the bookshop.

Pollock Toy Museum, 1 Scala Street W1 *Tel:* 0171 636-3452. Admission charge. A small and fascinating museum, with entrance in Whifield Street. It occupies two small houses joined together, with small rooms connected by narrow winding staircases. Entrance +1 step to two sections of the museum shop, linked by a narrow corridor (D65cm). The museum is on the first and second floors, with a minimum of +15.

Public Record Office Museum see chapter on *Places of interest.*

Queen's Gallery, Buckingham Palace Road SW1 *Tel:* 0171 799-2331. Admission charge. A changing exhibition of works from various parts of the royal collection. Flat to ticket office and shop, where Royal souvenirs can be bought. The galleries are on two levels, +11 steps to the first floor, then +17 to the second.

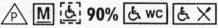

Royal Academy Of Arts, Burlington House, Piccadilly W1 *Tel:* 0171 439-7438. Admission charge. The oldest and most prestigious fine arts institution in Britain, known particularly for its Summer exhibition, although it has its own permanent collection. Two OB spaces in the forecourt if reserved in advance. Ramp 5m to the left bypasses +7 steps at the entrance. The main exhibition on the first floor can be reached by a glass lift (D80 W135 L280), which is itself worth having a look at. Lift access also to smaller second floor galleries. Flat access to other first floor galleries through private rooms. Most exhibitions have taped commentaries, and there are seats available throughout the 200m circle of the main gallery. Shop on first floor. Ramped access to the upmarket restaurant, and there is a **wheelchair loo (D98 ST80)** by the gents on the GF.

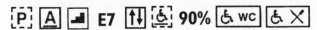

Science Museum, Exhibition Road, South Kensington SW7 *Tel:* 0171 938-8111 *Minicom:* 0171 938-9770 DisEnq 0171 938-8080. Admission charge. One of the country's most popular museums, with three excellent 'Hands On' galleries for children: the 'Launch Pad' on the first floor; 'On Air' and the 'Flight Pad' on the third floor; and on the lower ground floor, 'Interactions'. This is a new facility which opened in 1995 and is described as the most important development since the opening of the Children's Gallery in the 1930's. There's a spectacular Space Exploration gallery on the GF.

Access has been carefully thought about, and the management are keen for any ideas to improve things, with an ongoing programme to make all areas fully accessible. The museum is on seven floors, and over fifty galleries cover a total area of some eight acres. A *Guide for Disabled Visitors* is available at the entrance.

There are four OB spaces with a time limit directly outside the museum in Exhibition Road, and prior arrangement can be made to use the museum's own CP. Flat entrance, then a ramp bypasses –8 steps to main GF. The mezzanine gallery, which introduces the whole museum, can be reached by the lift (D110 W230 L300) which is to the right of the main restaurant. This lift goes to all floors except the lower ground. The glass lift (D87 W140 L180) is straight on from the main entrance, and serves the cloakroom in the lower ground floor and floors one to three. A more central lift (D130 W195 L200), serves the remainder of the lower ground floor, and floors one to three. Each floor contains a few galleries with +1. The gallery over the Space hall on the GF, and the one over the nuclear physics section on the second floor can both be reached via a platform stairlift.

A new restaurant opened on the GF in 1995; there is a picnic area on the first floor and a snack bar on the third, all with flat access. The café on the third floor has +7, which can be bypassed by an open lift. **One wheelchair loo (D85 ST110)** on the GF next to the central lift, another **(D90 ST70)** by the schools entrance, and others **(D75 ST70)** close to the main lift on both the second and the third floors. A further **wheelchair loo (D84 ST100)** is on the lower ground floor. An open lift (D90 L125) serves the shop, but can be bypassed through the entrance to the first exhibits. The three main floors are approximately 250m long, and there is some seating. Most of the exhibits have attached handrails.

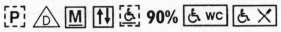

Serpentine Gallery, Kensington Gardens W2 *Tel:* 0171 723-9072. Changing exhibitions of contemporary art, in four spacious rooms, with a shop. Entrance +1 step, normally ramped. Flat inside.

Shakespeare's Globe Museum and Theatre, New Globe Walk, Blackfriars SE1 *Tel:* 0171 928-6406. Admission charge presumed. Opening is currently scheduled for June 1996, and following a windfall from the National Lottery, plans are now definite. The centre will contain a theatre and an underground exhibition. All levels of the complex will be accessible by lift, and there will be a **wheelchair loo**. The theatre itself will have a large area for seating or standing which will have flat access.

 80%

Sherlock Holmes Museum, 221b Baker Street NW1 *Tel:* 0171 935-8866. Admission charge. Celebratory museum of Sir Arthur Conan Doyle's fictional detective. Entrance +1 step, but no exhibits on the GF. First floor +17, then +18 to the second, and +16 to the third. The shop is in the basement, –18 from the GF.

 El8 N34

Sir John Soane's Museum, 13 Lincoln's Inn Fields WC2 *Tel:* 0171 405-2107. The house was left to the nation in 1837, with a stipulation that nothing should be changed. Full of artefacts of this great collector, but access is (inevitably) poor. The entrance has +2+5+1 steps, and 80% of the GF is flat. The other 20% is –3+3. There are some narrow doorways, including one W52cm. The basement is –17 (winding), the first floor +27. Even though only about 40% of the collection is visible from the GF, it is well worth a visit to step back into the dreamy and eclectic world of this great collector and architect.

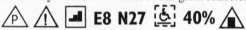 E8 N27 40%

Tate Gallery, Millbank SW1 *Tel:* 0171 887-8000. Charge for special exhibitions. One of the major art collections, with roughly 50 galleries including a fine exhibition of Turners in the Clore Gallery. **Management currently have a strict limit of six chair users in the Gallery at any one time, and one of our surveyors has twice been denied entry due to this.** Parking for visitors with disabilities can be booked. Entrance in John Islip Street, opposite Bolinga Street. Using entrance by the CP, disabled visitors are escorted to the Clore Gallery, where a public lift (D135 W175 L430) to the first floor gives flat access to the upper level of the Main Galleries, through the Turner collection.

The main entrance has +21 steps. Alternative flat entrance 50m to right into the Clore Gallery, which has a revolving door. A swing door can be opened. From here, the route to the Main Galleries is the same as that described above. All forty-four galleries on the main level, including the exhibition galleries and gallery shop, have flat access. Access to five lower galleries is through a staff area.

The café and the restaurant are both on the lower level, reached from the Clore Gallery entrance with staff escort. The eating places can also be reached by a staff operated lift (D100 W100 L200) in the Main Galleries level next to the Friends Room. **Wheelchair cubicle (D105 ST70)** in the ladies, nearby, and an **adapted cubicle (D80 ST30)** in the gents. Neither is signposted, nor is the **wheelchair loo (D80 ST120)** to the left of the information desk at the Clore Gallery entrance. Wheelchairs can be borrowed. A detailed map is available at either entrance, which is useful as signposting can be misleading. There is a tape tour, although sound quality is variable and it occasionally fades out altogether.

There are plans to open a new rear entrance to the Gallery by 1998 with flat or lift access to all galleries, and to install a new adapted loo. This may lead to a much-needed and permanent change in attitude by the Gallery management to the admission of chair users.

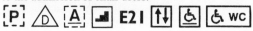

Theatre Museum, 1e Tavistock Street WC2 *Tel:* 0171 836-7891. Admission charge. On the corner of Wellington Street, the museum exhibits costume and make-up, as well as containing a theatre and booking agency. Flat or ramped access throughout. The main entrance is on Russell Street. The two floors are connected by a long ramp. **Wheelchair loo (D80 ST70)** to the right of the entrance. Ask for the key.

Victoria & Albert Museum, Cromwell Road, South Kensington SW7 *Tel:* 0171 938-8500. Admission charge (voluntary). Vast museum with seven miles of galleries and literally thousands of objects. Collections cover furniture, jewellery, china, prints, drawings, sculpture and dress from all over the world. The museum is split into three main sections: the main galleries (numbers 11 to 51 and 65 to 117), the Cromwell Road galleries (numbers 1 to 9, 52 to 64 and 118 to 145) and the Henry Cole wing.

There are four OB spaces and a flat entrance to the museum in Exhibition Road. The main entrance in Cromwell Road has +7 steps. A detailed plan can be obtained from the information desk near the entrance. Access is particularly complicated but, with detours, roughly 95% of the exhibits are step free.

The **main galleries** can be reached from the wheelchair ramp on the right once inside the Exhibition Road entrance. From this ramp there is an unmarked door (next to the service lift) which leads into room 21, usually locked. An alternative is to continue to the bottom of the ramp, then turn right, through the shop and to the right of the restaurant to room 11. All of the galleries on this level (numbers 11-51) have step free access, except for +22 to room 40A. There is a well hidden ramp between rooms 32 and 46. This floor contains the main shop and the Exhibition Courts which house temporary exhibitions. To get to the second floor of the main galleries it is necessary to return to the main ramp, and use the service lift (D76 W82 L122) to room 74. An open lift (W75

L117) bypasses –4 from room 74 to 73. From here the rest of the galleries on this floor have flat access, except for +9 from 109 to 111 to 117. Rooms 91 to 93 contain Jewellery and have narrow revolving security doors at each end. These can be bypassed through a door from room 83, but not all staff are aware of its existence. Flat access can be arranged in advance to the National Art Library through room 74A, and the Lecture Theatre is +21, although there is a lengthy step free route through staff areas. Ask for assistance.

The **Cromwell Road galleries** are reached via a well-signposted push button automatic door at the bottom of the main wheelchair ramp, which leads into room 1 (on level A East). These galleries are on four levels, and are split into two sections (East and West). There is a lift (D82 W160 L135) in room 6 which serves levels B, C and D East, and on level D it is possible to cross to the West side, where there is a different lift (D84 W134 L152) which serves levels A, B and C West (rooms 8, 9, 62 to 64, and 127 to 131). All of the Cromwell Road galleries have flat access, except for +16 to the glass displays in room 129. On level D there are narrow gaps (W60), which can be bypassed.

The **Henry Cole wing** is reached by the Exhibition Road ramp. It is served by two lifts (D80 W110 L150) between the Restaurant and room 11. On level 2 there are +5 to rooms 207 to 9, –4 to 202 and +6 to 220. Level 3 has –3 to all rooms except 305, and levels 4, 5 and 6 have flat access except for +8 to the Panorama of Rome on level 4.

The restaurant beneath the Henry Cole wing has flat access. There are **wheelchair cubicles (D75 ST75)** in the loos at the bottom of the main ramp (from the Exhibition Road entrance), and a **wheelchair loo (D80 ST90)** next to room 16 on the lower level of the main galleries. Induction loop in the lecture theatre, and a touch tour pack in Braille or large print available from the information desk near the main entrance. The museum is huge.

[P] △ [👜] [A] [↕] [👤] 90% [👤 WC] [👤 ✕] [👁] [👂]

Wallace Collection, Hertford House, Manchester Square W1 *Tel:* 0171 935-0687. An extensive private art collection bequeathed to the nation by Lady Wallace in 1897. A ramp at the entrance bypasses +3 steps. The exhibits are on two floors, both of which are flat, and connected by a staff lift (D127 W137 L104), which bypasses +33. The small central courtyard is –3.

△ [A] [▬] E3 [↕] [👤] 90%

War Museum see write-up on *Imperial War Museum.*

Wellington Museum (Apsley House), 149 Piccadilly W1 *Tel:* 0171 499-5676. Admission charge. The Duke of Wellington's former residence, known as 'Number 1 London'. It is situated on the north side of Hyde Park Corner, and somewhat isolated because of the swirl of traffic on almost all sides. There is ramped access to the 'island' from Exit 3 of the subway from Hyde Park Corner tube. The easiest other approach is from Hyde Park. Parking can be booked in the forecourt. The entrance has +7 steps then –9 to the lift (D85 W100 L105) which serves the other two floors. Despite extensive refurbishments in 1995 no access improvements were included.

 **E7 N9** 20%

Wimbledon Lawn Tennis Museum, Church Road, Wimbledon SW19 *Tel:* 0181 946-6131. Admission charge. Part of the All England Lawn Tennis and Croquet Club. Parking available inside the gates with advance warning. Step free via a lift (D76 W103 L130) to museum and shop which are on the second floor, except for –5 steps to one small display. **Wheelchair loo (D85 ST105 NKS)** by the cash desk. Tea room on the GF, with –4 or a ramp from outside the building, or –5 or platform lift from inside. On request chair users can be shown the centre court. For details of the Championships, see chapter on *Sport.*

P **M** **↑↓** 90% **wc** **×**

Winston Churchill Britain At War Theme Museum see chapter on *Places of interest.*

Outer London

Bethnal Green Museum of Childhood, Cambridge Heath Road, Bethnal Green E2 *Tel:* 0181 980-2415. A museum with all kinds of things of interest to children, and various holiday activities. Entrance +4 steps but a flat way in at the back. To use this, and the goods lift (D110+ W100+ L100+) which serves all four floors, you are asked to phone in advance. There is a mezzanine level with ramped access from the ground floor. The coffee shop is on the GF, as is the **wheelchair loo (D80 ST80).**

P **A** **E4** **↑↓** 90% **wc** **×**

Dulwich Picture Gallery, College Road, Dulwich SE21 *Tel:* 0181 693-5254. Admission charge. This building, designed by Sir John Soane, provides a wonderful setting for an art gallery, with large and peaceful grounds. Entrance +2 (steep) steps, but ramps are available. Step free everywhere, except –2 to one tiny section. A tea tent with flat access is erected in the garden in the summer months.

P **A** **E2** 90%

Geffrye Museum, Kingsland Road, Bethnal Green E2 *Tel:* 0171 739-9893. Built as almhouses in 1715, the museum now details the history of the evolution of interior design. Parking difficult. The –3 steps at the main gates can be bypassed by ramps 20m away either on the left or right. Ramped entrance to museum itself. 95% of the exhibits are on the GF, which is flat almost everywhere including the small shop. The coffee bar has +1. 1950s room has +20. **Wheelchair loo (D80 ST78)** in the education department. Staff have key.

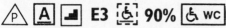

Horniman Museum and Gardens, 100 London Road, Forest Hill SE23 *Tel:* 0181 699-1892. A museum about people concerned with arts, craft, religion and history. Located at the top of a steep hill on a main road. The museum is in the middle of extensive refurbishments, which will continue until 2001. There are plans to install a **wheelchair loo** in the museum in summer 1996, and longer term plans include the installation of a lift.

Temporary access is flat to the reception area, and the +14 steps then +8 to level one can be bypassed by ramped entrance 20m to the left along the pavement. Ring bell, or visit reception first. The GF currently houses only one small exhibition, and the caféteria. Exhibits are displayed on three other levels, with platform stairlifts (W67 L84) connecting levels one and three (+12+13) and levels three and two (–8).

The CUE building (Centre for Understanding the Environment) was built in 1995 and is adjacent to the museum. It may be environmentally friendly but is +11 from the main section of the museum. There is a ramped entrance from the Gardens which means going 50m around the front of the museum on a main road. The Horniman Gardens are pretty and underused. The **wheelchair loo (D85 ST120)** is not signed, but is near the picnic area.

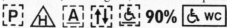

Kenwood House see chapter on *Places of interest.*

Kew Bridge Steam Museum see chapter on *Places of interest.*

National Maritime Museum see chapter on *Places of interest.*

Orleans House Gallery see chapter on *Places of interest.*

Royal Air Force Museum see chapter on *Days out.*

Whitechapel Art Gallery, Whitechapel High Street E1 *Tel:* 0171 522-7878. The site of David Hockney's first exhibition. Flat entrance, then staff operated lift (D200+ W200+ L200+) goes to all three floors. Café on the first floor renowned for its vegetarian food, and a **wheelchair loo (D80 ST74)** on the second floor.

Days out

Around London there are numerous castles, country houses, gardens, theme parks, and the extensive developments in the Lee Valley. The variety is immense and we have included just a small selection of places. We describe first those places outside the north and south circular ring roads, then, those beyond the M25, and finally a section on facilities in the Lee Valley.

Country Parks – a guide for disabled people available from RADAR (published 1994) has useful information. There is an excellent guide, updated annually, on *Facilities for Disabled and Visually Handicapped Visitors at National Trust Properties* available from the NT, 36 Queen Anne's Gate SW1H 9AS. The NT have gone to some lengths to improve the access at their properties.

Many places charge for entry, although there are commonly reductions for chair users. The three theme parks listed (Chessington, Legoland Windsor and Thorpe Park) have a substantial entrance charge, after which the rides are all free. As a result it's probably worth making it a whole day's visit.

Beyond the north and south circular roads

Chessington

Chessington World of Adventures, Leatherhead Road, Chessington, Surrey *Tel:* 01372-727227 M 01372-729560. A substantial theme park which has developed from what used to be a small zoo. Besides the zoo, there are many rides, a pub, a playground, cafés and numerous other attractions. Queues for the rides will be much shorter if you get there early. Closed during the winter months.

The main CP is well signed off the A243, and has sixteen OB spaces near the entrance. As the CP is huge, these are of considerable value. Flat/ramped access throughout the 35 acre site, with undulating paths that are mainly tarmac. Chairs are available for use.

A Guide for disabled visitors is available, and there are information signs at the entrance to each ride. Certain height restrictions apply on some of the rides, the largest minimum being 1m 40cm.

The park is split up into the following sections:

Animal Land 1 and 2. A ramp bypasses –6 steps to the *Children's Zoo*. Loos near the main entrance contain an **adapted cubicle (D78 ST57).**

Market Square. Safari Skyway has +19 at the exit. The *King's Head* pub has a small threshold. *Sea Storm* has +1 at exit and is a fast ride on which you have to hold on tightly. **Two wheelchair loos (D95 ST70 NKS).**

Calamity Canyon. *Runaway Mine Train* has +3 at exit. The *Rodeo* is a high G-force ride which requires a strong grip.

Forbidden Kingdom. *Rameses Revenge* has –17+5 at the exit. *Terror*

Tomb is a slow ride with a ramped exit, and +2 into the car.

Mystic East. *Magic Carpet* has +2 steps at the exit. *Dragon River* has +1 at the exit, and involves getting into a slow-moving car.

Toy Town. *Toy Town Truckers* has step free access at exit with +2 into the truck. *Flying Jumbos* has step free access and +1 into the car. *Toy Town Coaster* has +5+2+1. Old Crocks Rally has +2 and then +1 into the car. The *Chessington Railroad* has +1 to an adapted section on the last carriage, which measures W90 L100.

Smugglers Cove. *Smugglers Galleon* has ramped access at the exit.

Transylvania. *Professor Burps Bubbleworks* has ramped access, and the floating cars do not stop. Utterly bizarre ride. *The Vampire* ride has +6–12 –9–12–3 at the exit. **Wheelchair loo (D98 ST76 NKS).**

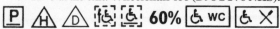

Chislehurst

Chislehurst Caves, Caveside Close, off Old Hill, Chislehurst, Kent *Tel:* 0181 467-3264. An extraordinary complex of caves, cut through chalk and flint. Exhibits include part of an Ichthyosaurus fossil, and an area associated with the Druids and Romans. During World War II the caves were used as a massive air-raid shelter with thousands of people living there. You can see the church and hospital, and where people kept their belongings by their bunk beds.

CP 50m away; rail station about 300m. At the entrance to the caves there's a gate (D68cm). Note that even the short tour will take you about 1km, with no seats. Inside, the caves are cool (always 8°C) and access is step free, although the surface is really rough and bumpy in places. Even the hardiest chair user would need a good pusher. The long tour involves going through some really low passages.

Ramp to the left bypasses +2–2 steps at the main door to the ticket office and café. **Adapted loo (D70+ ST57)** off the café area with flat access.

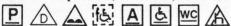

Enfield

Forty Hall Museum, Forty Hill, Enfield, Middx *Tel:* 0181 363-8196. A small museum of fine art and local history set in pleasant grounds. Two OB spaces immediately outside the house. Main entrance +2 steps, side entrance +1, and there is a ramp available. The GF, including the tea-room, is flat; the first floor has +22. **Wheelchair loo (D78 ST110)** in a toilet block 20m from the main entrance.

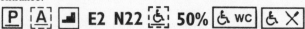

Hendon

Royal Air Force Museum, Grahame Park Way, Kingsbury NW9 *Tel:* 0181 205-9797. Admission charge. Britain's national museum of aviation housing one of the world's finest collections of historic aircraft. Large CP. The bulk of the museum is in the Main Aircraft hall and the Bomber Command hall. Flat entrance and step free access almost everywhere, except to the chapel (+1 step) and to one small exhibition (+2). There is ramped access to a flight simulator, and a theatre with two chair spaces. There are galleries on the first floor, reached by lift (D78 W140 L120), as well as a cinema with room for chair users at the back. The **wheelchair loo (D90 ST70)** is between the two halls, next to the gents.

The separate Battle of Britain hall, has two flat entrances, one to the display galleries and one to the restaurant, again, step free throughout. Lift (D85 W110 L145) to the first floor of display galleries. There is a mezzanine level containing a Sunderland Flying Boat, which is +13 from the GF. The restaurant contains a second **wheelchair loo (D90 ST85).**

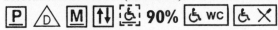 90%

Richmond & Kingston

Kew Gardens, Kew, Richmond, Surrey *Tel:* 0181 940-1171. Admission charge. The Royal Botanic Gardens is a world leader in plant research and conservation. The gardens are large, covering over 300 acres, and with distances of over 1.5km. Wheelchairs are available for use, but if you want one it is best to ring in advance (*Tel:* 0181 332-5121). There are quite a few benches and seats, and also some shelters in the event of rain. CP by the Brentford Ferry gate.

Three of the entrances are along the Kew Road, one off Kew Green and one by the river and CP. The area is fairly flat, and there are tarmac paths through much of the gardens. **The visitors centre** is by the Victoria gate on Kew Road, opposite Lichfield Road. There is a ramp to bypass +3 steps. It has the main information point, a shop and a **wheelchair loo (D85 ST70).** They have a large print map. The leaflet *Welcome to Kew* gives information on which plants are in bloom at different times of the year.

Going round clockwise on the map from the riverside (Brentford) gate:
Kew Bakery has flat access.
Kew Palace has +2+1 at the entrance and +11+3+11 to the first floor. The route to the 17thC garden is via some bumpy cobbled ramps (bypassing steps). **Wheelchair loo (D75 ST90)** nearby.
Orangery shop and restaurant, both +2 but with ramped bypass. **Adapted loo (D75 ST68)** around the back.
Filmy Fern House, +1 at entrance, –1 at exit.
Gallery, +2 at entrance.
Alpine House, ramped access.
Princess of Wales Conservatory gives a unique glimpse of tropical flora

in a house divided into ten habitats. Although the main route is flat, some parts can only be reached via stepped ramps (one step at a time).

By the Cumberland Gate there's an **adapted loo (D80 ST42).**

Waterlily House, ramp bypasses +4. Hot !

Palm House, built in 1850. A ramp bypasses +5, then mainly flat. Spiral staircase to marine display (–26) and to gallery (+52). Hot, and possibly difficult for asthmatics.

Temperate House, ramp bypasses +9+3. Sprial stairs to gallery (+45).

Marianne North Gallery, +5+5+1 to Victorian paintings of plants and landscapes. Flat inside.

Wheelchair loo (D75 ST85) between the gallery and the Lion Gate. Unisex, though signed as for gents.

The Pavilion restaurant/café, flat access. **Adapted loo (D70 ST55).**

Evolution House, which opened in 1995, takes you on a journey from Precambrian times, over 500 million years ago right through to the present. Step free throughout, including the shop. The surface is mainly smooth, except for some large 'footprints' set in the path.

Wheelchair loos (D80 ST73) over towards the lake.

[P] [F] [⚠ D] [👥] [M] [♿] 80% [♿ WC] [♿ ✗]

Kingston has a town centre which has been extensively redeveloped, see chapter on *Shops.*

Hampton Court Palace and Gardens, East Molesey, Surrey *Tel:* 0181 781-9500. A magnificent riverside Tudor palace with 50 acres of formal gardens surrounded by extensive wooded parklands. The main palace covers an area of about 200m by 100m. CP, with twelve OB spaces, approached from the main entrance near the end of the bridge. Hampton Court rail station is about 400m away across the bridge, and has +2 steps with a ramped alternative.

You can walk through some of the courtyards in the palace, and there are routes through the gardens at the side. The main formal gardens are at the back of the palace, and the area is generally flat.

To see the palace, the ticket office (with +2) is near the CP and main entrance. There are a substantial number of stairs involved, but disabled visitors can use the lift (D70+ W70+ L100+), although this means taking a slightly different route from other visitors. All four main sections of the palace (Henry V111's rooms, the Queen's rooms, the Georgian rooms and the King's rooms) can then be seen with step free access, with warders opening any necessary doors. The only step is –1 to the video room.

The Wolsey rooms and Renaissance Picture Gallery are +22 –1 with no lift. The Tudor Kitchens are at ground level, with +1 at the entrance in Clock Court, then –4 to see a model of the palace and a commentary. This can be bypassed by an entrance in Base Court with –1 –1 and then step free access to most of the kitchens. The Coffee Shop in the kitchens has a ramped entrance, bypassing +1. The seating is –2 but step free by coming in through the exit.

The **Gift Shop** is situated between Base Court and Clock Court. It has two entrances, one +5 from Anne Boleyns Gateway, the other +2 from the south side of Clock Court. **Wheelchair loo (D84 ST76)** by the south entrance to the shop.

Other noteworthy details are:

- the **Garden café, Tiltyard Restaurant,** and Gift Shop have ramped entrances (each bypassing +1).
- the **Tudor Tennis (Real Tennis) Court** has –1 at the entrance and +1 at the exit.
- the **Vine** has step free access, as does the Maze, although some of its tarmac paths are quite narrow with tightish turns.
- **wheelchair loo (D87 ST90)** close to the Maze, in an area known as The Wilderness. It is next to the ladies.

Ham House, Ham Street, Richmond, Surrey *Tel:* 0181 940-1950. Delightful house by the river, built in 1610. CP in the forecourt. The main entrance has +4+5 steps/ramped, then +1+1. The house is on three floors, with a small lift (D67 W87 L84) to the basement and first floor, bypassing –13 and +27 respectively. Most areas on the GF have +1.

The shop on the right hand side of the house has step free access. The route to the restaurant bypassing –5 is signposted, with a ramp to get inside. Paths around the gardens are gravelled, and you may prefer to use the grass. There are plenty of seats and wheelchairs available for use. **Wheelchair loo (D85 ST80)** opposite the shop and well signed.

Osterley Park House, Jersey Road, Isleworth, Middx *Tel:* 0181 560-3918. The entrance to the park is off the A4 via Thornbury Road. Fine neo-classical house set in a large park. CP some 300m from the house, and there is a shuttle bus. It is possible to reserve a space by the house itself.

The entrance is +10+10+1+3 steps, leading directly to the first floor. A Stairclimber is available, and we have been asked to say that as it requires two members of staff to operate, it must be pre-booked. It was unservicable when we surveyed (which is a reason for checking first), but we deplore the need for phoning. Most of the rooms are on the first floor, but there's also the GF (–23) and second floor (+36).

On the right of the house the shop has +1/ramped, and the tea room and information desk have flat access. **Wheelchair loo (D95 ST150)** behind the shop. Wheelchairs available, and on some days there are powered buggies for use in the grounds. Ring first to confirm.

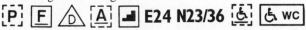

Richmond Park, Surrey TW10 5HS *Tel:* Superintendant 0181 948-3209. The park, to the west of London, provides a huge area over 2000 acres, of rough but attractive open ground and is well-known for its herds of deer. It was created by Charles I, and given over by Edward VII for public use in 1910. It's definitely a place to go to by car as there's no public transport in or through the park. There is a road running all the way round and several entrances and CPs, whose surfaces are uneven and gravelly. Refreshments are available near the Roehampton Gate and at Pembroke Lodge (between the Richmond and Ham gates) with step free access. The **Isabella Plantation** contains a magnificent collection of azaleas.

Pembroke Lodge is surrounded by level tarmac paths, and offers fine views over the river from an outside part of the restaurant. The area is particularly attractive during May with the rhododendrons. You can drive up to the Lodge if you need to. **Wheelchair loo (D70+ ST70+)** outside the Lodge, poorly signed at the back of the main toilet block. Near the Roehampton Gate there is ramped access to the restaurant. There are some awkward gates in the area designed to keep deer out. **Wheelchair loo (D70 ST70)** by the ladies loo at the side. At the **Sheen Gate** there is an **adapted loo (D70 ST45).**

If you want to visit the **Isabella Plantation**, the main CPs are about 300m away over rough ground. There are OB spaces in a special CP reached from the Ham Gate and near Peg's Pond.

P ☖ ⓓ ⚠ 👫 👫 ♿ WC

Thorpe Park, Staines Road, Chertsey, Surrey *Tel:* 01932-562633. A leisure park for the family, well signposted along the A320, with different rides and a small working farm. Closed through the winter months. A comprehensive guide for visitors with disabilities is available.

Large CP with nineteen OB spaces to the right of the entrance. Once inside it is generally flat or ramped, but is quite big, covering about 1km. Wheelchairs are available by the main entrance.

The first thing you come to is the 'Dome', with a restaurant, bar, cinema and children's show, all with flat access. There are numerous eating places throughout the complex. The farm can be reached on the ferry (step free to board, and –1 at the exit), or by a train, which has two adapted carriages (W70cm) and portable ramps.

Access to many of the rides is very difficult. It is the policy of the management, however, that although some rides are not recommended, if you are with friends who can assist you, it is your choice as to which rides you go on. Although the access guide produced by the management is good, it does not detail the steps involved. We have selected a few of the more popular rides to illustrate the access problems.

'Flying Fish' has +7 with a ramped alternative 5m to the left, and you need to transfer into a 'Fish' which has leg room of L45cm. 'Loggers Leap' has ramped access and involves transferring. 'Thunder River' has +15–16+59–4 and the guide says chair users can go on the ride if they have friends to carry them up and down the steps. What the guide does not say is that you need to hold onto a bar during this ride. 'Depth Charge' has +6, then a steep ramp going up 30m, then +12. Their guide suggests this is not suitable for chair users, but it may actually be more suitable than 'Thunder River'

Five wheelchair loos (D80+ ST80+) are scattered throughout the complex, and **adapted ones in the Dome, and the Farm (D80 ST30)**. They are not well signed, so it may be worth noting the loo on the left just before the entrance point.

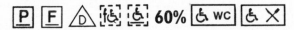 60%

Outside the M25

Bedfordshire

Whipsnade Wild Animal Park, near Dunstable, Bedfordshire *Tel:* 01582-872171. On the B4540 and well signed from the M1. A large zoo on the edge of the Chiltern Hills, with some species roaming freely. There's a big CP about 100m from the main entrance but you can take your car and drive round the main circuit (about 2km), which is undoubtedly the best way to see the park. Many of the animals can be seen from the road or from tarmac paths, and there is parking near some of the pens. There are a few rough and hilly paths, difficult if it's just been raining; to get to some places a chair user would need a strong pusher. It's a good idea to get a map and guide book of the site.

The train which goes round most of the site has +1 step and D75cm, and one coach provides three wheelchair spaces. This is a good way to get an overview, and you'll see some things you cannot see from a car. The *Café on the Lake* has ramped access and the *Spotted Pig* pub has +2. There is +1 into the Discovery Centre. The Children's Zoo has +1, and the Sea Lions building has heavy double doors and a steep ramp. In the Underwater Amphitheatre, there is +1 to the seats, but room for chair users at the front.

Three wheelchair loos (D80+ ST100+) all shown on the map. One is to the left just after the entrance, one is quite near, by the Discovery Centre and the third is by the Reindeer enclosure.

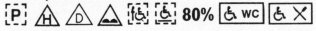 80%

Berkshire

Windsor & Windsor Castle are a great draw for visitors with its riverside, the castle, the Great Park and Eton just across the river. By car it is some 50km from central London. Alternatively you can take a Network SouthEast train to Windsor Riverside, a station with flat access but situated at the bottom of Castle Hill (and it is a long steep hill); or take a Western Region train to Windsor Central (changing at Slough), which is higher up and nearer the castle.

The Tourist Office, 24 High Street, Windsor SL4 1LH *Tel:* 01753-852010, has step free access. *The Access Guide to Windsor & Maidenhead* is available as a handout, but this is mainly for residents. It will tell you where there are some **wheelchair loos** in the area. Windsor Central station has flat access. In the forecourt there's a lively shopping and café/restaurant area.

River trips are operated by Salters and by others *Tel:* 01753-865832. Get other numbers from the tourist office. Access to the landing stage is ramped from the main road.

Windsor Castle *Tel:* RecM 01753-831118 DisEnq 01753-868286 Ext2235. Parking in the vicinity of the castle is difficult and the main CPs are at the bottom of the hill. Unfortunately no provisions can be made for disabled people to park inside the castle grounds, even though there is space in the Middle Ward. There's a CP in the Central station, and three OB spaces on the High Street about 150m from the castle. Quite a good ploy is to use the CP close to the coach park (which is well signed), and use the lift (D70+ W70+ L70+) up to the Central Station. **Access to the Castle grounds is generally fairly good, although it's hilly and big.** To see most of it you have to go 400/500m from the top of Thames Street. There are cobbles by the main gate, but most of the paths are then tarmac. The courtyard areas are largely accessible to chair users, but the viewpoint overlooking the playing fields of Eton may prove difficult.

St George's Chapel has superb perpendicular architecture. Entrance +1+2 steps. Alternative flat access from the north entrance (by prior request). Inside, there is step free access apart from one side chapel.

Albert Memorial Chapel, with beautiful marbled walls, has +2 –2 inside, avoided by ignoring the one-way system.

State Apartments. Tickets are obtained in the Middle Ward. The normal route is then to go via the North Terrace and +20 to the China Museum followed by a further +28 to the State Appartments. **It is possible to bypass these steps using an entrance from Engine Court (you may have to ask at the Police office).** A ramp bypasses +2 and leads to the China Museum level, then a lift (D70 W100 L95) with a tight 90° turn on exit goes to the State Appartments. Regrettably, it's wise to ring first to check that you can use this, and one of our chair-using surveyors has had bad experiences when just turning up. There is then step free access, and you can get a good view of the area damaged by the fire. We were told that there were plans for the provision of a new lift, which may make access rather easier.

Wheelchair loo (D85 ST70) in Engine Court, with the key available at the police office, through the door marked 'side door'. **Another (D85 ST85)** is in the ladies on the north terrace to the left of the Dolls House entrance. The **Gallery** is +7+2+1 from the north terrace, but there is an alternative step free route. Ask a warden for assistance.

The International Crown Jewels Exhibition, 47 Peascod Street, Windsor, Berks *Tel:* 01753-833722. Near the junction with William Street. The exhibition is on the first floor with +21 steps.

 **E21**

Eton College Chapel is nearby (over half a mile on foot, but considerably further by car). Gravelled or cobbled access to the front entrance, then +5+7+5+5+2 steps, and +1 in the main body of the chapel. The general area of Eton College school is flat and well worth a visit. Visiting is curtailed during the school term, and if you want to find out when it is open, *Tel:* 01753-671177. About 75m further on there's the cloister, via cobbles and –1. There are then +2 to the GF of the Brewhouse. Stairs to the upper levels. In the cloister the museum has –1, with a video presentation. **Wheelchair loo (D80 ST75).**

 **E24**

Savill Gardens, Windsor Great Park. *Enquiries to:* Keeper of the Gardens, Crown Estate Office, The Great Park, Windsor, Berks *Tel:* 01753-860222. These are some delightful and varied gardens, covering some thirty-five acres of woodland. They are well signposted. Large CP.

Ramped access to the main entrance, labelled 'Savill Garden Entrance'. The paths through the gardens are mainly tarmac, although some of the routes are grassed. **Wheelchair loo (D80 ST72)** on the right just after the marked entrance. The shop alongside has flat access, and sells a wide range of plants as well as gifts and books. There's an excellent restaurant/tea room, with a splendid view, about 60m from the garden entrance/shop. It has a small threshold at the entrance.

 **80%**

Legoland Windsor, near Windsor SL4 4AY *Tel:* 01753-626111 *Fax:* 01753-626113. Some two miles from Windsor off the B3022, and well signed. A large and impressive theme park, opened in 1996. The park area is about 800m by 600m, and there is a special, signed, CP with OB spaces about 100m from the entrance. The park is built on a hillside with the entrance near the top. Disabled visitors can make their way gently downwards, via various rides and attractions, and then take the **Hill Train** back to the top. The train has +1 step and includes a compartment for three chair users. Some of the rides such as the **Ferris Wheel** and the **I Spy Express Train**, have been designed so that chair users can get on without transfer. For some others, chair users would have to transfer. There are chair spaces if you want to see any of the shows. A detailed leaflet is available giving guidance for disabled visitors.

All the main cafés/restaurants have step free access, and all five toilet blocks include **wheelchair loos (D100 ST80+).**

Buckinghamshire

Bekonscot Model Village, Warwick Road, Beaconsfield, Bucks *Tel:* 01494-672919. A remarkable minature 'world', dating from the 1930s, with an enormous amount of detail, including a working model railway. Closed in Winter. Well signed from the M40, junction two, except the last turning into Warwick Road. There are OB spaces in the CP by the church, 120m from the entrance. The village includes rather narrow and slightly hilly tarmac paths and bridges, in keeping with the 'model' concept. A sign outside indicates that the maximum width of chair that can get around is W66cm; accordingly there are three wheelchairs available (W56cm), these are not suitable for self propelling. The route around the village is about 300m long, and there's a tea shop and **adapted loo (D75+, ST blocked by fixed bar)** about halfway round. A really interesting visit for children.

Hertfordshire

St Albans

St Albans is about 40km north of London. It has a combination of both old and modern shopping facilities (in and around the Maltings), a cathedral and unique Roman remains in Verulamium. Some parts of the city, such as St Peter's Street and High Street are hilly, and some streets are cobbled. The various sites are some way apart, and the best way to come is by car. If you come by train, the station is more than 1km from the city. There are several **wheelchair loos**, including in the Maltings, and at the station on platform 1. The main sights are shown on the diagram. **The Tourist Information Office** *Tel:* 01727-864511 is in the Town Hall, Market Place, at the end of St Peter's Street. They produce a useful leaflet detailing local accessible sites, and a CP map.

St Albans Cathedral, Sumpter Yard, St Albans *Tel:* 01727-860780. The abbey church can be approached from three directions. The first, for pedestrians only, is via the Waxhouse gate which is off the High Street opposite the clock tower. By going to the left (east) around the end of the abbey to the large cedar tree, there is flat access. Should the door be locked, ring the bell. The second way in is from Holywell Hill into Sumpter Yard, where there is limited parking. The third route is to the West entrance, by way of George Street and Romeland, and has +2+1+5 steps.

Once inside, there are several small groups of steps (up to 5) but these are nearly all ramped, giving step free access to about 80% of the interior. The shop, bookstall, refectory and tea shop all have flat/ramped access. **Adapted loo (D82 ST57)** to the right of the entrance, in the South Presbytery aisle with ramped access from the South Transept. There is a touch and hearing centre in the South Quire aisle. Ask a verger for a key. There are normally wheelchairs available for use in the cathedral. There are grassy slopes around the abbey but the paths include the odd step or so.

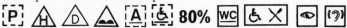 80%

Museum of St Albans, Hatfield Road, St Albans *Tel:* 01727-819340. Adjacent CP. A side entrance opened on request bypasses +2 steps. The staff will open locked doors, giving the GF step free access. First floor +9+9, second floor +5+7. **Wheelchair loo (D74 ST95)** on the ground floor.

E2 N30   40%

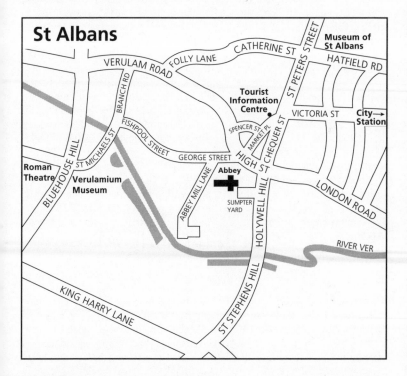

Verulamium is what remains of Roman St Albans. Verulamium Park is a large area, and is generally flat/ramped. Verulamium includes the remains of houses, a theatre, and hypocaust as well as parts of the town walls. What you see is mainly the building foundations, and some impressive mosaics. The **hypocaust** has a bumpy approach, +1 step and a narrow entrance (W66cm).

 80%

Verulamium Museum St Michaels Street *Tel:* 01727-819339. OB spaces in the CP about 50m from the museum. Step free access throughout. **Adapted loos (gents D82 ST60; ladies D78 ST130, but obstructed by fixed rail; NKS).** The **Roman Theatre** is under separate ownership. It is about 200m from the museum and has a ramped but narrow (W72cm) entrance. There are bumpy grass slopes inside with some quite steep ramps.

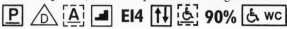 80% [WC]

Other interesting places in the area which are listed in the city guide as being fully wheelchair accessible, and with **adapted loos**, are the **Garden of the Rose**, Chiswell Green *Tel:* 01727-50461, and the **Mosquito Aircraft Museum,** Salisbury Hall, London Colney *Tel:* 01727-822051. These are not always open, and if you want to visit, you should either ring the number given, or the tourist office.

Hatfield House, Hatfield, Herts *Tel:* 01707-262823. A Jacobean mansion built in 1611 for the Cecil family, who still live there. From time to time it holds Elizabethan banquets (*Tel:* 01705-262055). The house lies just off the A1000 and is less than 1km from Hatfield town centre. Parking directly in front of the house. Hatfield BR station is nearly 400m. The entrance has +14 steps bypassed by a detour of about 150m round the back if you ask. Small lift (D70 W95 L115) to all relevant floors for the tour (otherwise it involves +31 and –31). There is a ramped outside route into the kitchen display.

About 150m away is the 'Old Palace' with an adjacent courtyard (Palace Yard) containing a cafe and a small shop, both with ramped access. The beautiful grounds and garden are nearly all on the same level. **Adapted loos (D78 ST100, but door opens in)** in the courtyard. The normal guided tour lasts about an hour.

[P] /D\ [A] [■] EI4 [↑↓] [占] 90% [占 WC]

Kent

Chartwell, near Westerham *Tel:* 01732-866368. Winston Churchill's country home from 1924. At busy times, entry is by 'timed ticket', and you may have to wait at peak periods. The CP is some 250m from the house, and the pathway to the house is steep with several flights of steps. Ring first if you want to park near the house. According to the National Trust information the GF of the house is readily accessible, and there's a small lift (W80 L80) to the first floor which was installed for Sir Winston. It may be possible to transfer to a smaller chair if necessary. The dining room and exhibition on the lower ground floor can only be reached via steps. There's a step free route from the front of the house to overlook the garden, which has many different levels linked by steps.

The restaurant by the CP is reached via steep slopes and a ramp. The shop has flat access, and there is an adapted loo (not seen) just behind it.

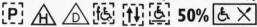 50% [占 X]

Ightham Mote, Ivy Hatch, Sevenoaks, Kent *Tel:* 01732-810378. Near the M20 junction 2A, and signed from the A25. Medieval stately home with a moat. On-site CP with three OB spaces, and a bumpy, stony surface. It is possible to negotiate a slightly closer dropping-off point near the shop if necessary. The easiest route to the cobbled central courtyard is to go down a stony path behind the house, about 100m long, and with −1 step at the start. There are GF rooms with step free access, but with +1−1 between some of them. First floor is +17.

Around the house are some attractive lawns, grounds and ponds, reached by gravel paths, or a steep grass verge. The tea lounge near the CP has step free access but fixed seating. The shop has a flat entrance through D67cm, then a +3 split level and an upstairs section (+14), so that only about 40% has step free access. **Wheelchair loo (D85 ST110)** near the shop, just before the entrance gate to the stony path described.

Leeds Castle, Maidstone, Kent *Tel:* 01622-765400. The castle dates back nearly 900 years, and the setting is breathtaking, in the middle of a lake. It has been owned by monarchs, including Henry V111, and by famous families including those of Sir Anthony St Leger, Lord Culpeper and Lord Fairfax. The last owner, Lady Ballie, left the castle to the nation. Since then, considerable efforts have been made to make the site accessible. A detailed leaflet and a braille guide are available. Special events, such as wine festivals, concerts, and a flower festival, are held from time to time.

The castle is well signposted from junction 8 on the M20. Large CP about 400m from the castle with OB spaces, and a minibus with lift access goes near to the entrance if necessary. Wheelchairs are available. The drawbridge has 45m of cobbles, and leads past the Dog Collar museum (+1step) to a circular 'courtyard' called the Inner Bailey. A ramp bypasses −15 into the castle, and the GF has been made accessible by the use of a platform stair lift by the Heraldry room bypassing −6. Part of the route takes you against the flow of people doing a standard tour, so you may have to wait a little. The upper floors are +2+14+14, then −15 −15 (spiralled).

The grounds have occasional steps and slopes, and a good number of seats. The Duckery has an artificial lake with a wooden walkway. Past the castle entrance the Culpeper garden is ramped throughout; the Aviary is up a gentle slope, and in the centre of the Maze there's a grotto with −15−7+13. There is also a 9-hole golf course which can provide facilities for blind or partially sighted players *Tel:* 01622-880467.

About 150m from the drawbridge around the Fairfax Courtyard are the restaurant (with ramp bypassing +2), and the shop. Both have split levels inside. **Adapted loos (D75 ST67)** by the OB spaces in the CP. There are three **wheelchair loos (D87 ST85)** just before the Fairfax courtyard. Another **wheelchair loo (D80 ST120)** is near the castle entrance by the Dog Collar museum; go through the archway and turn left and left again.

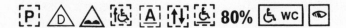 **80%**

Surrey

Claremont Landscape Garden, Portsmouth Road, Esher *Tel:* 01372-467806. One of the earliest surviving English landscape gardens, dating from before 1720. On the opposite side of the road from West End Lane. CP by the entrance. The gravel path and grassland immediately around the lake are flat and firm. Tea room and shop by the CP, and adapted loo (not seen). National Trust information used.

 **90%**

Guildford is a picturesque town with a steep cobbled High Street. Not an obvious place to recommend for accessibility. It does, however have step free access at the main station, and a *Shopmobility* (*Tel:* 01483-453993) scheme based in the Friary CP about 400m away. **Wheelchair loo (D70+ ST70+ NKS)** on the first floor of the CP alongside the *Shopmobility* office. A pedestrian bridge goes to the Friary Shopping Centre with lift access to all levels. You can then get to North Street and the High Street (which is pedestrianised for most of the day), as well as the castle and the river.

The town has a 'wheelchair tourist trail', updated in 1995, with details available from the Tourist Information Centre in Tunsgate (*Tel:* 01483-444007). This is some 700m from the Friary Centre, and has +1 step at the entrance. *Shopmobility* may have copies of the route.

Guildford Cathedral on Stag Hill just outside the town dominates the skyline. It is one of only four cathedrals built in Britain in the 20thC. CP outside, and a permanent ramp bypasses the steps at the entrance. Flat inside, except for +4 to the Lady Chapel, and –4 to the Brass Rubbing Centre. The shop and refectory, by the parking area, are step free. **Wheelchair loos** (D90 **ST70+**) by the shop.

⟦P⟧ ⟨H⟩ ⟦A⟧ ⟦♿⟧ **80%** ⟦♿ WC⟧ ⟦♿ ✗⟧

Polesden Lacey House, Polesden Lacey, Great Bookham, Dorking, Surrey *Tel:* 01372-458203. Approached from junction 9 on the M25, and well signed from the A24 to Dorking. An elegant 19thC house with formal Edwardian gardens. Open air theatre performances in the summer. OB parking spaces next to the shop and café, about 100m from the house. The main entrance is ramped bypassing +2 steps, and all the rooms with displays are on the GF with step free access. The shop, plant sales and restaurant have a ramp bypassing +2. **Wheelchair loo (D80 ST120)** nearby.

The garden has gravelled or grass paths, and is generally flat. The only steps are those to the former kitchen garden (+4). There is a wheelchair route with a hard surface which goes well over 1km. Most chair users would need a strong pusher. The open air theatre (*Tel:* 01372-457223) is about 200m from the house, and chair users are asked to book spaces in advance.

Wheelchairs, including one powered chair for use in the garden, are available.

[P] /D\ [&] [A] [&] [& WC] [& X]

Wisley Gardens, A3, Woking, Surrey *Tel:* 01483-224234. The Royal Horticultural Society Gardens are about 10km north of Guildford off the A3. Members only on Sundays. CP with OB spaces near the entrance. Wheelchairs and Batricars available.

Flat entrance. Over half the gardens are readily wheelchair accessible and a map is available showing hard surface paths, link routes over grass areas, and where the paths are steep. Broadly speaking, the northern part of the gardens is fairly flat while the southern part is hilly. Most chair users will need a pusher. It's not a bad idea to do the hilly bit first and then trundle gently down towards the restaurant. The Glasshouses have a longish push up, but flat access throughout. **There's a garden designed for disabled people.** For visually impaired people there's a special scented garden.

The restaurant and gift shop are both step free throughout. **Adapted loo (D85 ST65)** just outside the entrance. There are two **wheelchair loos (D82 ST72+)** between the garden for disabled people and the glasshouses, and **another (D82 ST76)** near the restaurant.

[P] /H\ /D\ [&] 60% [& WC] [& X] [👓]

Lee Valley

Lee Valley Park, Countryside Centre, Abbey Gardens, Waltham Abbey, Essex EN9 1XQ *Tel:* 01992-713838. A remarkable venture, established in 1967 to regenerate the then derelict valley into a 'green chain' stretching from London's East End (around Stratford), through Walthamstow and Tottenham right up past the M25 to Broxborne and Ware. Its extent, and some of the key facilities, are shown on the map. The river along which the Park has been developed is variously called the Lea or Lee. For the sake of consistency, we refer to everything here as Lee. *Because many facilities have the prefix 'Lee Valley' is is not always clear, initially, which part of the valley they are in.* Some of them sound very similar, and yet are 15km apart, and we have tried to use descriptive names to clarify their location.

The Park area provides a wide range of activities. There are nature reserves, sports and entertainment facilities, an excellent choice of places for fishing, a boating centre and camp sites. A pack of leaflets is published detailing facilities for disabled people, and giving a local map on the back. These are excellent, and cover:

• countryside sites and activities;
• fishing sites; and
• sports and recreational facilities.

The pack is available from the Countryside Centre listed above, or from the major centres mentioned. Just ring, and they'll be happy to send you a copy. The information seems to be updated regularly, so it should be reliable. We found it most helpful.

Because of the range of facilities, and the care taken to make as many of them as possible accessible to all, we have made a detailed survey of the area, and included descriptions of the various places, starting from the inner London part, and working outwards.

The south end of Lee Valley, around Stratford, Leyton and Hackney

Cycle Circuit, Temple Mills Lane, Stratford E15 *Tel:* 0181 534-6085. Opposite the Sports Centre. Steep slope up to the track from on-site CP. Changing facilities +2 steps, key available from office in left-hand block. **Adapted loo (D80 ST52, partially blocked by sink)** in the right-hand block.

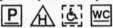

Sports Centre, Quartermile Lane, Leyton E10 *Tel:* 0181 519-0017/555-2636. Off the A106 Eastway, and well signed as Lee Valley Sports Centre. On-site CP. Ramped main entrance, and most facilities are step free, except the viewing gallery for the squash courts which has +14 steps. Health suite +1. No adapted changing/shower facilities. Café/bar to the left from reception. **Wheelchair cubicle in the gents (D90 ST80), adapted in the ladies (D85 ST52) loos.**

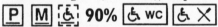

Ice Centre, Lea Bridge Road, Leyton E10 *Tel:* 0181 533-3154/553-3155. Situated on the east side of the River Lee Navigation, on the A104. On-site CP. Ramped main entrance to an ice rink, changing area and bar. Only 20% of the bar is step free. Limited space for chair users at the corners of the rink, with relatively poor view. The easiest seats have +3 to the back row, then –2 towards the front. Induction loop. **Wheelchair loo (D70 ST120)** behind reception.

| P | M | ♿ 50% | ♿ WC | (?) |

Riding Centre, Lea Bridge Road, Leyton E10 *Tel:* 0181 556-2629/539-1633. Some 100m east of the Ice Centre. On-site CP. Step free access throughout. There is a specially designed mounting block for riders with disabilities. **Wheelchair cubicles (D75 ST75)** in both the gents and the ladies opposite reception.

Middlesex Filter Beds Nature Reserve, south of Lea Bridge Road (A104) not far from Chatsworth Road. *Tel:* Countryside Centre 01992-713838, or the

South Area Ranger Base 0181 533-6937. There is a CP behind the *Prince of Wales* pub giving step free access to the towpath. All paths are surfaced, and ramps are provided along the 500m route. Panels describe the natural, industrial and archaelogical history of the Beds. Described by our surveyors as 'lovely!' Nearest adapted loo in the Ice Centre.

Mid-valley, between Chingford and Edmonton. Picketts Lock area.

Picketts Lock (Lee Valley) Sports & Leisure Centre, Picketts Lock Lane, Edmonton E9 *Tel:* 0181 345-6666. Off Meridian Way. The centre is signed from the North Circular Road (A406), and is close to Ponders End.

There's a whole range of facilities, including practically every sports activity you can think of, a UCI cinema with twelve screens, restaurants and a camping site. The London Hawks Sports Club for disabled people meets on Friday evenings, and there are a considerable number of events that disabled people can readily join in. Spectator events include sports competitions, dog and cat shows, fashion shows and concert and variety shows. Huge on-site CP, including some twenty-five OB spaces close to the entrance.

Flat main entrance into the main foyer with an information desk. Lift (D80 W130 L130) goes to all floors. The *Oasis restaurant* is step free from the foyer.

The swimming pool is reached via –6 steps, bypassed by using the lift. Family changing cubicle has D60 W125 L125 (note that the door is quite narrow for a chair). There's an **adapted loo (D75 ST95 but with an inward opening door)** in the changing area. A portable hydraulic lift *(not seen by our survey team)* is available to help people in and out of the pool, but there is no ramped or stepped access into the water. The Great Hall is –28 from the foyer, but can be accessed from the lift. There are **wheelchair cubicles (D90 ST80) in both gents and ladies loos** at this level. The snooker room is +8, with a ramped bypass but D67cm. **Bodylines Gym** is +16 from the foyer, with ramped bypass.

The UCI cinema is about 30m from the main entrance (see section on *Cinemas*). **Wheelchair loo (D90 ST80)** at the bar and restaurant by the petrol filling station next to the cinema. Also on-site is a *Deep Pan Pizza* restaurant which has step free access and a **wheelchair loo (D85 ST75).**

North of the M25

Lee Valley Park Countryside Centre, Abbey Gardens, Waltham Abbey, Essex EN9 1XQ *Tel:* 01992-713838. Situated inside the Waltham Abbey grounds, the entrance is off the roundabout where Sewardstone Road (A112) meets the Crooked Mile (B194), and also Parklands. The Abbey Gardens consist of a small orchard, a moat and grass areas with picnic tables.

On-site CP about 80m from the Centre with five OB spaces. Flat main entrance and step free access via ramps to meeting rooms. Information centre and shop on the GF. **Wheelchair loo (D80 ST70) behind the information point. Note that arrangements may be made at the Centre for making wheelchair access possible in various parts of the Lee Valley Park.**

⌈P⌉ ⌈M⌉ ⌈&⌉ ⌈&⌉ wc

Waltham Abbey Church, Church Street, Waltham Abbey, Essex. About 300m from the Countryside Centre described above. Flat access to a gate where there is +1–1 step, but this can be bypassed if another door is opened for you. Step free access inside, but –8 to the crypt, and Visitors' Centre. **Wheelchair cubicles (gents D95 ST120, and ladies D95 ST120)** in the toilets just opposite the church.

⌈P⌉ ⌈A⌉ ◢ E2 ⌈&⌉ 80% ⌈&⌉ wc

Lee Valley Park Farms, Hays Hill Farm, Stubbins Hall Lane, Holyfield, Waltham Abbey, Essex *Tel:* 01992-892291 (weekdays) 01992-892781 (weekends). CP about 100m away, and then there's a steepish slope up to the farm. There is a wide variety of cattle, sheep, pigs, goats, poultry and rabbits, including a few rare breeds. The shop and information point both have +1 step. **Adapted loo (D85 ST75 but obstructed by fixed rail).** There's also a picnic area.

⌈P⌉ ⌈H⌉ ⌈&⌉ 70% ⌈wc⌉

Leisure Pool, Old Nazeing Road, Broxbourne Herts *Tel:* 01992-446677. Just off the B194 Nazeing New Road. On-site CP. The main entrance is some 100m via a ramp (bypassing steps), and the foyer has step free access to a café, a poolside balcony, and beauty treatment rooms. The pool is reached by lift (D100 W150 L150). There is an alternative flat (and shorter) route if you go to the double-doors at the foot of the steps between the CP and the main entrance. This entrance is normally locked, so you either have to ring first, or get someone to 'alert' the staff of your need.

The pool level is flat. There are changing rooms for disabled swimmers on your right as you come out of the lift. There are two **adapted loos (D74 ST40)** at this level. During the summer there is access to an outdoor area, and it is possible to get there step free through a door by the entrance to the disabled changing room. The GF also contains a wet sauna (+1 step D62cm) and a dry sauna (+1+1 D53cm). The jacuzzi is +6.

⌈P⌉ ⌈A⌉ ⌈↑↓⌉ ⌈&⌉ 70% ⌈wc⌉

Boat Centre, Old Nazeing Road, Broxbourne, Herts *Tel:* 01992-462085. As implied, this is a centre for boat hire, and there's nothing quite so relaxing as a trip on the river. Our group has enjoyed several such trips in the past, and

Lee Valley

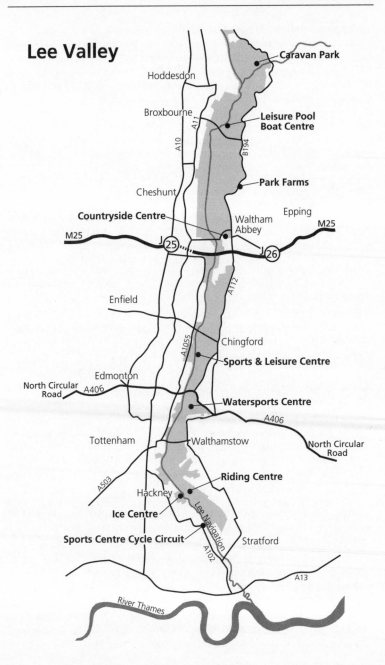

with judicious choice of boat, it is possible to ease possible access problems. There's a fully adapted passenger vessel with an adapted loo called the *Lady of Lee Valley* which does regular short trips, and may be available for hire as well. It is said to have a lift on board to facilitate access, and sounds really good. It was not there when we surveyed. **Adapted loo (D75 ST75 but partly obstructed by a fixed rail)** in the *Crown* pub about 100m away. This has a ramped entrance on the left side, although there's a split level of –3 to part of the GF bar. There's another **wheelchair loo (D80 ST75 NKS)** at the Old Mill and Meadows site about 200m away along the towpath. At this site there are four riverside chalets for hire. One is adapted for chair users with a shallow ramp at the front. See chapter on *Accommodation*.

[P] [&] [WC]

Rye House Gatehouse, and Marsh Nature Reserve, Rye Road, Hoddesdon, Herts *Tel:* 01992-713838. The gatehouse is a 15thC moated building. CP with two OB spaces. Access inside involves +23 spiralled steps to a first floor exhibition and then a further +31 to the roof. The Nature Reserve is run by the Royal Society for the Protection of Birds (RSPB), and has an information centre open every weekend (01992-460031). Most of the paths are well surfaced. There's a wheelchair accessible bird hide on the site overlooking the lake and marsh. It is possible to arrange similar facilities on the nearby Thames Water Sewage Works. **Wheelchair cubicles in both ladies and gents (D80+ ST110+)** in the loos across the road from the main CP.

[P] Gatehouse [◢] N54 Reserve [&] 80% [&] WC

Dobbs Weir Caravan Park, see *Accommodation* chapter.

Opportunities for fishing – angling sites with step free access.
There are areas allocated for fishing throughout the Lee Valley Park. All the normal regulations apply, which you will know about if you fish regularly. You need an NRA Rod Licence, for example. There are eleven species to be caught. A special permit for anglers with disabilities is available from the Countryside Centre, and for specific enquiries about fishing, phone 01992-893345 to speak to the head of fisheries. The Countryside Centre publishes an excellent leaflet summarising where the sites are, and what you can catch, and there are fuller details in the information pack mentioned at the start of the Lee Valley write-up.

If you need to get any gates unlocked so that you can get your car nearer to a particular site, contact the Countryside Centre in Waltham Abbey. There will be local rangers who can organise this. We looked at several sites, but bear in mind that some are quite large. There are some allocated angling stances' near to parking, but it will depend on what you want to do, and how much effort is involved, as you may wish to go further up the bank, or to another part of the gravel pit. By far the best thing is to talk to the experts in the Countryside Centre.

Entertainment

The chapter is split into sections on:

Arts centres where there are several adjacent facilities
Cinemas
Music venues, and
Theatres, divided into:
   central
   others inside the north/south circular roads, and
   outside the north/south circular roads.

Much of the information was originally gathered by Artsline with whom we have worked closely. For the central London theatres, there are location maps readily available, and most London guides have one. **The Society of London Theatre (SOLT),** Bedford Chambers, The Piazza, Covent Garden WC2E 8HQ publishes a fortnightly *London Theatre Guide* which includes a detailed location map. SOLT were partners, with Artsline, in producing the *Disabled Access Guide to London's West End Theatres* which will be regularly updated.

Artsline (*Tel:* 0171 388-2227) should be able to provide additional and updated information about most venues if you have further queries. They will also have (or be able to get) information about signed performances, concessionary prices, and whether or not guide dogs can be admitted to the auditorium. The staff have lots of experience and are interesting people to talk to.

Gaining access to entertainment in London is getting easier, and the situation has improved considerably since our last survey in 1988. Surveyors were frequently given a friendly welcome and were often impressed by the good intentions of theatre staff. This is partly due to visits over the years by Artsline staff.

Difficulties can arise, as box office staff are sometimes temporary employees. However, people are generally more aware than they were a few years ago. Although many house managers move around quite frequently, they are still the best people to negotiate with if you have special requirements. One tip when making arrangements by phone, is always to find out who you are talking to. It's so much more convincing to say *'Mr Thomas told me that…',* than it is to say, *'Someone said…'*.

The safety regulations governing the admission of chair users seem sometimes to have been formulated a little too officiously and specifically, as the chair user can be identified, whereas other people causing risk can't. **The licence arrangements are in fact the result of negotiation between venue owners, fire officers, licencing authority and management.** The criteria result from the application of conditions such as 'it should be possible to evacuate the entire building in three minutes (or some specific limit)'. The management view on what is possible plays a large part in determining what is imposed. In both

London Disability News and *Disability Now* the Fire Brigades Union fire safety adviser was recently quoted as saying that the decision about access rests effectively with the venue owner, and is in a sense a purely financial one. It was suggested that licensing authorities use excuses about fire regulations to hide their inaction in encouraging managers and owners to provide access, by making it a licence condition. Looking through the results of our survey, there would appear to be many anomalies. Accessibility on the day depends on the staff and managers on duty, and it may depend on whether the auditorium is full or not. The rules, however, are important and the manager has the right to refuse admission, and his licence may be at risk.

Note that special booking and seating arrangements cannot normally be made through ticket agencies. The Stoll Moss group, however, have a central booking system which is not an 'agency' like Ticketmaster, and booking through Stoll Moss should be secure, provided you make your needs known. **For anyone with special needs, it really is necessary to negotiate access with the venue management when booking and to do it in advance.** This is particularly true in places where seats have to be removed, which takes a little time. Fortunately for theatregoers, the culture is such that booking in advance is quite normal. That is not quite so true for cinemas, where people are more used to taking decisions on the spur of the moment.

Many venues provide for people who have impaired hearing, and have induction loops or Sennheiser infrared systems. Commonly there is good reception for both induction loops and infrared systems in only part of the auditorium. There is sometimes a problem with the output from loops overlapping between screens in a cinema, so that you see one film and hear the soundtrack of another. It is usually possible to get round this by moving to a different seat, but it may be that the loop needs adjustment, and you will have to ask the staff. Try to get it 'tuned' during the adverts before the main film if necessary. There are occasional signed performances for deaf people; both Artsline and the venue concerned will have details.

A few venues are no longer making it a condition of entry that a chair user should be accompanied, although many still do. It may be a condition attached to their licence. Ask the venue and/or Artsline. Quite often disabled people need to sit in the most expensive part of the auditorium. For people who are partially sighted it is normally best to sit at the front of the stalls, and chair users have to use the 'chair spaces' provided. Many venues offer concessionary prices because of this. Concessions for disabled walkers are not as common as for chair users. Pensioners can often go to some matinee performances at reduced rates. Many venues admit chair users and/or registered disabled patrons at a reduced price. **Artsline** will advise. We have not attempted to cover this, as concessions may vary at different performances in the same venue. In parallel with the variable cost is the fact that your special requirements preclude a wider choice of seat. In several venues the chair spaces provide only a restricted view, or are at the very front. Because of difficulties of classification in the theatres listing, we have taken the following postal districts as being central: EC1, EC4, SE1, W1, W2, WC1 and WC2. As elsewhere in the guide we have not generally tried to describe parking for central venues. Note that with phone numbers, BO means box office and M management. RecM indicates that there is a recorded message about programmes. If you have problems check the number in the phone book or in *Time Out*.

In our descriptions we have described the relation between the auditorium and the street level by which you would normally arrive. Quite a few theatres have the circle at street level, so you go down to the stalls and up to the upper circle. Fringe theatres and music venues are highly variable. Some are in a room over a pub, with only stepped access. Where possible, we've described their physical layout.

Arts centres

Many sites and venues have multiple functions – and include a cinema, theatre and a display space for exhibitions. The South Bank has about ten important venues and a major museum, all in the same area, and it seems sensible to list these together. The Barbican centre similarly has several venues and exhibition spaces, this time in one building. Some arts centres are smaller, but you'll find several facilities, often with a place to eat and, probably, parking space. Many of the buildings are relatively modern, or have been well adapted.

We describe the South Bank group of venues first, with the National Theatre and Festival Hall among other places, then we describe the Barbican, followed by Croydon. Finally we list the smaller centres in alphabetical order.

South Bank Complex

This includes the National Theatre, Festival Hall (RFH1), National Film Theatre, Hayward Gallery and the Museum of the Moving Image. The National Theatre has the Olivier, Lyttleton and Cottesloe auditoria, and there's the Queen Elizabeth (RFH2) and Purcell (RFH3) concert halls as well. It's a huge concentration of arts related venues on a site overlooking the Thames on either side of Waterloo Bridge.

Some of it was built for the Festival of Britain in 1951, so it is remarkable that the Festival Hall (in particular) incorporated a substantial number of chair spaces, since access and disability issues were not much thought about at that time. The riverside frontage is attractive, and there is now a riverside walk which stretches from County Hall (currently being developed into an Aquarium, among other things) under Hungerford and Waterloo bridges, right through to Blackfriars bridge and beyond.

There is an UGCP under the National Theatre with lift access to the ground level, and to upper levels which is probably the best place to park. While there are other CPs in the area this is particularly convenient. There are OB spaces in the road in front of both the National Theatre and the Festival Hall.

To get there from Waterloo station, (a rather vital route, as Waterloo has step free access), use the main central exit opposite platform twelve and by the clock. Turn left, down the pavement past the main station steps. There are steps down to a subway, with a lift by-pass. However, the lift has has a very poor record of availability, and is often not working. *Planners should note that the provision of a lift doesn't always solve access problems. There were other possible 'solutions' here, and simpler ones.* If the lift doesn't work, and you cannot manage the steps, then either go judiciously down the hill towards York Road on the road, or use a longer route (slightly safer) alongside the International Station. This brings you out at the end of Belvedere Road. Both routes involve using the road, and the direct route is more difficult because there are railings along the pavement for much of the way. In York Road, use the crossing by Lloyds bank, and turn right, then left under the railway arches. This takes you into Concert Hall Approach and the GF foyer of the Festival Hall. The National Theatre is further along the river to your right. The distance from the station to the Hall is about 500m. All other exits from Waterloo involve steps, except the very long ramp to the right towards Westminster. If you used that it would be well over 1km to the Festival Hall. Bearing in mind the distance and the problems with the lift, it might be worth taking a taxi, even though it's a relatively short distance.

How to get around:

At ground level, the Riverside Walk links to level one of the Festival Hall, via a gentle ramp. It links directly with flat access to the NFT restaurant and the NFT1 cinema. It also links to the MOMI, via the road, and to the GF of the National Theatre, including the Cottesloe, around the corner.

The upper level links across to the first floor of the National Theatre, and gives access to the main concourse of the Festival Hall (level two), the Hayward Gallery, the Purcell Room and the main entrance to the Queen Elizabeth Hall (although not the chair users entrance, which is at ground level opposite the MOMI).

It is one of those typical nonsenses that you need to take the lift in the National Theatre to the first floor, or in the Festival Hall to level two.

Venue details:

Hayward Gallery, South Bank Centre, Belvedere Road SE1 *Tel:* 0171 928-3144. CP underneath in Belvedere Road with a large lift for disabled visitors and an intercom. Our experience was that you don't always get an answer. Alternatively, access is step free from the RFH1, level two, or from the first floor of the National Theatre. The main entrance is flat, and +1 −12 steps on the lower floor has a ramped bypass. The gallery is basically on two levels, linked by a lift (D108 L300 W150). Other places nearby have **wheelchair loos**.

The South Bank Complex

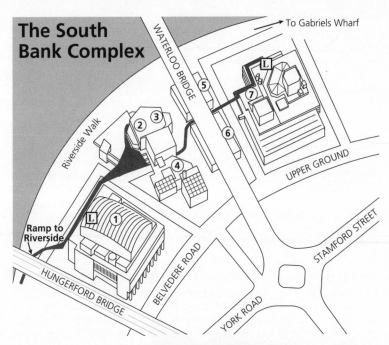

Ramp to Riverside

To Gabriels Wharf

WATERLOO BRIDGE

Riverside Walk

UPPER GROUND

STAMFORD STREET

BELVEDERE ROAD

YORK ROAD

HUNGERFORD BRIDGE

① Royal Festival Hall **RFH1**
② Queen Elizabeth Hall **RFH2**
   (Main entrance, upper level
   Wheelchair access, ground level)
③ Purcell **RFH3** (upper level)
④ Hayward Gallery (upper level)
⑤ National Film Theatre
⑥ Museum of the Moving Image
⑦ Royal National Theatre

━━━━ Step free access at
      upper level
- - - - Step free routes to and
      from Waterloo
☐L☐ Lift

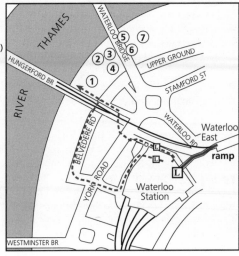

THAMES

RIVER

WATERLOO BRIDGE

HUNGERFORD BR

UPPER GROUND

STAMFORD ST

BELVEDERE RD

YORK ROAD

WATERLOO RD

Waterloo East

ramp

Waterloo Station

WESTMINSTER BR

Museum of the Moving Image (MOMI) South Bank Centre SE1 *Tel:* 0171 928-3535. Museum detailing the history of film and television from Javanese Shadow Theatre to Satellite Television. Interesting and well presented. Situated under Waterloo Bridge it is part of the NFT complex, and is best approached from the Festival Hall. There are +14 steps to the box office, then –18 to the beginning of the exhibition. Both can be bypassed by a ramp from the entrance. There is a help point, and staff are normally nearby. The museum is on two floors, and follows a chronological route. Access for disabled visitors involves a number of platform stairlifts and some circumnavigation, but 95% has step free access. It is possible to follow the first 70% chronologically. There are help points, and actors at various places to assist. The MOMI cinema has chair spaces in the front row. To record an interview with Barry Norman there is +1 and a gap of 70cm. To reach the shop there is either –14 or +6. The shop in the NFT nearby has flat access and stocks many of the same products. There is a **wheelchair cubicle in the gents (D78 ST90) and an adapted one in the ladies (D78 ST57).** Both are at the beginning of the exhibits. Audio cassette guides are available.

National Film Theatre (NFT), South Bank SE1 *Tel:* BO 0171 928-3232 M 0171 815-1347. There are two entrances, and two cinemas (NFT1 and NFT2). One entrance is the same as MOMI and leads to the box office and NFT2. The other entrance is on the riverside, under Waterloo bridge. Inside the building there is a split level with ±8 steps. To get to NFT1 from the box office you either have to use the steps, or go right round the outside of the building (about 100m) and use the step free route through the restaurant. There is a **wheelchair loo (D75 ST70)** just to the left after you have gone down the passage towards NFT1. At the lower level there's a large **adapted loo (D70 ST0)** to the right of reception, 10m down the corridor. The ST0 (no space for side transfer) is because of a vertical pole placed immediately adjacent to the WC. NFTI has two chair spaces and there are transfer possibilities in both cinemas. Induction loops in both cinemas.

National Theatre, South Bank SE1 *Tel:* BO 0171 928-2252; RecM 0171 633-0880; M 0171 928-2033; *Minicom:* 0171 620-0741. The complex contains an UGCP, three theatres, bars, buffets, a restaurant, a bookshop, and a GF foyer with temporary exhibitions and free evening performances. An *Access Guide* is available with an excellent cut-away diagram. OB holders have free parking if using the UGCP: get your ticket stamped at the venue you are visiting. The **Lyttelton/Olivier** main entrance is at ground (riverside) level facing the river. The **Cottesloe** theatre entrance is some 80m round the corner of the building. In the main building the levels are connected by lifts (D100 W210 L160), including the UGCP and the upper walkway. Some parts of the building can only be reached by steps. **All three theatres have infrared hearing systems covering all seats, and headsets for people with a hearing aid T switch.**

Olivier, The box office is on a mezzanine, reached via +11 steps from level one or –23 from level two. You can arrange to pick up Olivier tickets at the Lyttelton box office on the GF. The theatre is an amphitheatre is on two levels, linked by the main lifts. Three chair spaces in the rear stalls. **Wheelchair loo (D80 ST75)** outside the rear stalls.

Lyttelton, Box office and foyer on the GF. A traditional proscenium arch theatre, also on two levels. Flat access to rear stalls where there are four chair spaces. **Wheelchair loo (D90 ST85)** off the foyer, next to the ladies. To the right of this, there is a lift (D75 W115 L90) to the circle (level one), bypassing +22.

Cottesloe, Ramped entrance, bypassing +5, 100m to the left of the Olivier/Lyttelton main entrance. Flat to foyer and box office. A small studio-style theatre where a variety of layouts are used. The auditorium has three seating levels. It is flat from the foyer to two chair spaces, and six possible transfer seats. There are steps to both higher and lower seating levels. **Adapted loo (D65 ST80)** on the right inside front entrance.

In the National Theatre, the **Mezzanine restaurant** is –13 steps from level one, but a platform stairlift was installed in 1995. The alternative is to use a kitchen service lift (D111 W150 L145). Ask at the GF information desk. **Wheelchair loo (D85 ST95)** level with the restaurant. The **Terrace Café** is on level two with flat access via the small lift (D74 W119 L90) off the Lyttelton foyer, (near ladies loos on GF). There is –1 to the outdoor tables on the terrace. The **Lyttelton Long Bar** is on the GF with flat access and sometimes has free entertainment of one kind or another, often prior to evening performances.

The south bank concert halls are RFH1, RFH2 and RFH3. An *Access Guide* is available:

Royal Festival Hall (RFH1), South Bank Centre SE1 *Tel:* BO 0171 928-8800 M 0171 921-0639. There are OB parking spaces on the road by the riverside entrance to the Hall. Step free access both from riverside level, and from the upper walkway. The box office is to the left of the riverside entrance. There is a single lift linking the riverside level with the main concourse and auditorium. It was out of action when we surveyed. Bypassing it involved going round the building to the stage door and using a service lift (D300 W300 L300).

From the main concourse (level two, upper walkway level) there are three large lifts (D170 W170 L220) up to most of the auditorium. To get to levels three and four without steps there are two smaller lifts (D80 W160 L90). One is just past the cloakroom on level two, and the other is behind a small bar on the other side of the concourse. There are chair spaces with flat access in the balcony (level five) and terrace (level four). Level five is reached using the large lifts. To get to level four use the smaller (separate) ones. Row AA has the most leg room. On most floors the lifts lead to split levels and steps to the auditorium. Twin track Sennheiser system.

On the main concourse, there are free music and dance performances at various times, a bookshop, bar (–4 steps), and several food counters. The new restaurant on level three can only be accessed without steps using the smaller lift by the cloakroom. The lift is on the right of the building (looking from the riverside). **Wheelchair loos (D85+ ST80+)** on levels one, three and five. On level one, by the riverside, turn to the right as you come in through the main doors, and the loo is on the left opposite the lift.

Queen Elizabeth Hall (RFH2), South Bank Centre SE1 *Tel:* BO 0171 928-8800 M 0171 921-0639. Main entrance on the upper walkway level, and from the foyer, there are –11 steps to the hall. Access for people with disabilities is via the Artists' entrance at Riverside/Belvedere Road level opposite MOMI. This gives step free access via a large lift to five chair spaces. **Wheelchair loo (D80 ST75)** by the Artists' entrance. Row AA has good leg room. Twin track Sennheiser system in the front stalls.

Purcell Room (RFH3), South Bank Centre SE1 *Tel:* BO 0171 928-8800 M 0171 921-0639. Entrance on the upper walkway level. The QEH and Purcell Room share the same entrance. Then +4 steps bypassed by a platform stairlift. There are two chair spaces, and good legroom in rows A and D. The nearest **wheelchair loo** is on the riverside level of the Festival Hall. Induction loop.

The Barbican
Barbican Centre, Silk Street EC2 *Tel:* BO 0171 638-8891 *Minicom:* 0171 382-7297; M 0171 638-4141; Restaurant *(*Searcy's brasserie*)* 0171 588-3008; Library 0171 638-0569.
   The centre is in the north-east corner of the City in a complex which includes hundreds of flats, the Guildhall School of Music and Drama, and two Exhibition Halls. It is surrounded by a large pedestrian area on two levels which now has much improved maps at all the entry points. Car and taxi access is from Silk Street.

While this modern centre for theatre, concerts, cinema and art exhibitions was opened in 1982, access was considered only after all the main design parameters were fixed. There have been recent improvements, but it's an extremely confusing building. Signposting inside is not at all clear, and we found that the new plans and listings, which have been put in strategic places to clarify things, were cluttered, and contained far too much information. *A guide for disabled visitors is available,* and there is a cut-away diagram of each floor in the Barbican Centre Pocket Guide.
   The centre provides unique facilities. It is compact, and there are lots of things to see and do. If you follow certain basic principles, virtually everywhere can be reached reasonably easily, and the management have gone to some lengths to overcome the design shortcomings.

Parking in CP3, curently entered off Silk Street. The CP4 and CP5 are approached off Beech Street. They all form a multi-storey stack, and are linked by lift E. From the bottom level CP3, you come out, on level –1, and can go directly to the theatre and concert hall foyer. Signing is poor. From the top level, CP5, you can come out on the lakeside on level 0, and can enter the building near the *Waterside Café*. Again, signing is poor. From the OB spaces, go directly away from lift E, and find an exit to your left. There are plans to 'integrate' the three CPs, and possibly to have only one entrance and exit. For OB holders there are three spaces in CP5 and thirteen in CP3. Take your parking ticket and get it stamped at the venue you are visiting, to waive the parking charge.

Getting there by foot is now somewhat easier. There are good maps at each of the fourteen gates to the upper podium, five of which have ramps. See the write-up in *Recommended itineraries*. There is a step free route from the Museum of London over the upper podium.

Barbican Centre
The key links

w = wheelchair

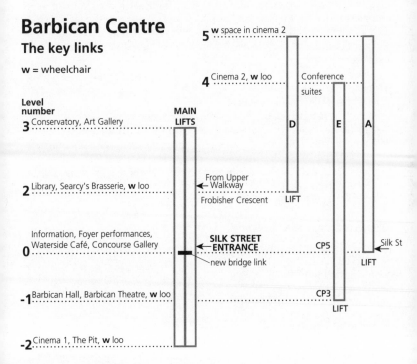

Level number

5 — **w** space in cinema 2

4 — Cinema 2, **w** loo — Conference suites

3 — Conservatory, Art Gallery — **MAIN LIFTS** — D — E — A

2 — Library, Searcy's Brasserie, **w** loo — From Upper Walkway / Frobisher Crescent — LIFT

0 — Information, Foyer performances, Waterside Café, Concourse Gallery — **SILK STREET ENTRANCE** — new bridge link — CP5 — Silk St — LIFT

-1 — Barbican Hall, Barbican Theatre, **w** loo — CP3 — LIFT

-2 — Cinema 1, The Pit, **w** loo

The main entrance to the centre is at the junction of Silk Street and Whitecross Street. Unfortunately, it is a bit of a mess. Even if you arrive in Silk Street right opposite it you can be confused. To the left is a road leading down into the building which is the route down to CP3. To the right is a two-lane covered road. Signs saying Main Entrance are not prominent. Follow the two-lane 'road' about 30m, apparently into the building, and then the main door is on your left. There's a plan and listing just outside. Go through the doors, and you are on level 0, the main GF level. In front of you is the new bridge link (an enormous improvement) which gives flat access to the main foyer and to the lifts. To your right is the ticket office and information desk, and there is a platform stairlift to bypass the –8 steps.

Since the building is big, it is important that you know where you want to go and how to get there. The diagram accompanying this section indicates where the various facilities are. People with disabilities are basically dependent on the four main lifts (D105 W160 L150), which are grouped together. By sticking to these lifts you can probably avoid getting lost ! It is assumed that you start either on level –1 (CP3 level); on level 0 from the main entrance, now linked to the lifts by a new bridge; on level 0, reached from CP5; or on level 2 from the high-level walkway. For both the Barbican Hall and the Theatre, you need to make your way to level –1 with the main foyer for major performances.

There are **wheelchair loos** on:
- level –2 (**D90 ST70**) close to the lifts;
- level –1, planned, to be sited off the theatre/concert hall foyer;
- inside the theatre area there are two loos (**D75 ST70**) at the circle level. Note that the wheelchair spaces are in the upper circle, one floor higher, so you have to use the lift;
- level 2 (**D90 ST70+**), from the lifts go out to Frobisher Crescent, and it's on your right; and
- level 4 (**D75 ST70**).

Detalis of facilities in the centre:

Barbican Hall, used mainly for concerts. On level –1. Thirteen chair spaces in row U of the stalls reached from level –1. If you arrive by lift you must then cross the service road via a steepish ramp to the kerb. Seats with step free access for disabled walkers are also in Row U. Induction loop.

Barbican Theatre, used mainly by the Royal Shakespeare Company. Foyer on level –1. It has a unique design with most seats reached via stepped access. Four chair spaces in the upper circle on level 0 reached via the internal theatre lift (D79 L95 W110). Each chair position has a device which can lower the floor to improve sight lines. However you are left with a stage view that is slightly obstructed. There is only one row of seats (T) with step free access in the main part of the theatre. It is at the back of the stalls (on level −1) and has a good amount of leg room. The **wheelchair loos** are on the circle level inside the auditorium; to use them during the interval you've got to be pretty quick, as it's down a level. The theatre has a Sennheiser infrared sound system, and headsets can be borrowed.

Pit Theatre and Cinema 1 are on level −2 reached via the main lifts. The **Pit** has one chair space, and step free access to front row seats. In **Cinema 1** there are boxes for two wheelchairs. Induction loop, which does not work in the boxes.

Cinema 2 is on level 4. The foyer can be reached by using the main lifts to level 2 and then lift D from Frobisher Crescent. One chair space on level 5 at the back of the raked auditorium. This is accessed via lift A (D80 W105 L150) either from outside the Silk Street entrance, or from the cinema foyer on level 4. To find the lift at street level you have to go back from the main entrance to Silk Street, and then into the administrative area through the glass panels. The security guard will show you. Induction loop.

Concourse Gallery on level 0, alongside the ticket/information desk just inside the Silk Street entrance. Numerous free exhibitions. Use the platform stairlift to bypass the −8. Alternatively it is step free at the other end from the main GF foyer. Art Gallery on level 3, right by the main lifts. The gallery is on two levels with −56 between them. There are plans to install a platform stair lift during 1995/6. Currently you can use a service lift.

Searcy's brasserie restaurant, near the main lifts on level 2, the library floor. View out over St Giles church and the lake. Flat access.

Conference suites are on level 4 which is a section primarily for private functions and conferences. You can get there from level 2. There are two lifts going to level 4: lift E which you can take from CP3, and lift D which you can take from Frobisher Crescent on level 2.

Library (a public library with a reference section) is on level 2. Flat access. Membership is open to those who live, work or study in the City, and to regular Barbican centre visitors. The Music library is accessed via a platform stairlift, bypassing −22.

Waterside Café is on level 0, with tables and chairs alongside the artificial lake. This is particularly attractive in the summer. The café is buffet-style and serves a variety of food. Flat access, but it can get congested.

Conservatory normally open at weekends and bank holidays. A garden 'in the sky' on level 3, reached via the main lifts. Flat/ramped access through most of the area, although a few narrowish gaps.

In the centre foyer there is a varied programme of free early evening and

Sunday lunchtime concerts, and also occasional exhibitions.

Croydon

Clocktower, Katharine Street, Croydon, Surrey, CR9 *Tel:* 0181 253-1030. The building is joined to the Town Hall and contains a library, cinema, museum, art gallery and music venue. Parking in the Surrey Street CP (entrance on Scarbrook Road), with eight OB spaces.

A ramp to the right of the main entrance bypasses –11 steps to the foyer. On the GF there is Tourist Information, a shop, and a **wheelchair loo (D90 ST85)**. The +3 to the café has a ramped alternative on the right. All floors can be reached by lift (D108 W98 L200+). Second **wheelchair loo (D90 ST80)** on the first floor to the right of the lift.

Library. Entrance from the foyer, then lift (D110 W173 L163) or escalator access between all four floors. **Wheelchair loo (D90 ST75)** on the first floor, and **another (D85 ST80)** on the third floor. Ask at enquiry desk for key.

Riesco Gallery. Step free access from foyer and throughout. Small gallery with permanent exhibitions of pottery and the like. Seats available. **Exhibition Gallery**. Flat access from foyer and throughout. Small gallery with changing exhibitions.

Lifetimes Museum. Small museum situated mainly on the first floor but with a small mezzanine level (+18) which can be reached with staff assistance by lift.

Braithwaite Hall. Step free access from first floor. Small jazz, chamber music and comedy venue.

David Lean Cinema. Flat access from the first floor. Art House film theatre. Removable front row seats which can accommodate three wheelchairs if advance warning given. Infrared hearing units available for hire.

Fairfield, Park Lane, Croydon, Surrey *Tel:* 0181 681-0821 with three major venues. Some parking directly outside the main entrance. Spaces can be reserved. Alternatively UGCP and MSCP signposted from Barclay Road. From UGCP steep ramp bypasses +28 steps to the ground level. From MSCP, lift (D92 W135 L106) from even floors only, gives access to street level. Flat main entrance to the box office. A steep ramp 5m to the right bypasses +6 to restaurant, bar and coffee shop. There are plans to install an open lift. All other floors are reached by lift (D100 W185 L115). **Wheelchair loo (D90 ST140)** on the GF near the restaurant, **another (D82 ST84)** in the ladies on the second floor, and an **adapted cubicle (D82 ST65)** in the gents on the third floor.

Arnheim Gallery. For public functions. Flat from the GF.

Ashcroft Theatre. Three wheelchair spaces in a separate box on the second floor. Circle seats are –2 then –2 for each row. Induction loop.

Fairfield Hall (concert hall). Eight wheelchair spaces on level three with seats in between. Front row of the lower stalls (level two) has step free access, as do the front six rows on level one. Sennheiser system.

Other arts centres

BAC, Old Town Hall, Lavender Hill, Battersea SW11 *Tel:* BO 0171 223-2223 M 0171 223-6557 *Minicom:* 0171 223-5311. Located by the junction with Theatre Street. Parking congested. Ramped entrance, bypassing +4 steps. It's an old Town Hall with a grand entrance and staircase. There are several performance areas, some accessed by lift (D75 W100 L140). Café and bar on the GF. There are +3+12+11 to the first floor, then more to the theatre but then step free via the lift and stage. Up to ten chair spaces. Both Studios one and two have step free access, and up to eight chair spaces if seats are removed. The gallery for exhibitions of pictures, photography and sculpture is on the first floor, with step free access. **Adapted loos** on either side of the main stairs, **gents (D67 ST74) ladies (D72 ST60),** both on the GF.

ICA (Institute of Contemporary Arts), The Mall SW1 *Tel:* 0171 930-3647. Modern gallery with changing exhibitions, films, and productions reflecting current ideas and themes. Flat entrance gives access to box office, shop and restaurant, the last of which has fixed chairs and tables, and pillars which partially block access to the food counter. The bar has +10 steps. The shop is flat but cramped. The +30 steps to Gallery one, can be bypassed by a small lift (D52 W89 L80). Gallery two is –7 from the GF. **Wheelchair loo (D86 ST87)** on the left by the entrance. At the time of writing a ramp is being built giving access to the theatre, bypassing +9. A further ramp is scheduled to be built to bypass +3 to reach the cinema and a smaller studio, both of which have two chair spaces. Other plans include the provision of a lift to bypass the –7 to Gallery two.

Riverside Studios, Crisp Road, Hammersmith W6 *Tel:* BO 0181 741-2255 M 0181 741-2251. An active fringe theatre in an old warehouse. Close to Hammersmith Broadway where there are CPs. Parking near the theatre can be congested. Hammersmith tube station has lift access from platform to pavement, and is about 400m away. Flat to the foyer and café. Studios one and two have flat/ramped access to the front row. The ramp bypasses +2 steps from the foyer. Studio three and the cinema are both about +45. There are normally chair spaces in Studios one and two, and there's a **wheelchair loo (D70+ ST70+)** just by the ramp from the foyer.

Watermans Arts Centre, 40 High Street, Brentford, Middx *Tel:* BO 0181 568-1176 M 0181 847-5651. The centre has a theatre, cinema, gallery and open performing space, bar and café. It is by the junction with the South Ealing Road, and overlooks the Thames. On-site UGCP with three OB spaces. The centre is on several levels. There is a flat entrance from the CP mid-level, near two of the OB spaces, but this is sometimes locked. The main entrance at an upper level can be reached up a ramp, and is some 80m from street level. From here there is a lift (D80 W90 L125) down to the main level. There is step free access throughout with ramps to bypass the split levels.

The theatre has four chair spaces. The cinema has ten. The bar and café are fully accessible, and there is an outside eating area and riverside balcony. There are even two small open lifts to get you over the 75cm wall to the outside balcony eating area. This is a unique installation, with one on each side of the flood prevention wall ! Induction loop in both the cinema and theatre. **Wheelchair loo (D75 ST75)** up the ramp and past the bar and theatre entrance.

Cinemas

Since the guide was last published, provisions at cinemas have improved enormously. Initially it was the UCI group who introduced multi-screen cinemas with chair spaces in every screen and step free access. MGM (now Virgin) also have accessible multi-screen cinemas. Recently it has been the Warner Brothers (WB) who have set the pace and standard, and their Leicester Square cinema, and the ones in Croydon, Park Royal and at Lakeside Thurrock are brilliant in every way. They are unequalled from an access viewpoint. Warner Brothers are planning new complexes in Dagenham, Finchley and Harrow (in St George's Leisure Centre), so that in a year or so's time there will be WB cinemas all round London. Add to that the UCI multiscreen cinemas at Whiteleys (Queensway), Lee Valley and Sutton; the MGMs at Staples Corner and the Trocadero, and it is clear that things are improving. Other cinemas also have really good access, such as the Premier in Peckham and the Rio in Kingsland. New UCI complexes are planned to open in Croydon Palace and Surrey Quays during 1997.

There are still problems because of the number of older 1930s cinemas which have been converted into several screens. The 'main' screen is often in the circle of the old cinema and accessed only by steps, often 30+. However, a good number of the GF screens (usually two and three) have chair spaces with flat access, or via a few steps, possibly through a side exit.

We have listed cinemas by location and name, putting the 'chain' name after, where applicable. Cinemas do change their numbers and booking arrangements from time to time. If you have trouble check in *Time Out* or with another cinema in the chain. Note that *The Reel Guide* was published by Artsline early in 1996, and this includes additional details about London's cinemas.

The main chains are:

Cannon and MGM/Virgin, Head Office, 84 Regent Street W1 *Tel:* 0171 915-1717. Note that MGM were taken over by Virgin in 1995, so the office may move.

Odeon Cinemas, Head Office, 439 Godstone Road, Whyteleafe, Surrey CR3 0YG *Tel:* 01883-623355.

United Cinemas International (UCI), Head Office, Lee House, 90 Bridgewater Street, Manchester M1 5JW *Tel:* 0161-4554000.

Warner Brothers, Head Office, 135 Wardour Street W1 *Tel:* 0171 437-5600

An increasing number of cinemas are using automatic computerised booking systems via the phone, where you can pay for your ticket by credit card and simply collect it on arrival. Some have an enquiry method for disabled patrons which puts you through to the management to make necessary arrangements.

Cinemas with access problems, involving 10+ steps to all screens are listed below:

Baker Street (MGM), Station Approach, Marylebone Road NW1 *Tel:* RecM 0171 935-9772 M 0171 224-0312.

Baker Street (Screen On), 96/98 Baker Street W1 *Tel:* 0171 935-2772.

Cannon Ionic, 612 Finchley Road, Golders Green NW11 *Tel:* 0181 455-1724.

Chelsea Cinema, 206 Kings Road SW3 *Tel:* 0171 351-3743.

Chelsea (MGM), 279 Kings Road SW3 *Tel:* 0171 376-4744.

Coronet, Notting Hill Gate W11 *Tel:* 0171 727-6705.

Curzon Mayfair, 38 Curzon Street W1 *Tel:* BO 0171 369-1720 M 0171 495-1722.

Curzon Phoenix, Phoenix Street, off Charing Cross Road WC2 *Tel:* 0171 369-1733.

Curzon West End, 93 Shaftesbury Avenue W1 *Tel:* RecM 0171 369-1722 M 0171 439-4805.

Ealing (Cannon), Northfield Avenue, West Ealing W13 *Tel:* 0181 567-1075.

French Institute, 17 Queensbury Place SW7 *Tel:* 0171 589-6211.

Harrow (Cannon), Station Road, Harrow, Middlesex *Tel:* 0181 427-1743.

Haymarket (MGM), Haymarket SW1 *Tel:* RecM 0171 839-1527 M 0171 839-1528.

Haymarket (Odeon), 48 Haymarket SW1 *Tel:* RecM 0426-915353 BO/M 0171 930-0365.

London Film Makers Co-op, 42 Gloucester Avenue NW1 *Tel:* BO 0171 586-8516 M 0171586-4806.

Odeon (Marble Arch), 10 Edgware Road, Marble Arch W2 *Tel:* RecM 0426-914501 M 0171 723-2011.

Minema, 45 Knightsbridge SW1 *Tel:* BO 0171 235-4225 M 0171 235-4226.

Phoenix, 52 High Road, East Finchley N2 *Tel:* RecM 0181 883-2233 BO/M 0181 444-6789.

Piccadilly (MGM), Piccadilly W1 *Tel:* RecM 0171 437-3561 BO/M 0171 287-4322.

Renoir, Brunswick Shopping Centre, Brunswick Square WC1 *Tel:* 0171 837-8402.

Shaftesbury Avenue (MGM), 135 Shaftesbury Avenue WC2 *Tel:* RecM 0171 836-6279 BO 0171 836-8606.

Tottenham Court Road (MGM), 30 Tottenham Court Road W1 *Tel:* RecM 0171 636-6148 BO 0181 970-6032 M 0171 636-6749.

West End (Odeon), 40 Leicester Square WC2 *Tel:* RecM 0426-915574 BO 0171 930-7615 M 0171 930-4994.

Central London and inside the N/S circular roads

Barbican Cinema see section on *Arts centres*.

Clapham Picture House, 76 Venn Street, Clapham Common SW4 *Tel:* RecM 0171 498-2242 BO 0171 498-3323 M 0171 627-2120. 100m from Clapham Common tube. Flat entrance, and step free to screens two and three, each with four chair spaces. Screen one has +26 steps and transfer seats. **Adapted loo (D85 ST68)** in the foyer.

Coronet, Turnpike Parade, Turnpike Lane N8 *Tel:* 0181 888-2519. 100m from Turnpike Lane tube station. Entrance +1 step, then flat to screens two and three. Each have four chair spaces. Screen one +18.

Electric Cinema, 191 Portobello Road W10 *Tel:* M 0171 792-2020. Near the junction with Cobble Terrace. Entrance +2 steps. Fire exit to the right of the main entrance gives step free access to screen. Up to four chair users can transfer or stay in the aisle.

Elephant & Castle (Coronet), New Kent Road SE1 *Tel:* RecM 0171 703-4968 M 0171 708-0066. Adjacent to the shopping centre. CP in the centre. Entrance +4 steps. Screens two and three have flat access from the foyer. Two chair spaces in each. Screen one involves over 20 steps.

Empire, Leicester Square WC2 *Tel:* RecM 0171 437-1234 M 0171 734-7123. One of London's premier cinemas. Three screens. Main entrance +14 steps, but there's an alternative for screen one (with six chair spaces) via a steep ramp accessed from Leicester Street. Screen two has +35 and screen three –48. Induction loop in all screens. **Wheelchair loo (D80 ST90)** off the main foyer, level with screen one, step free if you have come up the ramp.

Everyman, Holly Bush Vale, Hampstead NW3 *Tel:* 0171 435-1525. Entrance +3+5 steps then +8 to the auditorium. Side exit allows step free access into the auditorium. One chair space and four transfer spaces.

Finchley (Phoenix), High Road, East Finchley N2 *Tel:* BO 0181 883-2233 M 0181 444-6789. By the junction with Fairlawn Avenue. From street level +3 steps to BO then +8 to kiosk, then +13 to the auditorium. The stairs take you into the back of the cinema. Step free access via an exit in Fairlawn Avenue. Three chair spaces at the front.

Fulham Road (MGM), 142 Fulham Road SW10 *Tel:* 0171 370-2110. Near the junction with Drayton Gardens. Limited on-site parking on request. Entrance +1 step, then flat to screens two and four, each with two chair spaces. Screens one, three and five are reached by over 35 steps. Induction loop in screens one and three.

Gate, 87 Notting Hill Gate W11 *Tel:* 0171 727-4043. About 50m from Notting Hill Gate tube station. Step free to the auditorium. One chair space.

Greenwich, 180 Greenwich High Street, Greenwich SE10 *Tel:* BO 0181 235-3005 M 0181 853-0053. Between Royal Hill and Stockwell Street. Pay and display CP off Burney Street behind the cinema. Step free throughout. Screen two is on the GF, screens one and three are on the first floor reached by lift (D80 W105 L140). Two chair spaces in each screen. Induction loop in each screen. **Wheelchair loo (D85 ST90)** on the GF. Ask staff for the key.

Hammersmith (MGM), 207 King Street, Hammersmith W6 *Tel:* RecM 0181 748-0557 BO 0181 748-2388. 200m from Ravenscourt Park tube. Step free to the foyer and screens three and four. Both have two chair spaces. About +40 steps to screens one and two. **Wheelchair loo (D85 ST75)** in the foyer. Induction loops in all screens.

Hampstead (MGM), Pond Street, Hampstead NW3 *Tel:* BO 0171 794-6603 RecM 0171 794-4000. 150m from Belsize Park tube. On-site CP. Entrance +3 steps. Exit in Fleet Road gives step free access to screens two and three. Each has two chair spaces. Screen one is +31.

Haverstock Hill (Screen on the Hill), 203 Haverstock Hill, Hampstead NW3 *Tel:* RecM/BO 0171 435-3366 M 0171 435-9787. 80m from Belsize Park tube. Steepish ramp at the entrance, then +5 steps to the auditorium, with transfer seating in the aisles.

Holloway Odeon, 417 Holloway Road, Islington N7 *Tel:* RecM 01426-914042 M 0171 272-1172. At the junction with Tufnell Park Road. Step free through the foyer to screens one, two and three. Each has at least three chair spaces. Screens four and five +45 steps; +27 to screen six. **Wheelchair loo (D90 ST85)** in the foyer.

ICA see section on *Arts centres*.

Islington (Screen on the Green), Islington Green NW1 *Tel:* RecM 0171 226-3520 M 0171 226-3791. Entrance +3 steps, then +2 to the screen. One chair space.

Kensington (Odeon), Kensington High Street W8 *Tel:* RecM 01426-914666 M 0171 602-6460. Opposite the Commonwealth Institute, near the junction with Earls Court Road. Flat entrance. Exit doors give single step access to screens four, five and six where transfer into an aisle seat is possible. From the foyer: screen one has +46 steps; screen two +39; screen three +72; screen four

+8; screen five +6; and screen six +21.

Leicester Square (Odeon), Leicester Square WC2 *Tel:* BO 0171 930-6111/4. Flat entrance, and step free to the stalls, with four chair spaces. Circle +29 steps. Induction loop in the circle.

Lumiere, 42 St Martin's Lane WC2 *Tel:* BO 0171 836-0691 M 0171 379-3014. On the corner of Hops Gardens. Flat to foyer. Lift (D83 W150 L134) down to the cinema. Transfer into any aisle seat is possible.

Mall see under ICA in *Arts centres*.

Metro, 11 Rupert Street W1 *Tel:* RecM 0171 437-0757 BO 0171 734-1506 M 0171 287-3515. Between Shaftesbury Avenue and Coventry Street. Entrance −19 steps, but an exit gives flat access to both screens via a small lift (D80 but not working when we surveyed). Each screen has one chair space. **Wheelchair loo (D85 ST100)** next to the lift, at screen level.

Muswell Hill (Odeon), Fortis Green Road, Muswell Hill N10 *Tel:* RecM 01426-911885 M 0181 883-1001. Near the junction with Muswell Hill. CP at the rear. Entrance +1 step, then flat to screens two and three. Each have two transfer and three chair spaces. Screen one +26.

National Film Theatre see section on *Arts centres*.

Odeon Mezzanine, Leicester Square W2 *Tel:* RecM 01426-915683 BO 0171 930-3232 M 0171 930-2787. Flat entrance, then ramped to screen one with two chair spaces. Screen two has +40 steps, to screen three +34, and screens four and five +60. **Wheelchair loo (D75 ST100)** to the left of the entrance.

Panton Street (MGM), 11 Panton Street SW1 *Tel:* RecM 0171 930-0631 BO 0171 930-0632. Near the junction with Whitcombe Street. Main entrance +1 step. From the foyer, +6 to screens one and two; and +35 to screens three and four. Via exit doors, screen one is +1 and screen two is flat. Both have a chair space.

Plaza, Lower Regent Street W1 *Tel:* RecM 0171 437-1234 BO 0990-888990. On the corner of Jermyn Street. Entrance +2 steps. An exit door in Jermyn Street gives flat access to screen two where the Royal Box has two chair spaces. Screen one is +30; screens three and four −20. **Wheelchair loo (D75 ST95)** next to the Royal Box in screen two.

Premier, 95A Rye Lane, Peckham SE15 *Tel:* RecM 0171 732-1010 BO 0171 732-1313 M 0171 732-5956. About 150m from Peckham Rye BR station. CP behind cinema, 100m away; with access through Cerise Road. Step free entrance, and to all screens. Screen one has two chair spaces, and screens two to six have one chair space each. Staff will provide more chair spaces by prior arrangement. **Wheelchair loo (D85 ST90)** by the entrance to screen six. All screens have an induction loop.

Prince Charles, 7 Leicester Place WC2 *Tel:* BO 0171 437-8181 M 0171 494-4687. 50m from Lisle Street. Built as a theatre, with the circle at street level. Entrance +2 steps. Flat side exit in Lisle Street leads to the circle via +2. Transfer seats in the circle. From the foyer, +16 to the upper circle and –21 to stalls.

Rio, 107 Kingsland High Street, Kingsland E8 *Tel:* BO 0171 254-6677 M 0171 249-2722. At the junction with John Campbell Street. Step free entrance and to the stalls. Three chair spaces. **Wheelchair loo (D85 ST85)**. Induction loop.

Ritzy, Brixton Oval, Coldharbour Lane, Brixton SW2 *Tel:* 0171 737-2121. Reopened in late 1995, showing a mix of old and current films. 50m from Brixton tube station. Step free to screens via main entrance. Screens one to four on the GF. Screen five on the first floor is reached by lift (D80 W105 L140). All screens have removable seats in the front row, although when we visited there were teething problems. All seats are reservable. Induction loop in all screens. Step free to Ritzy bar on GF; Ritzy canteen on the first floor has some tables on the flat. **Wheelchair loo (D85 ST80)** on the GF.

Staples Corner (MGM), Geron Way, Staples Corner NW2 *Tel:* RecM 0181 208-2277 BO 0181 208-1367. Just 400m south along the Edgware Road, on the left. The other developments in the area are a group of shops and stores. On-site parking. Ramped entrance (medium gradient), then step free to all screens. Every screen has three or more chair spaces. Two **wheelchair loos** (D70+ ST70+) in the foyer. All screens have an induction loop.

Swiss Cottage (Odeon), 96 Finchley Road NW3 *Tel:* RecM 01426-914098 BO 0171 722-5905/586-3057. 50m from Swiss Cottage tube. Entrance +1 step. Flat route to screens three, five and six. Each has at least one chair space. Screen one is +35, screen two +26, screen four +9. **Wheelchair loo (D90 ST90)** in the foyer. Induction loop in screen one, currently out of order, but it should be repaired by 1996.

Trocadero (MGM), Coventry Street W1 *Tel:* RecM 0171 434-0031 BO 0171 434-0032 M 0171 434-0034. Built on the upper floors of a large complex described in the chapter on *Places of interest.* Flat entrance from Coventry Street, but if you come via the alternative in Shaftesbury Avenue, there are –5–5–5 steps to the Coventry Street level. Inside there are +3 to the escalators. The alternative is an ancient service lift with manual doors (D80 W120 L120). This can take you up to a level from which there is a ramp up to the ticket office.

Alternatively, there is a special (well disguised) way in, via a dedicated lift which only serves the cinema. You will find this near the junction between Shaftesbury Avenue and Great Windmill Street. Go past the window displaying the cinema programmes, and you will find three doors – a double and a single. By the single door is a 'press button and hold' intercom.

This links to the box office and someone will open the door for you which leads to a lift (D70 W100 L120).

The cinema has seven screens. Using the lift, screens one to five have step free access and designated chair spaces (though we're a little doubtful about the size of these, and you may have to sit sideways). Screen six has step free access to part of the auditorium, but screen seven has –2 then 1 inside. **Wheelchair loo (D85 ST85)** near the lift on the fourth floor. The route for walkers from the foyer to the screens is via steps and escalators. These can be avoided by using the lift.

In the smaller screens the chair spaces are created by removing seats, and it is not clear that the seats are always 'out'. If you ring first, they can remove seats to increase the number of chairs accommodated. All screens have an induction loop.

Walthamstow (Cannon), 186 Hoe Street, Walthamstow E17 *Tel:* 0181 520-7092 M 0181 520-3550. 200m from Walthamstow Central tube. Entrance +3 steps. Exit door gives flat access to screens two and three with two chair spaces each. From foyer: +28 to screen one; +7 to screens two and three.

Warner Brothers – Park Royale, Royale Leisure Park, Kendal Avenue W3. On the left of the A40 Western Avenue after Gipsy Corner. It is just before Park Royal station and the Hangar Lane underpass. You can approach it from one side of the A40 going out of London towards Oxford or from behind, from the residential area via Westfields Road and across the bridge. On-site CP with more than twenty OB spaces, but the place gets very congested over weekends.

It is a compact development including the cinema, a large bowling alley, a nightclub and several restaurants. Virtually all have step free access to facilities and **wheelchair loos**.

The Warner Brothers Cinema *Tel:* RecM 0181 896-0099 BO 0181 896-0066 M 0181 896-3255. Flat entrance and a spacious foyer, with step free access to all screens. All have several chair and transfer spaces. They can take out additional seats if you ring and ask. Two **wheelchair loos (D80 ST75)** off the foyer. All screens have an induction loop.

Other on-site facilities include:
Superbowl bowling alley and entertainments centre with step free access to almost everywhere. **Wheelchair loo (D70+ ST70+)** by the other toilets; **Pizza Hut,** with flat access to 25% of it. **Wheelchair loo (D80 ST70); Chiquito,** Mexican restaurant, flat throughout. **Wheelchair loo (D80**

ST100+);
Deep Pan Pizza, with flat access and some movable chairs. **Wheelchair loo (D80 ST80);**
Burger King, with flat access and an **adapted loo (D80 ST62).**

Warner West End, 3 Cranbourn Street, Leicester Square WC2 *Tel:* RecM 0171 437-4347 BO 0171 437-4343 M 0171 437-3484. 50m from Cambridge Circus NCP. Flat entrance into foyer, where there is a lift (D80 W100 L140) to all levels. All screens have four or more chair spaces. **Wheelchair loos** (D70+ ST70+) off the foyers on all levels except the GF. All screens have an induction loop. It's a superb facility in central London.

Whiteleys (UCI), Second floor Whiteleys Shopping Centre, Queensway W2 *Tel:* RecM 0171 792-3332 M 0171 792-3303. On-site parking at the centre off Redan Place, and three OB spaces on the second floor, level with the cinema. There is +1 step en route. The centre is described in the chapter on *Shops.* To get to the second floor, use the main lifts in the centre of the building. The cinema is level with a number of eating places. Screens five, six, seven and eight are on the second floor. The larger screens, one, two, three and four are on the third floor reached by lift (D78 W105 L135). All screens have at least two chair spaces. **Wheelchair loo (D85 ST80)** in the foyer.

Willesden Picture House, Willesden Green Library Centre, 95 The High Road NW10 *Tel:* RecM 0181 830-0822 BO 0181 830-0823. Somerfield CP behind the Centre has four OB spaces. Ramped entrance. Flat route via fire doors bypasses +7 steps into the cinema. Please ring first. Two chair spaces, and room for up to fifteen at the front. **Wheelchair loo (D85 ST80)** in main concourse.

Between the N/S circular roads and the M25

Barking (Odeon), Longbridge Road, Barking, Essex *Tel:* 0181 507-0533. Opposite Barking station. Five OB spaces at side of cinema. Access to screens three, four, five and six is via exit doors with a small step. Screens three, five and six each have two chair spaces. Screens one and two involve more than 20 steps.

Barnet (Odeon), Great North Road, Barnet, Herts EN5 *Tel:* RecM 01426-0911167 BO 0181 441-2574. Near the junction with Station Road. Entrance +3 steps. Flat access to screens three and four via exit doors. The +4 to screen two can be ramped if warning is given. Transfer spaces available in all these screens and a seat can be removed (with notice) in three and four for a chair space. Screens one and five have more than +30. Induction loop in screen one.

Beckenham (Cannon), High Street, Beckenham, Kent *Tel:* RecM 0181 650-1171 BO 0181 970-6030 M 0181 658-7114. Some on-site parking. Entrance

+3 steps, then −3 to screens two and three. Transfer possible. Screen three has one chair space. Screen one is +33.

Bromley (Odeon), 242 High Street, Bromley, Kent *Tel:* 0181 313-9599. Near Beckenham Lane. On-site parking possible if you phone first. Entrance +1+3 steps. Flat access through a side exit. Then flat to screens two and three with two chair spaces in each. Screen one +42, screen four +18.

Catford (Cannon), 1 Bromley Road, Catford SE6 *Tel:* BO 0181 697-6579 RecM 0181 698-3306. Near the junction with Culverley Road. CP in Canadian Avenue. Entrance +3 steps. Flat route possible to screen one, with two chair spaces. Screen two +26. Induction loop in screen two.

Croydon (Cannon), London Road, West Croydon *Tel:* RecM 0181 688-0486 BO 0181 688-5775. Near West Croydon Station. Flat entrance. Screen one +19 steps. Screens two and three both −8. Screen three can be entered through an exit on the CP side without steps. Screen two could be entered (via exits) either with −6 from the road or −3 from a gravel path round to the back of the cinema. No chair spaces, transfer only.

Croydon (Warner Bros), Lathams Way, off Beddington Farm Road, Purley Way, Croydon Tel: RecM 0181 680-6881 BO 0181 680-8090 M 0181 680-1968. In the **Valley Park Leisure Complex**, near Wadden Marsh station (and IKEA). On-site CP. Step free access to eight screens with at least four chair spaces in each. Two **wheelchair loos (D95 ST85)** in the foyer. Induction loop in every screen. Nearby in the Leisure Complex is a *Burger King* restaurant, *Frankie and Benny's* New York Italian Diner and the *Chiquito* (Mexican) restaurant and bar. All have step free access and a **wheelchair loo (D70+ST70+).**

Ealing (MGM), 61 Uxbridge Road, Ealing W5 *Tel:* RecM 0181 235-3003 BO 0181 970-6044 M 0181 579-4851. Opposite the Town Hall, and recently refurbished. Small step at the entrance, then flat to screens two (three chair spaces) and three (two chair spaces). Screen one is reached via +30steps. Induction loop in all screens. **Wheelchair loo (D90 ST200+)** by screen three.

Enfield (Cannon), Savoy Parade, Southbury Road, Enfield EN1 *Tel:* RecM 0181 363-4411 M 0181 367-4909. Entrance +1 step. Flat to screens three and four each with at least two chair spaces. Screens one and two have +26.

Ewell (MGM), Kingston Road, Surrey. *Tel:* RecM 0181 393-2211 BO 0181 970-6029 M 0181 394-1118. Near Stonely BR station. Large on-site CP. Slope and +2 steps at the cinema entrance. An exit gives flat access to screen two with two chair spaces. Roughly +30 to screen one.

Gants Hill (Odeon), Eastern Avenue, Gants Hill, Ilford *Tel:* RecM 01426-

939518 M 0181 554-2452. 30m from Gants Hill tube station. Some on-site parking, reservable by phone. Entrance +1 step. Then flat to screens two and three. Each has two chair spaces. Screen one +38. Screen four +6. Screen five +26.

Harrow (Cannon), Sheepcote Road, Harrow, Middx *Tel:* RecM 0181 427-1946 BO 0181 863-7261. At the junction with Station Road. NCP 100m away. Entrance +1 step, then flat to screens two and three. Each has two chair spaces. Screen one +37.

Hendon (MGM), Central Circus, Hendon NW4 *Tel:* RecM 0181 202-7137 BO 0181 202-4644. 50m from Hendon Central tube. You can use the small CP at rear by arrangement. Entrance +3 steps. Side exit gives step free access to screens two and three, each with five chair spaces. Screen one +27.

Kingston Options (MGM), 1 Clarence Street, Kingston-upon-Thames *Tel:* RecM 0181 546-0404 BO 0181 549-0388 M 0181 547-2860. 50m from Kingston Bus Station. Flat entrance, then flat to screens one and two which have two chair spaces each. Screen three +50. **Wheelchair loo (D80 ST80)** by screen two.

Lee Valley UCI (Picketts Lock Centre), Lee Valley Leisure Complex, Meriden Way, Edmonton *Tel:* RecM 0181 482-5282 BO 0181 482-5280 M 0181 482-5270. Large on-site CP with ramps and OB spaces. Flat entrance and step free to all twelve screens. All have at least two chair spaces. **Wheelchair loos (D90 ST80)** either side of the foyer. There are several other **wheelchair loos** in the complex, see the *Days Out* chapter. Induction loop in each screen and at the box office.

Purley (MGM), High Street, Purley, Surrey *Tel:* RecM 0181 660-1212 BO 0181 970-6024 M 0181 763-1620. OB parking in front. Entrance +3 steps, then +4 to screens two and three with transfer seats. Screen one +31.

Richmond Filmhouse, 3 Water Lane, Richmond, Surrey *Tel:* BO 0181 332-0030 M 0181 332-0316. Opposite the Watermans Arms pub. The street is slightly cobbled. Entrance +1 step with difficult camber. Then flat to the screen. One chair space. **Wheelchair loo (D85 ST95).**

Richmond Odeon and Richmond Studio, 72 Hill Street, Richmond, Surrey *Tel:* RecM 01426-915474 Odeon BO 0181 948-8143 Studio BO 0181 332-0055 M (both) 0181 940-3040. The Odeon entrance is opposite the bridge, while the Studio entrance is about 100m down Hill Street near the junction with Red Lion Street. Parking is difficult. The Odeon contains screens one to three. Flat entrance, but then steps to the screens. Using a side exit via +1 small step, there is access to screens two and three, both with three chair spaces. From the foyer: there are +5 to screens two and three and two flights of stairs lead to screen one.

The **Studio** contains screens four to seven. The entrance is near the police station. Entrance +6, bypassed via a ramp on the left of the entrance giving step free access to screens four and five. Each has two chair spaces. Screens six and seven are +22 from the box office. **Wheelchair loo (D85 ST75)** near the Red Lion Street entrance. Induction loop in all the Studio screens.

Sidcup (Cannon), High Street, Sidcup, Kent *Tel:* 0181 300-3603. On-site parking behind cinema. Flat entrance. Exit door gives flat access to screen one with three chair spaces. From foyer, screen one –4 and screen two +42.

Streatham (Cannon), 5 Streatham High Road, Streatham SW16 *Tel:* RecM 0181 769-1928 BO 0181 970-6033 M 0181 769-6262. Parking by arrangement. Entrance +1 step, then flat to screens two and three. Each has at least one chair space. Screen one +25.

Streatham (Odeon), 47 Streatham High Road, Streatham SW16 *Tel:* RecM 01426-912977 BO 0181 769-2221. By the junction with Pendennis Road. Entrance +4 steps, then flat to screens two and four. Each has three chair spaces. Screen one +36, screen three +22 and screen five +13.

Sutton (UCI), St Nicholas Centre, St Nicholas Way, Sutton, Surrey *Tel:* RecM 0181 395-4477 BO 0990-888990 M 0181 395-4488 *Minicom:* 0181 395-4477. Part of the shopping centre, see write-up on Sutton in the chapter on *Shops.* Adjacent MSCP. Lift (D105 W110 L135) to the GF. Flat entrance, and step free via lift (D70 W75 L150) to all six screens. All screens have four chair spaces. **Wheelchair loo (D95 ST80)** in the foyer. Screens one, four and six have induction loops.

Watermans Art Centre, see write-up in section on *Arts centres.*

Well Hall Coronet, Rochester Way, Eltham SE9 *Tel:* BO 0181 850-3351. Flat to entrance and screen two where two chair users can be accommodated. Screen one +23 then +8.

Wimbledon (Odeon), The Broadway, Wimbledon SW19 *Tel:* BO 0181 542-2277 M 0181 540-9978. Opposite the junction with Stanley Road. Sloped entrance, then flat to screens three to five. Each has one chair space. Screens one and two have +21 steps. **Wheelchair loo (D75 ST140)** just off the foyer. Screen five has an induction loop.

Woodford (Cannon), 60 High Road, South Woodford E18 *Tel:* RecM 0181 989-3463 M 0181 989-4066. On the corner of George Lane. Entrance +1 step. Flat access to screens two and three via an exit. Each has one chair space.

From the foyer, +4 to screens two and three and +36 to screen one.

Woolwich Coronet, John Wilson Street, Woolwich SE18 *Tel:* 0181 854-2255. At the junction with Woolwich Church Street. Entrance +2 +8 steps to the foyer. A side exit gives flat access to screen two with three chair spaces and others for transfer. Uneven surfaces en route. Screen one has +24. **Wheelchair loo (D90 ST150)** in screen two.

Music venues

A new multi-purpose venue has been built in Docklands, which we list first, along with Wembley.

London Arena, Limeharbour E14 *Tel:* 0171 538-8880 *Fax:* 0171 538-5572. By the junction with East Ferry Road, and 50m from Crossharbour DLR station. The Arena is a huge modern multi-purpose venue. It has a capacity of 13,000, and puts on a variety of events. As a result, various layouts are used. The ASDA CP about 200m away has ten OB spaces. Depending on the event, there are up to thirty OB spaces less than 100m away, under the DLR bridge. The management have gone to some lengths to assure adequate access for both chair users and disabled walkers. They will normally use the flat VIP entrance some 25m from the main entrance. Flat access everywhere on the GF to all bars, kiosks and loos. Lift (D80 W100 L150) to the first floor. There are usually up to thirty chair spaces, and seats with step free access. Five **wheelchair loos (all D70+ ST70+)** on the GF, one in the south stand, and two each in the west and east stands.

Wembley Arena, Engineers Way, Wembley HA9 *Tel:* 0181 902-8833, is used mainly for concerts and ice shows. Public transport and parking are much the same as for the stadium. The entrance for disabled people is to the left of the booking office through a barrier opposite Club Royale. This bypasses the normal turnstiles for getting in. The main area around the arena has step free access, and there are fast food kiosks and refreshment stalls.

For pop concerts there are three areas by gates 6, 26 and 36, for chair users and friends. Each can accommodate up to seven chairs and has step free access. For ice shows some twenty chair spaces are allocated in the west terrace. Other events may involve different layouts. There are relatively few seats with step free access, but if you want one, ask when booking.

Two **wheelchair loos (D85 ST70)** with a tight 90° turn en route by gates 17 and 38. The restaurant/bar on the second floor is reached by +12+12 steps.

Wembley Stadium see chapter on *Sport*.

Rock, jazz, rave and folk

Inside the north/south circular roads

Archway Tavern, 1 Archway Close, Archway Roundabout N19 *Tel:* BO 0171 272-2840. The pub is opposite Archway tube and specialises in Irish music. Side door on the right with a small step.

Astoria, 157 Charing Cross Road WC2 *Tel:* BO 0171 434-0403 M 0171 434-9592. Entrance +3+4 steps. The auditorium is well above street level. The lowest part is the dance floor which is +27 from the foyer. Best viewing is from the balcony which has two flat areas with tables and seats, with space for a couple of chair users to get a good view of the stage. This involves +50 –8 from the foyer, and the staff are willing to help if needed. No hearing system, as the music is likely to be very loud!

Apollo, Hammersmith, see Labatts Apollo, Hammersmith.

BAC see section on *Arts centres.*

Blue Note, 1 Hoxton Square N1 *Tel:* 0171 729-8440. Club and café. New jazz. Easy street parking in evenings. Entrance +7 steps, then flat to café. From here, –16 to the club which has three tiers with –2 or –3 steps between them. Two chair users allowed; very few seats.

Borderline, Orange Yard (off Manette Street) W1 *Tel:* BO 0171 734-2095 M 0171 287-2030. NCP at Centre Point. Step free from Manette Street. Then –23 to venue, bypassed via a service lift (D150 W150 L150) reached from Goslett Yard. The dance floor is +1.

Bottom Line, 58 Shepherds Bush Green W12 *Tel:* 0181 746-0255. Near the corner with Goldhawk Road. Step free throughout, apart from +20 to the balcony area. **Wheelchair loo (D85 ST85)** to the right of the bar but there was no lock on the door and no seat when we surveyed it. Maximum of twelve chair users at one time. People with disabilities can ring to reserve a seat. **Wheelchair loo (D90 ST80 NKS)** 40m away on the pavement.

Brixton Academy, 211 Stockwell Road, Brixton SW9 *Tel:* 0171 274-1525 BO 0171 924-9999 *Fax:* 0171 738-4427. One of London's premier venues. Opposite the junction with Bellefields Road. Entrance +5 steps, and staff will offer to carry chair users up these. Alternative step free entrance about 150m round to the left. Once inside step free throughout GF to bars and the main auditorium, which has a raised viewing area on the left with priority use for chair users. Excellent viewing point. First floor circle +20. **Wheelchair loo (D88 ST90)** in the foyer.

Bull's Head, Lonsdale Road, Barnes SW13 *Tel:* 0181 876-5241. Jazz. Near the junction with Barnes High Street. The bar has +1 step then +4 to the music venue. A side entrance in Barnes High Street has an easier +4. Maximum of three chair users.

Chestnuts Folk Club, Grove Green Road, Leytonstone E11 *Tel:* 0181 539-1369. In the *Heathcoat Arms* pub. Folk. Some on-site parking. There is +1 step to the spacious pub, and then +22 to folk club. Wider straighter steps at the side of the pub. Level upstairs. Maximum of four chair users.

Cellar Upstairs Folk Club, above the *Dolly Fossett's* pub, 291 Kentish Town Road NW5 *Tel:* Pub 0171 485-2802 Club 0171 281-770. 50m from Kentish Town tube. On-site parking. Flat access via the side entrance in Holmes Road into the pub. The club has +22 steps with awkward turns.

Dublin Castle, 94 Parkway, Camden NW1 *Tel:* 0171 485-1773. About half way along Parkway. The pub has +1 step, then +2 to the venue.

Earl's Court see chapter on *Exhibition halls*.

Forum, 9 Highgate Road, Kentish Town NW5 *Tel:* 0171 284-1001. Rock. 80m from Kentish Town tube and BR. You can book parking space. No restriction on chair users. It can get very crowded, so arrive early. Entrance +1 step. The hall floor has three levels. From the entrance there are –2 to the first level, then –4 –4 to other levels. Very little seating. There are +30 to the circle, which has transfer seats.

Garage, 20 Highbury Corner N5 *Tel:* 0171 607-1818. Rock. 50m from Highbury & Islington tube and BR. No restriction on number of chair users. Flat entrance then +3 steps to the hall, which has very few seats. Steps to the bar. It also contains **Upstairs at the Garage**, which is +25 from the GF. Rock, folk. No restriction on chair users. Very few seats.

Grand, Clapham Junction SW11 *Tel:* BO 0171 738-9000 M 0181 961-5490. Rock. Opposite Clapham Junction station. Box office flat, then +3 steps to the foyer, main hall, and bar. The –5 to the dance floor can be bypassed by prior arrangement (portable ramps can be installed). Café is +30, and then another +15 to the circle from which there is +81 to the balcony. Service lift (D80 W85 L140) goes up to the circle bar, allowing up to four transferees to sit upstairs. **Adapted loo** some 15m away in the Burger King at the Junction shopping centre.

Hale End Folk Club, County Arms Tavern, Hale End Road, Highams Park E4 *Tel:* 0181 503-3484. By Highams Park BR station. The side entrance in Hansworth Avenue has +1 step to the pub from where there is +19 to the music hall. Maximum of two chair users.

Half Moon Putney, 93 Lower Richmond Road SW15 *Tel:* 0181 780-9383. Rock, Blues and Folk. Pub and music hall +1 step, or flat around the back. Flat inside apart from +1 to the raised sections at either side of the hall where there are movable chairs and tables.

Heathcote Arms & Attic, Grove Green Road, Leytonstone E11 *Tel:* Pub 0181 539-1369. Jazz and comedy. On the corner of Richmond Road. The main bars have +1 step, then +22 to the club.

Labatts Apollo Hammersmith, Queen Caroline Street, Hammersmith W6 *Tel:* BO 0171 416-6080. On the corner with the Fulham Palace Road. Parking in nearby NCPs in the new centre, or under the flyover. Entrance +3 steps. Access via a side exit and +1 can be arranged. There are two chair spaces and three seats for transfer. Row L has good legroom. Public **wheelchair loos** in the new Hammersmith development just across the road.

Jazz Café, 5 Parkway, Camden NW1 *Tel:* 0171 916-6000. Jazz. Ticket office outside, then +1 step to enter the building which is flat apart from two small raised seating areas which are both +3. The split level balcony bar and restaurant have +15. **Adapted loo (D83, opening in ST79)**, next to the stage through the double doors.

Mean Fiddler, 22 High Street, Harlesden NW10 *Tel:* 0181 961-5490. Rock. Opposite Tavistock Road with a CP 50m away. There are +2 steps into the night time ticket booth down the alleyway on the right. Then –3 to the Acoustic Room' music venue. The Mean Fiddler itself has –3 to the main hall, and +15 to the balcony. Alternative step free access to the main hall via the street level wine bar and the double doors at the far end. Ask the staff. Four chair users allowed.

Orange, 3 North End Crescent, North End Road, West Kensington W14 *Tel:* 0171 371-4317/4528. The Fox, Rat & Carrot pub. Rock and jazz. 60m from West Kensington tube. Step free to the box office, then +28 to the main hall. Two chair spaces and two people can transfer.

Paradise Bar, 460 New Cross Road, New Cross SE14 *Tel:* 0181 692-1530. On the corner of Florence Road. Step free via a narrow door (W65cm).

Pizza Express, 10 Dean Street, Soho W1 *Tel:* 0171 439-8722. Jazz. One small step to the restaurant, and then –16 to the club and bar with space for two chairs, or for transfer.

Rock Garden, The Piazza, Covent Garden WC2 *Tel:* 0171 836-4052. Rock. 50m from Covent Garden tube. There are 20 steps to venue, and bar (+1). Little seating. Maximum of four chair users. Restaurant at street level.

Robey, 240 Seven Sisters Road, Finsbury Park N4 *Tel:* 0171 263-4581. Rock and rave. 20m from Finsbury Park tube. Flat throughout, including the bar next door. Six chair users allowed.

Ronnie Scott's, 47 Frith Street W1 *Tel:* BO 0171 439-0747. World famous Jazz venue. Entrance +3 steps, then +2, and –3 to a lower level. Quite cramped. There are –15 to the TV room/social bar and +24 to the dance club. Two chair users allowed.

Royal Standard, Blackhorse Lane, Higham Hill E17 *Tel:* 0181 503-2523. Rock. 15m from Blackhorse tube station with on-site parking (phone early to reserve a place in the CP). Entrance +1 step, then step free to the bar and music hall apart from +2 to raised section. Phone in advance to reserve a place.

Shepherds Bush Empire, Shepherds Bush Green, Shepherds Bush W12 *Tel:* BO 0181 740-7474 M 0181 740-1515. Near the corner of Goldhawk Road. Flat to the ticket office, then +2 steps to the foyer and –6 to a raised section at the back of the stalls where there is a bar. Alternative route via fire door 14, which is –2 from street level. From the raised section to the dance floor is –6. From the foyer: circle +21; upper circle +40–5; balcony +40–5+30. **Wheelchair loo (D94 ST79 NKS)** 50m away on the pavement.

606 Club, 90 Lots Road, Chelsea SW10 *Tel:* BO 0171 352-5953. Jazz & Blues. Members only, membership is about £50 per year. Entrance via 17+1 –2 steps, then +1 to the bar. Two chair users allowed.

Swan Pub, 215 Clapham Road, Stockwell SW9 *Tel:* 0171 978-9778. Opposite Stockwell tube station. Flat throughout.

Tufnell Park Tavern, 162 Tufnell Park Road N7 *Tel:* BO 0181 830-5233 Pub 0171 272-2078. On the corner of Campdale Road. Step free access to bar and **wheelchair loo (D85 ST85)**. Key from the bar. The Jazz section has +3 steps, the comedy club +21.

Outside the north/south circular roads

Amersham Arms, 288 New Cross Road, New Cross SE14 *Tel:* BO 0181 692-2047 M 0181 694-8992. Opposite New Cross tube station. Step free access via side doors to bar and music. **Wheelchair loo (D85 ST100)**.

Cartoon, 179 London Road, Croydon *Tel:* 0181 688-4500. Rock. Near the junction with St James's Road. Step free throughout.

Vortex Club, 139 Stoke Newington Church Street N16 *Tel:* 0171 254-6516. Opposite Grove Lordship Road. Entrance to the club is +15, then +1 to a seating area.

Woolwich Folk Club, *Crown and Cushion* pub, High Street, Woolwich SE18 *Tel:* 0181 854-1451. Entrance +2 steps, then +1 to the bar.

Classical music

Barbican Centre see section on *Arts centres.*

Blackheath Concert Halls, 23 Lee Road SE3 *Tel:* BO 0181 463-0100 M 0181 318-9758. By the corner of Blackheath Park. Parking by prior arrangement only. The +4 steps at the front entrance can be bypassed via a ramp on the left leading to the foyer, and **wheelchair loo (D80 ST100)**. The music hall is on the GF with three flights of stairs leading to the recital rooms. Induction loop planned.

Conway Hall, 25 Red Lion Square, Holborn WC1 *Tel:* 0171 430-1271. Used for classical music recordings and public meetings. Step free to the main hall with **wheelchair loo (D75 ST75)** and several chair spaces. Ring first. Balcony +27.

Purcell Room see section on *Arts centres.*

Queen Elizabeth Hall see section on *Arts centres.*

Royal Albert Hall, Kensington Gore SW17 *Tel:* DisEnq 0171 589-3203 ext2670 RecM 0891-500252. Eight on-site OB spaces which can be booked. Ramped entrance at door fourteen, bypassing +4 steps at other entrances. Twenty-two chair spaces in the G and O stalls. Two **wheelchair loos (both D85 ST 80)** by doors seven and eight. Large forty person lift at door eleven serves all floors, as does the goods lift at door five (D125 W180 L200). Single track Sennheiser system.

Royal Festival Hall see section on *Arts centres.*

Covent Garden (Royal Opera House), Bow Street WC2 *Tel:* BO 0171 304-4000. Access officer 0171 212-9307. The main centre for both opera and ballet in London, with an international reputation. It is due to close for a major refurbishment during 1997, and doubtless access provisions will improve. Even now, they have gone to considerable lengths to make the building, opened in 1858, more accessible.

There are regular performances, about once every two weeks, when a (very steep) ramp is put in. Seats are removed from Row A in the stalls circle to allow up to about eighteen chair users to get in. A team of friendly volunteers are on hand to help people negotiate the ramp safely. A free mailing list is available to disabled people, and advanced booking is essential. There is a concessionary price for these performances. You'll find it worth getting there early. If you go with a friend/escort, they may find that their sightlines are a bit restricted. **Wheelchair loo (D85 ST100)** in the stalls circle area of unusual but practical design. The door folds in half to increase the space available inside. Our surveyors thought that it was an excellent example of making good provision in a theatre designed long before access was ever thought of.

The box office is at 48 Floral Street with +1 step. The right hand door in Bow Street is step free into the main foyer. The −3+14 to the stalls and stalls circle seats can be bypassed by an open lift (W90 L100). This gives step free access to two seats in the stalls circle on a raised section in Row C, and to the loo. As you are unable to see the English translation of the opera arias from this position, they have provided lap-top translation screens instead. From the foyer +35 to the grand tier. The amphitheatre is about +90 from Floral Street. Infrared assisted sound system.

Sadlers Wells, Rosebery Avenue EC1 *Tel:* BO 0171 278-8916 M 0171 278-6563. Near St John's Street. One tiny step at the entrance then flat, with two chair spaces in the rear stalls and six more given notice. Transfer also possible. **Wheelchair loo (D90 ST90)** near the chair spaces. From foyer: stalls +3 steps or via the slope; dress circle +40; upper circle +65. Induction loop. Due to close in 1997 for rebuilding.

St John's Smith Square Concert Hall, St John's Smith Square SW1 *Tel:* BO 0171 222-1061 M 0171 222-2168. There is a minimum of +16 steps.

St Martin-in-the-Fields see chapter on *Places of worship.*
St Paul's Cathedral see chapter on *Places of worship.*

Wigmore Hall, 36 Wigmore Street W1 *Tel:* BO 0171 935-2141 M 0171 486-1907. Step free to foyer. A lift (D114 W160 L140) serves all floors; it goes to the two chair spaces in the auditorium, the restaurant and the **wheelchair loo (D89 ST79)**. Induction loop.

Theatres

London offers a huge range of theatre, and there is a somewhat blurred distinction between mainstream performances in the mainly Victorian and Edwardian theatres, and those in generally smaller venues, many of which are away from the West End, and are called the 'fringe'. We have adopted a strictly geographical approach, and the theatres listed as central are those in the West End and City areas. The theatres listed here can nearly all accommodate chair users, mostly with step free access, but where there are barriers, these are described. Many of the venues have an adapted loo and a good number have a loop or Sennheiser sound system.

Trying out some of the fringe shows has always been a slightly haphazard pleasure. The really brilliant shows tend to get noticed and are booked out very quickly, so if you want to get to these, keep your eyes open on the weekly *Time Out* reviews, among others. There are many other good shows, and others that don't quite come off, but may be interesting nonetheless.

Theatre staff should recognise the needs of a chair user fairly readily, as they're relatively clear. The needs of disabled walkers are rather more varied, and you're more likely to have to ask for help if you need it. **Usually the easiest access will be the same as for a chair user, and the easiest seats to get to will be on the same level as any chair spaces.**

Note the SOLT/Artsline *Disabled access guide to London's West End Theatres* which contains a great deal of additional information, and is regularly updated.

Central

Some small scale theatre takes place in a room over a pub or in a basement. These involve the barrier of (usually) more than 15 steps, as well as restricted space in the venue itself. These are listed below:

New Grove, Drummonds, Judd Street WC1 *Tel:* 0171 383-0925;

Old Red Lion, 417 St John's Street EC1 *Tel:* 0171 833-3053;

Royal Court Theatre Upstairs, Sloane Square SW1 *Tel:* 0171 730-1745.

Adelphi, The Strand WC2 *Tel:* BO 0171 379-8443 or via Ticketmaster 0171 344-0055. A 1930s theatre, recently refurbished, with the stalls at street level. Entrance +1 step. Then step free to the stalls, with two chair spaces (slightly restricted view). The stalls are sloped, and transfer is possible to any aisle seat. Two boxes at circle level are available for chair users, one +1+1, the other –4. Both are accessed from side entrances, and both have a side view of the stage. **Wheelchair loo (D70 ST70+)** off the foyer. From the foyer: dress circle +40; upper circle +80. Sennheiser hearing system.

Albery, St Martin's Lane WC2 *Tel:* BO 0171 867-1115. A Victorian/ Edwardian theatre with the royal circle at street level. Main entrance +3 steps, then +3 to the royal circle where aisle seats are available for transfer (in row G). Box M at royal circle level is available for chair users. It is accessed from a side exit, then +3 (which can be temporarily ramped, though it's quite steep). From the foyer: stalls –30; grand circle +30; balcony +50. Infrared hearing system.

Aldwych, Aldwych WC2 *Tel:* BO 0171 416-6003. Entrance +1+5 steps, then flat to the dress circle and boxes. Easier entry via Drury Lane exit door (over a slight edge) then –2 to dress circle with a portable ramp available. One chair space beside seat C1. From the foyer: stalls –25; +15 to rear dress circle;

upper circle about 50.

Ambassadors, West Street, Cambridge Circus WC2 *Tel:* BO 0171 836-6111. Small Victorian theatre with the dress circle at street level. Entrance +1 step, then +5 into the dress circle where seats F4 and F5 are available for transfer. Box available for chair users, +3 from dress circle with D65. From the foyer, stalls –25.

Apollo, Shaftesbury Avenue W1 *Tel:* BO 0171 494-5070 M 0171 734-2987. Entrance +1 step, then +12 to dress circle with four transfer seats (E5, E6, E17 and E18). Alternatively, enter through an exit door, then –12 to stalls with three transfer seats (O12, O13 and P11). No chair spaces. From foyer: stalls –15; upper circle +40; balcony +60. Eight infrared headsets.

Apollo Victoria, 17 Wilton Road SW1 *Tel:* Customer Relations 0171 828-7074 M 0171 834-6318. Two entrances, each with +4 steps. Alternatively, use an exit, which gives access via +1 to the dress circle with five small chair spaces; you may have to sit slightly sideways-on as the space is only 85cm deep. Eight transfer seats as well. From foyer: stalls –30; dress circle +15. **Wheelchair loos** in Victoria Station.

Arts, 6 Great Newport Street WC2 *Tel:* BO 0171 836-2132 M 0171 379-3280. Small theatre, partly sunk below street level. Flat entrance, but +5 steps to the circle and –19 to the stalls. The +5 can be bypassed by a ramped entrance. Seats can be removed to accommodate two chair users at the back of the circle. **Adapted loo (D75 ST60)** by the back of the circle.

Bloomsbury, Gordon Square WC1 *Tel:* BO 0171 388-8822 M 0171 383-5976. Small theatre with its auditorium well above street level. Ramped entrance, bypassing +4 steps, and a platform stairlift bypasses +7 to the box office and café. There is a further stairlift to the auditorium passing a further +7. Lift (D80 W135 L105) to the basement, where there are **adapted cubicle in gents (D80 ST40 with fixed rails) and wheelchair cubicle in the ladies (D80 ST120)**.

Cambridge, Earlham Street WC2 *Tel:* BO 0171 494-5080. 1930s theatre with the stalls at street level. Flat entrance, then –4 steps to the stalls. Alternatively, +1 using a side door in Earlham Street, then step free to stalls. Two seats in row N can be removed to make chair spaces, and aisle seats are available for transfer. **Wheelchair loo (D80 ST80)** by rear stalls. From the foyer: dress circle +30; upper circle +65. Infrared headsets.

Cochrane, Southampton Row WC1 *Tel:* BO 0171 242-7040 M 0171 430-2500 *Minicom:* 0171 242-7040. A small theatre on the corner with Theobolds Road. Ask about parking. Flat main entrance. Lift inside (D75 W130 L140) to all floors. Up to four chair spaces in the stalls, although seats need to be removed. Rows Q and R have step free access. Sennheiser hearing system, and an induction loop. **Wheelchair loo (D80 ST75)** on the GF near the CP entrance.

Coliseum, St Martin's Lane WC2 *Tel:* BO 0171 836-3161. Large Edwardian-style theatre used mainly for opera and dance. Stalls at street level. Ramped front entrance. Step free access to boxes at the back of stalls (D75cm), with up to two chair users per box. Stalls aisle seats available for transfer but there are –2 steps into the area, and then each row is stepped. Seven chair users allowed. **Wheelchair loo (D80 ST100+)** off the corridor leading to the ladies, by the stalls bar. From the foyer: dress circle +35; upper circle 60+, and balcony 90+ from an outside entrance. There is a service lift from the foyer which you may use with permission. It goes to within 4 steps of the back of the dress circle and within 14 steps of the rear upper circle. Both circles are themselves steeply stepped. The management are somewhat reluctant to allow those who really cannot manage stairs to use this facility, because of possible difficulty in the event of an evacuation. They are, however, both helpful and flexible. Infrared hearing system.

Comedy, Panton Street SW1 *Tel:* BO 0171 369-1731. A medium size Victorian theatre with the dress circle at street level. Entrance +2 small steps. One box (D65cm) for chair users on right of dress circle, reached via a portable ramp which takes you down –6. Slightly sideways view, and the ramp is quite steep! Dress circle seats F1 (with step free access from foyer) and E4, E5 and E6 (all –1 from foyer) are available for transfer. From the foyer: stalls –25; upper circle +35; balcony +55.

Criterion, Piccadilly Circus W1 *Tel:* BO 0171 839-4488. The theatre is built below ground level. There is +1 step to foyer, then –20 to the upper circle and –32 to the dress circle. An alternative entrance next to the stage door in Jermyn Street can be opened. It gives sloped access to the rear upper circle with one chair space next to C20, and is also the easiest access for a disabled walker. **Wheelchair loo (D80+ ST80+)** off the passage behind the upper circle. Induction loop.

Dominion, 269 Tottenham Court Road W1 *Tel:* BO 0171 636-2295 M 0171 580-1889. 50m from St Giles Circus. Flat entrance, then –10 steps to the stalls with spaces for two chair users in the rear right hand side with a slightly restricted view. Aisle seats available for transfer. Maximum of two chair users allowed. From the foyer: royal circle +40; centre circle +60.

Donmar Warehouse, Thomas Neal's, Earlham Street WC2 *Tel:* BO 0171 867-1150. A small new theatre in the heart of theatreland. It is in a block that has been rebuilt and is all above road level. The box office has +1 step, although you can gain flat access via the adjacent shopping precinct. Lift, staff operated in the evenings, (D75 W80 L100) to the stalls (first floor) and circle (second floor). This bypasses +25 to the stalls or +40 to the circle. One chair space in the stalls, another in the circle. **Wheelchair loo (D75 ST80)** off the circle bar. Induction loop.

Drill Hall, 16 Chenies Street WC1 *Tel:* BO 0171 637-8270 M 0171 631-1353. In a turning off Tottenham Court Road. Step free to auditorium, using a ramped bypass to +2 steps at the entrance. Up to twelve chair spaces by taking out seats. Induction loop. **Adapted loo (D75 ST56)** off the foyer. There are +23 to first floor with a rehearsal room and community dark room and a further +22 to the second floor with another dark room. Bar and vegetarian restaurant (*the Greenhouse*) on the GF.

Drury Lane Theatre Royal, Catherine Street WC2 *Tel:* BO 0171 494-5001. This has been a theatre site since Restoration times, and the current one is the fourth. It is very grand' with Edwardian and Victorian imperialism. It has been home to a series of hit musicals. Entrance +5 steps to the box office, then +3 to foyer. Flat access through side exit door on Russell Street, leading to the stalls which have four chair spaces. From the foyer: stalls –17+17; grand circle +40; upper circle +75, balcony even higher and very steep. **Wheelchair loo (D75 ST90)** near the Russell Street entrance. Infrared hearing system.

Duchess, Catherine Street WC2 *Tel:* BO 0171 494-5075. Small theatre built at the end of the 1920s. Entrance +1 step, then –21 to stalls, with two chair spaces. Or +12 to dress circle where aisle seats are available for transfer (but note the steep steps). Row A is nearest (up 3 steps). **Adapted loo (D73 opens in, ST55, but the cubicle is quite long) on stalls level. Infrared hearing** system.

Duke of York's, St Martin's Lane WC2 *Tel:* BO 0171 836-5122. Victorian-style theatre with the royal circle at street level. Flat entrance, then step free access into the back of the royal circle which has four seats that can be removed to make chair spaces. They put in a small platform to create an adequate area. A wooden rail prevents your chair from sliding down the slight slope. Restricted view sometimes, depending on the production. For walkers, there is step free access to row D seats. **Wheelchair loo (D80 ST70).** From the foyer: stalls –24; upper circle +23. Eighteen infrared headsets.

Fortune, Russell Street WC2 *Tel:* BO 0171 836-2238. A small art deco style theatre built in the 1920s. It is one of the smallest west end theatres. Flat entrance. Easiest chair access through Crown Court Alleyway side exit door, then +5 steps to the dress circle with two transfer seats at the right hand end of row F. No chair spaces. From the foyer: stalls –21; dress circle +7; upper circle +33.

Garrick, 2 Charing Cross Road WC2 *Tel:* BO 0171 494-5085. An old Victorian style theatre, partly sunk below road level. Entrance +2 small steps. One chair space at the back of the dress circle, when seat E25 has been removed. It is necessary to negotiate an extremely awkwardly angled step to get into the space, and as there is no 'depth' it is necessary to sit side on to the stage. Seat number E1 is available for transfer. From the foyer: −30 to stalls and +35 to the upper circle. Six infrared headsets.

Gielgud (Globe), 35 Shaftesbury Avenue W1 *Tel:* BO 0171 494-5067. An Edwardian theatre with the dress circle at street level. Recently renamed. Entrance +1 step. Two chair spaces, or transfer seats, B1 and B21 in the dress circle. Access to these is via +1 and through an exit door in Rupert Street. The seats have to be removed to make the space. From the foyer: stalls −20, dress circle +3, upper circle +70. Nine infrared headsets.

Haymarket, Theatre Royal, Haymarket SW1 *Tel:* BO 0171 930-8800. A beautiful Victorian theatre which has been completely refurbished and redecorated, restoring its original grandeur. Unfortunately the refurbishment did not go so far as to include the planned adapted loo or an improved hearing system. Stalls on street level. Main entrance +3 steps. Step free through exit doors leading to the stalls. There are ten chair spaces at the back. Stalls aisle seats are available for transfer. From the foyer: stalls −20+10; royal circle +25; upper circle +55; balcony +60.

Her Majesty's, Haymarket SW11 *Tel:* BO 0171 494-5400. Victorian/ Edwardian theatre with the stalls at street level. Flat entrance. A side exit door off Charles II Street gives step free access to the stalls with one chair space beside S12/S13. The view is distinctly restricted, with a pole in the way. Stalls aisle seats available for transfer. **Wheelchair loo (D80 ST74)** by rear stalls. From the foyer: stalls −22+18; dress circle +32. Twelve infrared headsets. The provision for chair users could be considerably improved by removing another seat or two from a spot giving a better view.

Lilian Baylis, Arlington Way, Rosebery Avenue EC1 *Tel:* BO 0171 278-8916 M 0171 278-6563 *Minicom:* 0171 713-0093. Bookings made via the Sadlers Wells Theatre office. Steepish ramp at the entrance. Gentle slope through the café to the theatre. Two chair spaces (H1 and H20) with step free access. Eight more can be provided by taking out some seats with adequate notice. **Wheelchair loo (D80 ST100)** off the café area. Induction loop.

Logan Hall, University of London, 20 Bedford Way WC1 *Tel:* BO 0171 580-1122 M 0171 612-6401. Main entrance ramped, then an open lift (W110 L175) bypasses +13 steps leading to reception on level four. Lift (D110 W110 L175) to level 1, with seven chair spaces when seats are removed. Induction loop. **Adapted cubicles in the gents (D77 ST45), and ladies (D75 ST69)** on level one.

London Palladium, Argyll Street W1 *Tel:* BO 0171 494-5020. Huge theatre, associated with 'variety', and recently with musicals. The stalls are at ground level. Front entrance +3+8 steps. Box Office +5. Ramillies Place exit almost gives step free access (there's a tiny step) from street level to the stalls. This is right round the other side of the theatre, and about 300m from the entrance via Oxford Street. Seats can be removed to create a chair space at V35 in stalls (restricted view sometimes). Other spaces at L46, S49 and W49, with side views. Stalls aisle seats are available for transfer. From the foyer: stalls –23; circle +15. **Wheelchair loo (D80 ST80)** by rear stalls. Infrared headsets.

London Television Studios, Upper Ground, Waterloo SE1 *Tel:* 0171 620-1620. On the South Bank just past the National Theatre. Both BBC and ITV shows are recorded and broadcast from here. Many of the shows are free. Contact the BBC Ticket Unit. Flat main entrance. Three studios on the GF, and there's a ramped side entrance to the studios area. The number of chair spaces depends on the studio/seating layout and this depends on the show. The normal route to seats is up a flight of stairs and then down to seats. This is presumably up behind the structure on which the seats are built. Disabled walkers would be sensible to ask to use the side entrance. Because of the variations in layout, disabled spectators are asked to contact the studios first to sort out the practicalities. **Wheelchair loo (D85 ST90)** on the second floor, reached by lift (D80 W180 L200). There are other **adapted loos** on the fourth and eighteenth floors, but they are smaller than the one on the second.

Lyric, Shaftesbury Avenue W1 *Tel:* BO 0171 494-5045. A traditional Victorian theatre with the dress circle on street level. Entrance +1 step, then +3 to the foyer. Shaftesbury Avenue royal entrance +1, and then step free to three boxes which can each accommodate a chair user and companion. All have D74cm and a side view. **Wheelchair loo (D70+ ST70+)** inside the royal entrance. From the foyer: stalls –25; flat to the back of the dress circle, and a minimum of +2 into seats; upper circle +30; balcony +50. Eight infrared headsets.

Mermaid, Puddle Dock, Blackfriars EC4 *Tel:* BO 0171 236-2211 M 0171 236-1919. Close to Blackfriars station, but the pedestrian approach is made difficult because of poor signing and a complete lack of dropped kerbs in the area. A chair user would have to use the road. Step free access at the main entrances. One goes to the box office and the other to the studio. Main auditorium reached via gently sloping corridors and there are up to twelve chair spaces. Induction loop. **Wheelchair loo (D80 ST85)** level with the auditorium. Other parts of the building, including the Studio theatre, Bridge bar, and the **wheelchair loo (D80 ST80)** on level two can be reached by lift from the studio entrance (D80 W110 L140). This bypasses some 60 steps between the GF and level two. The theatre complex includes a restaurant, open when there is a show on, and facilities for conferences and exhibitions. Access to the first and second floors is by lift from the entrance further down Puddle Dock.

National Theatre see section on *Arts centres.*

New London, Parker Street, Drury Lane WC2 *Tel:* BO 0171 405-0072 or 0171 404-4079. A modern and versatile theatre in the upper part of a modern block. Cats has been on there since May 1981, and is the longest running British musical ever. UGCP next door with two OB spaces. Flat entrance. For people with disabilities, there is step free access through the stage door in Parker Mews, leading to small lift (D60 W80 L105) which goes to level three for the stalls. A larger service lift goes to the second floor, where the original lift can be entered via a larger door (D70cm) to get to level three. The alternative is that there are +18 steps to the stalls from level two. Stalls seat number D38 can be removed to make a chair space. Stalls seats J15 and J18 are available for transfer. From the foyer, there is an escalator or +32 to the stalls, then a further +50 to the circle. Infra-red headsets and others for use with hearing aid T switch.

Old Vic, Waterloo Road SE1 *Tel:* BO 0171 928-7616. Forever associated with the name of Lilian Baylis, who took over the theatre in 1912 and established its classical tradition. Refurbished in 1983. Entrance +4 steps. Alternative entrance through Webber Street side exit with +1. Portable ramp available, giving step free access to the stalls and chair spaces at H1, L3 and W8 where the seats can be removed on request. Stalls aisle seats available for transfer. **Wheelchair loo (D85 ST100)** inside the Webber Street entrance. From the foyer: stalls +3; dress circle +32; upper circle +60.

Open Air, Inner Circle, Regent's Park NW1 *Tel:* BO 0171 486-2431/1933. Outdoor auditorium which can be delightful on a fine summer's evening. Open May to September. OB spaces on the Inner Circle opposite Chester Road, and also opposite Regents College. Flat entrance via the box office, or via a steepish ramp opposite 'The Holme'. Step free access to four chair spaces on either side of stalls. **Adapted cubicles (D85 ST65)** in both ladies and gents on the same level as the chair spaces.

Palace, Shaftesbury Avenue W1 *Tel:* BO 0171 434-0909. In Victorian times, the Royal English Opera House, now a home to many successful musicals. Entrance +2 steps. Alternatively go through a side exit (+1), to the rear stalls. Two chair spaces, with restricted view; so you may prefer to transfer into an aisle seat. The exit also gives step free access to Box Y (D64cm) with space for a chair user and companion, with side view. From the foyer: the stalls are normally –23+23, but these can be bypassed via –3, on request; dress circle +30; upper circle +55; balcony approx +75.

Phoenix, Charing Cross Road WC2 *Tel:* BO 0171 867-1044. A theatre strongly associated with Noel Coward, with the dress circle at ground level. Entrance +4 steps. Flat access through an exit, giving step free access to a box (D79cm), which can hold a chair user and companion. Slightly sideways view. Dress circle seat A28 available for transfer. **Wheelchair loo (D78 ST85)** next to the box. From the foyer: stalls –13; dress circle +21; upper circle +40.

Piccadilly, Denman Street W1 *Tel:* BO 0171 867-1118 M 0171 867-1128. Entrance +1 step. Two side exits in Sherwood Street without steps. One (on the right) leads to the royal circle with +1 en route, and one transfer seat at A28. The other on the left, leads via a ramp to Box C, on left of circle. This holds up to three chair users and three companions. For some productions it may house technical equipment and be unavailable. From the foyer: stalls –15; royal circle +11–10, grand circle +70.

Place, 17 Dukes Road WC1 *Tel:* BO 0171 387-0031 M 0171 380-1268. About 200m from Euston station, south and east. Small theatre venue. Entrance +1 step. Platform stairlift to the first floor, bypassing +12. Up to ten chair users can be accommodated. The café is –13.

Players, The Arches, Villiers Street WC2 *Tel:* BO 0171 839-1134 M 0171 741-2251. Small venue built below street level under Charing Cross station. Flat access to the foyer, but –16 steps to the auditorium. There's a flat entry to the balcony with three chair spaces, and a **wheelchair loo (D80 ST80)** off the foyer.

Playhouse, Northumberland Avenue WC2 *Tel:* BO 0171 839-4292. Recently refurbished medium size Victorian theatre. Stalls at street level. The +3 steps to the foyer can be bypassed by a portable ramp (quite steep). Then step free to the stalls, where up to eight chair spaces can be provided by removing seats. Advanced booking essential. **Wheelchair loo (D75 ST75)** at stalls level. From the foyer: dress circle +25; balcony +80. Induction loop.

Prince Charles see section on *Cinemas.*

Prince Edward, Old Compton Street W1 *Tel:* BO 0171 734-8951. Large 1930s theatre with the front of the circle at street level. Flat entrance. Easiest entrance for people with disabilities via a side exit door in Greek Street, giving step free access to Row A in the dress circle, where seats A2-A5 are available for transfer. The Royal Box has space for two chair users and companions. Slightly side-on view, but otherwise good. From the foyer: stalls –25 steps; dress circle +27; upper circle 80/100+. **Wheelchair loo (D70+ ST80+)** through the main foyer on the right. Infra-red hearing system.

Prince of Wales, Coventry Street W1 *Tel:* BO 0171 839-5972 M 0171 839-5957. Built in the 1930s on a grand scale. Stalls at street level. Flat entrance, then –4 steps to the stalls with six seats available for transfer. From the foyer: stalls –4, dress circle +23/40. Infrared sets available.

Queen's, Shaftesbury Avenue W1 *Tel:* BO 0171 494-5041 (Stoll Moss group).

Large Edwardian theatre partly reconstructed after the war. Dress circle at street level. Flat entrance. Side exit gives step free access to the dress circle. Chair spaces in a box (flat access D61cm). Dress circle seat D1 available for transfer, accessed via this entrance. From the foyer, stalls –18 steps; dress circle –3 and upper circle +19. Infrared hearing system. There's an adapted loo signed, but it is in fact a standard size cubicle.

Royal Court, Sloane Square SW1 *Tel:* BO 0171 730-1745. Small theatre, internationally known for presenting new plays. Dress circle at ground level. Entrance +4 steps. No chair spaces. Two dress circle aisle seats are available for transfer. From the foyer: stalls –20; upper circle +25. Induction loop. Also contains the **Theatre Upstairs** *Tel:* 0171 730-2554. Separate auditorium with +62.

Royalty, Portugal Street WC2 *Tel:* BO 0171 494-5090. The theatre was 'dark' (ie there was no show on) when we visited. We confirmed the details with the management, but without visiting. Rear circle at street level. Entrance +4 steps. Alternative via a side exit, initially flat, then +4. Staff can remove dress circle seats J19 and J20 to create two chair spaces. J8 and J9 available for transfer. From the foyer: dress circle –20+10; stalls –40.

Sadler's Wells see section on *Music venues.*

St Martin's, West Street, Cambridge Circus WC2 *Tel:* BO 0171 836-1443. Small Edwardian-style theatre with the dress circle close to street level. Entrance +3 steps, then +3 to dress circle. At this level, Box C (D76cm) holds one chair user and companion. Two seats in row F at the back of the dress circle are available for transfer. From the foyer: stalls –25; upper circle +45.

Savoy, Savoy Court, Strand WC2 *Tel:* BO 0171 836-8888. Built for the Gilbert and Sullivan light operas, the theatre has recently been refurbished, providing improved access. The theatre lies under the Savoy building, and the street is level with the upper circle. Step free access from the Strand to the BO. Ramped access is possible from Carting Lane to the dress circle. It's best to go there *first* if you need to use this entrance as it's a long way round the block from the BO. Contact the stage door in Carting Lane to gain access. Step free access to two chair spaces in the dress circle, and to row F seats. The adapted loo (D70 opening inwards, ST50) near the chair spaces has restricted space, particularly because of the door. From the foyer: upper circle +2 steps; dress circle –33 and stalls –75. Ten infrared headsets.

Shaftesbury, Shaftesbury Avenue WC2 *Tel:* BO 0171 379-5399. An Edwardian theatre with a somewhat troubled history. In 1973, part of the ceiling collapsed. When we wanted to resurvey the theatre was 'dark' (ie closed), so we are dependent on our past surveys and what we were told by management. The royal circle is at street level. Entrance +1 step, then –3 to boxes A, B, F and E. All can hold either one or two chair users and a companion. From the foyer, –2 to the royal circle row A in which two aisle seats are available for transfer; stalls –25; grand circle +50. A maximum of four chair users are allowed at any one performance.

Strand, Aldwych WC2 *Tel:* BO 0171 930-8800. An Edwardian theatre, built as a 'pair' with the Aldwych on either side of the Waldorf Hotel. Circle at street level. Entrance +8 steps. Easier access through Catherine Street side exit, with –2. Two chair spaces at the front of the dress circle. From the foyer: stalls –29; dress circle –7; upper circle +40.

Theatre Museum see chapter on *Museums & galleries.*

Theatre Upstairs see write-up on the Royal Court.

Vaudeville, Strand WC2 *Tel:* BO 0171 836-9987 M 0171 836-3191. Originally built in 1870, it was completely refurbished in 1969 and the stalls are close to street level. Main entrance +1 step. No chair spaces, but transfer is possible for one chair user to an aisle seat in the stalls. This is reached via –6. From the foyer to the dress circle is +27; upper circle +57.

Victoria Palace, Victoria Street SW1 *Tel:* BO 0171 834-1317. Built as an Edwardian music hall, it has the stalls on street level. Flat entrance over a tiny lip. Step free access through Allington Street exit, to the stalls. Staff can remove stalls seats M36 and O36 to make two chair spaces. Alternatively you can transfer to these seats. From the foyer: stalls –4; dress circle +15; upper circle +75. The theatre is licensed to accommodate up to six wheelchair users (inclusive of transferees). Infrared hearing system being fixed.

Westminster, Palace Street, Buckingham Palace Road SW1 *Tel:* BO 0171 834-7882. Built originally as a cinema in the 1920s, it was redecorated and refurbished in 1986. Stalls at street level. Main entrance +13 steps. A side exit gives access to the to stalls via +1. Then step free to two boxes with up to three chair spaces in each; good, slightly side-on view.

Chair space at stalls seat D1. Front stalls aisle seats available for transfer. Six chair users are allowed altogether. From the foyer: stalls –3; dress circle +35 –20. Private lift (D70 W73 L120) in the foyer goes to the circle, where there is –2 to the back row, and then it is stepped to other rows. Induction loop.

Whitehall, Whitehall SW1 *Tel:* BO 0171 867-1119. As the theatre was 'dark' when we resurveyed, we are basing this on previous information collected some time ago. Entrance +1 step. No chair spaces. The royal circle has +10 and some transfer seats. From the foyer: stalls –25.

Wyndham's, Charing Cross Road WC2 *Tel:* BO 0171 369-1736. An intimate theatre built for Charles Wyndham, a famous Victorian actor-manager. The stalls are just below ground level. Entrance +1 step to the foyer. Two exits can be opened to give easier access. One leads to the rear stalls via –9; the other gives access to technicians box via –3. This can sometimes be used and has chair space, limited by the fact that its quite cramped. The viewing area is only 120cm wide, and there's a restricted view. From the foyer: stalls –18; royal circle +18; grand circle +40; balcony +60. Infrared hearing system.

Young Vic, 66 The Cut SE1 *Tel:* BO 0171 928-6363 M 0171 633-0133. Located just opposite Short Street. Flat access to the main entrance, and stalls with two chair spaces, and possibilities for transfer. The circle has 20+ steps. The café is –3 from the foyer, with a platform stairlift. This was not operational when we visited, and provided a good example of where a ramp would have been a much better solution to bypass steps, especially as ramps are much cheaper. **Wheelchair loo (D85 ST70)** just past the stairs in the foyer. Sennheiser sound system.

Outer – but inside the n/s circular roads

Some small scale theatre takes place in a room over a pub or in a basement, and these involve the barrier of more than 15 steps, as well as restricted space in the venue itself. These are listed below:

Arts, Holy Trinity Community Hall, 170 Gloucester Terrace W2
Tel: M 0171 262-1429.

Barons Court, Barons Ale House, 28 Comeragh Road W14
Tel: 0171 602-0235.

Canal Café, Bridge House, Delamere Terrace, Little Venice W2
Tel: 0171 289-6054.

Etcetera, Oxford Arms, 265 Camden High Street NW1
Tel: 0171 482-4857.

Finborough, 118 Finborough Road, West Brompton SW10
Tel: 0171 244-7439.

Gate, 11 Pembridge Road, Notting Hill W11
Tel: 0171 229-5387.

Grace (over the *Latchmere* pub), 503 Battersea Park Road SW11
Tel: BO 0171 228-2620 M 0171 738-2919. Has four chair spaces.

Greenwich Studio, *Prince of Orange*, 189 Greenwich High Road SE10
Tel: 0181 858-2862.

Hen and Chicken, 109 St Paul's Road N1
Tel: 0171 704-2001.

Pentameters, 28 Heath Street, Hampstead NW3
Tel: 0171 435-3648. Above the *Three Horeshoes* pub.
Has three chair spaces.

Albany, Douglas Way, Deptford SE8 *Tel:* BO 0181 692-4446 M 0181 691-3277. Flat access at the entrance and to the GF of the venue. Inside there is a lift (D75 W110 L125) to get to most other parts of the theatre. No restriction on the number of chairs. **Wheelchair loo (D85 ST100)** on the GF opposite the front door. Induction loop.

Almedia, Almedia Street, Islington N1 *Tel:* BO 0171 359-4404 M 0171 226-7432. NCP about 50m away. Entrance step free over some cobbles, leading to the foyer and café. A lift (D70 W120 L90) bypasses steps to the stalls, where there are two chair spaces. The circle has at least +30 steps. **Wheelchair loo (D80 ST90)** off the foyer.

BAC see section on *Arts centres.*

Bridge Lane, Bridge Lane, Battersea SW11 *Tel:* BO 0171 228-5185. Entrance +1+2 steps but ramped bypass via an exit. Two chair spaces. Step free to bar from the ramp, through D65cm.

Chats Palace, 42 Brooksby Walk, Hackney E9 *Tel:* BO 0181 533-0227 M 0181 986-6714. Opposite Hommerton Grove. A venue putting on cabaret, comedy, poetry, jazz, soul and theatre performances. They involve people with disabilities in workshops and performances as well as spectating. Level access to foyer and bar. Step free to performance area with chair spaces. There are +27 steps to the first floor where there are meeting rooms and where some of the workshops take place. **Wheelchair loo (D75 ST85)** off the bar. Infrared sound system to be installed in 1995.

Cockpit, Gateforth Street, Lisson Grove NW8 *Tel:* BO 0171 402-5081 M 0171 262-7907. Some on-site parking possible. Step free to the foyer and bar. The –6 steps to the auditorium can be bypassed via exit door in Samford Street. Five chair spaces. **Adapted cubicle in the ladies (D65 ST74 obstructed by a fixed handrail inside the door).**

Courtyard, 10 York Way, Kings Cross N1 *Tel:* BO 0171 833-0870. About 700m north of Kings Cross station. Step free throughout. Two chair spaces.

Greenwich, Crooms Hill, Greenwich SE10 *Tel:* BO 0181 858-7755 M 0181 858-2265. On the corner with Nevada Street. Entrance +1 step. Lift (D80 W100 L140) to the auditorium. Two chair spaces if seats are removed. Access to the front of the theatre is via +33. Induction loop. **Adapted loo (D75 ST60)** on the GF. The theatre has an adapted minibus available with a tail-lift, and can bring disabled customers who live within 8km to the theatre. This applies to performances on any Wednesday. Book in advance !

Hackney Empire, 291 Mare Street, Hackney E8 *Tel:* BO 0181 985-2424 M 0181 986-0171. Opposite Morning Lane, by the Town Hall. Entrance +2 steps.

Alternative via exit door gives step free access to six chair spaces or for transfer. **Wheelchair loo (D80 ST80)** between the alternative entrance and the bar. Dress circle +25, upper circle +100.

Hampstead, Swiss Cottage Centre, 98 Avenue Road Hampstead NW3 *Tel:* BO 0171 722-9301. 150m from Swiss Cottage station. Step free to two chair spaces in the front row. Induction loop. **Wheelchair loo (D70 ST120)** off the foyer.

Hoxton Hall, Hoxton Street N1 *Tel:* BO 0171 739-5431. Nearly opposite Homefield Street. Parking at the Britannia Leisure Centre 100m away. Ramped entrance, and step free to the café, theatre auditorium and most workshop spaces. Balcony +20 spiralled. Induction loop in theatre, and in GF workshop space. **Wheelchair loo (D80 ST85)** at the rear of theatre.

Jackson's Lane, 269a Archway Road, Highgate N6 *Tel:* BO 0181 341-4421 M 0181 340-5226. Opposite Highgate tube station. Two OB spaces on site. Steep ramp to the entrance. Level inside to the café, bar and theatre. Plenty of chair spaces and transfer opportunities. The theatre has a lift (D78 W88 L130) by which you can get to the control box. Adapted cubicles in both gents and ladies, and there's a **wheelchair loo (D85 ST80)** by the gents. Induction loop. There's also a backstage changing room for disabled performers with a **wheelchair loo and shower (D85 ST100).**

Jongleurs Comedy Club, Middle Yard, Camden Lock, Chalk Farm Road NW1 *Tel:* 0171 924-2766. Underneath *Dingwalls,* with a cobbled ramp down from Camden Lock Place. Chair spaces at street level, where the bar and food counter are. Other levels drop down (with −2 steps) towards the stage. **Wheelchair loo (D85 ST80)** at street level.

Lee Valley Ice Centre, Lea Bridge Road, Leyton E10 *Tel:* BO 0181 533-3154. On-site CP with OB spaces. Step free through the entrance to chair spaces for viewing ice shows. There's a **wheelchair loo (D70 ST120)** next to the box office, where the key is kept. Chair users are encouraged to go on the ice when the centre is being used for general skating. The café and bar are +3 steps.

Lewisham, Rushey Green, Catford SE6 *Tel:* BO 0181 690-0002 M 0181 695-6000 ext3175. On the corner of Catford Road. MSCP with OB spaces at the back of the theatre about 100m away. Entrance +11 steps, but there's a platform stairlift (W66 L75) behind the theatre. This goes to the stalls with four chair spaces. Steps up to the circle, and −10 to the **Studio theatre** which also has four chair spaces. There are **wheelchair cubicles (D85 ST80)** in both ladies and gents loos off the foyer. We were told that there's an adapted loo in the Studio theatre, accessible by ramp. Induction loop.

Little Angel Marionette, 14 Dagmar Passage, Cross Street, Islington N1 *Tel:* 0171 226-1787. Neatly tucked away between Cross Street and Dagmar Terrace. Two OB spaces on-site if booked in advance. Entrance +1 step, but a step free alternative is available. The venue is all on one level, including the café. Up to four chair spaces if benches are removed. **Wheelchair loo (D75 ST70)** just off the foyer. Induction loop.

Lyric, King Street, Hammersmith W6 *Tel:* BO 0181 741-2311 M 0181 741-0824. Next to Hammersmith Grove with an NCP about 200m from the theatre. Step free to the box office. Lift (D80 W100 L130) goes to all floors. On the first floor, there's a bar, restaurant and outside garden. The **Studio** is on this level with level access, but no chair spaces. The second floor is the stalls level of the main theatre, with three chair spaces. The lift goes to both the circle and upper circle, but there are steps involved. Both theatres have induction loops. There are **wheelchair cubicles (D70 ST115)** in both the ladies and gents on the first floor.

Man in the Moon, 392 Kings Road, Chelsea SW3 *Tel:* 0171 BO 351-2876 M 0171 351-5701. The entrance, via the side of the pub on Park Walk, has +1 step, then +6 to the box office and –6 to the auditorium. Up to four chair spaces.

Oval House, 52 Kennington Oval SE11 *Tel:* BO 0171 582-7680 M 0171 735-2786. Right by the cricket ground. CP space if booked in advance. Level access to the foyer, café and Theatre Downstairs. Plenty of room for chair users. Induction loop. Theatre Upstairs is +17 (steep and narrow). **Two unisex loos, labelled gents (D76 ST42) and ladies (D76 ST110) on the GF.**

Riverside Studios see section on *Arts centres.*

Southwark Playhouse, 62 Southwark Bridge Road SE1 *Tel:* 0171 620-3494. Entrance +1–1, then flat to the auditorium. Up to four chair spaces.

Theatre Royal, Stratford, Gerry Raffles Square, Stratford E15 *Tel:* BO 0181 534-0310 M 0181 534-7374. About 150m from Stratford station on the DLR. Opposite Angel Lane. On-street OB spaces outside and CP about 100m away. Level to the box office. The stalls have –2 steps, but a step free route to be opened if needed. Six chair spaces in the stalls. Induction loop. **Wheelchair loo (D100 ST70)** next to the bar at the end of the corridor. From the foyer: +18 to the circle; +35 to the upper circle.

Theatro Technis, 26 Crowndale Road NW1 *Tel:* 0171 387-6617. Ramped access available, and the venue is all on one level. Six chair spaces. **Adapted loo (D78, opens in, ST85)** near the box office.

Tower, Canonbury Place, Islington N1 *Tel:* 0171 226-5111. Level entry to one chair space. Other parts of the theatre at different levels. The bar/coffee shop has +2 steps. Induction loop.

Turtle Key, 74A Farm Lane, Fulham SW6 *Tel/Minicom:* 0171 385-4905. Small arts centre near Fulham Broadway. Step free throughout. Induction loop.

Walthamstow Assembley Hall, Town Hall, Forest Road, Walthamstow E17 *Tel/Minicom:* BO 0181 521-7111 M 0181 527-5544 ext4556. OB spaces outside. Ramped entrance and step free to the auditorium. Up to twenty chair spaces. **Wheelchair loo (D75 ST90)** off the foyer. Induction loop.

White Bear (club), 138 Kennington Park Road, Kennington SE11 *Tel:* BO 0181 793-9193 M 0181 793-8139. Ramped access and then the venue is all on one level. Three chair spaces. Bar and café.

Between the N/S circular roads and the M25

Beck, Grange Road, Hayes, Middx *Tel:* BO 0181 561-8371 M 0181 561-7506. Turn right at the Crown if travelling east on the Uxbridge Road. Large CP with OB spaces. Level access throughout, and up to eight chair spaces. Bar/bistro. **Adapted cubicles in both ladies and gents loos.** Induction loop.

Charles Cryer, 39 High Street, Carshalton, Surrey *Tel:* BO 0181 770-4950 M 0181 770-4960. Theatre CP off Westcroft Road. Ramp to main entrance. Lift (D75 W110 L150) to the auditorium on the first floor. Three chair spaces, and more chair users can be accommodated on occasion. Induction loop. **Wheelchair loo (D85 ST110)** on the first floor. For those interested in the production side of theatre, the lift goes up to the lighting box, and there is a **wheelchair loo and shower (D75 ST70)** in both dressing rooms. The production studio behind the theatre is step free to the main GF area.

Chingford Assembley Hall, Station Road, Chingford E4 *Tel:* BO/*Minicom:* 0181 521-7111 M 0181 529-0555. On-site CP with three OB spaces. Level access to hall, loo, and ten chair spaces. Induction loop. **Wheelchair loo (D76 ST150+ NKS door opens in but spacious)** off the foyer. **Wheelchair loo (D89 ST100+ NKS)** outside.

Churchill, High Street, Bromley, Kent *Tel:* BO 0181 460-5838 M 0181 464-7131. In the pedestrian precinct, by the corner with Churchill Way. Five OB spaces in Churchill Place. Level access and step free to nine chair spaces in the circle, which is at street level. A staff lift (D80 W100 L140) serves both floors. Sennheiser sound system. **Adapted loo (D75 ST75, but fixed handrails)** off the circle foyer.

Croydon Warehouse, 62 Dingwall Road, Croydon *Tel:* BO 0181 680-4060

M 0181 681-1257. Adjacent to East Croydon station (which is step free). Flat entrance, but +9+6 steps to auditorium. Several chair spaces and staff will help lift people up the stairs (given notice).

Kenneth More, Oakfield Road, Ilford, Essex *Tel:* 0181 553-4466. About 400m from Ilford station. Step free to the auditorium. Three chair spaces. Induction loop. **Adapted loo (not seen)** near the chair spaces.

Millfield, Silver Street, Edmonton N18 *Tel:* BO 0181 807-6680 M 0181 807-6186. At the junction of the North Circular and the A10. On-site CP, but ring if you want to reserve a slot. Level access on the Silver Street side to four chair spaces and transfer possibilities. Bar. Induction loop. **Adapted cubicle in gents (D75 ST40) and wheelchair cubicle in the ladies (D75 ST155)** off the foyer

Orange Tree, 1 Clarence Street, Richmond, Surrey *Tel:* 0181 940-3633. 100m from Richmond station (with step free access to and from all lines). Possible on-site parking if booked. Entrance +5+6 steps. The normal route from the foyer to the theatre is via −7 steps, or about +25 if you are going to the gallery. Alternative ramped entrance from the courtyard CP, giving step free access to the chair spaces (up to four chairs, where seats are removed) in the main auditorium. Only one row is accessed this way without steps. The back entrance also leads to the lift (D80 W110 L160) which goes to the foyer/bar and up to the third floor. **Wheelchair loo (D80 ST80)** on the third floor, through two doors into the dressing room area. Induction loop. There's a second theatre space over the Orange Tree pub across the road, reached via +8+15. The pub has step free access.

Paul Robeson, Centre Space, Treaty Centre, High Street, Hounslow, Middx *Tel:* BO 0181 577-6969 M 0181 570-0622. Treaty Centre MSCP, about 200m away see write-up in *Shops* chapter. Theatre box office on the GF. Lift (D110 W155 L140) gives level access to the front row of first floor auditorium with up to nine chair spaces. Step free to café. Induction loop. **Wheelchair loo (D85 ST75)** on the first floor.

Polka, 240 The Broadway, Wimbledon SW19 *Tel:* 0181 543-4888. A unique children's theatre some 600m from Wimbledon station (which is step free). Level access to the GF where there is a café, play area and a workshop for children with special needs. **The Adventure theatre** of the GF is simply a large empty room. There are exhibitions from time to time. Lift (D75 W100 L130) to the auditorium with six chair spaces. Induction loop. **Wheelchair loo (D80 ST110)** on the GF.

Questors, Mattock Lane, Ealing W5 *Tel:* BO 0181 567-5184 M 0181 567-0011. A long-established theatre club about 500m from Ealing Broadway station. Small on-site CP with OB spaces. Level entrance and lift (D90 W110 L150) to the back of the auditorium with four chair spaces. The lift bypasses about +30 steps. The bar and gallery are on this level. The lift also gives access to the Grapevine bar (for members) and a **wheelchair loo (D85 ST85)** on this level. Sennheiser infrared sound system. The small **Studio** theatre has flat access, and uses movable seating.

Richmond, The Green, Richmond, Surrey *Tel:* BO 0181 940-0088 M 0181 940-0220. Richmond station (which is fully accessible) is about 400m away. Parking difficult, and there's a CP off the A316 Twickenham Road, also some 400m. A traditional-style theatre, recently renovated. There are +5 steps at the main entrance, then step free to the rear stalls; +23 to the dress circle and +40 to the upper circle. Alternative entrance to the left gives level access to the rear stalls with four chair spaces. Flat to the bar. **Wheelchair loo (D70 ST80)** next to the rear stalls entry. Induction loop.

Studio, 28 Beckenham Road, Beckenham, Kent *Tel:* BO 0181 663-0103 M 0181 663-0901. About 150m from the Clockhouse station. There are +9 steps at the entrance, but once inside, the venue is on one level. Some chair spaces. **Adapted loo (D75 ST30)** between the front entrance and box office.

Tara, 356 Garrett Lane, Earlsfield SW18 *Tel:* 0181 871-1458. A small arts centre opposite Earlsfield station. There is +1 step at the entrance. Six chair spaces by removing a row of seats.

Tricycle, 269 Kilburn High Road NW6 *Tel:* BO 0171 328-1000 M 372-6611. A fringe theatre with good access. Entrance ramped. There are +6 steps into the theatre, but given notice, some seats can be removed and there is a lift for chair users giving access to four spaces. The catering facilities, bar and exhibition space all have flat/ramped access. Induction loop available. **Wheelchair loo (D70+ ST70+)** to the left of the entrance.

Waltham Forest, Lloyd Park Pavilion, Winns Terrace, Walthamstow E17 *Tel/Minicom:* BO 0181 521-7111. Off Forest Road, by the park, with on-site CP and OB spaces. Step free throughout including the café/bar. Twelve chair spaces in the theatre. Induction loop. **Wheelchair loo (D85 ST80)** to the right of the auditorium as you face the stage.

Watermans Arts Centre, see section on *Arts centres*.

Wimbledon, The Broadway, Wimbledon SW19 *Tel:* BO 0181 540-0362 M 0181 543-4549. About 250m from Wimbledon Station (which is fully accessible) by the junction with Russell Road. Small on-site CP. There are +7 steps to the box office and +6 to foyer bar. Alternative for chair users via a fire exit on Russell Road involving –5 (steep steps), with a platform stairlift to bypass them. Eight chair spaces. Induction loop. Two **wheelchair loos (D95ST90)** at the back of the stalls, step free from the chair spaces.

Pubs and wine bars

The English pub is a unique institution. They vary a great deal. Some have a mainly 'local' clientel while others are full of passing trade because of their location. Most have a core of 'regulars'. Some depend on business trade, and **many in and around the City and Docklands are closed at weekends**, while others only serve food during the week. *We have included phone numbers, so if you want to find out about eating or are in doubt about whether they'll be open, you can ring to check.*

This listing has seen enormous change. We are now able to list well over 150 pubs inside the M25 which have either flat or single step access, and which have a well adapted loo. Several of the brewers have made it a policy to include a disabled persons toilet in the specification for all new premises. Sometimes they will include one when a pub is refurbished. All the loos are unisex unless specifically described as being inside the 'ladies' or 'gents' area. Note that some of the newest pubs are adopting an 18+ policy or even a 21+ policy, particularly at busy times. As these things tend to change we have not indicated this. If it's an issue, ring first to find out.

We intend to produce an updated list in mid-1997, and, hopefully, annually after that. Without such a list it is difficult to find out which are accessible. If you want a new list, write to **Access Project,** 39 Bradley Gardens, West Ealing W13 8HE.

The *Evening Standard London Pub Guide,* has good pub descriptions, and includes information about access. Unfortunately they have not adopted any specific criteria, and so some of it is misleading.

We have included several pub/restaurants in the *Beefeater* chain, partly because they had gone to the trouble of marking their 'accessible' places on their general brochure. As with other listings, it was somewhat inaccurate, as no consistent criteria were applied. Also the *Beefeater* pubs make an architectural feature of having split levels everywhere. Nonetheless, the ones we have included have some parts of the bar and restaurant accessible without steps, and also have an adapted loo. It is hoped that other chains will provide similar facilities, and in particular that consistent and practical criteria are applied when people use the 'wheelchair' symbol in their listing.

In order to make the list easily used we have grouped the pubs in geographical areas:

London's West End and centre, comprising the postal districts W1, W2, WC1, WC2, SW1, SE1, NW1 and N1;

the **City area** comprising postal districts EC1, EC2, EC3, EC4 and E1;

inner areas including:

the northern Docklands, and the Isle of Dogs (E14), and inner postal districts E, N, NW, W, SW, SE;

outer areas north of the river, comprising:
Brentford, Greenford, Hayes and Hounslow,
Denham, Ickenham, Rickmansworth, Ruislip and Uxbridge,
Borehamwood, Edgware, Harrow, Kenton and Stanmore,
Barnet, Chingford and Enfield,
Chigwell and Loughton,
Barking, Brentwood, Dagenham, Hornchurch, Ilford and Romford;

outer areas south of the river, comprising:
Chessington, Kingston, Richmond, Surbiton, Walton and Worcester Park;
Mitcham, Morden, Putney, Wandsworth and Wimbledon;
Croydon, Purley, Sutton and Wallington;
Beckenham, Bickley, Bromley, Orpington and West Wickham;
Bexley and Dartford.

London's West End and centre
(W1, W2, WC1, WC2, SW1, SE1, NW1 and N1)

All Bar One, 1 Liverpool Road, Islington N1 *Tel:* 0171 278-5906. On the corner
with Upper Street, almost opposite the Angel station. Entrance +1 step, then
step free throughout. **Adapted loo (D70+ ST55)** en route to the other toilets.
Fortunately the cubicle is quite big. The WC was placed in the centre, preventing
ST from either side, and the 'support' bars were on the walls, too far away to
be useful to anyone ! Apart from that, it's a good place.

Burlington Berties (Regent Inn), 39 Shaftesbury Avenue WC2 *Tel:* 0171
437-0847. Next door to the Queen's theatre. Step free to 40%, including the
main bar. **Wheelchair loo (D85 ST70)** to the right of the bar.

Crown & Anchor (Bass), 137 Drummond Street, Regents Park NW1 *Tel:*
0171 387-6474. By the junction with North Gower Street. Ramped entrance
on the right was locked when we visited. Easiest other entrance has +2 steps.
Then 100% step free access. **Adapted loo (D75 ST61)** at the rear, on the left.
Side transfer was blocked by an old fridge when we visited!

Finnock & Firkin (Taylor Walker), 100 Upper Street, Islington N1 *Tel:* 0171
226-3467. By the junction with Theberton Street. Step free on the GF.
Wheelchair loo (D80 ST75) on the right, by other toilets; key from bar. Upper
floor has +20 steps.

Flyman & Firkin (Taylor Walker), 166 Shaftesbury Avenue WC2 *Tel:* 0171
240-7109. 150m north of Cambridge Circus, just past the junction with Mercer
Street. Entrance +1 step, and then step free. Most tables have long benches, or
are high up. Three/four tables are of standard height with movable chairs.

Wheelchair loo (D80 ST85) opposite the bar, on the right.

Henry's Café Bar (Greenalls), 27 Endell Street WC2 *Tel:* 0171 379-8500. Towards the Long Acre end of the road. Flat entrance, and over 50% is step free. **Adapted loo (D80 ST64).**

Jack Horner (Fullers), 236 Tottenham Court Road SW1 *Tel:* 0171 636-2868. On the junction with Bayley Street. Ramped entrance and **wheelchair loo (D80 ST90)** on the GF. Key at bar.

Lord Moon of the Mall (Wetherspoons), 18 Whitehall SW1 *Tel:* 0171 839-7701. About 50m from Trafalgar Square and next to the Whitehall theatre. It is a listed building which presented problems relating to access. A bell is discretely placed outside if you need help to get in, and we have suggested the provision of portable ramps. Entrance +3 steps. Step free inside. **Wheelchair loo (D80 ST120+)** just past the bar on the left.

Man in the Moon (Wetherspoons), 40 Chalk Farm Road NW1 *Tel:* 0171 482-2054. 30m from the junction with Harmood Street. Ramped entrance on the right, giving 30% step free access. **Wheelchair loo (D77 ST82)** is unfortunately on a level –3 steps below the entrance level. To reach it, go through the door 3m to left of bar and it is on your left.

Moon and Sixpence (Wetherspoons), 185 Wardour Street W1 *Tel:* 0171 734-1098. Near Oxford Street, on the corner of Noel Street. Tiny step at the entrance, then step free. **Adapted loo (D80 ST55 blocked by a bin)** to the right of the bar.

Moon under Water (Wetherspoons), 28 Leicester Square WC2 *Tel:* 0171 839-2837. Next to the Odeon cinema. Relatively long thin pub which can get very crowded. Entrance +2 steps, then flat throughout. **Wheelchair loo (D80 ST80+)** past the bar and through the swing doors.

Old Orleans (Pub/restaurant), 29 Wellington Street, Covent Garden WC2 *Tel:* 0171 497-2433. On the corner with Tavistock Street. Entrance +3 steps, then step free access to 50%, with an **adapted loo (D80 ST55)** to the left. When surveyed the loo was being used for storage.

179 Upper Street (Wetherspoons), 179 Upper Street, Islington N1 *Tel:* 0171 226-6276. Opposite Islington Town Hall, 40m south of the junction with Tyndale Lane. Ramped entrance and step free inside. **Wheelchair loo (D75 ST80)** on the left, near the rear of building. To reach it, go to the right of the bar, turn left and it is the first door on the left.

Sheila's (Bar/Restaurant), 41 King Street WC2 *Tel:* 0171 240-8282. Located in the northwest corner of Covent Garden. +1 step at the entrance, then step free. **Wheelchair loo (D80+ ST80+)** past the bar and on the left.

Southampton Arms (Bass Charrington), 1 Camden High Street NW1 *Tel:* 0171 387-2749. Located where Hampstead Road meets Camden High Street. Step free throughout, using left hand entrance. Unmarked **wheelchair loo** at rear LHS of building, just to right of gents; key from bar. The barman said the **wheelchair loo** wasn't in "mint condition" and we didn't see it. When we rang, we were told that the loo was usable, but partly used for storage. It is scheduled for renovation.

Wetherspoons, Victoria Station concourse, SW1 *Tel:* 0171 931-0455. The two storey building in the centre of the station with a W H Smiths, has a Wetherspoon pub upstairs. Access is by escalator or stairs (10+11). However, there is a lift (D80 W95 L140), in the corner of the building by platform 8, giving step free access to the pub/restaurant. **Wheelchair loo (D86 ST75)**; key from the bar.

City area
(EC1, EC2, EC3, EC4 and E1)

Banker (Fullers), Cousin Lane EC4 *Tel:* 0171 283-5206. On the riverfront, under the arches of Cannon Bridge, carrying the lines going from Cannon Street Station. Flat access to a bar which only has high stools and tables. An upper section is +9 steps, overlooking the river, and there's an outside riverside area (+7). **Wheelchair loo (D90 ST70)** by the entrance; key from the bar.

Bishops Wine Bar (Whitbread), 160 Bishopsgate EC2 *Tel:* 0171 256-7279. On the Arcade (see *Sir Paul Pindar* pub). Split level with +3 steps to get to the bar, but some tables have step free access. **Wheelchair loo (D80 ST80)** on the left.

Bull Bear & Broker (Bass Charrington), 24 King William Street EC4 *Tel:* 0171 623-0714. On the corner with Arthur Street and at the end of London Bridge. Step free from Arthur Street to about 20% of the whole (other bars are up many steps). In the accessible bit all the tables and chairs are 'standing' height. **Wheelchair loo (D90 ST80)**.

Captain Kidd (Samuel Smith), 108 Wapping High Street E1 *Tel:* 0171 480-5759. About 100m west of Wapping tube station, set back from the street and next to the river. Cobbled street. High kerb, then step free access to pub, or +2+2 steps to the beer garden. **Wheelchair loo (D90 ST70)** to the right of the entrance, but –5 steps to get there !

Dickens Inn (Courage), St Katherine's Way E1 *Tel:* 0171 488-2208. This is in the centre of St Katherine's Dock right by Tower Bridge. It is open most of the day and includes restaurants as well as bars and is accessible via a ramp (away to the right and bypassing the +12 steps). There is a lift (D75 W100 L130) behind the food bar in the part of the pub near the ramp, leading to a **wheelchair loo (D75 ST85)** in the basement, and the first floor restaurant.

Exchange Restaurant (Scottish and Newcastle Wine Bar), Exchange Square, Broadgate Centre EC2 *Tel:* 0171 377-9958. On the corner of Exchange Square and Exchange Place, overlooking some fairly dramatic architecture around the railway. At the end of Exchange Place there's an 'ansaphone controlled' lift to and from Appold Street. Step free access to 70%. **Wheelchair loo (D80 ST70).**

49 Gresham Street (Fullers), 49 Gresham Street EC2 *Tel:* 0171 606-0399. Near the Guildhall. Flat access to part of the GF bar. **Adapted loo (D85 ST60 obstructed by sink)** just to the left of the entrance, unsigned. Key at the bar.

Hamilton Hall (Wetherspoons), Unit 32, Liverpool Street Station EC2 *Tel:* 0171 247-3579. In a high and splendidly decorated hall, on the upper level of the station (which is ground level if you're coming from outside), towards Bishopsgate. Step free access from the station side. It is step free from Bishopsgate, from near the clocktower, and then into the station. **Wheelchair loo (D80 ST70)** but blocked by mop and bucket storage. "There's nowhere else to put them," according to the manager.

Kings Head (Whitbread), 49 Chiswell Street E1 *Tel:* 0171 606-9158. At the junction with Whitecross Street. Step free to the pub from either street, but split level inside involves –2–2 steps. **Wheelchair loo (D80 ST80)** by the Whitecross Street entrance; key at bar.

Kings Stores (Whitbread), 14 Widegate Street E1 *Tel:* 0171 247-4089. At the junction with Sandys Row. Step free only from White Rose Court. **Adapted loo (D90 ST25, blocked by fixed handrail)** at the end of the bar next to the gents; key at bar.

Magpie and Stump (Bass Charrington), 19 Old Bailey Road EC4 *Tel:* 0171 248-5085. Opposite the Old Bailey, with step free access throughout via a lift (D80 W100 L140) just inside the entrance. This bypasses +9 steps to the top level, –13 to the lower GF, and another –20 to a basement level. You need staff assistance to use the lift to the 'lower GF' which contains one **wheelchair loo (D70 ST70).** There's **another** on the lower lower GF (or basement) **(D70 ST70).**

Masque Haunt (Wetherspoons), 168 Old Street EC1 *Tel:* 0171 251-4195. At the junction with Bunhill Row. Most doors have +1 step, but the Bunhill Road one is ramped, giving step free access to 70%. **Adapted loo (D84 ST70,**

but door opens in), behind and to the left of the bar, next to the gents.

Melton Mowbray Pie & Ale House (Fullers), 18 Holborn EC1 *Tel:* 0171 405-7077. About 100m from Chancery Lane station and opposite Holborn House. Entrance +1 step and only part with step free access, as it is on three levels. Some tables outside in the summer. **Wheelchair loo (D85 ST130)** on the right, after the entrance.

Mint (Fullers), East Smithfield EC3 *Tel:* 0171 702-0370. Main entrance +16 steps, bypassed by a lift (D90 W90 L160) accessed from a side entrance. **Wheelchair loo (D90 ST90)** to the right of the bar.

Old King Lud (Whitbread), 78 Ludgate Hill EC4 *Tel:* 0171 329-8517. At Ludgate Circus, on the junction of Ludgate Hill and Farringdon Street. Flat from Farringdon Street. The **wheelchair loo (D85 ST85)** is through a door about three-quarters of the way down the bar, and at the bottom of the steps leading up to Ludgate Hill. Key at bar.

Sir Paul Pindar (Bass Charrington), 180 Bishopsgate EC2 *Tel:* 0171 496-0269. In the Bishopsgate Arcade near the junction with Primrose Street (there's ramped access about 50m from the junction by the mulitcoloured sculpture). Step free access. **Wheelchair loo (D80 ST70)** to the left from the corner entrance, with 90° turns.

Wynkyn de Worde Wine Bar and Restaurant (City Court Restaurants), Bride Lane, off Fleet Street EC4 *Tel:* 0171 936-2554. Under St Bride's Church, Fleet Street. Flat entrance and step free inside. **Wheelchair loo (D80 ST100)** by the entrance.

Inner areas
The northern Docklands, and the Isle of Dogs (E14)

Cat and Canary (Fullers), 1 Fishermans Walk, Canary Wharf E14 *Tel:* 0171 512-9187. About 50m from Cabot Square on the waterfront. Flat entrance then 60% is step free. **Wheelchair loo (D80 ST70).**

Drummonds (Charrington), Marsh Wall, Heron Quays E14 *Tel:* 0171 538-3357. Located at the junction with West Ferry Road and opposite the *City Pride*. The small CP becomes a 'garden' in the summer. Entrance +1 step, then step free to 60%. **Adapted loo (D80 ST56).**

Henry Addington (Bass Charrington), 20 MacKenzie Walk, Canary Wharf E14 *Tel:* 0171 512-9022. Located some 50m from Cabot Square on the waterfront. Step free throughout, including the waterfront patio. **Wheelchair loo (D80 ST80).**

Pier Tavern (Whitbread), 299 Manchester Road E14 *Tel:* 0171 515-9528. At the junction with Pier Street. Flat way into both the pub and garden from Pier Street. 80% with step free access. **Wheelchair loo (D80 ST70).**

Spinnaker (Greene King), Harbour Exchange Square E14 *Tel:* 0171 538-9329. Situated in the square which is on Limeharbour. Flat entrance with step free access to the pub and to the balcony overlooking the quay. **Wheelchair loo (D90 ST80)** opposite the bar.

Waterfront (Fullers), South Quay Plaza, Marsh Wall E14 *Tel:* 0171 538-8449. The pub is in the middle of the plaza, next to the river. Entrance +1 step, then flat to the lift (D80 W100 L120). First floor bar step free, though there's −1 to the balcony and patio. Thai restaurant on the second floor. **Wheelchair loo (D80 ST80)** on the first floor near the patio.

Inner postal districts E
East Ham, Forest Gate and Stratford

Earl of Wakefield (Charrington), 72 Katherine Road, East Ham E6 *Tel:* 0181 472-2382. At the junction with Wakefield Street. There is +1 step to the bars, flat to garden. **Wheelchair loo (D85 ST80)** to the right, at the back of the lounge bar.

Goldengrove (Wetherspoons), 146 The Grove, Stratford E15 *Tel:* 0181 519-0570. At the junction with Great Eastern Road. Step free throughout, including the garden, via ramps. **Wheelchair loo (D85 ST120)** at the rear of the pub.

Holly Tree (Bass Charrington), 141 Dames Road, Forest Gate E7 *Tel:* 0181 555-8548. Opposite the junction with Sidney Road. CP off Pevensey Road. Kerb between CP and rear entrance. Steep ramp at the rear entrance gives 95% step free access. Raised area +2 steps. From the rear entrance level, ledge then −1 to the garden. **Wheelchair loo (D80 ST75)** on the right just after rear entrance.

Miller's Well (Wetherspoons), 419 Barking Road, East Ham E6 *Tel:* 0181 471-8404. Opposite the Town Hall. Step free inside, −1 step to small garden. **Wheelchair loo (D85 ST75)** past the bar at the back of the pub.

Railway Tavern (Taylor Walker), 173 Forest Lane, Forest Gate E7 *Tel:* 0181 555-1177. At junction with Woodgrange Road. Step free. **Wheelchair**

loo (D80 ST90) at the rear, on the left. Staff said it is normally usable, but it was blocked by music equipment when we visited.

Tollgate Tavern (Whitbread), Mary Rose Mall, Beckton E6 *Tel:* 0171 476-3716. At the back of the ASDA supermarket, and about 200m from Beckton DLR station. CP outside. Step free to 90% of pub. **Wheelchair loo (D85 ST80)** by the shopping mall exit.

Inner postal districts N

Edmonton, Highgate, Holloway and Tottenham

Dagmar Arms (Whitbread), 36 Cornwall Road, Tottenham N15 *Tel:* 0181 800-7785. 30m from junction with Dagmar Road. On-site CP. Entrance +1 step, then 90% step free. **Wheelchair loo (D80 ST100)** at the rear through the family room. The garden has −1.

Gate House (Wetherspoons), 1 North Road, Highgate N6 *Tel:* 0181 340-8054. By the mini-roundabout at the junction with Hampstead Lane. Step free. **Adapted loo (D85 ST67) by the gents**; key at the bar.

Lamb (Wetherspoons), 52 Church Street, Edmonton N9 *Tel:* 0181 887-0128. Near the junction with Victoria Road. Flat front entrance, giving 35% step free access; −3 steps to rear area. **Wheelchair loo (D79 ST91)** to the left of the bar.

Nags Head (Bass Charrington), 456 Holloway Road, Holloway N7 *Tel:* 0171 607-2855. On the junction with Seven Sisters Road, near the Odeon. Step free from Holloway Road. **Wheelchair loo (D90 ST95).**

New Moon (Wetherspoons), 413 Lordship Lane, Tottenham N17 *Tel:* 0181 801-3496. Near the junction with Walpole Road. Step free. **Wheelchair loo (D85 ST90)** on the left.

Stag & Hounds (Taylor Walker), 371 Bury Street West, Edmonton N9 *Tel:* 0181 360-1740. 40m from junction with West View Crescent. Sloped on-site CP. Step free to 80% of the pub. **Wheelchair loo (D80 ST135)** on the right.

Toll Gate (Wetherspoons), 26 Turnpike Lane, Harringay N8 *Tel:* 0181 889-9085. Near the junction with Waldegrave Road. Small step, then flat access. **Wheelchair loo (D95 ST100)** in the back left hand corner.

Woodbine (Bass Charrington), 215 Blackstock Road, Highbury N5 *Tel:* 0171 226-0373. By the Police Station. Step free. **Wheelchair loo (D80 ST80)** at the back of the pub. Key at the bar.

Inner postal districts NW
Cricklewood, Golders Green, Hampstead, Harlesden, Maida Vale and Muswell Hill

Beaten Docket (Wetherspoons), 50 Cricklewood Broadway NW2 *Tel:* 0181 450-2972. 15m from junction with Skardu Road. Step free via ramped entrance on the right. **Wheelchair loo (D80 ST80)** at the rear, on the left.

Café Toto (Taylor Walker), 190 Muswell Hill, Broadway, Muswell Hill N10 *Tel:* 0181 444-7171. 20m north of the roundabout where Muswell Hill meets Muswell Hill Broadway. Flat entrance on the right, then 90% step free. **Adapted loo (D83 ST68)** at the rear, on the left.

Coliseum (Wetherspoons), 26A Manor Park Road, Harlesden NW10 *Tel:* 0181 961-6570. Near the junction with High Street. Step free via ramped entrance on the left. **Adapted loo (D72 ST62)** at the rear, on the left; key at the bar.

Crockers (Regent Inn), 24 Aberdeen Place, Maida Vale NW8 *Tel:* 0171 286-6608. On the corner of Cunningham Place and Aberdeen Place. Entrance with small step, then step free. **Adapted loo (D84 ST66)** to the right of the entrance in the far corner.

Flask (Youngs), 14 Flask Walk, Hampstead NW3 *Tel:* 0171 435-4580. Step free. **Adapted loo (D90 ST115, large, but the door opens in)** off the saloon bar.

Maid of Muswell (Bass Charrington), 121 Alexandra Park Road, Muswell Hill N10 *Tel:* 0181 883-9442. By the junction with Grosvenor Road. Entrance +1 step, then step free. **Wheelchair loo (D70 ST85)** at the rear, on the right.

Moon under Water (Wetherspoons), 10 Varley Parade, Colindale NW9 *Tel:* 0181 200-7611. Near the centre of the Parade. Step free. **Wheelchair loo (D70 ST200)** at the rear, on the left.

Old Bull & Bush (Taylor Walker), North End Road, Golders Green NW11 *Tel:* 0181 455-3685. Near the Hospital. Flat or ramped entrances, including from the CP at the rear. 90% step free. **Wheelchair loo (D85 ST80)** by the door to the CP.

Royal Oak (Bass Charrington), 95 High Street, Harlesden NW10 *Tel:* 0181 965-2278. By the junction with Park Parade. Entrance +1 step, then step free. **Wheelchair loo (D86)**; key at bar. When we visited the key was 'unavailable', so we were unable to measure it. When we rang, we were told that the loo was currently available for chair users.

Three Hammers (Taylor Walker), The Ridgeway, Hammers Lane, Mill Hill NW7 *Tel:* 0181 959-2346. By junction of Hammers Lane and The Ridgeway. On-site CP. Ramped entrance on the left, then 45% step free. Higher levels are +2 or +3 steps; –2 to lower level, then –1 to garden. **Wheelchair loo (D74 ST73)** on the left, just inside ramped entrance.

Inner postal districts W
Acton, Chiswick and Ealing

Better Half (Free House), 2 Central Chambers, Ealing Broadway W5 *Tel:* 0181 567-4859. Opposite Ealing Broadway station. CP 200m away off Spring Bridge Road. Step free access and **wheelchair loo (D80 ST80),** but restricted width of 70cm in the corridor leading to it when bar stools are stored there.

Fidlers Three (Bass), 28 New Broadway, Ealing W5 *Tel:* 0181 567-9438. Less than 100m from the Town Hall, towards Christ Church. Step free. **Wheelchair loo (D70+ ST70+)** just past the other toilets.

Kent (Fullers), 2 Scotch Common, West Ealing W13 *Tel:* 0181 997-5911. CP. Near the junction with Kent Avenue. Entrance +1 step, then step free to about 60% of the bar. **Wheelchair loo (D70+ ST70+).** A ramp outside leads down to the large garden, bypassing roughly –15 steps.

J J Moons (Wetherspoons), 80 Chiswick High Road, Chiswick W4 *Tel:* 0181 742-7263. By the junction with Ennismore Avenue. Ramped, but somewhat bumpy way in on the left, to bypass the +1 step at the entrance. **Adapted loo (D80 ST42)** en-route to the ladies, at the end of the bar. NKS key, kept at the bar.

Old Orleans, 26 Bond Street, Ealing W5 *Tel:* 0181 579-7413. 50m from the roundabout where Mattock Lane meets Bond Street. Ramped entrance gives 80% step free access. **Wheelchair loo (D75 ST70)** at the rear by other toilets.

Photographer & Firkin (Taylor Walker), 23 High Street, Ealing W5 *Tel:* 0181 567-1140. Some 50m north of the junction with Bond Street. Step free to 85%, via entrance on the right. **Wheelchair loo (D80 ST90)** to the right of the bar. Key from the bar.

Red Lion and Pineapple (Wetherspoons), 281 High Street, Acton W3 *Tel:* 0181 896-2248. Located by the junction with Gunnersbury Lane and the Uxbridge Road. One entrance with a slight bump. **Wheelchair loo (D80 ST70).** There is +1 step to small garden, though step free from outside.

Tabbard (Taylor Walker), 2 Bath Road, Chiswick W4 *Tel:* 0181 994-3492. By the junction with Turnham Green Terrace, and 100m from Turnham Green station. Entrance +3 steps, but ramped way in via the garden. Slightly congested bar. **Wheelchair loo (D80 ST80)** to the right of the bar. The key was at the bar (among some 50 others, and it took them a little time to find the right one !).

Yates Wine Lodge (Yates), 5 Mattock Lane, Ealing W5 *Tel:* 0181 840-0988. 50m from the junction with Bond Street. Step free access to about 50%, including the bar but no tables or chairs. These are on upper levels, with either +1 or +2 steps. The +2 level can be reached by using an alternative entrance on the left, where there is simply a small ridge en route. Lift (D77 W100 L135) from the bar level to first floor, then step free to 60%. **Adapted loo (D75 ST66)** to the right of the bar on the GF, at the bar level.

Inner postal areas SW
Balham, Fulham, Norbury, Streatham and West Brompton

Half and Half (Regent Inn), 90 Streatham High Road, Streatham SW16 *Tel:* 0181 677-5600. Near the junction with Leigham Avenue. Entrance +1 step, then 60% step free. **Wheelchair loo (D70 ST80)** through the door at the back of the pub marked private ! Key at the bar.

Moon Under Water (Wetherspoons), 194 Balham High Road, Balham SW12 *Tel:* 0181 673-0535. Step free with **adapted loo (D80 ST60)** past the bar and the other toilets. Key at the bar.

Moon under Water (Wetherspoons), 1327 London Road, Norbury SW16 *Tel:* 0181 765-1235. At the junction with Northborough Road, opposite Windsor House and a petrol station. CP behind the pub off Northborough Road. Ramped entrance to the pub bypassing +3 steps, then step free. **Wheelchair loo (D85 ST85)** at the back, on the left.

Prince of Wales (Charrington), 467 Brixton Road, Stockwell SW9 *Tel:* 0171 326-1462. Near the corner with Coldharbour Lane and across from Lambeth Town Hall. Entrance +1 step then step free to the bar. **Wheelchair loo (D85 ST190)** with inward opening door but very large space. It is at the back on the right, beyond the bar.

Stargazey (Fullers), 236 Fulham Road, West Brompton SW10 *Tel:* 0171 376-5827. On the junction with Hollywood Road, opposite St Stephens Hospital. Step free, with **wheelchair loo (D70+ ST70+)** on the GF just to the left of the main toilets.

Windmill on the Common (Youngs), Clapham Common South Side SW4

Tel: 0181 673-4578. CP. Flat access through the conservatory entrance. Spacious GF area. **Wheelchair loo (D85 ST85)** in the corner of the conservatory.

Inner postal districts SE
Camberwell, Catford, Greenwich, Grove Park and New Cross

Amersham Arms (Courage), 288 New Cross Road, New Cross SE14 *Tel:* 0181 694-8992. Opposite New Cross tube station. Step free via side doors to bar and music. **Wheelchair loo (D85 ST100).**

Fox on the Hill (Wetherspoons), 149 Denmark Hill, Camberwell SE5 *Tel:* 0171 738-4756. Large CP. Step free from CP to bar, but +7 steps to garden. **Wheelchair loo (D85 ST75)** at the back of the pub.

Gipsy Moth (Taylor Walker), 60 Greenwich Church Street, Greenwich SE10 *Tel:* 0181 858-0786. Some 80m from the Cutty Sark. Step free via a ramp in the garden. **Wheelchair loo (D85 ST90).**

Green Man (Beefeater), 335 Bromley Road, Catford SE6 *Tel:* 0181 698-3746. At the junction with Beckenham Hill Road. On-site CP. Flat entrance at the front, facing the road. 60% step free inside. **Adapted cubicle (D90 ST60)** in the gents at the back of the pub.

Grove Park Tavern (Whitbread), Marvels Lane, Grove Park SE12 *Tel:* 0181 857-6416. At the roundabout and junction with Chinbrook Road. Large CP on-site. Step free from the CP to the lounge bar. Two split levels, each +2 steps. The back one can be bypassed by a ramp to the left of the children's play area, past the arcade machines. **Wheelchair loo (D80 ST110)** at the top of the ramp on the left.

Tiger's Head (Wetherspoons), 350 Bromley Road, Catford SE6 *Tel:* 0181 460-3768. By the junction with Southend Lane. On-site CP. Step free access at the front, through the garden (there's a small threshold). Flat to most of the bar. **Wheelchair loo (D75 ST150).**

Outer areas north of the river
Brentford, Greenford, Hayes, and Hounslow

Ballot Box (Taylor Walker), Horsendon Lane North, Greenford, Middx *Tel:* 0181 902-2825. Roughly half way along Horsendon Lane North. On-site CP. Step free access into the pub, with +1 to 50% inside. **Adapted loo (D85 ST43),** through the door marked 'gents' to the left of the bar. Normally unlocked.

Chariot (Fullers), 34 High Street, Hounslow, Middx *Tel:* 0181 572-8044. 50m from the junction with Kingsley Road. Small CP behind pub but +10 steps from there. Step free from the front to 50% of the bar. **Wheelchair loo (D85 ST100+)** just inside the entrance. Normally locked, key from bar.

Globe (Fullers), 104 Windmill Road, Brentford, Middx *Tel:* 0181 560-8932. By the junction with Boston Park Road, 50m north of the A4. Entrance +1 step. **Adapted loo (D80 ST60)** just to the left of the bar. Garden –7.

Moon & Sixpence (Wetherspoons), 1250 Uxbridge Road, Hayes End, Middx *Tel:* 0181 561-3541. By the junction with Newport Road. Step free. **Wheelchair loo (D75 ST100)** at the front, on the right.

Moon Under Water (Wetherspoons), 10 Broadway Parade, Coldharbour Lane, Hayes, Middx *Tel:* 0181 813-6774. 50m west of the junction with Birchway. Two flat central entrances, giving 85% step free access; –3 steps to rear area. **Adapted loo (D80 ST67)** on the left.

Moon Under Water (Wetherspoons), 84 Staines Road, Hounslow, Middx *Tel:* 0181 572-7506. 40m east of the junction with Cromwell Street. Step free throughout. **Wheelchair loo (D80 ST75)** at the rear, on the right; key from the bar.

Myllet Arms (Taylor Walker), Western Avenue, Perivale, Middx *Tel:* 0181 997-4624. No access from Western Avenue, CP reached from Perivale Lane. Ramped entrance to bar and restaurant. Step free to 40%. **Adapted loo (D80 ST40)** to the left of the entrance.

Noble Half, (Regent Inn) High Street, Hounslow, Middx *Tel:* 0181 570-0169. By the junction with Gilbert Road, where there are some OB spaces. Entrance +1 step, then step free to 60%, although there's +1 to the bar. **Wheelchair loo (D85 ST90)** at the back of the pub on the right.

Denham, Ickenham, Rickmansworth, Ruislip and Uxbridge

Coach & Horses (Taylor Walker), High Road, Ickenham, Middx *Tel:* 01895-623559. By junction with Swakeleys Road. On-site CP. Step free to 90%. **Adapted loo (D85 ST49)** to the left of the bar.

Good Yarn (Wetherspoons), 132 High Street, Uxbridge, Middx *Tel:* 01895-239852. 100m from roundabout at east end of High Street. Step free to bar area and +3 steps to dining area. Alternative side entrance to dining area in Johnson's Yard with +1. **Wheelchair loo (D81 ST77 NKS)** to the right of the bar; key at the bar.

J J Moons (Wetherspoons), 12 Victoria Road, Ruislip Manor, Middx *Tel:* 01895-622373. Opposite Ruislip Manor tube. Entrance +1 step, then 70% flat. **Wheelchair loo (D85 ST75)**, left after main entrance.

Middlesex Arms (Taylor Walker), Long Drive, South Ruislip, Middx *Tel:* 0181 845-0667. 50m east of the railway bridge over Long Drive. Rear CP. Step free entrances. GF has a split level of one step. **Adapted loo (D87 ST67)** by the side entrance near the food bar; key at bar.

Orchard (Beefeater), Ickenham Road, Ruislip, Middx *Tel:* 01895-633481. By roundabout at the junction with Kingsend. CP. Entrance +1, then 70% step free in the bar area and 20% in the restaurant. Raised areas are up several steps. **Wheelchair loo (D80 ST85)** on right side of the building, through the restaurant.

Scotsbridge Mill (Beefeater), Park Road, Rickmansworth, Herts *Tel:* 01923-778377. Signposted turn-off is about 300m east of roundabout at the junction with the High Street. On-site CP. Ramped entrance on the right, then step free to 15% of the bar and 30% of the restaurant. Several steps to higher or lower levels. **Adapted loo (D77 ST60)** on the left of bar.

Sylvan Moon (Wetherspoons), 27 Green Lane, Northwood, Middx *Tel:* 01923-820760. By junction with Dene Road. Step free. **Wheelchair loo (D75 ST85)** at the rear, on the left.

Vine (Taylor Walker), 121 Hillingdon Hill, Hillingdon, Middx *Tel:* 01895-259596. By the junction with Vine Lane. Sloped on-site CP. Entrance +1 step, then 50% with step free access. **Wheelchair loo (D73 ST90)** to the right of bar; key at the bar. From entrance level, ramped access to outdoor seats.

Waggon & Horses (Taylor Walker), 37 Oxford Road, New Denham, Bucks *Tel:* 01895-233168. Opposite the junction with Oakside. On-site CP. Ramped entrance giving 75% step free access; +2 to pool tables area. After entering the pub, turn left to reach **adapted loo (D84 ST67)**.

Borehamwood, Edgware, Harrow, Kenton and Stanmore

Blacking Bottle (Wetherspoons), 122 High Street, Edgware, Middx *Tel:* 0181 381-1485. 30m from the junction with Manor Park Crescent. Step free. **Wheelchair loo (D85 ST200)** at the rear of pub, on the left; key at bar.

Change of Hart (Taylor Walker), 21 High Street, Edgware, Middx *Tel:* 0181 952-0039. 30m from junction with Spring Road. Rear CP; kerb, then +1 step. Flat front entrances. GF has split level of 1 step. 30% step free from CP entrance.

Wheelchair loo (D80 ST95) at the rear of the pub. If not open, ask for key at bar.

Everglades Exchange (Taylor Walker), Hale Lane, Edgware, Middx *Tel:* 0181 959-6403. By the roundabout where Selvage Lane meets Hale Lane. On-site CP. Step free to 95%. Fixed tables in bar. Small raised section (+3) in the dining area. **Wheelchair loo (D80 ST100)** 10m straight ahead from main entrance.

Fat Controller (Regent Inn), 362 Station Road, Harrow, Middx *Tel:* 0181 426-0161. Just by the junction with College Road. Step free to 80%. **Adapted loo (D80 ST56)** to the left of the bar.

Hart & Spool (Wetherspoons), 148 Shenley Road, Borehamwood, Herts *Tel:* 0181 953-1883. Step free. **Wheelchair loo (D70 ST75)** at the back of the pub, normally unlocked.

Leefe Robinson VC (Beefeater), Brockhurst Corner, 76 Uxbridge Road, Harrow Weald, Middx *Tel:* 0181 954-6781. 30m from the junction with Elms Road. CP. Ramped central entrance, giving 60% step free access in the bar and 45% in the restaurant. Higher levels are +2 or +3 steps. **Adapted loo (D86 ST68)** just inside the main entrance, on the left.

Man in the Moon (Wetherspoons), 1 Buckingham Parade, Stanmore, Middx *Tel:* 0181 954-6119. Opposite the junction with Church Road. Entrance +2 steps, then step free. **Wheelchair loo (D76 ST96)** at the rear, on the left.

J J Moons (Wetherspoons), 397 High Road, Wembley, Middx *Tel:* 0181 903-4923. Opposite junction with Park Lane. Entrance +1 step, then step free via ramp. **Adapted loo (D78 ST67)** on the right of the pub, by the ladies.

Moon on the Hill (Wetherspoons), 373 Station Road, Harrow, Middx *Tel:* 0181 863-3670. 30m from the junction with Gayton Road. Entrance +1 step, giving 50% flat access. **Wheelchair loo (D72 ST92)** to the right of bar.

Sarsen Stone (Wetherspoons), 32 High Street, Wealdstone, Middx *Tel:* 0181 863-8533. 25m from junction with Palmerston Road. Flat entrance, giving 100% step free access. **Wheelchair loo (D80 ST80)** at the rear, on the right.

Travellers Rest (Beefeater), Kenton Road, Kenton, Middx *Tel:* 0181 907-1671. By junction with Carlton Avenue. Sloping CP. Ramped right hand entrance giving 45% flat access in the bar area and 100% in the restaurant area. **Wheelchair loo (D80 ST110)** on right of building; key from the bar.

Village Inn (Wetherspoons), 402 Rayners Lane, Harrow, Middx *Tel:* 0181 868-8551. 20m from the junction with Village Way East. Small CP at the rear. Flat main entrance; rear entrance from CP has +1 step. Bar area +6 above dining area. Flat to bar from Rayners Lane main entrance; flat to dining area from CP entrance. **Adapted loo (D80 ST51)** to the right of bar, not signed.

Barnet, Chingford and Enfield

Duke of York (Beefeater), Ganwick Corner, Barnet Road, Barnet *Tel:* 0181 449-0297. By the junction with Dancers Hill Road. CP. Step free via ramped side entrance by the CP. After entering, turn right for the **wheelchair loo (D80 ST70)**.

Ridgeway (Taylor Walker), 76 The Ridgeway, Enfield, Middx *Tel:* 0181 363-1209. 50m south of roundabout where Lavender Hill meets The Ridgeway. On-site CP. Ramp and +1 step at main entrance, then 80% step free. **Wheelchair loo (D83 ST78)** on the left. From main entrance, −1 to garden.

Royston Arms (Bass Charrington), 83 Chingford Mount Road, South Chingford E4 *Tel:* 0181 531-6461. By the junction with Westward Road. On-site CP. Step free via ramped entrance on the right. **Wheelchair loo (D95 ST135)** on the right, by pool tables; key from bar. −1 to garden, then ramped down to outdoor seating.

Chigwell and Loughton

Last Post (Wetherspoons), 227 High Road, Loughton, Essex *Tel:* 0181 532-0751. About 150m north of the junction with Forest Road. Step free. **Adapted loo (D80 ST67)** at the rear, to the left of the bar.

Maypole (Taylor Walker), 171 Lambourne Road, Chigwell Row E11 *Tel:* 0181 500-2050. By the junction with Gravel Lane. On-site CP. Step free to 85% of bar and to seats outside. **Wheelchair loo (D75 opens in, ST75)** to the left of the bar.

Plume of Feathers (Taylor Walker), 123 Churchill, Loughton, Essex *Tel:* 0181 508-3618. Opposite junction with Sedley Rise. Rear CP, but rear entrance has +6 steps. It is easier to go round to ramped front entrance. Inside, 55% is step free. **Wheelchair loo (D90 ST80)** on left of the pub.

Retreat (Whitbread), Retreat Way, Chigwell Row, Essex *Tel:* 0181 500-2716. At the end of Retreat Way furthest from Lambourne Road. On-site CP. Family entrance on the right is ramped but with a steep lip. Step free inside. **Wheelchair loo (D79 ST130)** on the right of the pub.

Barking, Brentwood, Dagenham, Hornchurch, Ilford and Romford

Barking Dog (Wetherspoons), 61 Station Parade, Wakering Road, Barking, Essex *Tel:* 0181 507-9109. Right beside Barking station. CP in Vicarage Field shopping centre just opposite. Step free. **Wheelchair loo (D84 ST70)** at the back of the pub. Redevelopment means that the loos will move, hopefully not eliminating the unisex cubicle.

Bear (Bass), Noak Hill Road, Romford, Essex *Tel:* 01708-381935. About 100m from the junction with North Hill Drive. On-site CP. Entrance +10 steps, or a steep ramp to the main door from the CP, and a small step through a side entrance. Step free access through a door on the extreme left. Flat throughout, and there's a large garden. **Wheelchair loo (D90 ST85)** near the main entrance. Follow the bar all the way round.

Black Horse (Charrington), 420 Ongar Road, Pilgrims Hatch, Brentwood, Essex *Tel:* 01277-372337. From the junction of Noak Hill Road and Ongar Road, the pub is over 1km on the right. On-site CP. Step free except for +3 steps to garden. **Wheelchair loo (D75 ST80)** at the back of the pub, following the bar round to the left.

Bull (Taylor Walker), 76 Market Place, Romford, Essex *Tel:* 01708-740476. 100m down Market Place from the subway interchange. Sloped cobbled pavement leading through an archway to a ramped entrance, then step free to 90%, including the small patio at the back. **Adapted loo (D80 ST70, but the door opens inwards)** just to the left of the bar if you come in via the ramped entrance; key at bar.

Colorado Exchange (Taylor Walker), 69 Epping New Road, Buckhurst Hill, Redbridge *Tel:* 0181 504-9886. By junction with Brook Road. On-site CP. Step free to dining area and 40% of the bar area, but there are +3 steps to the bar itself. To reach the **wheelchair loo (D70 ST70),** turn right after the main entrance.

Dick Turpin (Beefeater), Aldborough Hatch, Aldborough Road North, Newbury Hatch, Ilford, Essex *Tel:* 0181 590-1281. About 150m north of the junction with Applegarth Drive. On-site CP. Step free to the bar, but +2 steps to the dining area which can either be bypassed by using a back route or by a temporary ramp. You'll have to ask ! **Wheelchair loo (D85 opens in, ST120)** to the right as you enter, then right again, level with the bar.

Great Spool of Ilford (Wetherspoons), 114 Cranbrook Road, Ilford, Essex *Tel:* 0181 518-0535. 30m west of the junction with Wellesley Road. CP off Wellesley Road. Rear entrance by CP has +1 step. Front entrance on the right is flat. 90% inside is step free; raised area is +2. **Adapted loo (D80 ST56)** on the right of the pub near the front (as you face towards rear).

Greengate (Bass Charrington), Horns Road, Barkingside, Ilford, Essex *Tel:* 0181 518-6078. By the junction with Eastern Avenue, on the east side of Horns Road by the lights. On-site CP. Flat rear entrance from the CP, others have +1 step. 50% is step free. **Wheelchair loo (D85 ST300)** to the right of the bar and kitchen area. It is 10m past the kitchen.

Hinds Head (Whitbread), 2 Burnside Road, Chadwell, Dagenham, Essex *Tel:* 0181 590-2465. Located on a corner of the roundabout at the junction with Station Road. Nearby pay and display CP, free to OB holders. Quite a steep slope from the CP to the pub. Step free. **Adapted loo (D80 opening in, ST150)**. Picnic tables outside with step free access.

J J Moons (Wetherspoons), Unit 3, 46 High Street, Hornchurch, Essex *Tel:* 01708-478410. Situated in the middle of Unit 3 building including Pizza Hut and McDonalds, by the junction with Abbs Cross Gardens. CP behind, entered via Appleton Way. Step free to 90%. **Wheelchair loo (D80 ST80)** in the middle of the pub, on the left.

Lord Denman (Wetherspoons), 270 Heathway, Dagenham, Essex *Tel:* 0181 984-8590. Located on the High Street about 100m from Heathway station, on the other side of the road. Ramp bypasses +2 steps. There are –7 to the food area and loos, but there's a platform stairlift. **Wheelchair loo (D85 ST80)** towards the back of the pub at the lower level.

Moon and Stars (Wetherspoons), 99 South Street, Romford, Essex *Tel:* 01708-730117. 50m from Romford station, towards Market Place. Step free to 70%. There's a limited number of low tables with movable chairs. **Wheelchair loo (D85 ST75)** to the right of the main entrance. Key at bar.

Unicorn (Taylor Walker), 91 Main Road, Gidea Park, Romford, Essex *Tel:* 01708-740131. Located about 100m from Balgores Lane, on the left. On-site CP. Step free to 90%. **Adapted loo (D90 opening in, ST66).**

Outer areas south of the river

Chessington, Kingston, Richmond, Surbiton, Walton and Worcester Park

All Bar One, 9 Hill Street, Richmond, Surrey *Tel:* 0181 332-1121. On the corner of Whittaker Avenue, and opposite the old Town Hall. Open lift (W80 L120) bypasses +3 steps at the entrance. Step free. **Wheelchair loo (D80 ST70)** by the lift.

Flicker & Firkin (Taylor Walker), Dukes Yard, Richmond, Surrey *Tel:* 0181 332-7807. Just off Richmond High Street. Ramped entrance, over a few cobbles, then step free to about 70%. **Wheelchair loo (D80 ST100)** just before the main doors, on the right. Key kept at bar.

Harts Boatyard (Beefeater), Portsmouth Road, Surbiton, Surrey *Tel:* 0181 399-7515. Opposite the junction with St Leonards Road. On-site CP. Ramp at the entrance, bypassing +3 steps giving step free access to 15% of the bar. There are split levels to the eating areas, but you can arrange to eat in the bar. To get to the balcony overlooking the Thames there is –4. The restaurant is +4+4 above the entrance level. **Wheelchair loo (D80 ST75)** to the left of the main entrance. Tables and chairs on the riverside behind the pub are step free via the CP and a 10m long slope.

Hogsmill (Beefeater), Worcester Park Road, Worcester Park, Surrey *Tel:* 0181 337-5221. By the junction with Cromwell Road. On-site CP. Flat access from the CP only on the left side of the building. The bar entrance gives step free access to 20% of the bar. There is a separate door giving step free access to the lower part of the restaurant which the staff can open if you ask. Other routes to the restaurant involve steps. The **wheelchair loo (D80 ST100)** is by the restaurant reception desk on the lower level.

Maypole (Whitbread), Hook Road, Surbiton, Surrey *Tel:* 0181 399-2906. At the junction with Ditton Road. Entrance +1 small step, then 75% step free. **Adapted loo (D85 opens in, ST75)** to the left of the bar, where the key is kept.

Monkey Puzzle (Beefeater), Leatherhead Road, Chessington, Surrey *Tel:* 01372-744060. Situated some 600m north of the junction with Rushett Lane. Flat entrance giving step free access to 70% of bar area. There are six dining tables at the bar level reached along a corridor to the left of the bar. Most of the restaurant is +20 steps. **Adapted loo (D80 ST66)** is underneath the staircase as you come in the main entrance.

Philadelphia Exchange (Taylor Walker), Bucklands Wharf, Kingston Bridge, Kingston, Surrey *Tel:* 0181 547-3733. On the riverfront below the John Lewis store, with lift access. Step free to 40% of the American diner, and **wheelchair loo (D80 ST75, but with large bin)** to the right of the entrance.

Regent (Wetherspoons), 19 Church Street, Walton-on-Thames, Surrey *Tel:* 01932-243980. 30m from the junction with Bridge Street. Step free to 90%. **Wheelchair loo (D78 ST80)** to the right of the bar; key at the bar.

Royal Barge (Taylor Walker), Kingston Bridge, Kingston, Surrey *Tel:* 0181 547-3191. Sited on the riverfront below John Lewis with lift access from the store. Step free to 90% of the pub and **wheelchair loo (D80 ST80)** towards the back of the pub.

Mitcham, Morden, Putney, Wandsworth and Wimbledon

Abbot (Taylor Walker), 1 Abbotsbury Road, Morden, Surrey *Tel:* 0181 687-0852. Large pub at the junction with London Road. Step free to 60%. **Wheelchair loo (D80 ST75)** to the right of the bar.

All Bar One, 57 Wimbledon Hill Road, Wimbledon SW19 *Tel:* 0181 947-8654. On the corner with Compton Road. Flat entrance from Compton Road leads to +2 steps bypassed by an open lift (W80 L125). **Wheelchair loo (D80 ST80).**

Brewers Inn (Youngs), 147 East Hill, Wandsworth SW18 *Tel:* 0181 874-4128. Opposite the Town Hall and on the junction with St Anns Hill. Small CP. Step free to saloon bar, but –1 step to the other bar. **Wheelchair loo (D80 ST100)** just inside saloon bar door.

Castle (Youngs), 38 High Street, Tooting SW17 *Tel:* 0181 672-7018. 50m from the junction with Tooting Broadway station towards Tooting Bec. Step free access, and a **wheelchair loo (D80 ST90)** by the gents.

County Arms (Youngs), 345 Trinity Road, Wandsworth SW18 *Tel:* 0181 874-8532. At the junction with Alma Terrace. CP. Lounge bar entrance has +1 step, then a **wheelchair loo (D85 ST70)** just inside. Spacious, and garden with a ramped entrance to the pub.

Cricketer (Beefeater), Lower Richmond Road, Putney SW15 *Tel:* 0181 788-0925. Just by Putney Hospital, and at the junction with Commondale. On-site CP. Small thresholds en route through entrance from CP. Step free to 30%, and **wheelchair loo (D80 ST100+)** off the corridor leading to the ladies. Small garden area outside, which is +2 steps.

Grid Inn (Wetherspoons), 22 Replingham Road, Southfields SW18 *Tel:* 0181 874-8460. At the junction with Heythorpe Street. Step free from Replingham Road. **Wheelchair loo (D85 ST85)** at the far end of the bar.

Halfway House (Youngs), 521 Garratt Lane, Earlsfield SW18 *Tel:* 0181 946-2788. On the junction with Magdalen Road. Step free access and **wheelchair loo (D85 ST70)**. Small garden, step free from street but –1 step from pub.

Hand & Racket (Whitbread), 25 Wimbledon Hill Road, Wimbledon SW19 *Tel:* 0181 947-9391. Almost opposite the end of Worple Road and about 200m from Wimbledon station. Step free to 80% of pub. **Wheelchair loo (D75 ST75)** at the back.

Mill House (Whitbread – Brewers Fayre), 1 Windmill Road, Mitcham Common, Mitcham, Surrey *Tel:* 0181 288-0491. 80m from the junction with Croydon Road. Large CP. Flat through the bar entrance and for the restaurant area. 30% step free inside. Small garden, and also a children's room and play area with flat access. **Wheelchair loo (D85 ST120)** to the right of the bar.

Oak & Acorn (Whitbread), Chestnut Grove, Pollards Hill, Mitcham, Surrey *Tel:* 0181 764-5816. At the junction with Conway Gardens. Entrance +1 step then step free to 90%. **Wheelchair loo (D75 ST100)** to the right of the bar, near the family room.

P Shannon & Sons (Fullers), 46 Putney High Street, Putney SW15 *Tel:* 0181 780-5437. Opposite the end of Putney Bridge Road. Step free to 70%. **Well adapted loo (D80 ST68)** to the right of the bar, and then it's on your left.

Railway (Wetherspoons), 202 Upper Richmond Road, Putney SW15 *Tel:* 0181 788-8190. At the junction with Putney High Street. Step free to 40% of the pub from the High Street. **Wheelchair loo (D80 ST150+)** past the bar, and turn right. The first door is to the right of the staircase. Then the loo door is on your left. Not well signed.

Ravensbury Arms (Taylor Walker), Croydon Road, Mitcham, Surrey *Tel:* 0181 648-6900. At the junction with Carshalton Road. On-site CP. Step free access to 80% of pub and half the garden. **Adapted loo (D80 ST40)** to the left of the entrance.

Spotted Dog (Wetherspoons), 72 Garrett Lane, Wandsworth SW18 *Tel:* 0181 875-9531. Adjacent to the Arndale shopping centre with a MSCP. Flat entrance and GF. **Wheelchair loo (D80 ST80).**

Croydon, Purley, Sutton, and Wallington

All Bar One, 2 Hill Road, Sutton, Surrey *Tel:* 0181 642-6510. Off St Nicholas Way, and close to the shopping centre. See chapter on *Shops*. The pub is next to Dillons bookstore, and is step free. **Wheelchair loo (D90 ST75)** at the far end.

Alma Tavern (Taylor Walker), 129 Lower Addiscombe Road, Croydon, Surrey *Tel:* 0181 654-5842. At the junction with Grant Road. Entrance +1 tiny step, then 90% step free. **Wheelchair loo (D90 ST80)** to the right, behind the bar where the key is kept.

Cricketers Inn (Bass Charrington), 36 Addington Village Road, Croydon, Surrey *Tel:* 01689-842057. Situated at the Addington Village roundabout on the A2022. Take the village exit. Large CP and flat main entrance. Step free everywhere including the garden except for the children's play area outside (+3). **Adapted loo (D85 ST62)** is on the right of the pub from the entrance. Follow the bar round to the right.

Foxley Hatch (Wetherspoons), 8 Russell Hill, Purley, Surrey *Tel:* 0181 763-9307. South of the junction with Purley Way. Step free to the main bar. **Wheelchair loo (D85 ST90)** at the back of the pub.

George (Wetherspoons), 17 George Street, Croydon, Surrey *Tel:* 0181 649-9077. About 300m from the station going towards the main shopping area. Step free to about 50%. **Wheelchair loo (D80 ST100)** just inside the pub on the left.

Hare and Hounds (Taylor Walker), 325 Purley Way, Croydon, Surrey *Tel:* 0181 688-0420. Situated at the junction with Mill Lane. Large on-site CP. Step free to 90%. **Adapted loo (D85 ST60)** is marked 'ladies' and is opposite the main entrance.

Moon on the Hill (Wetherspoons), 5 Hill Road, Sutton, Surrey *Tel:* 0181 643-1202. Opposite the Civic Centre, off St Nicholas Road. Step free to about 25% of the pub. **Wheelchair loo (D80 ST85)** clearly marked to the right of the entrance.

Town House (Whitbread), 36 High Street, Croydon, Surrey *Tel:* 0181 688-0595. Located between Katherine Street and St George's Walk, but on the opposite side of the road. Ramped entrance on the left side, bypassing +1 step. Pub on three floors with a lift (D90 W110 L87), reached via +2 –3. Portable ramps are available. Step free access on the GF to 70%. The lift goes to a basement function room, and a first floor bar. **Wheelchair loo (D75 ST90)** on the GF. Key at the bar.

Whispering Moon (Wetherspoons), 25 Ross Parade, Wallington, Surrey *Tel:* 0181 647-7020. Located on the corner with Woodcote Road. Step free from Ross Parade to the main bar. **Wheelchair loo (D85 ST85)** on the right as you enter; key at the bar.

Beckenham, Bickley, Bromley, Orpington and West Wickham

Bird in Hand (Taylor Walker), 3 Bickley Road, Bickley, Kent *Tel:* 0181 467-3665. On-site CP. Main entrance –1 step, but bypassed by a ramp on the right side of the building. This leads to the restaurant, and there is +1 to the bar. **Wheelchair loo (D85 ST70)** by the ramped entrance.

Crown (Beefeater), 155 Bromley Common, Bromley, Kent *Tel:* 0181 460-1472. On the A21, about 4km from Bromley. On-site CP. Lip at the entrance, step free access inside. **Wheelchair loo (D75 ST75)** on the far side of the restaurant.

Harvest Moon (Wetherspoons), 141 High Street, Orpington, Kent *Tel:* 01689-876931. On the main shopping street. Small lip at the entrance, then step free. **Wheelchair loo (D83 ST100 but door opens in)** on the left at the far side of the bar.

Pamphilon (Regent Inn), 196 Bromley High Street, Bromley, Kent *Tel:* 0181 313-0795. At the junction with Church Road and Market Square, opposite Allders. Step free to 80% of the pub. **Wheelchair loo (D80 ST115)** at the end of the bar on the left.

Plough (Youngs), Croydon Road, Beddington, Surrey *Tel:* 0181 647-1122. At the junction with Plough Lane. On-site CP. Step free from the garden, or from a side entrance. **Wheelchair loo (D85 ST75)** on the left side of the pub from the garden entrance.

Queen's Head (Taylor Walker), 73 High Street, Green Street Green, Orpington, Kent *Tel:* 01689-859866. At the junction with Worlds End Lane and opposite the Baptist Church. Large CP with two OB spaces on the left of the pub. Ramped entrance from here (+2 steps at the front) gives step free access to 90%. **Wheelchair loo (D80 ST75)** immediately inside the ramped entrance.

Queen's Head (Taylor Walker), 2 High Street West, Chislehurst, Kent *Tel:* 0181 467-3490. On-site CP. Ramped entrance from the CP with small lip. Step free to pub and garden. **Adapted loo (D70 ST60)** on the right of the entrance.

Railway (Taylor Walker), Red Lodge Road, West Wickham, Kent *Tel:* 0181 777-2764. At the junction with Hawes Lane. Very near West Wickham station. CP alongside. There are +2 steps from Red Lodge Road, +1 −1 from Hawes Lane. Some split levels, but they are building an extension which we were told would include an **adapted loo**.

Bexley and Dartford

Golden Lion (Whitbread), 258 The Broadway, Bexley Heath, Kent *Tel:* 0181 303-4268. About 450m from the shopping centre, at the junction with West

Lane. Two OB spaces outside. Step free to 95% of the pub. **Wheelchair loo (D85 ST100)** at the rear, behind a small stage.

Jacobean Barn (Beefeater), Hall Place, Bourne End, Bexley, Kent *Tel:* 01322-552748. On the A223 between the intersection of the A220 and A207. On-site CP. The entrance to the restaurant has +1 small step, then –5 to bar, but there is an alternative ramped route involving only +1. Using both entrances, there is 90% step free access. **Wheelchair loos (D85 ST120)** off the bar, and **(D85 ST70)** off the restaurant area.

Paper Moon (Wetherspoons), 55 High Street, Dartford, Kent *Tel:* 01322-281127. By the junction with Market Street. CP in Market Street within 100m. Slight lip at the entrance, then step free. **Wheelchair loo (D85 ST75).** Key at the bar.

Wrong'un (Wetherspoons), 234 The Broadway, Bexley Heath, Kent *Tel:* 0181 298-0439. Some 400m from the shopping centre, just past the Midland Bank. Step free. **Wheelchair loo (D85 ST75)** at the back of the pub near a fire exit.

Places for afternoon tea

Taking afternoon tea has long been an established British institution. There are, sadly, far fewer tea shops these days, and those remaining tend to be small and congested. We are listing here a few central hotels where it is possible to get tea served under generally genteel and upmarket conditions. You probably cannot afford to stay in the hotels mentioned, nor to have dinner there (they are certainly beyond our budget!), but having a relaxing tea in the middle of the afternoon can be an experience. Even for this the bill will be significant, but it could make a really special treat.

We have surveyed a few of the 'classic' places for tea, like Brown's and the Ritz (which do not have adapted loos), and we've included some of the more expensive central hotels with **wheelchair loo** facilities. The intention is to suggest people ideas, and not to present a comprehensive listing.

Brown's, Albermarle Street and Dover Street W1 *Tel:* 0171 493-6020. The Dover Street entrance was temporarily closed, and via Albermarle Street there is +1 step. Tea is served in the lounge, reached by the lift (D80 W105 L110).

Capital, 22 Basil Street, Knightsbridge SW3 *Tel:* 0171 589-5171. The hotel is only 50m from Knightsbridge tube station, off Sloane Street. UGCP down a ramp next to the entrance, with a service lift (D90 W120 L100) providing step free access to the GF. When we visited, the lift was nearly blocked off by a car, and staff assistance is needed to use it. There are +4 steps at the main entrance or +3+1 at the side. Tea room on the GF. No adapted loos.

Claridges, Brook Street W1 *Tel:* 0171 629-8860. Entrance has +1 step, and side doors bypass the revolving door. Inside there are +3 to the tea room, with a portable ramp available. **Wheelchair loo (D90 ST80).**

Intercontinental, Hamilton Place W1 *Tel:* 0171 409-3131. Situated on the corner of Park Lane and Piccadilly. UGCP with lift access. There are –5 steps at the Hamilton Place entrance, but step free through the Coffee House entrance, on the corner of Park Lane and Piccadilly. Afternoon tea is served in the Lobby lounge (turn right and follow the route from the Coffee House entrance. **Wheelchair loo (D80 ST120).**

Lanesborough, Hyde Park Corner SW1 *Tel:* 0171 259-5599. Situated just off Grosvenor Place. The UGCP does not have lift access, but it may be possible to park in the forecourt while having tea. Flat entrance. The tea room is on the GF, with 60% with step free access and movable chairs. **Wheelchair loo (D95 ST80)** past reception on the right.

Meridien, 19-21 Piccadilly W1 *Tel:* 0171 734-8000. Near Piccadilly Circus. Flat entrance and tea room on the GF with movable furniture. **Wheelchair loo (D85 ST140)** on the lower ground floor accessed by lift (D80 W110 L150).

Ritz, 150 Piccadilly W1 *Tel:* 0171 493-8181. 50m from Green Park station. Entrance +2 steps, with a ramp available. A side door can be used to bypass the revolving door. Then step free access to about half the tea room, with movable chairs. No adapted loos. We were told that a disabled person could use a toilet in one of the rooms if necessary. This is not totally reliable.

Savoy, Savoy Place WC2 *Tel:* 0171 836-4343. Half way along the Strand. Entrance flat, through a side door, but –10 –4 steps to get there. These can be bypassed by the use of two lifts (D80 W95 L105) and the kitchen! No adapted loos.

You might also consider the **Cumberland,** or the **Mount Royal Hotel,** for an up-market tea. They are both near Marble Arch, see *Accommodation* chapter.

Shops

One of London's main attractions are the long streets full of shops, many of them famous throughout the world. Our survey teams found that access to shops has improved over recent years, although the greatest improvement has been in the numerous newly built shopping centres around London, particularly with the advent of *Shopmobility*.

The National Federation of *Shopmobility* is a growing movement. Each scheme is independently run and financed, but the Federation coordinates information, and publishes a directory with brief details of each *Shopmobility*. Contacts are listed under *General information*.

A *Shopmobility* scheme usually has an office with adjacent OB parking spaces, and offer manual or electric wheelchairs for hire and use. Most have some electric scooters which are particularly useful to elderly people who cannot walk very far, or who find that carrying things is difficult. Some schemes can provide volunteer escorts if necessary, some of whom are trained to guide people with visual impairments. Opening times are variable, and depend both on demand, and on the availability of staff and of finance. Some schemes open every day, others open for perhaps two or three days a week.

All of the out-of-town shopping centres we have included in the guide have a *Shopmobility* office. The one in Hounslow is due to open early in 1996. There are plans to open offices in Enfield, Hillingdon, Richmond and Wandsworth. Schemes outside the M25 which we have not included are Bedford, Brentwood, Guildford, Watford and Woking.

In the write-ups, we have given the location of *Shopmobility* offices, and the CP with which it is associated. We have then described the centre starting from this point. Note that the office will almost certainly be centrally situated. Its OB spaces may well be in the main MSCP, and on Saturdays, and other times, there may even be a queue of cars trying to get in. It means that access is effectively blocked off, and you'll either have to wait in the queue, or choose to shop at some other time.

In the Central Shops section we have concentrated mainly on the Oxford Street and Kensington areas, as well as including famous shops like Harrods, Harvey Nicols, and Fortnum and Mason. We have only surveyed a tiny percentage of London's shops, so please do not be limited by listings in this section. Access is generally good, although the majority of big stores have central escalators and less obvious lifts. Most big department stores have a store guide near the main entrance. These do not normally take account of access problems. Departments are sometimes moved around without the list being amended.

For shop locations, see the map, and note that the numbering along Oxford Street (which is very long) is shown. Shops get extremely busy, particularly during sales and throughout the whole Christmas period. Car parking also gets difficult. Near Oxford Street there are CP's attached to Selfridges, one behind Debenhams and a UGCP at Cavendish Square.

There is a Lloyds Bank with step free access at 32 Oxford Street, W1 (*Tel:* 0171 636-8696). Banking facilities are on the first floor with escalator access, or alternatively a platform stair lift (W70 L74) to the basement, then a lift (D80 W120 L120) to the first floor. Have a look at the *Good loo guide* for toilets.

Near Kensington High Street, there's an UGCP on Hornton Street with lift (D90 W125 L140) access to the street. There are **wheelchair cubicles (D86)** in the loos at the exit. The key is supposedly with the attendant, but when our survey team visited he couldn't find it!

Remember the street and open-air markets for shopping, which have, in principle, good access. They are listed in the chapter on *Open-air activities.*

In the text, shops are listed in alphabetical order. Where there is more than one branch in the same area (eg C & A in Oxford Street) we have listed them together, but shown them separately on the map.

Central Shops

Army and Navy Stores, 101 Victoria Street SW1 *Tel:* 0171 834-1234. Large department store split between two buildings with an upper level link. The main building has a flat entrance and step free access throughout its three floors, via two lifts (D135 W190 L160) at the back of the store. Second floor restaurant near an **adapted loo (D90 ST55)** which is by the lifts.

The second building is across Howick Place and on two floors. Entrance +1 step and escalator/stair access only. The easiest way to reach the upper floor is probably to use the link (+4 –7) from the second floor of the main building. Café on the GF.

Barkers Of Kensington, 63 Kensington High Street W8 *Tel:* 0171 937-5432. Houses a variety of separate shops. Flat entrances from the High Street. Central escalators serve all four floors, but there is a well-hidden lift (D110 W139 L135) at the very back of the store. Restaurant on the second floor and coffee shop in the basement.

British Home Stores (BHS), 101 Kensington High Street W8 *Tel:* 0171 937-0919. Flat access everywhere. A lift (D120 W170 L170) at the back of the store serves all three floors. Restaurant on the first floor, with a nearby **wheelchair loo (D85 ST80)**.

British Home Stores (BHS), 252 Oxford Street W1 *Tel:* 0171 629-2011. Department store with flat entrance and two floors. Lift (D80 W185 L185) at the back of the store on the left. Restaurant on the first floor with a **wheelchair loo (D90 ST120)** nearby. The sliding door is somewhat temperamental.

C & A, 200 Oxford Street W1 *Tel:* 0171 631-4576. Near Oxford Circus. Clothes shop with step free access via a lift (D80 W150 L200) to all six floors. The **C & A**

near Marble Arch at 505 Oxford Street, W1 (*Tel:* 0171 629-7272) is on three floors. Flat front entrance and lift (D120 W145 L180) access throughout, including to the coffee shop on the first floor. The **C & A** at 376 Oxford Street, W1 (*Tel:* 0171 408-0047), has step free access to all three floors, using the lift (D110 W190 L170). None have loos.

Debenhams, 334 Oxford Street W1 *Tel:* 0171 580-3000. Large department store on five floors. Flat entrance on Vere Street corner. The GF has a split level with +5 steps, and there's another in the basement (+8). Both can be bypassed by open lifts (W80 L100) at the front left of each floor. The main lifts go from the upper GF level. There is a well hidden lift (D90 W200 L140) before the split level, on the left after the main entrance, signposted 'Exit to Marylebone Lane'. This lift gives access to all floors except the basement. On the upper floors you can cross without steps to the lifts (D80+ W160 L135+) at the back of the store, and get down to the upper level of the GF, and to the basement. If you want to go straight to floors one, two or three, it's simpler to use the hidden lift.

Restaurant and café on the second floor, both with flat access to the food counters, and to 50% of the tables. **Adapted cubicles (ladies D60 ST30), (gents D65 ST100),** in the main loos on the third floor. Although access has been improved with the provision of the open lifts, the decision of the management not to provide ramps remains disappointing, but it took a lot of pressure to get anything done. They carried out a multi-million pound development only a few years ago, and access issues were clearly not a priority.

DH Evans, 318 Oxford Street W1 *Tel:* 0171 629-8800. Flat/ramped entrances. Seven floors served by six central lifts (D142 W170 L142). A small section on both the second and third floor has a split level with +2 steps, and the lower ground floor has a section with +4. The lift nearest Oxford Street is the only one to serve this floor. Neither eating place in the store has flat access. The Terrace café on the GF has +3 whilst the Coffee Shop on the lower ground floor is flat from the escalator, but –4 from the lift. There is an **adapted cubicle (D80 ST69)** in the ladies on the fifth floor.

Dickins & Jones, 224 Regent Street W1 *Tel:* 0171 734-7070. Large, spacious and somewhat exclusive clothes store. Step free access everywhere. Two lifts (D110 W190 L140) on the left of the store from the Regent Street entrance serve all six floors. It contains various eating places, on the third, second, ground and lower ground floor, all of which have flat access. **Wheelchair cubicle (D70 ST105)** in the ladies on the third floor, but no equivalent facility for men, even though staff told us there is!

Dillons The Bookstore, 82 Gower Street WC1 *Tel:* 0171 636-1577 *Fax:* 0171 580-7680. The most accessible of London's big bookstores. Flat main entrance, and from Gower Street, although +1 step (steep) from Malet Street. Two lifts give access to all five floors (D90 W135 L95 at Malet Street, D80 W110 L140 at Gower Street). The odd step on the GF and in the basement can be easily bypassed. The shop is surprisingly roomy for a bookstore. There is a poorly signed **wheelchair loo (D75 ST150)** in the middle of the basement.

Fenwick, 63 New Bond Street W1 *Tel:* 0171 629-9161. Two flat entrances in New Bond Street, or –6 steps in Brook Street. The entrance on the corner only gives flat access to 10% of the GF. The other entrance in New Bond Street gives flat access to the lift (D90 W170 L105) and some 30% of the GF. Then there is –4 to a tiny section, +2 to about 60% of the floor, and a further +2 to the remaining 10% and the other flat entrance. Access is marginally better on the other four floors, all of which are accessed by the lift: the lower ground floor is flat; there is +2 to 10% of the first floor; 30% of the second floor is flat, with 60% being +4, and the remaining 10% either +3, or –1 from the +4; there is +8 to all clothes departments on the third floor.
    Using a staff lift (D80 W110 L150) greatly improves access. This is –8 from the GF, but if you take the other lift to the lower ground floor you can transfer step free. From the staff lift, the 60% with +4 on the second floor is then step free, as are all departments on the third floor. It may sound complicated, but by using both lifts about 90% of the store is step free, although there is still +2 to 60% of the GF. Café on the lower ground floor and restaurant and bar on the second floor. **Wheelchair loo (D85 ST130)** on the third floor, flat access from the lift, just past the standard loos and signposted by personnel.

Fortnum & Mason, 181 Piccadilly W1 *Tel:* 0171 734-8040. One of London's traditional shops with its own unique style. Flat entrance on Piccadilly, avoiding steps at the other entrances. Three lifts (D80+ W140+ L85+) on the right of the store give step free access to all six floors. The lower ground floor is cramped and full of fragile looking items. The upmarket St James Restaurant on the fourth floor has flat access. The Fountain Restaurant is –12 from the GF, but only +1 from the entrance on the corner of Duke Street and Jermyn Street. The Patio Restaurant is +10 from the GF but step free via a staff lift (D80 W120 L160).

Hamleys, 188 Regent Street W1 *Tel:* 0171 734-3161. The world's largest toyshop is on seven floors. There is flat access everywhere, although the shop is nearly always busy. It has central escalators. Two lifts (D105 W185 L145) on the left go to all floors. **Wheelchair loo (D80 ST100)** on the fourth floor.

Harrods, 87 Knightsbridge SW1 *Tel:* 0171 730-1234. A unique institution with a world wide reputation, where you can buy almost anything from a horse to a house to a hearse. Harrods have recently prevented people using electric Batricars and buggies from entering the shop. A detailed guide is available at all entrances. It is not reprinted very often and not 100% reliable. Flat entrances on the Brompton Road. The store has seven floors and is simply massive, measuring about 200m by 200m. There are numerous sets of lifts, all of which are at least D80 W165 L135, and they give step free access to about 95% of the store.

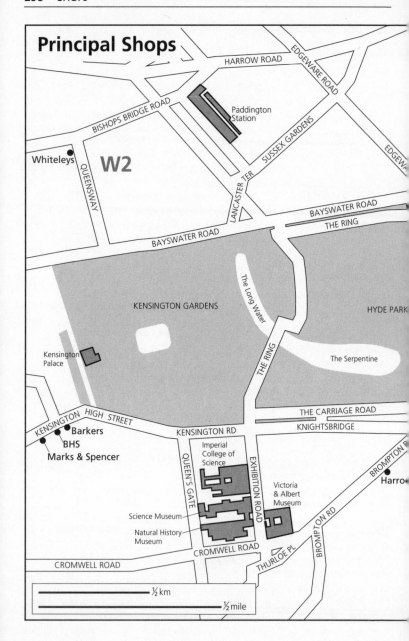

Principal Shops

HARROW ROAD

EDGEWARE ROAD

BISHOPS BRIDGE ROAD

Paddington Station

SUSSEX GARDENS

EDGEWA

Whiteleys

W2

QUEENSWAY

LANCASTER TER

BAYSWATER ROAD

THE RING

BAYSWATER ROAD

KENSINGTON GARDENS

The Long Water

HYDE PARK

Kensington Palace

THE RING

The Serpentine

THE CARRIAGE ROAD

KENSINGTON HIGH STREET

KNIGHTSBRIDGE

KENSINGTON RD

Barkers

BHS

Marks & Spencer

QUEEN'S GATE

Imperial College of Science

EXHIBITION ROAD

Victoria & Albert Museum

BROMPTON R

Harro

Science Museum

Natural History Museum

CROMWELL ROAD

BROMPTON RD

THURLOE PL

CROMWELL ROAD

½ km

½ mile

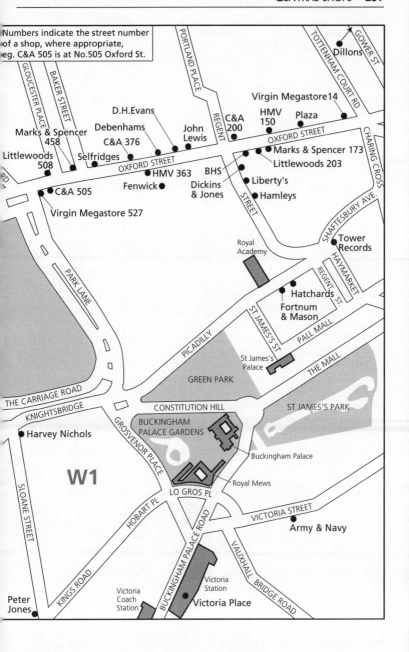

Numbers indicate the street number
of a shop, where appropriate,
eg. C&A 505 is at No.505 Oxford St.

Dillons

Virgin Megastore14

D.H.Evans

Debenhams

C&A 376

Marks & Spencer 458

Littlewoods 508

Selfridges

John Lewis

C&A 200

HMV 150

Plaza

OXFORD STREET

Marks & Spencer 173

Littlewoods 203

Fenwick

HMV 363

Dickins & Jones

BHS

Liberty's

Hamleys

C&A 505

Virgin Megastore 527

Royal Academy

Tower Records

Hatchards

Fortnum & Mason

St James's Palace

GREEN PARK

Royal Academy

BUCKINGHAM PALACE GARDENS

Buckingham Palace

Royal Mews

ST JAMES'S PARK

THE MALL

Harvey Nichols

W1

KNIGHTSBRIDGE

THE CARRIAGE ROAD

VICTORIA STREET

Army & Navy

Peter Jones

Victoria Coach Station

Victoria Station

Victoria Place

PORTLAND PLACE

REGENT STREET

GLOUCESTER PLACE

BAKER STREET

TOTTENHAM COURT RD

GOWER ST

CHARING CROSS

SHAFTESBURY AVE.

HAYMARKET

REGENT ST.

PALL MALL

ST JAMES'S ST

PICADILLY

PARK LANE

GROSVENOR PLACE

HOBART PL

LO GROS PL

CONSTITUTION HILL

BUCKINGHAM PALACE ROAD

VAUXHALL BRIDGE ROAD

KINGS ROAD

SLOANE STREET

Starting from the bottom, and working upwards, the:
- lower ground floor is made up of four separate sections of which only the Pantry is accessible by lift, the other three having at least –20 steps (the lift currently shown in the store guide as going to the main lower ground floor no longer exists);
- GF is step free, and the bridge (+17–17) from Men's Suits to the Food Hall, can be circumnavigated;
- first floor is flat throughout;
- second floor is flat except for +1 to a tiny display area;
- third and fourth floors are 99% step free by using different lifts, but this is not at all obvious, as there are split levels involved (staff can assist);
- fifth floor is flat apart from +3 to a small part of the sports department.

There are sixteen different eating places all with flat access, except for the Green Man Pub on the lower ground floor. All six on the GF have fixed stools, and only in the Bar Fromage are these low. Access to all four eating places on the fourth floor is more complicated, but not a problem if you use either of the two lift areas nearest to Hans Road. The Upper Circle restaurant appears to have +5 or +4 to get to it, but has flat access from the Terrace Bar. There is one **wheelchair loo (D95 ST80)** on the first floor at the back right of the shop, and another is listed in the ladies loos on the fourth floor but this actually has D70 ST30. For a store of this size (and reputation), the provision of only one **wheelchair loo** seems more than a little stingy. The store has recently introduced a fee of £1 for using their loos, but apparently not for the **wheelchair loo**.

Harvey Nichols, 109 Knightsbridge SW1 *Tel:* 0171 235-5000. Exclusive store known for ladies outfitting, but with some general departments and a comprehensive food store on the fifth floor. Flat entrances on Knightsbridge. Two central lifts (D78 W128 L122) serve all seven floors. About a quarter of the GF has +4. Floors one to five are step free except for –2 to a small section of the fourth floor. The lower ground floor has a number of split levels. From the lift there is flat access to only about 10%, then –4 or –5 to other parts. The fifth floor restaurant, café and separate bar all have step free access. There is a direct lift (D85 W160 L130) from the GF to the fifth floor by the corner entrance with Sloane Street. Near the bar, there are **wheelchair cubicles** in the loos **(gents D85 ST150, ladies D95 ST75).**

Hatchards Booksellers, 187 Piccadilly W1 *Tel:* 0171 439-9921. A smallish but well-stocked bookstore whose customers include the Queen. Flat entrance, then a lift (D80 W105 L140) at the back of the store goes to all five floors. The second and third floors both have +1+1 steps to a quarter of the area.

Hays Galeria see chapter on *Places of interest.*

HMV, 363 Oxford Street W1 *Tel:* 0171 629-1240. Near Bond Street. Flat to the GF, and lift (D107 W200 L105) to the first and second floors. A service lift (D80 W80 L140) goes to the basement. Ask for assistance. **HMV** near Oxford Circus at 150 Oxford Street, W1 (*Tel:* 0171 631-3423) has three floors linked by escalators, although there is a further –3 to the basement. A service lift (D180 W120 L200) is available. Ask for assistance.

John Lewis, 278 Oxford Street W1 *Tel:* 0171 629-7711. Between Oxford Circus and New Bond Street. Large department store on seven floors, with a flat main entrance and seven lifts (D115 W157 L182); three at the front on the left, and four at the back on the left. The restaurant, on the third floor is flat except for +2 steps to two small balcony areas. **Wheelchair loo (D100 ST100 NKS)** on the fourth floor.

Liberty's, 210 Regent Street W1 *Tel:* 0171 734-1234. On the corner of Great Marlborough Street. A store with wonderful character. Liberty designs and patterns are known the world over. It consists of two separate buildings, the Tudor Wing in Great Marlborough Street, and the Regent Street building. Some departments are congested and displays are often cramped.

On Great Marlborough Street, the entrance on the left is flat, avoiding +3 steps at the right hand entrance and a revolving door at the main entrance. Once inside both the lift (D80 W150 L120) near the entrance on the left, and the lift (D80 W120 L110) to the right of the main entrance give access to all six floors of the Tudor Wing. The Regent Street building has three floors with step free access throughout, linked by a lift (D80 W170 L190).

Most of the floors in the Tudor Wing have a split level although none take up more than 5% of a floor:
- on the GF +1 to the gift section on left from main entrance;
- shoes section on the first floor –4;
- café and prints section on second floor –2, both with a ramped alternative;
- beds section on the third floor –2 ;
- small section of the fourth floor +4 .

Access between the two buildings appears to be difficult. There is a link in the basement which is –4 from the Tudor Wing, and there is +8 –3 if you use the link on the first floor. There is, however, a flat link between the two buildings, which is unsigned. The Regent Street lift has doors at either end, and serves both buildings on the second floor, albeit at slightly different levels. From the Tudor Wing take any lift to the second floor, then transfer to the Regent Street lift by following the sign to Customer Services. From the Regent Street building ask the lift attendant to go to the second floor of the Tudor Wing. It may sound complicated, but is actually quite simple, and saves leaving from one entrance and coming back into the store around the corner.

The store contains three eating places, all in the Tudor Wing. There is step free access to all three, in the basement, and on the second and fourth floors. The second floor café has bar service and some high chairs. There is a **wheelchair**

loo (D78 ST75) on the first floor of the Regent Street building, which is unsigned. It is off the shop floor, so you will need to ask.

Littlewoods, 203 Oxford Street W1 *Tel:* 0171 434-4301. Flat entrance. Two lifts (D135 W200 L125) on the right after the entrance give step free access to all four floors. Restaurant on the second floor as well as a **wheelchair loo (D85 ST75)** on the right from the lift. **Littlewoods** at 508 Oxford Street is on two floors, with a flat entrance but no lift, and no wheelchair loo.

Marks & Spencer, 113 Kensington High Street W8 *Tel:* 0171 938-3711. Alongside Kensington High Street station. Step free to all four floors via two lifts (D90+ W105+ L160+) on the left. A split level (+3 steps) on the first floor, can be bypassed by a ramp. We were told that the wheelchair loo is now on the second floor next to other toilets. The exit to the Underground leads to Kensington Arcade, which has flat access to eight shops and a café.

Marks & Spencer, 173 Oxford Street W1 *Tel:* 0171 437-7722. Some 200m from Oxford Circus towards Tottenham Court Road. Step free throughout via a lift (D90 W132 L175) to all four floors. **Wheelchair loo (D105 ST90)** half way along the GF on the left. Not signed, and kept locked. The **Marks & Spencer** near Marble Arch at 458 Oxford Street W1 (*Tel:* 0171 935-7954) also has four floors with lift (D140 W190 L100) access. The two central lifts go to all floors, but the lift at the back of the store does not go to the basement. The second floor is on a split level but has a ramped bypass. No wheelchair loo.

Peter Jones, Sloane Square SW1 *Tel:* 0171 730-3434. Large department store on seven floors with flat access almost everywhere. Flat entrances, then two sets of well-signposted lifts (D100 W140 L135) go to all floors. Split level (3 steps) in the basement bypassed by open lift. The fourth floor has three separate areas. The two shopping areas are split by 5 steps but can be reached step free by using the different sets of lifts. The restaurant is a further –5. **Wheelchair loo (D100 ST200+)** on the fourth floor.

Plaza, 120 Oxford Street W1 *Tel:* 0171 637-8811. A development on four floors containing a wide variety of shops and an excellent food court in the basement. It is in the shell of an old department store called Bournes. Flat main entrance, then lift (D80 W80 L150) access to all floors. Two of the outlets in the food court have +1 step (steep). There are two **wheelchair loos (D85 ST100)** in the basement and **another (D85 ST75)** on the first floor.

Selfridges, 400 Oxford Street W1 *Tel:* 0171 629-1234. One of London's biggest department stores. Each of the five floors measure roughly 200m by 200m. It has its own seven storey CP (entered from Duke Street), which gives flat or lift (D80 W133 L130) access to the shop. It's not cheap to use. The entrance on Duke Street and the central one on Oxford Street both have flat access, as does the entrance to the food hall from Orchard Street. From the food hall to the main store there is a minimum of –10 steps, bypassed by an open lift (W80 L100) located by the exit to the Stationery Hall.

The main shop has two lifts (D120 W190 L150) in the centre of the store. The café by the food hall and the restaurant by Duke Street have stepped access. The other seven eating places have flat access and only on the ground and first floor is the furniture fixed. **Wheelchair loo (D95 ST170 NKS)** in the Dome Restaurant near Miss Selfridge on the GF, and an **adapted loo (D90 ST57)** on the third floor.

Immediately opposite Selfridges main entrance on Oxford Street is a 24-hour **wheelchair loo (D70+ ST70+ NKS)**, at the end of Balderton Street.

Tobacco Dock, 50 Porters Walk E1 *Tel:* 0171 702-9681. Being refurbished and due to reopen in early 1996 as a parade of factory shops on two levels, selling cheap goods through wholesalers. MSCP with OB spaces on level six with step free access to the upper level of shops, due to an open lift (W130 L130) bypassing –6 steps. Flat main entrance then either +16 to upper or –15 to lower level, bypassed by a lift (D85 W90 L165). Most shop units have +1, although this may change with the new building work. There are no fixed plans at the time of writing. **Wheelchair cubicle (D80+ ST70+)** in both the gents and ladies.

Tower Records, 1 Piccadilly Circus W1 *Tel:* 0171 439-2500. Ramp bypasses +4 steps at the main entrance, avoiding –7 from Regent Street and –4 from Piccadilly Circus underground. Once inside, a poorly signed lift (D80 W170 L155) on the right from the main entrance gives access to all three floors and the mezzanine level. All have flat access. In the basement there is +1, bypassed by turning left out of the lift.

Victoria Place, Eccleston Bridge SW1 *Tel:* 0171 931-8811. Two floors of shops and eating places built above Victoria Station with ramped access from Eccleston Bridge. From the station there appears to be only escalator access, but there is a lift (D110 W150 L220) to the first floor from half-way down platforms 13/14 (for the Gatwick Express). The platforms are open, so just walk or wheel down.

On the first floor, apart from the British Airways check-in, there's a range of shops, virtually all with flat access. On the second floor there's a whole range of eating places (from McDonalds and Garfunkles to Luigi Malones, and there are several other cafés and restaurants). There's also a pub, the Molly O'Grady's. All have flat access. On the same level, between Deep Pan Pizzas and Pontis there's a **wheelchair loo (D80 ST130 NKS)**. Access to the second level is by escalator or steps, and there is a service lift (D75 W100 L150). There is no indication anywhere that this exists, and you're supposed to be clairvoyant. Ask any shopholder to get someone from security to take you there. The lift is accessed from outside by the taxi drop-off point on the first floor, and from quite near the pub on the second floor. It is, however, quite absurd that you have to guess that it is there.

Virgin Megastore, 14 Oxford Street W1 *Tel:* 0171 631-1234. Flat entrances, with escalator or lift (D90 W110 L150) access throughout the four floors. The store has been refurbished and is step free throughout. The **Virgin Megastore** near Marble Arch, at 527 Oxford Street W1 (*Tel:* 0171 491-8582) is on three floors with a flat entrance but no lift. Escalator access throughout.

Whiteleys, 151 Queensway W2 *Tel:* 0171 229-8844. Shopping and eating centre on three floors built in the shell of a once famous department store. It contains an eight screen cinema complex (see chapter on *Entertainment*). CP is approached from Redan Place and has three OB spaces near the entrance on the second floor. There are three flat entrances, and flat/lift (D105 W200 L115) access throughout. Lifts are near the main central entrance from Queensway. Shops are on the ground and first floors, the cinemas and restaurants are on the second floor, and the third floor contains an art gallery and offices. **Wheelchair loo (D85 ST75)** to the right of the management office on the third floor. Due to become NKS. Another **wheelchair loo (D85 ST75)** is on the second floor next to *McDonalds.* The complex covers an area of approximately 150m by 50m.

Out of town centres

These have been chosen because they have a *Shopmobility* scheme at the time of writing. All have adjacent parking with OB spaces, covered shopping areas and big stores.

Bexley Heath

A compact centre when compared with some others, with an area of roughly 200m by 70m. The Broadway Shopping Centre (*Tel:* 0181 301-2956) is fully covered, and mainly on one floor. Large CP on two levels, approached from Albion Road, with OB spaces on both levels. On the lower level there are four spaces in the middle and eleven at the eastern end. Lifts (D110 W200 L170) give step free access to the centre.

Shopmobility (*Tel:* 0181 301-5237) is based on the first floor. Either take lift number eight to level one, or use one of the buzzers in the CP, and someone will come along to assist. There's another buzzer for *Shopmobility* by a drop-off point on Townley Road.

There is flat access at all entrances, and throughout most of the eighty or so stores. British Home Stores, WH Smiths and Marks & Spencers have two floors, with lift (D90+ W120+ L140+) access. There's a café on the first floor of BHS. The main Centre Restaurant has fixed seating, a third of which is +6 steps.

There are two **wheelchair loos (D80 ST70)** on the GF, and others on the first floor in BHS **(D95 ST85)**, and by the café in Asda, located separately from the centre **(D85 ST180)**. Also note the write-ups on the *Wrong'un* and the *Golden Lion* in the *Pubs* chapter.

Bromley

Apart from being on a hill Bromley has good facilities for people with disabilities, particularly in the Glades Shopping Centre (*Tel:* 0181 313-9292). The centre has over a hundred shops on two floors and well-signposted parking on two levels above the shops. The numerous parking areas are named after animals.

The *Shopmobility* office (*Tel:* 0181 313-0031) is in CP level one in Frog Zone, approached from Kentish Way. There are fifteen OB spaces. Lift (D110 W180 L130) access to the middle of the centre. There is lift access (D75+ W115+ L170+) from all other parking areas to both levels.

All entrances to the centre have flat access, as do all the shops. On the lower level is an information desk (*Tel:* 0181 466-8589), a food court and various restaurants, the Pavilion Leisure Centre, and a **wheelchair loo (D90 ST70)** outside Boots. On the upper level there are two **adapted loos (D90 ST60)** opposite McDonalds, and one inside, although the latter was out of order when our survey team visited. There is another **wheelchair loo (D80 ST75)** on the High Street opposite the Churchill Theatre (see section on *Theatres*). The centre itself is approximately 400m long.

Croydon

Of the shopping areas we have covered Croydon is biggest. The town centre has seven major CPs. The recently refurbished Whitgift Centre (*Tel:* 0181 688-0990) contains about 150 shops on two main levels. Note that East Croydon station is fully accessible and only about 200m from the main shopping area.

Shopmobility (*Tel:* 0181 688-7336) is located in the lower level of the Whitgift CP, clearly signed on Wellesley Road. There are twenty-nine OB spaces and it is step free to the north end of the Centre. *Shopmobility* can arrange for chairs and scooters to be available at a number of the central CPs including the Drummond Centre, the Surrey Street CP, and also at East Croydon station. To go to the south end of the Centre, the Allders CP is closer. This has twenty-two OB spaces on the third floor, with flat access to the second floor of the centre, or lift (D80 W125 L150) access to the first floor.

The main entrance to the Whitgift Centre is flat from the pedestrianised North End High Street. The centre has three clearly signposted sets of lifts (all at least D90 W120 L100). It has a central café on the first floor.

The Centre contains four **wheelchair loos**/cubicles:
- on the GF in the ladies **(D85 ST195)**;
- on the first floor in both ladies and gents **(D85 ST80)**;

• on the second floor **(D95 ST85)**. At time of our survey only the lifts nearest Woolworths served this floor and it contained nothing other than this loo. There are plans to provide a loo in the Whitgift CP.

If you are coming into Croydon from the south, the Surrey Street CP on Scarbrook Road is convenient. It has eight OB spaces on level 1, and flat access to the Surrey Street Market. The CP has lift (D110 W160 L150) access throughout, and from level 4 there is a step free footbridge of about 50m which comes out 50m from the Croydon Clocktower (see section on *Arts centres*). *Shopmobility* vehicles are available.

The Dingwall Road MSCP, entered from Lansdown Road, is some 300m from East Croydon station. It provides the best parking if you want to use the train. Twenty OB spaces on the GF, and lift (D90 L96 W140) access between floors. **Wheelchair cubicles (D85 ST115)** in both ladies and gents loos on the GF.

There are numerous **wheelchair loos/cubicles** in Croydon town centre (unisex unless stated):

Allders, third floor **(D80 ST180)**. Lift (D105 W200 L158) access at back right of store.

Debenhams, second floor **(D90 ST100)**. Lift (D108 W160 L220) access from central glass lift. Follow signs for toilets, **wheelchair loo** not signposted.

Drummond Centre, GF, on right after entrance, gents **(D85 ST80)**, ladies **(D80 ST120)**.

East Croydon Station, platform 3/4 **(D90 ST110 NKS)**, ask at the office for key.

The George Pub, George Street **(D85 ST100)**, flat from the Whitgift Centre through Allders Mall.

Marks & Spencer, GF **(D90 ST85 NKS)**, not signposted.

Mothercare, GF **(D100 ST110)**, marked 'toilet'.

One-Stop Reception, Taberner House **(D85 ST95)**, key at reception.

Register Office, first floor **(D85 ST95)** via lift (D80 W170 L105).

There are **wheelchair/adapted loos** in Fairfield and in the Croydon Clocktower (see section on *Arts centres*).

Epsom

A substantial area containing the Ashley Centre (*Tel:* 01372-742548), well signed on the High Street. It is mostly on one level although a few of the larger stores have other floors, linked by lift. There is a MSCP, the Ashley Centre CP.

The *Shopmobility* office is by the CP entrance (*Tel:* 01372-727086). There are around twenty OB spaces on level one, and more on other levels. Step free access to the shops is via five large lifts (all D100+ W150+ L150+). **Wheelchair loo (D85 ST70)** near the lifts by the entrance from the CP. The café on the ground level is step free.

Guildford

For a brief description of Guildford and of the *Shopmobility* there, see chapter on *Days out*.

Harrow

A centre with a covered precinct (the St Ann's Shopping Centre) about 150m long, and a pedestrianised shopping area some 200m long, leading to a large Debenhams department store. It is surrounded by a one-way traffic system. The MSCP off Clarendon Road has four OB spaces on level two.

Shopmobility (*Tel:* 0181 861-2282) is based in an office round the corner from the OB spaces. There's a bell. As you have to go outside to reach it, staff prefer to come to you. From the CP, there is step free access via a lift (D100 W150 L130) to all parts of the centre. The ramp down from College Road, opposite Harrow-on-the-Hill station is 20m long. Most of the shops off the pedestrianised St Ann's Road have flat access, and Debenhams (on Station Road) has step free access throughout via lifts (D95 W200 L130).

Wheelchair loo (D70 ST90) on the GF of the shopping centre near the CP lifts, and **another (D80 ST85)** on the first floor. Debenhams has an **adapted loo (D63 ST80)** on the second floor.

Hatfield Galleria

A shopping and cinema complex situated near Hatfield over the A1 and just off the A1001 (*Tel:* 01707-278301). CP with OB spaces under a covered section between the cinemas and the shops. There is also a MSCP which serves both floors of the centre via four lifts (D110 W170 L180). The Galleria is roughly 500m from end to end and has seats throughout. It is fully covered and contains about 100 shops. The centre has flat entrances and a variety of shops and restaurants, all with flat access.

Shopmobility is run from an office in Hatfield town (*Tel:* 01707-262731). There is an office in the Galleria on the first floor (*Tel:* 01707-336688). At the time of writing they had not found a permanent 'home' in the centre.

There are +4 steps from the lower level to the escalators, but this can be bypassed by the lifts. The centre has a number of **wheelchair loos (all D70+ ST70+)**, one in McDonalds on the lower level, and another in a staff area. There is one on the upper level by the CP, and another in the cinema.

Hounslow

When we surveyed, the 1km long High Street was being pedestrianised. There is a large covered shopping mall called the Treaty Centre towards one end, measuring about 200m by 80m. The attached MSCP, off Grove Road has twelve

OB spaces on level six. This gives step free access to the centre via lifts (D100 W200 L200). The centre is mainly on the GF, but Debenhams is on three floors with a lift (D90 W135 L240) inside. There's another lift inside the Paul Robeson theatre (see chapter on *Theatres*).

Shopmobility is due to start in April 1996, based on level six of the Treaty Centre CP. Enquiries to *Tel:* 0181 862-5950. Loos are next to the CP lifts on the GF, one is a **wheelchair (D90 ST70 NKS) loo**, while the other is **adapted (D90 ST40 NKS).**

As described, the High Street is long, with the Treaty Centre near one end. It's about 300m to Marks & Spencer, and another 300m to the end of the pedestrian area. There are numerous other CPs with OB spaces along the length of the street, the biggest of which is the Alexandra Road CP with six OB spaces on ground level. There are also three OB spaces in Gilbert Street and a further four in Fair Street, next to M & S.

Ilford (Redbridge)

The Exchange Shopping Centre is about 350m long and on three floors with over 100 stores. *Tel:* 0181 553-3000. MSCP entered from Myrtle Road has OB spaces on levels one and four. All entrances are flat, and the four sets of lifts (all D90+ W100+ L130+) go to all floors. This includes the CP lift, and the lift inside the department store Owen Owen, on three floors. Step free access throughout. There is a large food court area on the third floor as well as the Centre café.

Somewhat confusingly it comes under the auspices of **Redbridge** *Shopmobility* (*Tel:* 0181 500-1919. *Fax:* 0181 500-1002). It is based on level 1 (ground level) of the CP. Three **wheelchair loos** on the GF, (all D75+ ST80+), one is signed, near W H Smith, the others are to the left as you enter from the CP level one. A signed door leads to two unmarked doors containing the loos.

Kingston

The town centre has been extensively redeveloped. Much of the shopping area has been pedestrianised, and there are many peripheral CPs. The central area is about 500m square. There is also a river frontage with accessible pubs and restaurants. The development has produced a good blend of old and new, and accessibility is generally good. It has a good Access guide – *What's Where*, available from the Guildhall (*Tel:* 0181 547-4699) or from *Shopmobility*. There are considerable distances from the CPs to some shops and facilities. Signposting is not particularly good, but an excellent map is available from *Tel:* 0181 547-5928 (Guildhall Parking) or from *Shopmobility*. This shows the OB spaces.

Shopmobility (*Tel:* 0181 547-1255) is on level two of the Eden Walk CP which has OB spaces on level two; lift access to ground level or ramped access to the upper level of Marks & Spencer. It is reached from Wheatfield Way via Ashdown

Road. The CP is in the Market area, but is not well signed.

Alternatively, the Bentalls CP in the Horsefair area gives access to a huge multi-level covered precinct. Both A and B sections of the CP have OB spaces on level 8. The Bentalls centre is a covered precinct on four floors with lift access throughout containing over 40 shops in addition to the Bentalls department store. Just across the road is John Lewis, another large department store. This has slightly more complicated access because the shop goes over a main road and there is a split level on the first floor. The floor plans and diagrams do not clarify access. There is lift access and step free access to 95% if you approach from Horse Fair or the John Lewis CP. Marks & Spencer and British Home Stores have lift and step free access throughout.

There are numerous **wheelchair loos** throughout the shopping area of which we will mention a few:

M & S, second floor **(D85 ST80 but obstructed by a bin).**

BHS, first floor **(D90 ST150)** off the restaurant.

John Lewis, first floor on both Townside and Riverside **(D85 ST75).**

Bentalls Centre, level 8 of CP-A near the OB spaces **(D85 ST80 NKS),** and on the second floor, one unisex **(D85 ST85)** and one in the ladies **(D87 ST110).**

Royal Barge (riverside pub) **(D85 ST80).**

Philadelphia Exchange (riverside American-style bar-diner) **(D85 ST75)**

Gazebo (riverside pub) adapted loo **(D75 ST59).**

Bus station Cromwell Road **(D95 ST135 NKS).**

Lakeside Thurrock

West Thurrock Way, West Thurrock, Grays, Essex. *Tel:* 01708-869933. Clearly signposted from junctions 30/31 off the M25 and from the A13. There are sixteen CPs surrounding the centre with OB spaces in 3, 5, 6, 9, 10, 11 and D. Although signposting is not particularly good, maps/plans of the centre are readily available, adjacent to information displays. These list the shops and show which level they are on.

The *Shopmobility* office (*Tel:* 01708-869933 ext 566) is on the GF in CP10 or the 'Blue Car Park'. This is at one end of the complex, and the office is about 30m from an entrance to the centre, next to Debenhams. The centre is on three floors, with lifts (D110 W190) in the central atrium. It contains over three hundred shops. There are also lifts between levels one and two (GF and first floor) near both Debenhams and House of Fraser, and inside Marks & Spencer (D110 W115 L200). In addition, there's a lift linking the Lakeside Pavilion with level two at the end of Brompton Walk. The centre measures about 200m by 100m. The main floors are levels one and two, and the Pavilion has smaller specialist shops.

On level three there is a selection of food stalls and eating places. About 50% of this area has step free access, and movable chairs and tables. The rest is either

–3, or has fixed seating, or both.

There are **wheelchair loos (all D80+ ST80+)** at each end of the GF (level one), on level two near the lift at the end of Brompton Walk, and on level three near the main toilets. All are clearly marked on the plans available.

Outside the centre is a lake, and a Warner Brothers cinema complex with step free access to all screens.

Lewisham

Development of the town centre is ongoing, until 2000, including the continuing pedestrianisation of the High Street. The main shopping area is the fully covered and compact **Lewisham Centre** (*Tel:* 0181 852-0094) situated between the High Street and Molesworth Street, and roughly 100m from Lewisham station. It is about 350m by 150m and contains over 90 shops, cafés, a play area and the Leisure Centre. Lewisham market operates just outside the main entrance. The five storey CP above the centre is entered from Molesworth Street and well signed. Levels one to four each have nine OB spaces. Each floor has six lifts (all D100 W110 L200) giving step free access everywhere.

The *Shopmobility* scheme is currently based in a wooden hut near the central lifts on floor three of the CP (*Tel:* 0181 698-3775 *Minicom:* 0181 698-7384).

All shops are on the GF and all have flat access and are reached by any of six step free entrances from the street. Customer information is centrally placed next to café with fixed tables and chairs. **Wheelchair loo (D85 ST95 NKS)**, by the entrance on Molesworth Street near Endgate Street, and **another (D85 ST80)** which is not signposted, in the cafeteria of BHS.

Redbridge see write-up on Ilford.

Romford

Includes a large shopping area, which spreads out over nearly 2 km. There are two main shopping precincts, Liberty One which is pedestrianised but open air, and Liberty Two which is a covered mall on three floors. They are next to each other and have step free access links. *Shopmobility* is based in an office in the Angel Way MSCP (*Tel:* 01708-739431). There are ten OB spaces on the GF, but it is about 400m from the main shopping centre. A closer alternative simply for parking is to use the Liberty Two CP where there are eight OB spaces on levels two and three with step free access into the centre. The Liberty Two centre has two lifts (D90 W120 L135) in the central atrium, giving step free access to all floors, and to about 95% of the wide variety of shops. There is a further lift on the left as you enter from the CP which serves levels two and three only.

There are several NKS **wheelchair loos** in the area, including:

- **Liberty Two** centre, level one, behind the escalators (**D85 ST160**). Ignore the sign on level two which implies that the loo is on that floor;
- **Liberty One** precinct, along a lane to the right of Boots (**D90 ST150**);
- **South Street,** near Marks & Spencer (**D95 ST80**);
- next to the **Angel Way CP (D75 ST75)**;
- next to **Romford Market Hall,** an adapted loo, in a cobbled area (**D90 ST67**).

Sutton

As well as the pedestrianised High Street, the town contains as the St Nicholas Centre, a large new covered shopping centre on three floors. Traffic goes round on a large ring and, to find the St Nicholas CP, follow the parking signs either for 'town centre' or for the St Nicholas Centre. Some OB spaces on the first and third levels.

Shopmobility office on level three (*Tel:* 0181 770-0691). This is by the bridge leading to the covered area which is about 50m long. The centre is about 200m long and has step free access throughout via ramps and lifts (D90 W100 L240) near the bridge.

There are **wheelchair loos (D70+ ST70+)** on level one (near C & A) and on level three, signed from the bridge area. When we surveyed, about half the shop spaces in the centre had not been occupied.

Just across the High Street from the exit by C & A there is another, smaller, covered shopping area called Times Square. This has two floors and an adjacent CP. Lift (D120 W200 L200). **Wheelchair loo (D80 ST80 NKS)** just opposite the lift on the first floor. Also just across the High Street is Marks & Spencer. The largest supermarket is Tescos at the north end of the High Street with its own CP.

Adjacent to the St Nicholas Centre is a UCI multiplex cinema, with accessible screens, and an accessible pub, the *Moon on the Hill,* in Hill Road opposite the Civic Centre (see chapter on *Pubs).*

Sport

Access to the main sports venues is of great importance. Even though the TV coverage of big events may be good, there's nothing quite like 'being there'. You may see less (and you don't often get the action replays), but the atmosphere is entirely different, and usually much more interesting.

The emphasis in this chapter is on spectating, but participation is also a vital interest for many. The **British Sports Association for Disabled People (BSAD),** Solecast House, 13 Brunswick Place N1 6DX *Tel/Minicom:* 0171 490-4919 is the central co-ordinating body. Many new sports centres have provided facilities for disabled people, particularly changing facilities, wheelchair loos and access to swimming pools. There will be local clubs and events in most sports.

The **Sports Council, London and South East Regions,** PO Box 480, Crystal Palace National Sports Centre, Ledrington Road SE19 2BQ *Tel:* 0181 778-8600, has an officer whose responsibilities include sports for disabled people. London boroughs have a department for the provision of sports facilities in its area and may have a section encouraging participation by disabled people. Also, many Adult Education Institutes have programmes and activities for disabled people to participate in. The **Greater London Sports Association**, Leroy House, 436 Essex House N1 3QP *Tel:* 0171 354-8666 *Minicom:* 0171 354-9544 develops and coordinates sport and recreation for people with learning difficulties. In addition, both GLAD and RADAR may have contacts and information.

Wembley complex

The centrepiece of Wembley is the Stadium, built for the 1924 British Empire Exhibition, and beginning to show its age. It stages the Cup Finals, and most international matches, as well as major events, concerts and greyhound racing. For 'big' events, the atmosphere can be brilliant.

Also on the site are Wembley Arena, mainly used for concerts, Wembley Conference Centre, and three Exhibition Halls. Parking and public transport access is the same for all the venues and is described here. The whole complex is under the same ownership and administration, so the address, telephone and fax numbers are the same for all the venues. An assessment is currently being made as to whether Wembley should get a large slice of money from the National Lottery to fund rebuilding.

Parking and public transport details: OB spaces are usually at the end of the Royal Route accessed off Empire Way near the Hilton hotel. Arrangements for parking at various events may differ, so if you want to reserve an OB space contact *Tel:* 0181 902-8833 ext 5108. They will send you a CP pass in a designated area. As you get close to the complex, there's a real cluster of small signs pointing to all kinds of things, so don't be surprised if you get confused, particularly when it is dark. Hopefully the diagram will help.

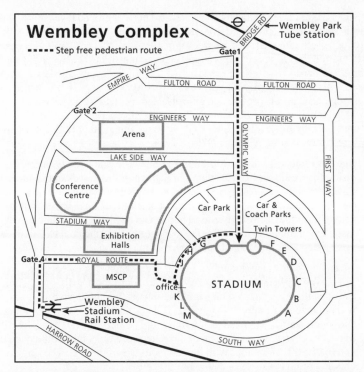

Wembley Park tube station, nearly 1km away with a mainly pedestrianised route down Olympic Way, has about +25 steps. Wembley Complex rail station, on the Marylebone to High Wycombe line has **step free access** (apart from getting on and off the train itself), with a long, steepish ramp to road level. The station is about 400m from the stadium.

Wembley Stadium

Wembley stadium, Wembley HA9 *Tel:* 0181 902-8833 Box office 0181 900-1234 *Fax:* 0181 903-3234. For football matches, the stadium is now an 'all seater', and the view from some of the cheaper seats isn't brilliant. There are a minimum of about 20 steps to most seats, and a maximum of around 100.

For chair users and other disabled spectators things really have improved enormously. Nearly thirty years ago it was members of PHSP who became the first chair users ever to get into a Cup Final, and people were lifted up dozens of steps so that they could transfer on to a seat. Chairs were stowed away. Our presence was completely against the wishes of the management! For a long time, facilities were minimal, although they improved slowly.

Now, an extensive area which can accommodate about 100 people (for football matches) is allocated to disabled spectators. This is at ground level, and at the front, so you are not protected from rain by the canopy. The entrance is usually through the Stadium Offices, between turnstiles J and K. The offices are about 100m from the OB spaces, up a slope with a roughish surface in parts. From the office there is step free access via the Royal Tunnel to the disabled spectators area. This is the best place if you have difficulty with steps. For concerts, a ramped raised area is provided to give disabled spectators a better view.

Wheelchair loo (D85 ST85) in the Stadium Offices. Two more in the Royal Tunnel, one in the 'hospital' area, and one in the Banqueting Hall area where Wembley Tours start. **All have D75+ ST75+.**

Stadium tours *Tel:* 0181 902-8833 Ext 3284 provide a really interesting visit, and give an idea of the history, and also of how the crowds are monitored and controlled for a really big event. On the route, not quite everything is step free, but a chair user can join in most of it without huge hassle with the help of a couple of strong friends. Help would be needed to go through the three 'event monitor' rooms for the management and the police. There are up to 3 steps at a time in and out of the rooms.

When our survey team including a chair user 'dropped in', we were shown a rather limited version of the tour. While we understand that disabled people can slow things down a bit on a tour, we felt that we could have seen more without much difficulty. It is sensible to check that the tours are operating, and to tell staff if you need a step free route (which cuts out a number of things) *or* if you can manage up to three steps at a time, this would enable you to do 90% of the tour with the judicious use of the lifts. The England dressing room is +1 step.

Wembley Arena see section on *Music venues.*

Wembley Conference Centre and **Wembley Exhibition Halls** see the chapter on *Exhibition halls.*

Athletics

Crystal Palace National Sports Centre, Ledrington Road, Crystal Palace SE19 *Tel:* 0181 778-9876. A large sports complex which, among other events, holds international athletics meetings in the main stadium. Access is somewhat complicated as the area is hilly. Extensive parking, the easiest of which is by Gate F of the Jubilee stand (the one furthest from the main entrance). A staff member will show chair users the way through Gate F to the wheelchair area in front of the Jubilee stand. The seats with the fewest steps in this stand are Row A (+1 step) and Row B (+3). The only other stand, the West stand, has +8 from the centre CP. We were told there is a **wheelchair loo** just outside the Jubilee stand.

The other main building contains the sports hall and swimming pools, with two OB spaces near the main entrance. There is step free access to all sports activities, and **two wheelchair loos (D90 ST120)** near the swimming pools.

Cricket

Lord's Cricket Ground, St John's Wood Road NW8 *Tel:* General enquiries 0171 289-1611 BO 0171 289-8979 *Fax:* 0171 266-3459. The home of the MCC (Marylebone Cricket Club), and host to Test Matches and county games. The office will have details of matches from January, and for the big games you need to make early enquiries about chair access and spaces. The ground is large, and has been extensively redeveloped with new stands being built. It measures roughly 100m by 150m, and the nursery ground area is another 100m square.

Step free access, avoiding turnstiles, is through the Grace Gate in St John's Wood Road, or through the North Gate off Wellington Place. Facilities for disabled spectators are quite limited. There are four areas with flat access for chair users: on the grass in front of the Warner Stand; in the first row of seats in that stand; in the Edrich Stand – although this is not always available, as the view may be blocked depending on which strip of the ground they are using for the pitch; in the Mound Stand (about twelve spaces). The first seven rows of seats in the Warner Stand are normally kept until lunchtime for disabled walkers. The only 'general' bar with step free access is in the Warner Stand.

Wheelchair loo (D87 ST70) in the Warner Stand, and a second **(D87 ST70)** in the North Clock Tower some 50m from the Edrich Stand and behind the Compton Stand. **Adapted loo (D85 ST64)** behind the Mound Stand, but it's kept locked, and the key is in the office six doors away (and +1 step).

Given the complexities of making arrangements, and the size of the place, it is obviously essential to negotiate with the ticket office, and probably to get them to send you a plan of the ground.

The Oval, Kennington SE11 *Tel:* 0171 582-6660 *Fax:* 0171 735-7769. A regular Test Match venue and home to Surrey County Cricket Club. By prior arrangement with the Stadium Manager a limited number of parking spaces are available inside the Vauxhall West Gate on Test Match days. Drivers entering from the Hobbs Gates can arrange to have their car met and driven round by a staff member, thus remaining near the Pavilion end. This is potentially a good arrangement provided the staff member can deal with the hand controls (if that is necessary). Otherwise, parking is difficult. As with Lords, and other big venues, it is sensible to contact the Stadium Manager in advance to get up to date details, and ask for a map/plan to be sent.

Entry is normally via turnstiles, but the Vauxhall West Gate and the Hobbs Gate both have flat access. There are chair spaces for members only in the Pavilion suites. For non-members there are six chair spaces at the front of the Laker Stand with step free access through reception. There are a further six spaces in the front row of the Bedser Stand reached via a gap between the stand and the Surridge Enclosure. On Test Match days there are a further 120 spaces on the grass in front of the 'blue seat area' of the Surridge Enclosure.

There is step free access to seats in the front row of all stands except the Surridge Enclosure, the Lock Stand and the Peter May Enclosure. It may be necessary to have certain barriers opened by staff on Test Match days to reach these seats.

The Mound Bar and the Middle Bar, both at the Pavilion end, have +1 step. The only restaurant available to non-members is on the third floor of the Bedser Stand, accessible by lift (D75 W110 L140). **Wheelchair loo (D75 ST140)** in the main reception, and **another (D75 ST85)** on the first floor of the Bedser Stand. We have been told that there are three further **wheelchair loos**: on the third floor of the Bedser Stand; just outside the Bedser Stand; and behind the Fender Stand at the other end of the ground.

Fishing see write-up on Lee Valley in the chapter on *Days out*.

Greyhound racing

Catford Stadium, Adenmore Road, Catford Bridge, Catford SE6 *Tel:* 0181 690-2261. CP by the main entrance with eight OB spaces on the left. Turnstiles at the entrance can be bypassed by a gate on the right.

There are two enclosures, the Main Enclosure and the Popular Enclosure. The only step free area is the video lounge on the GF of the Popular Enclosure. This, as it sounds, has live videos of the races, as well as betting facilities, but it is not possible to see the track. **Adapted cubicles in the ladies (D100 ST68) and gents (D100 ST55) loos.** The terraces on both stands have +1 step for each row of seats and visibility of the track is better the higher up you get. It is only really worth it if you can get up at least five rows. The restaurant in the Main Enclosure has +13.

Walthamstow Greyhound Stadium, Chingford Road, Walthamstow E4 *Tel:* 0181 571-4255. There is a two-tier CP in front of the stadium, and OB holders can reserve spaces in either of two private CPs. One is off the Chingford Road just in front of the North Stand, the other off Rushcroft Road, behind the North Stand. The stadium itself has two stands, North and South. Both have bars, betting areas, and seats with flat access, and an area that can be used by chair users. The view may be a bit restricted for those who do not wish to transfer. The only loos with flat access are the unadapted ones in the centre of the North Stand.

Wimbledon Stadium, Plough Lane, Summerstown SW17 *Tel:* 0181 946-5361. Greyhound racing all the year round, motorcycle speedway from March to October, and various car races including hot rods, bangers and stock cars almost every week. Facilities are the same for all events.

Large CP outside the main entrance, and the nearest spaces can be reserved in advance. Flat entrance from the CP, following the sign 'Restaurant/Executive seats'. This leads to a three-tier stand containing the executive seats with a trackside view from the GF. Lift (D80 W110 L135) access to the offices on the first floor and a restaurant with viewing and betting areas on the second floor. Chair users who are not eating can see the races on video screens. The easiest seats to reach are –4 steps from the restaurant. **Wheelchair loo (D80 ST70)** at the end of the restaurant on the left. **Another is on the GF (D85 ST90)** off the Diamond Room, and there's an a**dapted loo (D65 ST67)** off the bar on the GF.

The other, cheaper stand is step free from the CP to the edge of the track, then has steps up to seats and bars.

Horse racing

Ascot Racecourse, Ascot, Berks *Tel:* 01344-22211. Situated some 400m from Ascot station which is in the middle of town. Flat and National Hunt racing. Nine OB spaces by CP3 which is some 20m from the Grandstand entrance, across a busy road. There are four entrances, all to different parts of the complex. The Members entrance and the Grandstand entrance both have flat access. The silver ring entrance, and all facilities in this section have stepped access, and the Heath entrance involves –22 then +22 steps.

The grandstand has flat access to the shop, a bank, various bars and restaurants, and to betting areas. A lift (D120 W225 L155) goes to about a hundred chair spaces on the top of the grandstand, giving a panoramic view. The members stand, on five floors, has step free access to various bars and betting areas via a lift (D120 W225 L155). There is a wheelchair enclosure on the fifth floor and another on the front lawn with a view of the Winning Post. The Tattersalls is a large mobile stand with ramped access to six wheelchair spaces. The Winner's enclosure has flat access, as does the GF of the parade ring area, with six chair spaces and flat access to bars. The first floor is +20. The Queen Anne's building was not open when we surveyed.

Numerous **wheelchair loos** around the course, and two **adapted loos** in the Members Stand (on the GF **D95 ST60**, and on the fourth floor **D110 ST65**). There are two loos in the Balcony Restaurant (**D85 ST90**) in the Grandstand, and a further two reached by a service lift underneath this restaurant. These were shut when we visited. The parade ring has **wheelchair cubicles** in both the gents and ladies loos, and Queen Anne's building has a **wheelchair loo (D95 ST70)** on the GF.

Epsom Racecourse, The Grandstand, Epsom Downs, Surrey *Tel:* 01372-726311. Off Grandstand Road. Home to the Oaks and the Derby, and generally step free around the course. OB parking is normally available at the back of the Grandstand. On big race days it is on the grass at the back of the Queen's Stand. Phone first to confirm.

Entrance to the grandstand is through turnstiles and then –9 steps. There is a step free route to the course at either end of the grandstand, and we were told the +3 to the grandstand itself are usually ramped. It may be sensible to check.

Once past the +3 there are various bars and betting areas with step free access. The first floor, including Tattersalls Restaurant, is only reached via steps. Boxes are reached from a separate entrance at the back of the stand, with lift (D110 W190 L110) access. In the Queen's Stand there is a ramp on the left of the entrance and an open lift to bypass +5+5. From here, two lifts (D85 W130 L180) give step free access to all six floors. The first floor has a bar with a wheelchair enclosure on the balcony. Other floors contain private boxes and function rooms.

Six wheelchair loos (all D75+ ST80+) in the Queen's stand, and five in the grandstand **(all D70+ ST70+)**. We were told that additional portable **wheelchair loos** are put in the paddock area for the Derby.

Kempton Park Racecourse, Sunbury-on-Thames, Middx *Tel:* 01932-782292. On the A308, nearly a km east of junction 1 on the M3. The main CP is 700m from the course. OB holders can use a CP within 50m of the Grandstand. On race days, trains stop at Kempton Park station with flat access on one side only. Coming from London you can leave the platform with step free access, but for the return journey there are +29–29 steps. It would be possible to take a taxi the 4km or so to either Kingston or Hampton Court stations, both of which have step free access to London-bound trains.

The turnstiles at the main entrance can be bypassed by a gate. Once inside it is step free almost everywhere, except to the members-only clubhouse (+7/escalator). The grandstand has a steep slope bypassing +17, then flat access all along the front and to the Winners Bar. There is another steep slope to the wheelchair viewing area by the finishing line. It is also step free to the pre-parade ring, the parade ring, and various bars and betting areas. The Silver Ring at the other end of the grandstand has +1 –1. **Wheelchair loo (D74 ST90)** at the base of the members enclosure in the grandstand, and an **adapted loo (D84 ST obstructed)** in the Hampton suite.

Royal Windsor Racecourse, Maidenhead Road, Windsor, Berks *Tel:* 01753-865234. Situated on the A308 Maidenhead to Windsor Road, the course holds both Flat and National Hunt races, including some evening meetings. Access is good, due mainly to the new Royal Windsor Stand opened in 1995. OB holders can park in or near the members CP which is near the main stand.

The Royal Windsor stand has a ramped entrance and is step free throughout via a lift (D75 W100 L135) to a bar and refreshment area on the GF, and a restaurant on the first floor. A platform stairlift leads to the tables overlooking the track. The first and second floor both contain boxes. The club building has a ramped entrance, then –2+1, or +3 to all bars, except the buffet bar which has ramped access. The silver ring and picnic area has flat access, as does the parade ring which contains four wheelchair spaces. There is a further viewing area by the finishing line, currently with eight spaces, and with more planned.

Four wheelchair loos, one (D85 ST120) in the paddock pavilion with flat access from a staff operated lift, and one on each floor of the Royal Windsor stand, **each (D70+ ST70+).**

Sandown Park Racecourse, Portsmouth Road, Esher, Surrey *Tel:* 01372-463072. The complex, situated on the Portsmouth Road (A307), just off the A3, includes an exhibition centre, golf course, go-Karting and a dry ski slope. The main entrance for visitors with disabilities is about 400m from Esher station, next to the main turnstiles, with twelve OB spaces nearby.

Once inside, access is generally good. The grandstand is on three floors and step free everywhere via a lift (D115 W170 L170), except to the paddock bar and restaurant (+5 steps). Six chair spaces on the GF (three by the finishing post and three mid-way along the stand) and three spaces outside the Cobham bar on the first floor. There are various bars, betting areas, and boxes. It is also step free to the rails of the course, via a steep slope.

Adapted cubicles (gents D90 ST65, ladies D90 ST60) at the Esher Hall end of the GF of the Grandstand. **Adapted cubicles (gents D90 ST65, ladies D90 ST60)** at the Cavalier end.

The ski slope, golf course and go-Karting have a separate entrance off Esher Green. Large CP. Ski centre has +2 at the entrance, then −2 to the slope. The golf driving range has −2, and there is −7 to the go-Kart range.

Motor racing

Brands Hatch, Brands Hatch Circuits Ltd, Fawkham, Longfield, Kent *Tel:* 01474-872331. Famous motor racing circuit just off the A20 from junction three on the M25. Facilities cover the full range of the motor sports spectrum. Reservable OB parking in the Clearways area, signposted (unbelievably) the 'invalid area'. Turn right after the main entrance and follow the perimeter road for about 1km, and then left after the bridge. The main area for chair users is on the grass in the Clearways area, and it is possible to get a good view and remain in your car. The grass area is one of the major viewing areas for all spectators. The main grandstand is more than 500m from any parking area, and has step free access to one row of seats, which are unfortunately unreservable.

Because of the size of the complex, the management ask that visitors with disabilities phone in advance (they suggest at least a week). There is a minibus which can be used to transport people around the complex as necessary, but this is not adapted. The principal restaurant/bar is called the Kentagon, and is 1km straight on from the main entrance. A ramp bypasses +8 steps, then there is step free access throughout.

Wheelchair loo (D85 ST75) in the John Foulston centre immediately on the right after the main entrance. While the centre is not normally for public use, if you ask at the desk on the right after entering the building there should be no problem. For visitors with a pit pass there is a further **wheelchair loo (D85 ST85)** with flat access in the Nigel Mansell centre.

Rowing

Henley Royal Regatta is the most important event in the rowing calendar and usually takes place in early July. The town gets extremely crowded, as do pubs, restaurants and hotels in the area, and parking is difficult. It is possible to hire a boat and moor alongside the course, but book it months in advance and arrive very early in order to get a mooring. Similarly with parking, the trick is to arrive really early, and make a day of it. Bring a picnic to avoid hassles with getting food. Parking concessions to OB holders may be suspended locally because of the volume of traffic.

The towpath which, of course, gets crowded, is tarmac for about 500m on the side of the river farthest from the town. Thereafter it gets narrower and rougher. There are two temporary enclosures set aside for watching the race by the bridge on the Berkshire side. Both are grass and get muddy when it is wet. There is a general enclosure with seating, mainly in deck-chairs. The stewards enclosure (basically for members and friends) has a small area set aside for chair users. For membership, or other information, write to the Secretary, Regatta Headquarters, Henley-on-Thames, Oxon RG9 2LY *Tel:* 01491-572153 *Fax:* 01491-575509.

Rugby

Twickenham, Rugby Road, Twickenham, Middx *Tel:* 0181 872-8161. The 'home' of English rugby football. The stadium has been extensively redeveloped, and access for chair-bound spectators has been extremely well provided for, although access for disabled walkers, and those with other disabilities, has not really been thought through. Tickets for chair spaces are allocated from Twickenham. For international matches, it is advisable to get there really early, as some of the surrounding roads are closed well before the match. There are nearly 300 chair spaces, and a similar number for helpers. Over 200 spaces are at pitch level, and there are others on level three, accessed by lift (D120 W150 L170). There are two lifts on either side of the South stand.

Those using the chair spaces will be allocated parking space either in the North CP between Rugby Road and Whitton Dean, or in the smaller West CP through Gate 1. There is a low bar specifically for chair users on level two, reached by the same lifts.

Six wheelchair loos on ground level on either side of the North stand, and **four wheelchair loos** on level 3. Although they were not all completed when we surveyed, the ones we saw were **D70+ ST70+.**

For the **Rugby museum** and **Stadium tour** (*Tel:* 0181 892-2000) use the North CP. The museum is about 100m and well signed. It is on the first floor. If the gate to the lift (D100 W170 L120) is locked, ask at the shop. Step free throughout. The museum includes memorabilia and numerous video and film presentations. **Wheelchair loo (D90 ST70)** on level 2A via the lift. Tour tickets from the museum. The standard tour involves well over 100 steps, but disabled visitors can take a step free route and see most of the interesting parts. These include the view from the top of the stadium, and the England dressing room. It may be worth ringing first. The GF restaurant/café and shop both have a step free entrance.

Soccer grounds

Following the modernisation of all the Premier League and First Division grounds in the early 1990s, the facilities for disabled spectators at most grounds have improved considerably. Wheelchair spaces (with step free access) are provided at all grounds, and nearly all have a **wheelchair loo** nearby. Booking procedures vary, and you will need to check with the club over individual matches. Some major games and local derbys may be 'all ticket'. The clubs vary somewhat in their attitude to disabled spectators. Prices also vary, some admitting both chair users and a helper for free, whilst some charge. Whilst a reduced entry cost is a well intended gesture, *what is important is that all potential spectators with disabilities can get in.* A couple of clubs say that chair users must be accompanied, and in the text we have used the word 'helper' since in many cases, this is the justification for free entry. If you came with a 'friend' (possibly a more accurate description), then reduced price entry is largely unjustified. Many clubs now have a match commentary for blind or partially sighted supporters.

At the main grounds there are no longer any terraces, where spectators were able to stand to watch a match. As a result a group of disabled people who may have a problem are those with arthritis. This is because most seats are small, with cramped leg room, stopping you from stretching your legs! Access to most seats is via steps.

There may be some seats close to the chair spaces with step free access, which may have extra leg-room. There will be a few seats scattered around the ground where you can sit more comfortably. When you get to know a particular ground, you can identify the best ones for you, and book them in advance. It is not usually easy to get particular seats if you just turn up at the turnstiles on the day.

Many grounds have an area nearby where chair users and other disabled people can use their OB. These arrangements are usually somewhat ad hoc, and vary from match to match. Check when you book. Many grounds are situated in residential areas and were built long before most of us had cars. As a result, the approaches can get blocked up long before kick off. Be warned!

Arsenal FC, Avenell Road, Highbury N5 *Tel:* 0171 354-5404. Home of the 'Gunners'. OB parking in Elwood Street, but the streets around are all closed at least an hour before kick off.

The disabled spectators enclosure is in the East stand with step free access through Gate 8 in Avenell Road. It has space for roughly a hundred chair users and helpers, but is not covered. It is for both home and away fans. Seats with the least number of steps are also in the East stand, the minimum having +15 in Block L. **Adapted loo (D85 ST67)** by Gate 8, and **another (D90 ST30)** behind the wheelchair enclosure. No charge for chair users (who must be accompanied) or for helpers. Commentary available through headsets from the East stand lower entrance.

Barnet FC, Underhill Stadium, Westcombe Drive, Barnet, Herts *Tel:* 0181 441-6932. The newest (and smallest) London league club, with step free access at both the Barnet Lane and Westcombe Drive entrances. Parking can be arranged. There is room for two chair users outside the social club. An alternative viewing area with step free access is next to the Westcombe Drive entrance and can accommodate ten chairs. The lowest level of the stands have +1 step, and there are steps up to the seats. Ramped access to the café in the social club with a **wheelchair loo (D80 ST80). Wheelchair cubicles (D70 ST100+)** in both gents and ladies loos at the far corner from the Barnet Lane entrance. A commentary is being considered. No charge for chair users or helpers.

Brentford FC, Griffin Park, Braemar Road, Brentford, Middx *Tel:* 0181 560-2021. Reservable parking for OB holders outside the Braemar Road entrance. Chair users can use the Directors Gate giving step free access to about twenty covered chair spaces 80m away. Flat access to the terraces, or a minimum of +24 steps to seats in blocks D and E. Unmarked **wheelchair loo (D85 ST85)** by the entrance to Block E. A sign is put up on match days. Commentary available through headsets from the Officials Gate entrance. No charge for chair users or helpers.

Charlton Athletic FC, The Valley, Harvey Gardens, Charlton SE7 *Tel:* 0181 293-4567. The stadium was completely rebuilt a few years ago. Ten OB spaces at the West stand entrance from Harvey Gardens, and eight at the East stand entrance from Lansdowne Mews. Then step free to twenty chair spaces in the East stand through Gate 8, and eleven in the West stand through Gate 5. Away supporters can enter at Gate 6, and ask to use the touchline to get to the East stand enclosure. Spaces in the West stand are usually taken by season ticket holders. The East Stand enclosure is at the top of the stadium, reached by a long ramp. The easiest seats for disabled walkers are in the West Stand, in blocks C, D or E, and have +11 steps followed by –2 to –20 depending how near to the pitch you want to be. **Two wheelchair loos (D85 ST105)** halfway between the Harvey Gardens entrance and the wheelchair enclosure, and **another (D70+ ST70+)** at the top of the East stand. Commentary available through headsets. No charge for chair users, reductions for helpers.

Chelsea FC, Stamford Bridge, Fulham Road, Fulham SW6 *Tel:* 0171 385-5545. Like several other stadiums, Stamford Bridge is still being developed. Some parking can be reserved for OB holders inside the ground.

Entrance one on the Fulham Road gives flat access to forty covered chair spaces at the front of the East stand, by the touchline. Six are held for the 'away' club. There are five further covered chair spaces with an excellent 'birds-eye view' in the corner of the North and East stands on level four, reached by lift (D78 W135 L130). The easiest seats for disabled walkers are probably in the lower tier of the North stand, but involve steps. **Two wheelchair loos (D85 ST125)** on ground level between entrance one and the wheelchair enclosure. We were told there is another next to the bar on level four. The function rooms on level two contain two further **wheelchair loos (D85 ST75)**. Reductions for chair users, helpers pay full price.

A new UGCP is due to open in January 1996. The continuing development will result in a 'wraparound' stand between the North and West stands, a new South stand, and ultimately, a new West stand. It is intended to provide as many as two hundred chair spaces.

Crystal Palace FC, Selhurst Park Stadium, Crystal Palace SE25 *Tel:* 0181 653-1000. Situated off Whitehorse Lane and Park Road. The ground is currently shared with Wimbledon FC, and the main stand was being rebuilt when we visited. Work was due to be completed by the end of 1995. The CP is shared with Sainsburys, on the same site, with twenty-one OB spaces.

The wheelchair enclosure is entered from Park Road, with flat access to twenty-eight covered chair spaces in the Arthur Wait stand. We were told that there are twenty more in the Holmsdale Road stand and that there is an adapted loo in the Arthur Wait stand and two more in the Holmsdale Road one. Flat access to the front row of seats in the main stand. Commentary available in the Arthur Wait stand. Chair users pay half-price in the Holmsdale Road stand, and are admitted free in the Arthur Wait stand. Helpers pay full-price.

Fulham FC, Craven Cottage, Stevenage Road, Fulham SW6 *Tel:* 0171 736-6561. Street parking only. Step free access through the main gate in Stevenage Road to covered chair spaces in the Riverside stand via about 150m round the edge of the pitch. The terraces in the Stevenage stand are +5 steps, and seats in the Riverside stand a minimum of +7. **Wheelchair loo (D95 ST80)** between the entrance and the pitch, next to the first aid room. Commentary normally available if booked in advance. Free admission for chair users, reductions for helpers.

Leyton Orient FC, Leyton Stadium, Brisbane Road, Leyton E10 *Tel:* 0181 539-2223. A small and friendly club with an emphasis on creating a family atmosphere. Two OB spaces on Buckingham Road, 140m from entrance JK. The council runs a free adapted 'leisure-mobile' minibus service to matches, *Tel:* 0181 527-5544 and ask for the Arts and Leisure department.

Chair users should use entrance JK giving step free access to the covered wheelchair enclosure some 30m away, with space for at least eighteen chairs. The seats with the least number of steps are in the family enclosure, some 50m from entrance JK. The bottom row has +6 steps. **Wheelchair loo (D85 ST90)** by the wheelchair enclosure. Commentary available through an induction loop in the family enclosure. No charge for chair users or helpers.

Millwall FC, The New Den, Zampa Road, Rotherhithe SE16 *Tel:* 0171 231-9999. An impressive all-seater stadium opened in 1993. Ten OB spaces by the West stand and five behind the sports centre, inside the ground. Phone in advance to book. There's a huge CP in Juno Way some 400m away.

The entrance at the corner of the West and North stands gives step free access via a staff operated lift (D100 W110 L200) to the first floor and covered wheelchair enclosure in the West stand. Space for nearly eighty chairs, and more in the front row of the North and South stands, with entrances at the NW or SW corners. There are seats with flat access in the front row of the North, South and East stands. **Seventeen wheelchair loos (all D70+ ST70+)** scattered around. Commentary available on the first floor of the West stand. Free admission for chair users, reductions for helpers.

Queens Park Rangers (QPR), Rangers Stadium, South Africa Road, Shepherds Bush W12 *Tel:* 0181 743-0262. Small and friendly club with good facilities for disabled supporters. Reservable parking in the BBC CP if you make prior arrangements through the club.

Two wheelchair enclosures, with about nine spaces in each. The first, not covered, is below the South Africa Road stand, with priority for season ticket holders. **Wheelchair loo (D85 ST200)** nearby. The second is a covered enclosure in the Ellerslie Road stand, and is split. Home fans enter through the main South Africa Road gate some 80m from the enclosure. Away fans should use the School End gate (at the west end of the ground). The club advise phoning first to ensure a place. The only seats in the ground with step free access are those adjacent to the two wheelchair enclosures. Commentary available through an induction loop. Free admission for chair users and helpers.

Tottenham Hotspur FC, 748 High Road, Tottenham N7 *Tel:* 0181 365-5000. Known the world over as *White Hart Lane,* and home to a famous club. Reservable parking for OB holders in Thorns CP in Paxton Road. Alternative parking in Worcester Avenue in St Paul's School CP, the St Francis CP, or in the Northumberland Community CP.

From the entrance in Paxton Road, the wheelchair enclosure in the North stand has step free access and twenty-seven chair spaces. To reach the enclosure in the South stand (with sixteen spaces) go through the double doors from Park Lane or through the staff CP. Both enclosures are covered. There are no seats with flat access, and we were told that the least number of steps was about +10 to the lower tier of the West stand. **Two wheelchair loos (D80 ST80)** near the chair spaces in the North stand, and **another (D90 ST110)** near the chair spaces in the South stand. Chair users must come accompanied. Full-price for chair users, free for helpers.

West Ham FC, The Boleyn Ground, Green Street, Upton Park E13 *Tel:* 0181 548-2700. Home to the Hammers, a club with a really strong local East End following. Street parking only. Three areas with wheelchair spaces, all reached through gate 7A which is off Green Street. The Bobby Moore stand has thirty chair uncovered spaces in the front row; twenty covered spaces are in the West stand. Both areas have seats with flat access. The Centenary stand has thirty covered chair spaces. **Wheelchair loo (D75+ ST75+)** near both the Bobby Moore and West stand enclosures. Free admission for chair users, reductions for helpers.

Wimbledon FC, *Tel:* 0181 771-2233. See entry on *Crystal Palace* with whom Wimbledon share a ground. The phone number is different.

Tennis

The All England Lawn Tennis and Croquet Club, Church Road, Wimbledon SW19 *Tel:* 0181 946-2244. This is where the most famous tennis tournament in the world takes place for two weeks towards the end of June. The club is undergoing extensive development, the first stage of which should be completed in 1997.

There is no on-site parking, but spaces should be available between 100m and 500m away. To reserve the nearest spaces, contact the Automobile Association, Wimbledon parking, Norfolk House, Priestly Road, Basingstoke, Hants RG24 9NY as soon as you have tickets. There is a drop-off point directly outside the main Somerset Road entrance (Gate 13).

To obtain tickets, write to the ticket manager by January of the relevant year, and mark both the letter and the envelope 'Wheelchair'. All chair users are asked to come accompanied, and centre court tickets are half price for both. If you are queueing on the day, or even the night before, when you finally reach the front, a steward can take you through a step free entrance if necessary, avoiding turnstiles. Once inside, the area is generally flat.

In 1995 there were six reservable chair spaces on Centre Court, and ten spaces on both Courts Six and Thirteen which are not reservable. By 1997 the new Court Number One will provide a further forty chair spaces. All other courts except Courts Two and Fourteen have flat access to viewing points but, until the redevelopment plan is complete, the crowds make viewing (and moving around) quite difficult. There is ramped access to refreshments and to buy your strawberries and cream in marquees by the main gate.

There are four **wheelchair loos** spread around the complex. All have D85, but at the time of our survey, barriers stopped any ST. We were told that these barriers would be removed before the 1996 championships. There is another **wheelchair loo (D85 ST105 NKS)** in the museum, on the first floor. See the chapter on *Museums & galleries.*

Annual events

We include simply a fraction of the events that take place every year. In general, provision for disabled spectators is now made at most events, and certainly things have improved. Sometimes you have to make enquiries and arrangements in advance. Currently, chair users are better provided for than disabled walkers, in the sense that there are sometimes special arrangements made and enclosures at viewing points provided. A practical suggestion is for disabled people who can walk a bit but who find crowds and steps and distances a problem to use a wheelchair just occasionally, in order to go to the Proms, Beating the Retreat or even to Wimbledon tennis championships. It's not cheating and it might open up possibilities of getting around that you just hadn't thought of.

There's a more comprehensive list in Nicholson's *The London Guide* or the *Eyewitness Guide,* but we mention most of the principal ones here. You can also get information from the LTB. We have included many venues for major shows and sporting events in the guide text. Some of the events are open-air, and therefore accessible. For details of the venues for the Cup Final, Derby Week, Royal Ascot and Wimbledon, see chapter on *Sport.*

The Chinese New Year is celebrated in the streets of Soho with paper dragons, processions and a mini-carnival. Can be vey crowded. *Jan/Feb.*

Pancake races are held at Lincoln's Inn Fields on Shrove Tuesday, six weeks before Easter. *Feb/Mar.*

The Oxford & Cambridge Boat Race is rowed from Putney to Mortlake. To get a view, get there early (Hammersmith Bridge is often a good spot) but remember that you'll only get a brief view of the crews and the pursuing launches and there'll be a lot of people around, crowding the local pubs and making parking awkward. It's a good idea to bring a small radio to keep yourself informed about the race. *Late Mar/Apr.*

A parade of old cars is held on Easter Sunday in Battersea Park and a carnival procession. Generally very colourful. The London Harness Horse Parade is on the following day with brewers' vans, drays and other horse-drawn vehicles on show. The parade goes twice round the Inner Circle in Regent's Park at about midday. *Mar/Apr.*

The London Marathon has become the world's largest road race, with over 25,000 participants. All sorts of people enter, from the serious athlete, to celebrities, and fun runners wearing a variety of fancy dress. The Marathon is an event which a chair user always completes the quickest! It provides a marvellous atmosphere for spectators, drawing large crowds at the start (Greenwich) and finish (Westminster Bridge). There are numerous street parties en route, and an excellent spot to view is just by Tower Bridge. *April.*

The Chelsea Flower Show is organised by the Royal Horticultural Society (RHS) and is held in the grounds of the Royal Hospital, Chelsea. Parking in the area is difficult and entrance is not cheap. It may be possible for OB holders to negotiate parking with the organisers (RHS, 80 Vincent Square SW1P 2PB *Tel:* 0171 834-4333; Flower Show Information 0171 828-1744). The show gets extremely crowded. A good time to go, to avoid the crowds, is early in the morning; or you could become a member of the Society and go to the preview day. It's a glorious show and access is generally good. Main entrance on the Embankment, with flat access. Paths are either tarmac or grass but there are some kerbs and gentle slopes. There are two well signposted portable **adapted loos**, not quite big enough for sideways transfer but very adequate. If you can cope with the crowds and want to see a fantastic flower show, this is the place to go. There are picnic areas, plenty of shade and bands playing. Note that guide dogs are not allowed to go round, but the organisers can normally provide an escort if needed. Contact them in advance. **A special evening for disabled people is arranged every year.** Call the organisers for details. *Late May.*

Trooping the Colour is the best known of the several events held during the summer in Horse Guards Parade. Temporary stands built on scaffolding are erected around the square. Access is up steps and there are bench-type seats and few handrails. A procession also goes to and from the palace along the Mall. *Saturday nearest 11 June.* The other events include **Beating the Retreat** by various regiments. Disabled spectators for the military events should contact the HQ London District, Horse Guards, Whitehall SW1 (0171 930-4466). For Trooping the Colour ask for the brigade major; chair users are normally admitted only to the rehearsal for this event. For Beating the Retreat contact the public information office (PIO) (ext 2396/57). The PIO can arrange for wheelchair spaces and for seats to be put alongside for friends, if needed. They say that chair users can be accommodated but that chairs are not available for disabled walkers or friends and escorts. We suggest that this may change if disabled people start to go to the performances and the difficulties are evident.

City of London Festival, 230 Bishopsgate EC2M 4QH *Tel:* 0171 377-0540. The festival consists mainly of concerts and exhibitions in various churches and halls, some of which aren't otherwise open to the public. The main box office is situated in the Barbican Centre *Tel:* 0171 638-8891 *Minicom:* 0171 382-7297. Although most of the concerts and events take place in old buildings where there are steps (at one or two venues there are quite a lot of steps), the organisers say that they can help any disabled person to get in, provided they know about it. The organiser we spoke to was very clued up and knew how many steps there were at most of the halls and where there was a lift to bypass them. If he didn't know precisely, he would find out. As they use different places each year, there is little point in giving too much detail. Many of the venues used are described elsewhere in the guide. *June/July.*

Richmond Festival. Amateur and professional performances in venues around Richmond, including the Orange Tree and Richmond theatres. For information *Tel:* 0181 332-0534. *July.*

Notting Hill Carnival. A huge event in the Ladbrook Grove and Notting Hill area, W11. There are carnival processions with colourful floats and participants, and much street dancing and partying. It is primarily a celebration of the local West Indian community and its traditions, but it has grown from being a purely local event into something that attracts tens of thousands of people. Can be great fun, though local parking is a nightmare ! *August bank holiday weekend.*

Fair on Hampstead Heath NW3 (near North End Way). This is held on August bank holiday and there are likely to be other fairs at other places on spring and summer bank holidays. See the local press and *Time Out* or *What's On.*

Promenade Concert season takes place at the Albert Hall during *August* and *September.* The famous 'last night of the Proms' is on the *Saturday nearest 15 Sept.* (See Royal Albert Hall under *Music venues - classical).*

The State Opening of Parliament, usually at the end of *October,* provides an uncrowded opportunity to see pageantry and the Queen. We recommend viewing from the south side of the Mall.

Guy Fawkes' night commemorates the attempt in 1605 to blow up monarch, lords and commons when assembled in Westminster. There are both private and public firework displays. All generally accessible. *5 November and over the adjacent weekend/s.*

The London to Brighton Veteran Car Rally starts at Hyde Park Corner. It commemorates the Anniversary of Emancipation and is an opportunity to see period costumes as well as cars. *First Sunday in November.*

The Lord Mayor's Show is a large carnival-style procession through the City. The City Information Centre can advise about the precise route. S*econd Saturday in November.*

Christmas decorations. There are usually spectacular ones in Oxford Street and Regent Street, and traditionally there is a Norwegian pine tree in Trafalgar Square *during December.*

Open air activities

Open-air events and venues have the dual attraction of being generally accessible and surprisingly varied. There's music, politics, art and shopping, in addition to the parks, historical statues and architecture. Doing things in the open can enable you to get a real feel for London, and to see and experience many things that the visitor intent on the standard tourist circuit will miss. We have mentioned elsewhere the potential interest and variety of London's statues, and if you follow this up you will find out a great deal more than most people who either visit or even live in London.

Boating and river trips

Around London there are numerous rivers, canals and waterways which, with planning and organisation, can be used to provide an enjoyable way of touring some scenic, out-of-the-way parts of London. The Thames passes through the centre of London, and a particularly attractive trip is to take a boat from either Charing Cross or Westminster pier down to Greenwich. There are also some 80km of canal in London and a day spent cruising around parts of them is unlikely to be dull.

One of our survey teams did the river trip from Westminster pier to Greenwich. There are several problems, principally that the boats operating vary in their accessibility on a fairly random basis and the piers up and down the river are not all at the same height in relation to the boats ! Most of the main ones have ramped access from the pavement, although at low tide this can be quite steep.

At Westminster there are several companies operating, from separate ticket booths. Not designed to make booking easy! If you know roughly when you may want to make the trip, it's worth phoning up first and asking when the 'accessible' boats will be operating that day. The companies are:

Circular Cruises, Westminster *Tel:* 0171 936-2033
Red Fleet *Tel:* 0171 930-9033
Royal River Thames *Tel:* 0171 930-4097
Westminster Passenger Services *Tel:* 0171 930-2062.

Approach the **Westminster pier** entrance from about 50m along the Embankment from Westminster Bridge. The +5–5 steps over the flood barrier can be bypassed by a ramp. It is step free from the pavement down to the pier. **Wheelchair loo (D95 ST85)** at the bottom of the steps from Westminster Bridge by the pier entrance. It uses an NKS key, but there is a second lock, and you need to use the intercom to contact the attendant. When another team tried to use this, the attendant wasn't there, so we didn't get in.

On the boat our survey team encountered +1 from the pier, then either +6 or

–5 to the upper or lower deck. Several of the boats which operate have an area which can accommodate a chair user after the +1, and if this is important to you, you'll have to wait until a suitable one comes along. On the very popular routes like Westminster to the Tower and to Greenwich, there should be a boat every twenty minutes or so. Because of the difference in pier heights there may be up to ±3 to get on or off the boats. The Greenwich pier is higher than the one at Westminster.

Charing Cross pier is similar to Westminster, and there is a step free route down from the Embankment, although it can be quite steep at low tide. Catamaran Cruisers who operate from this pier have two boats (out of five, in 1995) with virtually step free access, one of which is completely flat and has a glass cover. Give them a ring (*Tel:* 0171 987-1185) to find out what the schedule is for the accessible boats on a particular day.

Tower pier has more difficult access because there are 3 steps built into the pier edge, and there is no provision for a gangway to provide a ramped route for getting on or off.

Greenwich pier is more straightforward than the one at the Tower, but is at a different height from either Westminster or Charing Cross so, if you got on step free, you'll have a step to get off.

There are a number of groups that hire specially adapted boats. We have compiled a list, but it is not exhaustive.

The Docklands River Project, St John's Centre, Albert Road, North Woolwich E16 *Tel:* 0171 511-2911, has an adapted narrowboat available for both day trips and five-day cruises. The showers, loo and kitchen are all adapted, and there's an open lift to get chair users in and out of the boat. There is accommodation for up to ten people, of whom up to six can be chair users.

Islington Boat Club, 16 Graham Street N1 8JX *Tel:* 0171 253-0778 have an adapted launch that can take up to five chair users. They have adapted changing rooms, and canoes and other craft available.

Lee Valley Boat Centre, Old Nazeing Road, Broxbourne, Herts *Tel:* 01992-462085, has a large fully adapted boat the *Lady of Lee Valley* which can take up to fifty people for a cruise. It has a lift on board to facilitate access, and an adapted loo.

Richmond Boat Project, 66 Hill Street, Richmond, Surrey TW9 1TW *Tel:* 0181 940-3509. This uses a converted 90-year-old Dutch barge the *Richmond Venturer*. It can take up to six chair users. Access is via a ramp and then an open lift. They have an **adapted loo**. During 1996 they are hoping to get it fitted out with bunks and a **wheelchair shower**, so that it can provide accommodation for longer trips.

Markets

Street markets tend to be crowded but the stalls are all basically accessible and they are lively and interesting places. If you're selective you can often pick up a bargain. It's advisable to arrive early to avoid the worst of the crush. Around the big markets there will be parking restrictions, even on a Sunday. A useful book is *The London Market Guide* by Andrew Kershman, published by Metro Publications, PO Box 6636, N1 6PY. Bear in mind that, even for chair users, crowds can be a pickpocket's delight.

There are numerous small markets scattered around the city, but the main ones are:

Brick Lane E1 and E2, operates on Sunday mornings, covering a substantial area. It is off the Bethnal Green Road just north of Shoreditch station. It includes Sclater Street and Cheshire Street. Some of the market is in the street and some in covered areas. It is a general market with a strong East End flavour. Included are electrical goods, hardware, fruit and veg, clothes, cameras, books and old furniture etc.

Brixton SW9. Mainly around Brixton station off Atlantic Road, Electric Avenue and Coldharbour Lane. Dominated now by the local black community, with all kinds of food stalls, African fabrics and clothes and stalls where soul, rap and reggae are played and sold.

Camden N1. A group of markets running the length of Camden High Street into the southern part of Chalk Farm Road. Some are on derelict land off the road with roughish surfaces. You'll find everything you need to make you trendy and give you street cred – but you may find yourself paying a trendy price.

Covent Garden WC2 see chapter on *Places of interest* under Holborn and the Strand areas.

Greenwich SE10, has a Flea Market in Thames Street open on Sundays, an Antiques market in Greenwich High Road open Saturdays and Sundays, and an indoor Crafts Market in Bosuns Yard, Greenwich Church Street, also open on Saturdays and Sundays. There's also the Central Market in Stockwell Street.

Petticoat Lane, Middlesex Street E1, and surrounding streets. Usually crowded, and parking nearby can be a problem. Something of a tourist trap, but very varied stalls and quite an atmosphere. Main market on Sunday, some stalls during the week as well

Portobello Road W11. This spills over into the surrounding streets. Like Camden it is really a group of markets with different things to sell and different opening times. Antiques and bric-a-brac on Saturday is the really big event, but also clothes, fruit and vegetables, hardware, etc. Monday to Saturday.

Other markets include:
Atlantic Road SW9;
Chapel Market, White Conduit Street N1;
Columbia Road E2;
The Cut SE1;
East Street SE17;
High Street Walthamstow E17;
Kingsland Waste E8;
Leather Lane EC1;
Ridley Road E8;
Shepherd's Bush W12;
Vallance Road E1;
Whitecross Street EC2.

Parks

London has several large and delightful parks. Even near the centre you can get right away from the traffic and bustle. The main parks were all parts of royal estates and books published specifically on the Royal Parks are available from The Old Police House, Hyde Park W2 2UH.

Battersea Park SW11 A lovely spot with a lake, zoo and river frontage on the south side of the Thames. Ample parking. Good for picnics and relaxing. Most of the paths are paved, and odd steps can be bypassed. There are just a few slopes.

On the riverfront is the **London Peace Pagoda**, a magnificent structure with gold tableaux depicting the birth, enlightenment, preaching and death of the Buddha. It's +14 steps to the walkway around it, but you can see perfectly well from ground level.

There's a small zoo for children south of Parade, and east of the pagoda. Ramp bypasses the −10 at the entrance. In the zoo itself there is ramped access everywhere, bypassing the odd step, and it is step free to the animal contact area and the reptile house.

The restaurant to the east of the boating lake has step free access, but fixed seating inside. **Wheelchair loo (D85 ST90)** directly opposite the disused pier, 400m west of the Chelsea Bridge entrance, but poorly signed. A second **wheelchair loo (D75 ST70)** is located with other toilets in the southwest corner of the park. It is 30m west along Carriage Drive from the all-weather sports pitches.

Greenwich Park see chapter on *Places of interest, outer London.*

Hampstead Heath see chapter on *Places of interest, outer London.*

Holland Park W8 & W14. Access from Kensington High Street or the CP with four OB spaces in Abbotsbury Road. Pleasant area with tarmac paths. Café with flat access from the side, near Holland House. Open-air theatre nearby, +15 at the entrance or a 30m slope on the left. **Wheelchair loo (D80 ST125 NKS)** 50m from the café.

Hyde Park & Kensington Gardens W2 & W8. This vast stretch covers over 240 hectares. It is fairly flat and there are tarmac paths throughout. Limited parking on the road running between the two parks (West Carriage Drive), with small CPs either side of the Serpentine Bridge. There is also a large UGCP with entrances off Park Lane and North Carriage Drive; but note that there's a longish walk of approaching 500m to get out.

There are some seats in the park and many more deck-chairs, for which there is a small hire charge. In summer, it's nice just to sit on the grass – you can almost forget that you're in the middle of an enormous city. There is also a track for horse-riding, and the small Serpentine Gallery alongside West Carriage Drive. See chapter on *Museums and galleries.*

Marble Arch is at one corner of the park, and Hyde Park Corner at another. If you want a long 'green' route through central London, you can start from the Black Lion Gate in the north-west corner of Kensington Gardens, and go past the Serpentine to Hyde Park Corner. There is a ramped pedestrian route under this linking via the underground station ticket office level to Green Park. You can find the ramped entrance by the bus stops which are on the northern corner of Knightsbridge where the slip road comes up from the underpass entrance. You can then go almost all the way to Westminster Bridge via parkland.

Some of the parks' principal features are:

Boating on the Serpentine from the north side of the lake. Rowing boats and canoes available for hire. Flat access.

Fishing is allowed at the eastern end of the Serpentine.

The Lido is an open-air swimming area on the south side of the Serpentine. There were, in the past, big marquees for changing and ordinary loos. Water only 1.3m deep. Children's pool and sandpit were +6 steps but otherwise easy access. When we visited, the Lido area was shut for redevelopment. It was due to reopen late in 1995.

Open-air art market on Sundays, by the park railings, right down the Bayswater Road as far as Queensway.

The Orangery in front of Kensington Palace, with its attractive sunken gardens. There is a tea room nearby with ramped access, past some gravel.

Refreshments are available at the Dell, a self-service restaurant at the east end of the Serpentine with flat access, and tables and chairs inside and out. It sometimes closes in winter. Several kiosks near Marble Arch and by the Black Lion gate, Queensway.

The Round Pond for model boats, ducks and swimming dogs is over towards Kensington on high ground approached by a broad tarmac path.

Speaker's Corner is near Marble Arch with easy access. Here you can listen to people talking about anything and everything, particularly on Sunday afternoon.

There are **wheelchair/adapted loos** as follows:

in Kensington Gardens
- behind the shrubbery between the Serpentine Gallery and the Albert Memorial; **adapted cubicle** in the gents **(D80 ST46 NKS)**. The ladies also has an **adapted cubicle**, not seen;
- in the southwest corner by Palace Gate. Flat access from Kensington Gore, but 5 from the park. The attendent has the key. Both ladies and gents have quite large cubicles, but with inward opening doors (D75) and a fixed bar alongside preventing ST altogether;

in Hyde Park
- at the Dell Café, **adapted loo (D90 ST50)** when the baby changer is retracted;
- **wheelchair cubicles (D80 ST85 NKS)** in both the ladies and gents about 100m east of The Dell;
- **adapted cubicles** in both ladies and gents some 200m northwest of the Dell. Both NKS, **ladies D80 ST59**, **gents D90 ST75**. There is a tiny step en route to each;
- in the ladies on the south side of Kensington Gardens opposite Hyde Park gate.

Regent's Park NW1 see chapter on *Places of interest* under Regent's Park.

Richmond Park, Surrey see chapter on *Days out* under Richmond & Kingston.

St James's Park & Green Park SW1 see chapter on *Places of interest* under Westminster and St James's.

Bandstands

Details of performances are available from the various parks superintendants, and also from the LTB. To get details of all the events in all the royal parks, send a stamped addressed envelope to Old Police House, Hyde Park W2 2UH *Tel:* 0171 298-2000, and ask for a list of 'Summer entertainment programmes'.

Some of the performances are of very high quality and to stop and listen to an open-air concert can provide a welcome contrast and rest. Bandstands are to be found in many places in central London, including the following:

Hyde Park W2, just north of Dell restaurant.

St James's Park SW1, near the north side of the bridge over the lake.

Tower Place EC3, opposite the Tower of London.

Victoria Embankment Gardens WC2, near Embankment station. Further out, stands are to be found in a number of parks, including Battersea Park SW1, the Regent's Park, Victoria Park E9 and on Parliament Hill NW3.

Street art displays

There are several large displays of painting, sculpture and handiwork to be seen in London, mainly on Sunday. All are easily accessible. It's fun to wander along to look even if you don't intend to buy. The main ones are:

- in the Bayswater Road along the railings of Hyde Park, stretching sometimes almost the entire length from Marble Arch to Queensway;
- in Piccadilly along the Green Park railings from Hyde Park Corner; and
- in summer only in Heath Street, Hampstead, starting at Whitestone Road.

Exhibition halls

Exhibitions and special events are held at various places in London throughout
the year. The five main ones are listed below. Access provisions have improved
considerably during the past few years, but for some exhibitions the problem
is simply the number of people who want to go and therefore the parking problem
outside and the difficulty of seeing inside. Exhibitors at an exhibition often
build special temporary stands inside the hall, and sometimes build-in steps
rather than provide a ramp. This is something we cannot guide you round, as
it is highly variable.

Obviously, an off-peak visit (such as on a weekday morning) has its attractions,
but not all disabled people and their friends can avoid the crowded peak periods,
and organisers need to take note of this. The responsibility for the use of the
building lies with the exhibition or event organiser and not primarily with the
building manager or owner. The user hires the hall lock, stock and barrel and
decides how it shall be organised and used – and that includes the use of lifts,
catering facilities and so on. The number of chair users admitted is at the
discretion of the hall management and the event organiser.

Alexandra Palace Wood Green N22 *Tel:* 0181 365-2121. At the top of a
steep hill, the only real barrier is a fairly severe slope as you go up through the
CP to the entrance, but it is no great distance (about 20m) and OB holders can
park in the small CP near the Palace. There are +4 steps to the Palm Gallery
where exhibitions are held, but with a ramped bypass. Inside the distances are
quite considerable and if you find walking difficult you may well want to use
the wheelchair available. The Ice Rink similarly has +4 with a ramped bypass.
  Near the entrance there is flat access to a **wheelchair loo (D85 ST130)**, the
bar and snack bar, both with movable chairs and tables. The exhibition space
is simply vast, but flat everywhere, with bars and snack bars all round the side
of the hall. There is another **wheelchair loo (D85 ST75)** near the lift (D110
W135 L190), through the door marked Roman bar/restaurant, and a third **loo
(D90 ST100)** in the basement near the lift.

Barbican Exhibition Halls, Golden Lane EC1 *Tel:* 0171 382-7058 (or via
the Barbican administration), have flat/lift access everywhere and **wheelchair
loos**. For a general write-up on the Barbican area and the Barbican Centre see
chapters on *Places of interest*, and on *Arts centres*.

Central Hall, Westminster, SW1 is quite often used for exhibitions and meetings,
and has much improved access. See chapter on *Places of worship*.

Earls Court, Warwick Road, SW5 *Tel:* BO 0171 370-8079 M 0171 385-
1200. This is one of London's major exhibition centres, and includes a cavernous
hall where various events are staged. It is in a residential area, so parking is

very limited. There are OB spaces next to the building, approached from the Warwick Road entrance, and these are allocated on a 'first come first served' basis. Earls Court Piccadilly line platforms have step free access to street level via a lift. Earls Court and Olympia come under the same management, and they produce a useful leaflet entitled *Visitor information.* This includes diagrams of the halls and the area around, and has a section for disabled visitors. They operate a dedicated phone line in the box office for handling bookings from people with disabilities *Tel:* 0171 370-8078.

From the foyer/reception area, two ramps bypass +3+3 steps. The turnstiles can be bypassed by going through a gate (W76cm). A platform stairlift (W66 L85) followed by a ramp bypasses +8+2 into the main inner foyer. From here it is step free to the main hall (EC1) where most of the big exhibitions and concerts are held. Two large lifts (D100 W150+ L150+) serve all six floors of the building.

   Wheelchair loos and wheelchair cubicles in loos in several parts of the building. The one we saw was **(D80+ ST80+).** These include **two unisex** on the west side of hall EC1 near B Gate and lift 12, and cubicles in the loos on the south side of the hall near the Brompton entrance and lorry lifts 9 and 10. On level two in EC1 there are **unisex loos** on the east side of the hall near Bar 12 and on the west side by the first aid post, and lift 12. In the smaller hall, EC2, there are **adapted loos** at each end of the GF on the west side.

   Overall, facilities have improved here enormously over the years. The number of chair users allowed in at any one time is at the discretion of the organisers of particular events, and as these vary widely, it may be best to check.

Olympia, Hammersmith Road, West Kensington W14 *Tel:* 0171 370-8402. This is the larger of the two exhibition and event halls in west London. Both Earls Court and Olympia are under the same management, see the write-up above mentioning the visitors leaflet and dedicated phone line. Olympia has three separate halls, which may be linked for some of the biggest events like the annual Ideal Home exhibition. The hall is in a residential area, so parking is a problem. There is a CP at the end of Olympia Way called Olympia Parking. This has, notionally, six OB spaces allocated, but they are unmarked. There are also six OB spaces allocated outside the Grand Hall, but these are also unmarked.

The **Grand Hall** in Olympia Way (alongside the railway line) has step free access to the foyer. From here there are several steps to the main GF level, but you can be taken through Gate B where a ramp gives step free access. The Grand Hall is used, among other things, for show jumping and for computer exhibitions. **Four wheelchair/adapted loos** well signed on the GF. The one we saw was **D80 ST140**. There is both a passenger lift (D80), which was switched off when we visited, and a huge service lift. Either gives step free access to the upper galleries.

The **National Hall** off Hammersmith Road has step free access to the foyer. From here, an open lift (W75 L110) bypasses –4 steps to the hall. **Adapted loo (D85 ST67)** on the GF, and a larger **wheelchair loo (D80 ST100+)** on the first floor and reached via a lift (D80). Again the lift was switched off when we visited as there was no 'event' at the time.

Olympia 2, also off Hammersmith Road, has step free access to the foyer. As with the National Hall, an open lift (W75 L115) bypasses the steps into the hall. The hall has four floor levels, step free via two lifts (D100 W100+ L100+). **Wheelchair loos (D70+ ST70+)** on all levels, generally well signed.

Wembley Conference Centre, Empire Way, Wembley HA9 *Tel:* 0181 903-8833. The centre was built in the 1970s when access was not really considered. Consequently there are some split levels and steps. For some events, there may be temporary ramping in places. There is a small dedicated CP outside. Ramped front entrance. Inside there are three floors, and four lifts (D150 W300 L200).

Access to the Grand Hall from the GF is via +16 steps. There are up to eight chair spaces in the hall reached with step free access from the lift on the second floor. They are, however, right at the back of the hall.

Access to most other conference suites involves steps, except the Thames suite which has step free access. There are **three wheelchair loos (D70 ST80)**. From the foyer, follow the red side corridor (to the left), and the loos are just past the main toilets on the right.

Wembley Exhibition Halls, Empire Way, Wembley HA9 *Tel:* 0181 903-8833. Parking, etc as for the stadium. There are three halls, all with step free access to the main facilities. Ramped entrance to hall one from Stadium Way, near the Conference Centre. With different exhibitions, some of the stands may involve steps or other access barriers. There are lifts in each hall (D80 W150 L110 in halls one and two) and (D80 W250 L110 in hall three). **Wheelchair loos (D75 ST75)** in each hall. The restaurant facilities are accessed by lift and are on the first floor in each case.

Car Tours

These two tours are designed as alternatives to standard organised sightseeing tours (by bus, for example). They're aimed at people who have the use of a car and may only have a few hours or for whom the effort of visiting places is too much. Some people may not be able or may not have the time to explore all the buildings or places of interest separately; others are, perhaps, visiting London for the first time and want to get a general and relatively quick impression of the London sights. Car tours also avoid the hassles of parking.

It is obviously recommended that the routes shouldn't be followed at peak times or on popular shopping days. Also, be careful not to cause an obstuction if you stop briefly. Virtually the whole area will have double yellow lines. The researchers found Sunday mornings an ideal time to drive through central London without facing delays. We found that solo driving while following the map is considerably more complex and difficult than going with a companion who can map read. A good street map is essential. Don't be afraid to pull in for a minute or two to get a better view of places. You can often do this without causing obstruction, but you must obviously be aware of the safety and needs of other road users.

Tour 1

Giving a view of major sites along the Thames, in less than a couple of hours. Start at Trafalgar Square and take the exit which leads to Whitehall, passing the Banqueting House on the left and then Downing Street on the right. The Cenotaph, commemorating Britain's war dead, is on an island in the middle of the road. Further on to the right is the east end of Westminster Abbey. Whitehall is quite wide and it may be possible to pull in and stop for a short time.

Passing the Houses of Parliament on the left, carry on via Parliament Square into Margaret Street, which soon becomes Millbank. Continue to the mini roundabout at the foot of Lambeth Bridge and turn left over the bridge. The view from car level is not ideal, but if you pull in as soon as you have turned left off the bridge (into Lambeth Palace Road) there's a layby from where you have an excellent view across the river of the Houses of Parliament, and also of Lambeth Palace nearby.

Carry on straight along Lambeth Palace Road and York Road, following signs for Waterloo Bridge, then bear left for Waterloo Bridge, passing the South Bank complex (the National Theatre and Hayward Gallery among others) on either side of the Road. From Waterloo Bridge there is a very good view of St Paul's and the City on the right, and it may well be a good place to pull in briefly. Coming off the bridge, Somerset House is on your right.

Bear right into the Aldwych and follow the semicircle round past a couple of theatres and Kingsway on the left. There then comes a fairly tricky piece of the route: going straight on across the Strand, make sure that you are in the left hand lane so you can turn into Arundel Street, the entrance to which is almost straight across the Strand from the Aldwych. Follow Arundel Street down to Temple tube station and turn left into Temple Place and then left again onto Victoria Embankment.

Continue along Victoria Embankment passing the Temple on the left. To turn onto Blackfriars Bridge, go under the bypass, then left up Puddle Dock, then left again at Queen Victoria Street. At the traffic lights turn right up Queen Victoria Street. Then left into Friday Street and left again into Cannon Street, thus passing St Paul's Cathedral. Continue down Ludgate Hill and then left at Ludgate Circus, to go over Blackfriars Bridge. On the bridge itself there is not really enough room to pull over, but the view to the right is a good one.

At the crossroads on the south side of Blackfriars Bridge turn left into Southwark Street, go straight across Southwark Bridge Road and follow Southwark Street until it joins Borough High Street. Continue towards London Bridge, going under the railway bridge and passing Southwark Cathedral on the left. Don't go onto London Bridge, but just after passing the Cathedral turn right into Duke Street Hill, which becomes Tooley Street. In order to get a view of HMS *Belfast* you have to park and walk/wheel down Battle Bridge Lane.

Continue on to Tower Bridge where you have a superb view of the Tower of London on your left, but a relatively poor one of the docklands on the right. To get a closer look at St Katherine's Dock, follow the one way system right down Royal Mint Street, then right at Dock Street, then right again at East Smithfield. At the end of East Smithfield turn left as if you were going back across Tower Bridge, and then take the immediate left (St. Katherine's Way) which is a slip road that goes down by the side of the bridge and leads past the Tower Thistle Hotel to give you a good view of the docks complex. If you have the time, you might consider parking at the hotel or at the Minories CP and taking the Docklands Light Railway to Island Gardens, as it gives a superb view of the whole dockands development.

From St Katherine's retrace your route back to Tower Hill and go straight on down Byward Street, Lower Thames Street and Upper Thames Street until you drive down a tunnel. Get into the right hand lane and turn right immediately when the tunnel finishes, turning into Puddle Dock. Then turn left at Queen Victoria Street, and instead of following the road round to the left to go over Blackfriars Bridge, TURN RIGHT at the elongated roundabout going north up New Bridge Street. Turn left at Ludgate Circus into Fleet Street (where all the newspaper headquarters used to be). Drive straight along Fleet Street, with the Law Courts on your right. Turn left down Arundel Street, then right on to Victoria Embankment to go past Cleopatra's Needle. To return to Trafalgar Square, turn right up Northumberland Avenue.

Tour Route 1

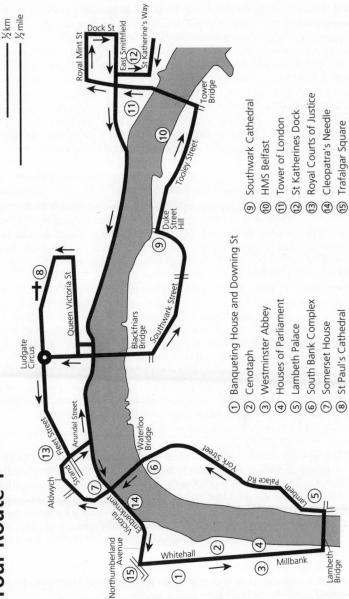

½ km
½ mile

Dock St
Royal Mint St
East Smithfield
St Katherine's Way
Tower Bridge
Tooley Street
Duke Street Hill
Queen Victoria St
Ludgate Circus
Blackfriars Bridge
Southwark Street
Fleet Street
Arundel Street
Strand
Aldwych
Waterloo Bridge
York Street
Victoria Embankment
Palace Rd
Lambeth
Northumberland Avenue
Whitehall
Millbank
Lambeth Bridge

① Banqueting House and Downing St
② Cenotaph
③ Westminster Abbey
④ Houses of Parliament
⑤ Lambeth Palace
⑥ South Bank Complex
⑦ Somerset House
⑧ St Paul's Cathedral
⑨ Southwark Cathedral
⑩ HMS Belfast
⑪ Tower of London
⑫ St Katherines Dock
⑬ Royal Courts of Justice
⑭ Cleopatra's Needle
⑮ Trafalgar Square

Tour 2

Covering the West End, South Kensington and Regent's Park, and slightly shorter than the first tour. The starting point is Trafalgar Square. Pass under Admiralty Arch and drive up the Mall: the Institue of Contemporary Arts, Clarence House and St James's Palace are on your right. Bear right in front of Buckingham Palace onto Constitution Hill and then round part of the Hyde Park Corner roundabout. Take the third exit from the roundabout, which is the entrance to Knightsbridge. (At Hyde Park corner, passengers will be able to see the Wellington Museum; drivers will need to concentrate to negotiate the roundabout!).

Take the left filter onto Brompton Road and you pass Harrods on the left, and then Brompton Oratory, the Victoria and Albert Museum and the impressive facade of the Natural History Museum on the right. There is no right turn into Queen's Gate so a detour to the left via Queensbury Place is necessary. Then turn left into Queensbury Way and left again into Queen's Gate. Towards the top of Queen's Gate, a right turn into Bremner Road allows you to see the Albert Memorial and the Royal Albert Hall (opposite each other). Turn right into Kensington Gore and take the next left into Hyde Park.

The Ring in Hyde Park takes you over the Serpentine, from where there is a good view of the lake and the park. Follow the Ring on towards Bayswater Road, but carry on to the right, past Victoria Gate, and this leads you to Marble Arch.

Turn left past Marble Arch, right into Oxford Street and then left into Portman Street, which leads into Gloucester Place. At the junction with Marylebone Road a right turn takes you past the dome of the Planetarium, then take the first left after Madame Tussaud's into York Gate and turn left again onto the Outer Circle. Follow this round Regent's Park, where it is easy to stop for a moment. You pass some fine terraces (including Cornwall Terrace and Hanover Terrace) and then the London Mosque on your left. At the top of the Outer Circle, on the right, is the entrance to the London Zoo.

Carry straight on south, across Marylebone Road and into Portland Place. You pass All Souls in Langham Place with the BBC on your left. Continue across Oxford Circus and down Regent Street, following the bend round into Piccadilly Circus. Go round the roundabout and bear off to the left into Coventry Street and then turn right into Haymarket past the Theatre Royal. Turn right at the bottom of Haymarket into Pall Mall and as you turn right again at the corner of St James's Street and Pall Mall, St James's Palace is on the left.

Go right again into Piccadilly, passing the Royal Academy on your left, round the Circus again and this time a left turn at the end of the Haymarket returns you to Trafalgar Square.

TOUR ROUTE 2

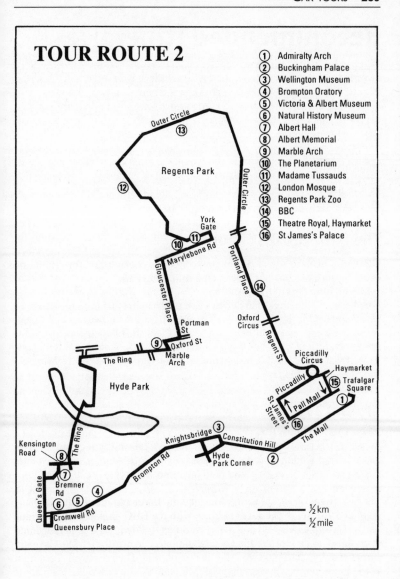

1. Admiralty Arch
2. Buckingham Palace
3. Wellington Museum
4. Brompton Oratory
5. Victoria & Albert Museum
6. Natural History Museum
7. Albert Hall
8. Albert Memorial
9. Marble Arch
10. The Planetarium
11. Madame Tussauds
12. London Mosque
13. Regents Park Zoo
14. BBC
15. Theatre Royal, Haymarket
16. St James's Palace

Recommended itineraries

We have tried to identify and suggest smallish areas where there are a number of varied sights, where you will find **wheelchair loos** *en route,* and where the majority of the places to be seen are described in this guide. Obviously you must study the map, because only you know what sort of distance you can cope with. The A-Z super scale map is particularly good for detail. In each case we have suggested places to park. We have in mind the visitor who has only two or three days in which to see London. It's difficult to represent everyone's interests, and you'll have your own ideas about what you want to see. We hope that with the judicious use of other guides, you can plan your visit to make the most of your time and resources, doing the things of most interest to you.

The Barbican & St Paul's

One varied group of sights is centred on the Barbican area. Parking is possible at the Barbican Centre. Alternatively you might be able to reserve a parking space at the Museum of London. Around the Barbican Centre are St Bartholomew-the-Great and St Giles Cripplegate churches (NB +3 steps at St Giles) and the Museum of London. There are **wheelchair loos** in the Barbican Arts Centre and in the Museum of London. Postman's Park offers a possible shady picnic spot, although a good number of office workers will probably have the same idea. A little further afield are the Guildhall, the Clock Museum and St Paul's Cathedral.

Around Tower Bridge

At the east end of the City there's a compact area to see including the Tower (where access is very limited inside), the Tower Bridge walkway, St Katharine's Dock and All-Hallows-by-the-Tower church. A possible extension to this visit could take in HMS *Belfast,* the London Dungeon and Hays Galleria. Parking is possible in the UGCP at the Tower Thistle Hotel, or the Minories MSCP. The area can be accessed by the new DLR to Tower Gateway, and you could park near one of the Docklands stations, all of which are step free. There are **wheelchair loos** at the Tower, in the Tower Thistle Hotel, Dickens Inn, Hays Galleria, and in the Tower Bridge Museum.

Westminster to Piccadilly

Westminster to Piccadilly is a somewhat larger area containing, again, a wide variety of sights. Parking is possible on the South Bank, see under *Arts centres.* It's a very congested area during the week and CPs are used mainly by season ticket holders and are often full by 09.30. One way of getting quite close is to come in by train to Charing Cross.

If you decide to take in the whole area, St James's Park provides a good place for a rest or a picnic. Interesting places en route could include the Westminster sights, the Cabinet War Rooms, Horse Guards Parade with its guard, and the galleries on Trafalgar Square. Whitehall itself is interesting with the Cenotaph, which is the national war memorial, government offices and numerous statues to famous people. Alternatively, you may prefer to concentrate on the Westminster area. The Abbey is largely accessible, although somewhat congested. Down Victoria Street, to the west, is the Army & Navy store and Westminster Cathedral. **Wheelchair loos** are detailed in the *Good loo guide,* and there are also loos in the Cabinet War Rooms

A river trip to Greenwich

Again it is possible to park on the South Bank, or to take the train to Charing Cross. Alternatively you might park at Greenwich and do the boat trip the other way round, possibly visiting either Trafalgar Square or Covent Garden. A river trip is an ideal way to see London, provided the weather is OK. At Charing Cross and Westminster piers there is (steep) ramped access. Some of the boats operating are accessible. See the write-up on river trips. The trip itself enables you to see much of central London in a really relaxed way, and Greenwich has some amazing buildings, as well as the park and National Maritime Museum. Don't miss seeing the pedestrian tunnel under the Thames, with its Victorian lift. **Wheelchair loos** en route are detailed in the Greenwich write-up. The ones around Charing Cross are in the *Good loo guide.*

The good loo guide

This section brings together the information on accessible loos in central London, which is scattered through the guide, and there are a few more that did not justify a mention anywhere else. To be accessible, there are two major criteria. The first is that the cubicle is large enough for a chair user or other disabled person. It should have support rails and lever taps and various other equipment, but we do not have enough space to give full details of every one. The second criteria is that it should be open, or use the NKS lock.

We strongly recommend that you get an NKS key, as this will open a large percentage of **adapted loos** in both in London and elsewhere. A key can be obtained from RADAR and costs less than £5, including postage. RADAR publishes the *National Key Scheme Guide* listing over 4000 NKS loos around the country, saying where they are.

Central London

We have highlighted public wheelchair loos that are available 24 hours of the day, such as the 'Tardis' loos found on some pavements, **by putting them in bold** in the listing. Loos in rail stations are usually available for most of the day, while those in pubs and shops are only accessible during opening hours. Note that some pubs get extremely crowded at certain times, as do fast food outlets such as Burger King and McDonalds. On Friday and Saturday nights they may even have 'bouncers' to control the number of people allowed in. Where we have mentioned a hotel loo, we have tried to give the precise directions of where to find it. This will enable you to go straight it without asking, as if you were staying there (or, of course, if you were planning to meet someone in the lobby).

In the last edition, we listed many accessible loos that are in museums. Unfortunately, many of these have started charging for entry, making them effectively less accessible. We have not included them in this list, nor those in theatres or cinemas, unless they are in what is effectively a 'public' part which is commonly open.

The *Good loo guide* covers the central London area, and is split up according to postal districts. If you don't happen to know which postal district you are in, then it is normally written on street name signs, for example, Oxford Street W1.

W1

1   Cumberland Hotel, Marble Arch see page 62 and Mount Royal Hotel, Marble Arch see page 63.

2   Selfridges, Oxford Street see page 242 and **immediately opposite Selfridges there's a Tardis loo (NKS, 24 hrs) at the end of Balderton Street.**

3   Debenhams, 334 Oxford Street see page 236

4   John Lewis, 278 Oxford Street see page 241 and BHS, 252 Oxford Street

see page 235.

5   Littlewoods, 203 Oxford Street see page 242.

6   Marks and Spencer, 173 Oxford Street see page 242.

7   Plaza, 120 Oxford Street see page 242.

8   Heals, Tottenham Court Road on the first floor. Enter the shop, turning right to reach the lifts (D68 W100 L120) at the far end. Out of the lift on the first floor, ask for the Café at Heals, and the wheelchair loo (D80 ST90) is just by the entrance on the right.

9   *Jack Horner* 236 Tottenham Court Road see page 211.

10   *Moon and Sixpence* 185 Wardour Street see page 211.

11   *Burlington Bertie,* 39 Shaftesbury Avenue see page 210.

12   Piccadilly Circus see page 89.

13   Royal Academy see page 134. And Meridien hotel, 19 Piccadilly see page 233.

14   Hamleys, 188 Regent Street see page 237.

15   Fenwick, 63 New Bond Street see page 237.

16   Hilton hotel, 22 Park Lane. Ramp bypasses –3 steps at entrance. On the first floor with lift access (D100 W200 L200). The lifts are directly in front of you as you go in. Get out at the first floor and turn left. There are wheelchair cubicles in both the ladies (straight ahead) and the gents (to the right). Both D70 and ST80+.

17   Intercontinental Hotel, Hamilton Place see page 233.

W2

18   Marble Arch. In the ramped subway which runs from Speakers Corner (by the park), under the roundabout to the west side of Edgware Road. Wheelchair cubicles (D85 ST75) in both ladies and gents.

19   Hyde Park: 200m northwest of the Dell café see page 274.

20   Hyde Park: 100m east of the Dell café see page 274.

21   Hyde Park: at the Dell café see page 274.

22   Kensington Gardens by the Serpentine Gallery see page 274.

23   Royal Lancaster Hotel, Bayswater Road by Lancaster Gate Station. Unisex on first floor with lift access. Go left from the lifts then right. Follow the signs to the Gloucester and Somerset suites, through the fire door, and it's on your right.

24   London Toy and Model Museum, 23 Craven Hill see page 129.

25   Whiteleys, 151 Queensway see page 244.

26   Paddington Station see page 32.

W8

(All are just off the map)

27   Copthorne Tara Hotel see page 66.

27   BHS Kensington, 101 Kensington High Street see page 235.

27   Marks and Spencers, 113 Kensington High Street see page 242.

SW3

28   National Army Museum, Royal Hospital Road see page 131.

SW1

29   Peter Jones, Sloane Square see page 242.

30   Victoria Coach Station see page 30.

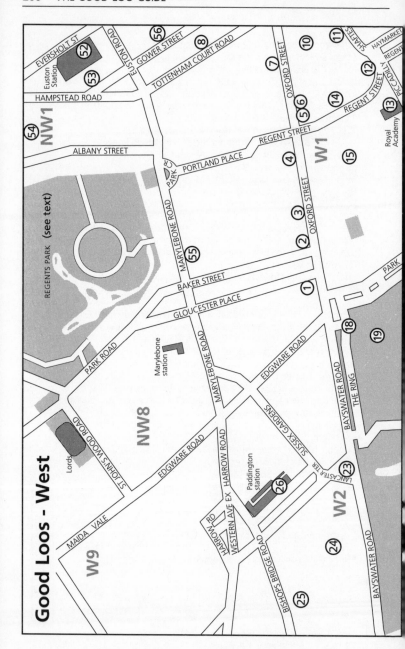

Good Loos – West

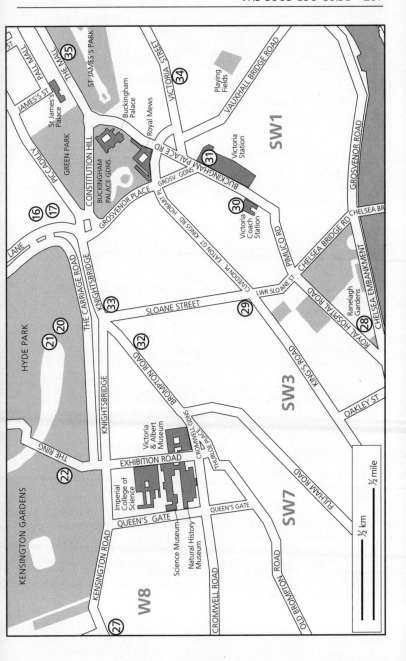

31	Victoria Station and *Wetherspoon* pub see pages 35, and 212. And Victoria Place see page 243.
32	Harrods, Brompton Road, Knightsbridge see page 237.
33	Harvey Nichols, 109 Knightsbridge see page 240.
34	Army and Navy Stores, 101 Victoria Street see page 235.
35	St James's Park see page 97.
36	Outside QE2 Conference Centre, opposite Westminster Abbey see page 116.
37	By Westminster Pier see page 269.
38	Banqueting House, Whitehall see page 98.
39	*Lord Moon of the Mall*, 18 Whitehall see page 211.

SE1

40	Royal Festival Hall see page 167.
41	NFT1 see page 166.
42	National Theatre see page 166.
43	Waterloo Station see page 35.
44	Gabriel's Wharf, next to the *Studio Six* pub.
45	London Bridge Station (under reconstruction) see page 35.
46	Hays Galleria, Tooley Street see page 83.

E1

47	*Dickens Inn*, St Katherine's Way see page 212 and Tower Thistle Hotel, St Katherine's Way see page 66.
48	*Kings Stores*, 14 Widegate Street see page 213.

N1

49	Kings Cross Station, York Way see page 34.

NW1

50	St Pancras Station see page 33.
51	**Euston Road by the corner with Chalton Street, Tardis loo, NKS 24 hrs.**
52	Euston Station see page 33.
53	*Crown and Anchor*, 137 Drummond Street see page 210 and Ibis Hotel, Euston see page 66.
54	Jewish Museum, Raymond Burton House, 129 Albert Street see page 129.
55	**Marylebone Road, opposite Cannon Cinema and 50m west of the Planetarium NKS, 24 hrs.**

WC1

56	Dillons bookshop, 82 Gower Street see page 236.
57	**Russell Square, by the corner of Bernard Street and Southampton Row. Tardis loo, NKS, 24hrs.**
58	Bonnington Hotel, 92 Southampton Row see page 65.
59	Montague Park Hotel, 12 Montague Street see page 65.
60	British Museum, Great Russell Street see page 125.
61	Marlborough Crest Hotel, junction of Bloomsbury Street and Great Russell Street. Entrance has +1 step. Loos on GF to your left towards the Brasserie.

WC2

62	*Flyman and Firkin*, 166 Shaftesbury Avenue see page 210.

63   Photographers Gallery, 5 and 8 Great Newport Street see page 134.
64)   Leicester Square see page 88.
64)   *Moon under Water*, 28 Leicester Square see page 211.
65   By Trafalgar Square: National Gallery see page 132 and National
       Portrait Gallery see page 133.
66   St Martin-in-the-Fields, St Martin's Place see page 119.
67   Charing Cross Station see page 35.
68   Victoria Embankment, 50m east of Embankment station (D80 ST80NKS)
69   Covent Garden see page 87. Also the Theatre Museum nearby where the
       loo is before you get to the pay desk see page 137, and *Sheila's,* 47 King
       Street see page 211.
70   *Old Orleans*, 29 Wellington Street see page 211.
71   *Henry's Café Bar*, 27 Endell Street see page 211.
72   Royal Courts of Justice, Strand see page 89.

EC1
73   *Melton Mowbray Pie and Ale House*, 18 Holborn see page 214.
74   **West Smithfield, signposted from miles around. On the east side of the
       circle. Tardis loo, NKS, 24hrs.**
75   *Masque Haunt*, 168 Old Street see page 213.
76   *Kings Head,* 49 Chiswell Street see page 213.

EC2
77   The Barbican Centre see page 170.
78   *49 Gresham Street*, 49 Gresham Street see page 213.
79   Guildhall, Gresham Street see page 78.
80   Bank of England Museum see page 124.
81   Liverpool Street Station see page xxx and *Hamilton Hall*, see page 213.
82   *Exchange Restaurant*, Exchange Square, Broadgate Centre see page 213.
83   *Bishops Wine Bar*, 160 Bishopsgate see page 212 and *Sir Paul Pindar*,180
       Bishopsgate see page 214.

EC3
84   Fenchurch Street Station see page 34.
85   *Mint,* East Smithfield see page 214.
86   Tower Hill, almost opposite the ticket office for the Tower, see page 80.

EC4
87   *Bull Bear and Broker,* 24 King William Street see page 212.
88   *Banker,* Cousin Lane see page 212.
89   **By St Paul's Cathedral, on the corner of the churchyard and New
       Change. Tardis loo, NKS, 24hrs.**
90   *Magpie and Stump*, 19 Old Bailey Road see page 213.
91   *Old King Lud*, 78 Ludgate Hill see page 214.
92   *Wynkyn de Worde Wine Bar* and Restaurant, Bride Lane see page 214.
93   City Thameslink station see page 33.

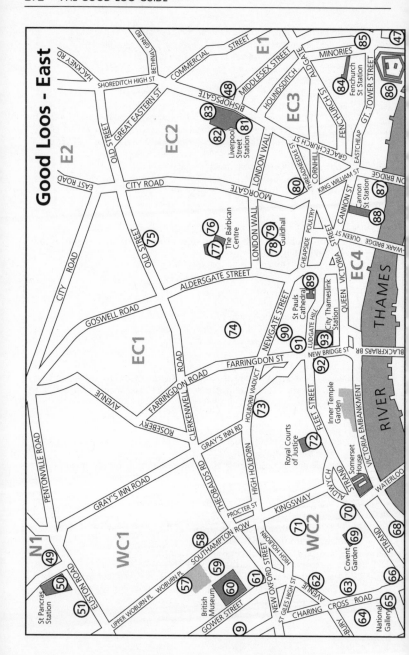

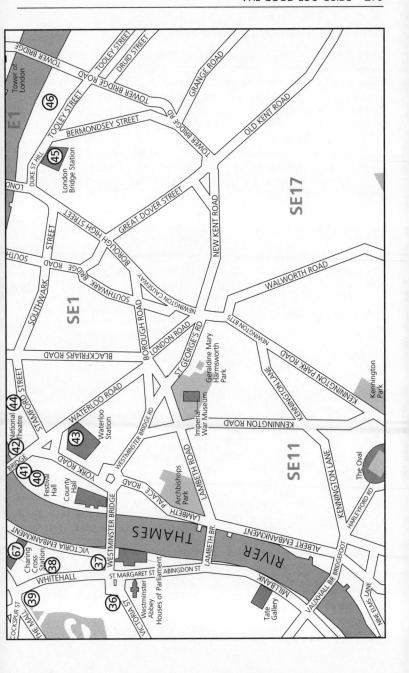

NKS loos in London boroughs

The listing of NKS loos was published in 1995 by RADAR, and covers the whole of the country. We have included here the ones in London boroughs. The list is derived from information supplied by local authorities. There is no indication how long the road is where they are situated, and a few have access barriers en route. We happen to know about the one listed on Ealing Broadway station which is down 32 steps, and you can only get to it by train ! However, the vast majority will have step free access, and the list is a good starting point if you are staying in or passing through an area. Note also the loos in the shopping centres we have listed. Most modern shopping precincts have adapted/wheelchair loos, and usually attached parking. There are also the pubs listed earlier in the guide with adapted loos.

Barking & Dagenham

Barking	Beacontree Heath
	Fanshawe Avenue
	Farr Avenue
Chadwell Heath	Ashton Gardens (to be replaced)
Dagenham	Hedgemans Road (to be replaced)
	Stamford Road
	Wood Lane

Barnet

N12 North Finchley	Stanhope Road
NW7 Mill Hill	Hartley Avenue, next to library
Barnet	Wood Street
Elstree	Scratchwood Open Place

Bexley

Abbey Wood	Lesnes Abbey
Bexleyheath	Brampton Road
	Broadway, Superbowl
	Townley Park
	Broadway Shopping Centre
Blackfen	Westwood Lane
Crayford	Waterside
Erith	Franks Park
	High Street
	Northumberland Heath Colyers Lane
Sidcup	St John's Road
	Sidcup Station
Welling	Bellegrove Road
	Danson Park

Brent

Wembley	The Church of the Ascension, The Avenue

Bromley

Beckenham	High Street/Kelsey Road junction
Biggin Hill	Main Road

Bromley	Hill CP, Beckenham Lane
	Bromley South Station
Chislehurst	High Street CP
Farnborough	Church Road
Locksbottom	Pallant Way
Orpington	Station Road CP
Penge	High Street
Petts Wood	Station Square
West Wickham	Glebe Way

Camden

| NW3 Swiss Cottage | Swiss Cottage Community Centre |
| NW5 Hampstead | Parliament Hill Fields, Running Track |

Ealing

| W3 Acton | Acton College, Woodlands Building |
| W5 Ealing | Ealing Broadway Station [but there are 32 steps] |

Enfield

N9 Edmonton	Edmonton Green Shopping Precinct
	Tramway Avenue
	Picketts Lock Campsite (Lee Valley)
N11 New Southgate	Arnos Park
N13 Palmers Green	Broomfield Park
	Triangle, Green Lanes
N14 Southgate	Grovelands Park
N18 Upper Edmonton	Angel Road
	Sterling Way/Kendal Parade
	Victoria Road
Enfield	Civic Centre
	Enfield Town Shopping Centre
	Forty Hall
	North Pavilion, Enfield Playing Field
	Sydney Road
	Town Park, Cecil Road

Greenwich

SE2 Abbey Wood	Bostall Gardens
	Knee Hill
	Abbey Wood Station
SE3 Blackheath	Batley Park, near *The Standard*
SE9 Eltham	Avery Hill Park
	Elm Terrace, off Eltham High Street
	Eltham Church, Well Hall Road
	Well Hall Pleasance, near Tudor Barn
	William Barefoot Drive
	Eltham Station
SE9 New Eltham	Southwood Road, by the library
SE10 Greenwich	Greenwich Pier
	Rodmere Station
SE18 Plumpstead	Abery Street
	Slade
SE18 Woolwich	Beresford Square
	Calderwood Street

Woolwich Arsenal Station

Hackney
E8 Dalston   Birkbeck Road, off Ridley Road

Hammersmith and Fulham
SW6 Fulham   Vanston Place, Fulham Broadway
W6 Hammersmith   Hammersmith, Broadway Centre
                                King Street, by the National Westminster Bank
                                Lyric Theatre
                                Social Services Department, 45 King Street
W12 Shepherds Bush   Shepherds Bush Green

Harringey
N4 Finsbury Park   Finsbury Gates
N8 Crouch End   Hatherley Gardens/Haringey Park
N10 Muswell Hill   Summerland Gardens Car Park
N15 South Tottenham   Downshills Park, West Green Road/Philip Lane
                                High Cross, Tottenham High Road
                                St Anns Road, Chestnuts Park
N17 Tottenham   Apex Corner, Tottenham High Road/Seven Sisters
                                Road
                                Tottenham Hale Station, on the platform
N22 Wood Green   Ducketts Common
                                Lordship Lane/High Road
                                Turnpike Lane Station
                                Safeway Store, Wood Green

Harrow
Edgware   Whitechurch Lane
Harrow   Greenhill Way, behind Debenhams
                                Harrow Bus Station, College Road
                                Reference Library, Civic Centre
Harrow Weald   High Road, by Bus Station
North Harrow   Pinner Road, at Car Park entrance
Pinner   Chapel Lane, Car Park
Rayners Lane   opposite the underground station
South Harrow   Northolt Road, near Sainsburys
Wealdstone   Gladstone Way, behind Safeways

Havering
Cranham   Front Lane
Elm Park   Station Parade
Harold Hill   Hilldene Avenue
Hornchurch   Appleton Way
                                Elm Park Broadway, Elm Park
Rainham   Tesco Store
Romford   Angel Way MSCP
                                Central Library
                                Market Place/North Street A12
                                Rear of Boots the Chemist
                                South Street
                                Western Road MSCP

Hillingdon

Eastcote	North View
Harefield	Park Lane
Hayes	Botwell Lane
Hayes End	Uxbridge Road
Hillingdon	Western Avenue
Ickenham	Community Close
Northwood	Oaklands Gate
	Pinner Road
Ruislip	Manor Farm
Uxbridge	Charter Place
	Pavilions Shopping Centre

Hounslow

W4 Chiswick	Chiswick Park, Great West Road
Brentford	The Watermans Art Centre
Feltham	The Centre, High Street
Hanworth	Country Way, A316
Hounslow	Treaty Shopping Centre

Islington

N1 Islington	White Conduit Street, Chapel Market
N4 Finsbury Park	Finsbury Park Station
N5 Highbury	Highbury Fields by Highbury Corner

Kensington and Chelsea

SW3 Chelsea	Sydney Street, by the ladies loo
SW7 South Kensington	Gloucester Road/Courtfield Road
W10 North Kensington	Ladbroke Grove
W11 Notting Hill	Westbourne Grove
W14 West Kensington	Kensington Olympia Station

Kingston-upon-Thames

Kingston	Bentalls CP, Footbridge Level
	Bittoms CP, Penrhyn Road
	Cattle Market CP
	Eden Walk CP, Union Street
	Bentalls Centre, second floor
	John Lewis Store, Wood Street
	Kingston Station, Platform 3
Surbiton	Claremont Road, by the Clock Tower

Lewisham

SE6 Catford	Catford Broadway/Catford Road
SE8 Deptford	The Albany Centre
SE13 Lewisham	Lewisham High Street
SE14 New Cross	New Cross Station

Merton

Mitcham	Sibthorp Road
Motspur Park	Station Road
Rayners Park	Approach Road
South Wimbledon	Kingston Road

Newham

E6 Beckton	Beckton District Park North, Boat House
	Beckton District Park South, Will Thorne Pavilion
	New Beckton Way, Stroud Pavilion
E6 East Ham	Central Park outside ASDA superstore
	St John's Road CP
	Town Hall, by old Cashiers Office
E12 Manor Park	High Street North/Romford Road
E13 Plaistow	Barking Road Recreation Ground
	Greengate Street/Barking Road
	Queens Market
E15 Stratford	Bus Station, Great Eastern Street
	Stratford Mall, by Subway to Station
E15 West Ham	Memorial Recreation Ground, Pavilion
	West Ham Park
E16 Canning Town	Cundy Road Open Space
	Rathbourne CP, by Market
	Royal Victoria Gardens
E16 North Woolwich	King George V Park

Redbridge

Chadwell Heath	Eastern Avenue/Barley Lane
	Wangey Road
Goodmayes	Goodmayes Park, Green Lane
	High Road/Barley Lane
Hainault	Forest Road, by Sailing Lake
	Fullwell Cross, Fencepiece Road
	Manford Way
Ilford	Chapel Road/Ilford Lane
	Clarence Avenue, Gants Hill (ladies only)
	Clayhall Park
	Clements Road MSCP
	High Road, by Flyover
	Horns Road
	Ilford Central Library
	Loxford Park, Loxford Lane
	Pearl Assurance Building
	South Park Road/South Park Crescent
	Town Hall CP, Chadwick Road
	Valentines Park, Emerson Road
	Valentines Park, Melbourne Road
	The Wash, Cranbrook Road
	York Road
	Ilford Station, Ticket Hall
Seven Kings	High Road, opposite "Pembroke"
Wanstead	Woodbine Place, Christchurch Green (ladies only)
Woodford	Eastwood Close CP (ladies only)
	Hillside Avenue
	Joyston Road/Broomhill Road

Richmond-upon-Thames

Barnes	Rocks Lane
Richmond	Buccleuch Gardens
	Princes Street, behind Waitrose

	Riverside, Old Town Hall
	Victoria Place
	Richmond Station
Teddington	Broad Street
Twickenham	The Green (café hours)
Whitton	Whitton Library

Southwark
SE21 Dulwich   Dulwich Park, Central Toilets

Sutton
Wallington   Stanley Park Road
                        Wallington Station

Tower Hamlets
E1 Whitechapel   Whitechapel Market
E2 Bethnal Green   Bethnal Green Road/Redchurch Street
E3 Bow   Roman Road/Parnell Road
                        Victoria Park, Grove Road
E14 Poplar   Pigott Street Bus Stand, East India Dock Road

Waltham Forest
E4 Chingford   Albert Crescent, Old Church Road
                        Kings Head Mill/Mansfield Hill
                        Larkshall Road/The Broadway
                        Station Road/The Green
                        Chingford Station
E10 Leyton   Coronation Gardens, Leyton High Road
                        Leyton Green Road, opposite Bus Garage
E11 Leytonstone   Green Man, Bus Station
                        Kirkdale Road
E15 Stratford   Crownfield Road/Leytonstone High Road
                        Eastway Sports Centre (Lee Valley)
E17 Walthamstow   Forest Road/Bedford Road junction
                        Higham Hill/Forest Road junction
                        Selbourne Road Bus Station
                        Willow Walk, by Railway Bridge
                        Wood Street/Forest Road junction

Wandsworth
SW11 Battersea   Falcon Road, Clapham Junction
SW17 Tooting   Tooting Broadway, by Garratt Lane
                        Tooting Common, by Dr Johnson Avenue
SW18 Wandsworth   Garrett Lane/Magdalen Road junction
                        Wandsworth High Street, by Arndale Centre

Westminster City Council
NW8 Maida Vale   Salisbury Street

Symbols

Although the guidebook is written in English, much of the information about accommodation and about the main sights is summarised in the form of symbols. It is intended that this will enable you to use much of the information, as the symbols have clear criteria. Their precise meaning is described in the list which follows.

The symbols define the information which you may need before you reach a building or area, followed by details of the entrance and then of access inside a building. The existence of a lift, of steps and of accessible toilets and eating facilities is defined. Where appropriate, any special facilities for visually handicapped people or those who are hard of hearing is noted.

In the vast majority of situations, facilities which are suitable for the wheelchair user will also be OK for those with other disabilities or access problems. The information that a building has a flat entrance and is 80% wheelchair accessible is represented by:

 80%

The information that parking is difficult and that the area is hilly; that there are two steps at the entrance; that the ground floor representing 60% of the whole has no split levels but that there are −19 steps to the basement is represented by:

 **E2 N19** **60%**

French

Bien que ce guide soit publié en anglais, la plupart des renseignements concernant le logement et les sites principaux á visiter sont représentés sous forme de symboles. Cette méthode a été choisie afin de rendre l'emploi de ce guide aisé. Chaque symbole est expliqué de façon précise dans la liste qui suit.

Ces symboles définissent les informations dont vous pourrez avoir besoin avant de visiter certains endroits ou bâtiments, suivies par les détails concernant l'entrée et les facilités d'accès à l'intérieur même du bâtiment. La présence d'ascenseurs, d'escaliers, de toilettes et de cafétérias est également indiquée. Les aménagements spéciaux pour les non-voyants et les mal-entendants sont également spécifiés.

Dans la majeure partie des cas, les aménagements convenant aux utilisateurs de fauteuils roulants seront aussi très pratiques pour ceux qui souffrent d'autres handicaps ou de difficultés d'accès.

Les cas pour lesquels un bâtiment dispose d'une entrée de plain pied et étant accessible à 80% par fauteuil roulant sont représentés par:

 80%

Les cas pour lesquels le parking est difficile d'accès ou le sol est accidenté; pour lesquels il y a deux marches à l'entrée; pour lesquels le rez-de-chaussée représentant 60% de l'ensemble ne s'étend que sur un seul niveau mais pour lesquels il y a – 19 marches jusqu'au sous-sol sont représentés par:

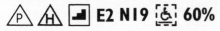 **E2 N19** **60%**

German

Obwohl der Reiseführer in englischer Sprache veraßt ist, wird ein großer Teil der Informationen über Unterkünfte und die wichtigsten Sehenswürdigkeiten in Form von Symbolen zusammengefaßt und dargestellt. Da die Symbole klare Merkmale haben wird es Ihnen ermöglicht, größten Nutzen aus den Informationen zu ziehen. Ihre genaue Bedeutung wird in der nachstehenden Liste erläutert.

Die Symbole geben Informationen, die Sie wahrscheinlich benötigen, bevor Sie ein Gebäude bzw. Gebiet erreichen. Sie sind ergänzt durch Einzelheiten über den Zugang und den Gegebenheiten innerhalb des Gebäudes bzw. Areals. Etwaige Fahrstühle, Treppen sowie zugängliche Toiletten und Eßgelegenheiten werden aufgeführt. An gegebener Stelle wird auf besondere Einrichtungen für visuell Behinderte oder Schwerhörige hingewiesen.

In den häufigsten Situationen werden Einrichtungen, die für den Rollstuhlfahrer geeignet sind, auch für Besucher mit anderen Behinderungen zweckmäßig sein.

Die Information, daß ein Gebaüde einen ebenen Eingang hat und zu 80% für Rollstuhlfahrer zungänglich ist, wird wie folgt dargestellt:

 80%

Die Information, daß das Parken problematisch und das Gebiet hügelig ist; daß der Eingang zwei Stufen hat; daß das Erdgeschoß 60% des gesamt zugänglichen Bereiches ist; keine Zwischengeschoße vorhanden sind aber 19 Treppenstufen zum Untergeschoß führen sind, wird wie folgt dargestellt:

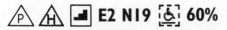 **E2 N19** **60%**

Symbols key:

P Parking with flat, lift or ramped access, normally attached to, or part of the building.

[P] Parking normally possible within 200m.

⟨P⟩ Parking may well be difficult.

⟨H⟩ Hilly area.

F Flat area.

⟨D⟩ Long distances may be involved.

⟨▲⟩ Bumpy surfaces.

[♿] A friend or escort for a chair user is advised eg. because of the size or surface.

⟨!⟩ Access is particularly difficult.

[I'] Good signposting.

⟨A⟩ Poor/non-existent signposting.

M Main entrance without steps.

A There is a step free way in or flat approach. Normally open.

[A] There is step free entrance on request. May require portable ramps or a stair climber.

Symboles clefs:

Schüssel für die Symbole:

Parking avec accès plat, par rampe ou par ascenseur; le plus souvent inclus ou attaché à l'ensemble.	Parken mit ebenem Zugang, Lift oder Rampe, normalerweise angrenzend an das Gebäude oder Teil des Gebäudes.
Parking normalement disponible à moins de 200 mètres.	Parken normalweise innerhalb von 200m möglich.
Parking pouvant être difficile.	Parken könnte schwierig sein.
Aire accidentée.	Hügeliges Gebiet.
Surface plate.	Flaches Gebiet.
Longues distances possibles.	Möglicherweise müssen größere Entfernungen zurückgelegt werden.
Surfaces bosselées.	Unebenes Gelände.
Personne ou ami conseillé à cause de la longueur ou de la surface de l'ensemble.	Es ist empfehlenswert, für einen Bekannten bzw. Begleiter mitzubringen, z.B. aufgrund der Größe oder aufgrund von Unebenheiten.
Accès particulièrement difficile.	Der Zugang ist besonders schwierig.
Bonne signalisation.	Gute Beschilderung.
Signalisation mauvaise voire inexistante.	Beschilderung schlecht/fehlt.
Entrèe principale plate.	Ebener Haupteingang.
Surface ou approche plate, normalement ouverte.	Es gibt einen stufenlosen Eingang oder Zugang. Normalerweise offen.
Surface plate ou par rampe à l'intérieur, sur demande.	Es gibt einen stufenlosen Eingang auf Anfrage. Möglicherweise tragbare erforderlich Rampen oder andere Hilfsmittel.

Symbols key:

◢	Steps.
E	Entrance E3 or E1+1 etc indicate the steps at the main entrance. Alternatives are indicated thus: E12/2.
N	Inside. Where numbers are added, they indicate the steps up or from the GF. If you can go either way it is indicated thus: N+25/–14 (25 steps up or 14 steps down).
⇅	Lift, larger than D70 W90 L110. Flat from the foyer or equivalent.
⇅	Lift, but there are possible problems eg. stepped access or small size.
♿	Flat /ramped/lift access everywhere, after any steps at the entrance.
♿	Flat/ramped/lift access to part of the building, after any steps at the entrance.
⚠	Narrow doors or gaps less than 70cm. Cannot be by-passed.
♿ WC	Special loo facility for a wheelchair user, with side transfer and door width over 70cm.
WC	Loos with flat access.
♿ ✗	Café/restaurant facilities accessible to a wheelchair user.
⊓	Seats available.
⚠	Few/no seats available.
👁	Special exhibitions/facilities for people who are partially sighted.
(?)	Equipment provided for deaf people eg. an induction loop or special hearing aids.

Symboles clefs:

Schüsselfür die Symbole:

Marches.	Stufen.
Entré E3 ou E1+1 etc indiquent les marches de l'entrée principale. Les alternatives sont indiquées de la façon suivante: E12/2.	Eingang E3 oder E1+1 etc. weist auf Stufen am Haupteingang hin. Alternativen werden wie folgt angezeigt: E12/2.
A l'intérieur. Lorsque les nombres sont additionnés, ils indiquent le nombre de marches pour descendre ou monter au rez-de-chaussée. Lorsque la montée ou la descente n'est pas practicable, ceci est indiqué comme cela: N+25/–14 (par exemple: 25 marches pour monter, 14 pour descendre).	Innen. Etwaige Zahlen beziehen sich auf Stufen, die hinauf ins Erdgeschoß bzw. hinunter vom Erdgeschoß führen. Wo beide Richtungen benutzbar sind, ist dies wie folgt angegeben: N+25/–14, d.h. 25 Stufen hinauf oder 14 hinunter.
Ascenseur dont la capacité est supérieure à 70 cm (porte), largeur 90cm et profonder 110 cm. Accès plat à partir du foyer ou équivalent.	Lift, größer als Tür 70cm Weite 90cm Länge 110cm. Flach vom Foyer o.ä.
Ascenseur pouvant présenter quelques difficultés, par exemple: marches à gravir ou capacité réduite.	Lift, aber mögliche Probleme wie z.B. Zugang mit Stufe oder kleine Abmessungen.
Accés plat, par rampe ou par ascenseur dans tout le bâtiment, une fois les marches de l'entrée gravies.	Überall flacher Zugang/Rampe/Lift, nach etwaigen Stufen am Eingang.
Accés plat, par rampe ou par ascenseur dans certaines parties du bâtiment, une fois les marches de l'entrée gravies.	Teilweise flacher Zugang/Rampe/Lift, nach etwaigen Stufen am Eingang.
Portes ou espaces étroits ne pouvant être contournés <70cm.	Unumgehbare schmale Türen oder Zwischenräume 70cm.
Sanitaires spéciaux pour utilisateur de fauteuil roulant, avec transfert latéral >70 cm.	Besondere Toiletteneinrichtung für Rollstuhlfahrer, die an sed Seite ausreichenden Platz für einen Rollstuhl bietet 70cm.
Sanitaires accessibles par surface plate.	Toiletten mit ebenem Zugang.
Café/restaurant accessible aux utilisaters de fauteuil roulant.	Café/Restaurant für Rollstuhlfahrer zugänglich.
Sièges disponibles.	Sitzmöglichkeiten.
Peu ou pas de siéges.	Kaum/keine Sitzmöglichkeiten.
Exhibitions/aménagements spéciaux pour non-voyants.	Besondere Ausstellungen/Einrichtungen für Sehbehinderte.
Equipement fourni pour les personnes mal-entendantes; par exemple: séance explicative ou équipementes spéciaux.	Einrichtungen für Schwerhörige, z.B. Induktionsschlaufe oder besondere Hörgeräte.

Index